VICTORIAN FAIRY TALES

❦ *Edited by Jack Zipes* ❦

VICTORIAN
FAIRY TALES

The Revolt of
the Fairies and Elves

Routledge
Taylor & Francis Group
New York   London

Routledge is an imprint of the
Taylor & Francis Group, an informa business

Routledge
Taylor and Francis Group
270 Madison Avenue
New York, NY 10016

Routledge
Taylor and Francis Group
2 Park Square
Milton Park, Abingdon
Oxon OX14 4RN

Typeset by C. R. Barber & Partners (Highlands) Ltd,
Fort William, Scotland

Library of Congress Cataloging in Publication Data

Victorian fairy tales.
Bibliography: p. 372
Summary: A collection of fairy tales by Victorian writers,
including Lewis Carroll, Charles Dickens, Oscar Wilde, and Rudyard Kipling,
with illustrations from the same period.
1. Fairy tales—Great Britain. 2. English fiction—19th century.
[1. Fairy tales. 2. Short stories] I. Zipes. Jack David.
PR1309.F26V5 1987 823'.8'08 [Fic] 86-23849
ISBN 0-415-90140-5

British Library Catloguing in Publication Data
Victorian fairy tales:
the revolt of the fairies and elves.
1. Children's stories, English
2. Fantastic fiction, English
I. Zipes, Jack
ISBN 0-415-90140-5

For Klaus Doderer,
my good friend and mentor,
who has created wonderful magic
in the realm of children's literature

CONTENTS

	Note on the Illustrations	ix
	Preface	xi
	Introduction	xiii
1	CATHERINE SINCLAIR *Uncle David's Nonsensical Story about Giants and Fairies*	1
2	JOHN RUSKIN *The King of the Golden River, or The Black Brothers*	13
3	GEORGE CRUIKSHANK *Cinderella and the Glass Slipper*	37
4	ALFRED CROWQUILL *Heinrich; or, The Love of Gold*	59
5	LEWIS CARROLL *Bruno's Revenge*	73
6	CHARLES DICKENS *The Magic Fishbone*	89
7	ANNE ISABELLA RITCHIE *Cinderella*	101
8	JULIANA HORATIA EWING *The Ogre Courting*	127
9	JEAN INGELOW *The Prince's Dream*	135
10	EDWARD H. KNATCHBULL-HUGESSEN *Charlie Among the Elves*	145
11	MARY DE MORGAN *A Toy Princess*	163
12	GEORGE MACDONALD *The Day Boy and the Night Girl*	175
13	HARRIET LOUISA CHILDE-PEMBERTON *All my Doing; or Red Riding-Hood Over Again*	209

14   ANDREW LANG
      The Princess Nobody   249

15   MARY LOUISA MOLESWORTH
      The Story of a King's Daughter   263

16   OSCAR WILDE
      The Happy Prince   285

17   LUCY LANE CLIFFORD
      Wooden Tony   295

18   RUDYARD KIPLING
      The Potted Princess   307

19   LAURENCE HOUSMAN
      The Rooted Lover   317

20   KENNETH GRAHAME
      The Reluctant Dragon   327

21   EDITH NESBIT
      The Last of the Dragons   351

22   EVELYN SHARP
      The Spell of the Magician's Daughter   359

      Select Bibliography   372

ILLUSTRATIONS

The King of the Golden River
illustrated by Richard Doyle (1851)

Cinderella and the Glass Slipper
illustrated by George Cruikshank (1853–4)

Heinrich; or, The Love of Gold
illustrated by Alfred Crowquill (1860)

Bruno's Revenge
illustrated by Henry Furniss (1889)

The Magic Fishbone
illustrated by John Gilbert (1868)

The Ogre Courting
illustrated by A. W. Bayes (1882)

The Prince's Dream
illustrator unknown (1872)

Charlie Among the Elves
illustrated by William Brunton (1871)

A Toy Princess
illustrated by William De Morgan (1877)

The Day Boy and the Night Girl
illustrated by Arthur Hughes (1882)

All my Doing; or Red Riding-Hood Over Again
illustrator unknown (1882)

The Princess Nobody
illustrated by Richard Doyle (1884)

The Story of a King's Daughter
illustrated by Walter Crane (1884)

The Happy Prince
illustrated by Walter Crane (1888)

The Potted Princess
illustrator unknown (1893)

The Rooted Lover
illustrated by Laurence Housman (1895)

The Reluctant Dragon
illustrated by Ernest Shepard (1930)

The Spell of the Magician's Daughter
illustrated by Alice B. Woodward (1902)

PREFACE

LTHOUGH VICTORIAN fairy tales have recently drawn a great deal of critical attention from literary scholars, there are surprisingly few anthologies of the tales available to the general reader. The lack of good representative anthologies may paradoxically be due to the plethora of Victorian fairy tales. Indeed, there were hundreds of fairy-tale books published during the Victorian period, and it is difficult to make an adequate selection that might give the present-day reader a sampling of the various types of tales produced at that time. Furthermore, there was also an abundance of fascinating illustrations that contributed to the rise of the literary fairy tale in nineteenth-century England, and they, too, must be taken into consideration in designing a representative collection of Victorian fairy tales.

In choosing the tales and illustrations for this anthology, I endeavored to adhere to two goals: a) to present a chronological picture of those tales (along with the illustrations) which were typical of the work being produced by different kinds of writers of the Victorian period; b) to include tales that are exceptional on an artistic and ideological level. This last point involved giving free rein to my own personal bias, for I wanted to demonstrate in my selection how the Victorians dreamed of better worlds and consciously reproduced their dreams as fairy tales which hold a unique position in literary history.

The Victorian fairy-tale writers always had two ideal audiences in mind when they composed their tales—young middle-class readers whose minds and morals they wanted to influence, and adult middle-class readers whose ideas they wanted to challenge and reform. It was through the fairy tale that a social discourse about conditions in England took form, and this discourse is not without interest for readers today.

I have included with the tales illustrations by Richard Doyle, George Cruikshank, Walter Crane, Alfred Crowquill, Arthur Hughes, Laurence Housman, and other significant artists. Like the authors of the tales, their works were part of the utopian quest for better worlds, and their illustrations demand careful attention in their own right. Since it would mean writing another book to do full justice to the illustrations, I have not commented in any detail about them but have simply tried to provide a sample of some of the more interesting works.

In the course of collecting and analyzing the tales, I have been helped by numerous people. U. C. Knoepflmacher, Anita Moss, and Catherine Gallagher made important critical suggestions with regard to my interpretations and selection of the tales. Michael Patrick Hearn gave me sound advice about Dickens and Cruikshank and shared his thoughts freely with me about the tales of this period. I also benefited a great deal from reading the works of Gillian Avery and Humphrey Carpenter, two of the leading critics in the field. My editor, Janice Price, made significant suggestions about the format of the book and acted as the guiding "fairy spirit" behind the entire project. Brigid Bell put the finishing touches on the book with her insightful comments and fine editorial work. As always, my wife, Carol Dines, contributed wise counsel and support from the beginning of the project to the very "happy end."

The illustration on p. 338 by Ernest Shepard is from *Dream Days* by Kenneth Grahame and is reproduced here by permission of The Bodley Head.

INTRODUCTION

N CONTRAST TO France and Germany, England did not experience the flowering of the literary fairy tale for children until the middle of the nineteenth century. This late flowering is somewhat puzzling, for Great Britain had been a fertile ground for folklore in the Middle Ages. Dazzling fairies, mischievous elves, frightening beasts, clumsy giants, daring thieves, clever peasants, cruel witches, stalwart knights, and damsels in distress had been the cultural staple of the peasants who told their tales at the hearth and in the fields throughout the British Isles. Extraordinary characters, miraculous events, superstitions, folk customs, and pagan rituals made their way quickly into the early vernacular English works by renowned authors such as Chaucer, Spenser, Swift, Marlowe, and Shakespeare; works which became part of the classical British literary tradition. However, the literary fairy tale failed to establish itself as an independent genre in the eighteenth century, when one might have expected it to bloom as it did in France. The fairies and elves seemed to have been banned from their homeland, as if a magic spell had been cast over Great Britain.

Yet it was not magic so much as the actual social enforcement of the Puritan cultural code which led to the suppression of the literary fairy tale in England. The domination of Calvinism after the Revolution of 1688 led to a stronger emphasis on preparing children and adults to be more concerned with moral character and conduct in this world rather than to prepare them for a life hereafter. Through virtuous behaviour and industry one would expect to be able to find the appropriate rewards in temporal society. Above all, Christian principles and the clear application of reason were supposed to provide the foundation for success and happiness in the family and at work. Rational judgment and distrust of the imagination were to be the guiding principles of the new enlightened guardians of Puritan culture and utilitarianism for the next two centuries. Despite the fact that the Puritans and later the utilitarians cannot be considered as monolithic entities, and despite the fact that they each often viewed the Enlightenment itself as a kind of utopian fantasy, they often assumed the same hostile position toward the fairy tale that bordered on the ridiculous. Here a parallel can be drawn to the situation described in E. T. A. Hoffmann's marvelous tale, *Little Zaches Named Zinnober*, where a fanatical prime minister representing the new laws of the Enlightenment, which are to be introduced into Prince Paphnutius' realm, argues that fairies are dangerous creatures and capable of all sorts of mischief. Consequently, the pompous prime minister declares:

> "Yes! I call them enemies of the enlightenment. They took advantage of the goodness of your blessed dead father and are to blame for the darkness that has overcome our dear state. They are conducting a dangerous business with wondrous things, and under the pretext of poetry, they are spreading uncanny poison that makes the people incapable of serving the enlightenment. Their customs offend the police in such a ghastly way that no civilized state should tolerate them in any way."

Obviously, England after 1688 was not entirely a police state, but the laws banning certain types of amusement in the theater, literature, and the arts had a far-reaching effect on the populace. In particular, the oral folk tales were not considered good subject matter for the cultivation of young souls, and thus the "civilized" appropriation of these tales which took place in France during the seventeenth and eighteenth centuries, undertaken by eminent writers such as Charles Perrault, Madame D'Aulnoy, Madame Le Prince de Beaumont, and many others, did not occur in England. On the contrary, the stories, poems, and novels written for children were mainly religious and instructional, and if literary fairy tales were written and published, they were transformed into didactic tales preaching hard work and pious behavior. Moreover, most of the fairy tales which circulated in printed form were chapbooks and pennybooks sold by peddlers to the lower classes. It was not considered proper to defend the fairies and elves—neither in literature for adults nor in literature for children.

The denigration of the fairy tale in England during the seventeenth and eighteenth centuries was in stark contrast to the cultivation of the tale in France and Germany, where it gradually came to express a new middle-class and aristocratic sensibility and flourished as an avant-garde form of art. In Great Britain the literary fairy tale was forced to go underground and was often woven into the plots of novels such as Richardson's *Pamela*. As an oral folk tale it could still dwell comfortably among the peasants, but the literary institutionalization of the fairy-tale genre had to wait until the Romantic movement asserted the value of the imagination and fantasy at the end of the eighteenth century. Here it should be stressed that the English utilitarians of the late eighteenth century and the Romantics actually shared the same utopian zeal that emanated from the principles of the Enlightenment. However, they differed greatly as to how to realize those principles in the cultural life of English society. The Romantics sought to broaden the notions of the Enlightenment so that they would not become narrow and instrumentalized to serve vested class interests. In contrast, the utilitarians did indeed view the Romantics as "enemies of the Enlightenment" à la Hoffmann because they questioned the Protestant ethos and the prescriptions of order conceived by the utilitarians to establish the good society on earth. The questioning spirit of the Romantics enabled them to play a key role in fostering the rise of the literary fairy tale in Great Britain, for the symbolism of the tales gave them great freedom to experiment and express their doubts about the restricted view of the utilitarians and traditional religion. Robert Southey, Charles Lamb, Thomas Hood, Samuel Coleridge, and Hartley Coleridge all wrote interesting fairy tales along these lines, while Blake, Wordsworth, Keats, Byron, and Shelley helped to pave the way for the establishment of the genre and created a more receptive atmosphere for all forms of romance. In time, the return of the magic realm of the fairies and elves was viewed by the Romantics and many early Victorians as a necessary move to oppose the growing alienation in the public sphere due to industrialization and regimentation in the private sphere. Indeed, the Victorians became more aware of the subversive potential of the literary fairy tale to question the so-called productive forces of progress and the Enlightenment, for it was exactly at this point that the middle and upper classes consolidated their hold on the public sphere and determined the rules of rational discourse, government, and industry that guaranteed the promotion of their vested interests. Supported by the industrial revolution (1830–90), the rise of the middle classes meant an institutionalization of all forms of life and this in turn has had severe ramifications to the present day.

We tend to think of the industrial revolution mainly in economic and technological terms, but the impact of the industrial revolution was much more pervasive than this. It changed the very fabric of society in Great Britain, which became the world's first urban as well as industrial nation. Whereas the landed gentry and the rising middle classes benefited greatly from the innovations in commodities, techniques, and occupations that provided them with unprecedented comfort and cultural opportunities, such "progress" also brought its penalties with it. As Barry Supple has pointed out in *The Victorians*:

> the impersonalization of factories, the imposition of a compelling and external discipline, the prolonged activity at the behest of machinery, the sheer problem of mass living in cities, the anonymity of the urban community, the obvious overcrowding in the badly built housing devoid of the countryside, the unchecked pollution—all these must have amounted to

a marked deterioration in the circumstances, and therefore the standards of life for large numbers of people.

Such negative features of the industrial revolution did not go unnoticed by early Victorian writers and led to what is commonly called the "Condition of England Debate." In actuality, this was not a single debate but a series of controversies about the spiritual and material foundations of English life and it had a great effect on literary developments. For instance, as Catherine Gallagher has shown in her book *The Industrial Reformation of English Fiction 1832–1867*, disputes about the nature and possibility of human freedom, the sources of social cohesion, and the nature of representation were embraced by the novel and "unsettled fundamental assumptions of the novel form." Just as the novel developed a certain discourse and narrative strategies to respond to the Condition of England Debate, the literary fairy tale conceived its own unique aesthetic modes and themes to relate to this debate. Writers like Charles Dickens, Thomas Hood, Thomas Carlyle, John Ruskin, and William Thackeray were among the first to criticize the deleterious effects of the industrial revolution. Interestingly, they all employed the fairy tale at one point to question the injustice and inequalities engendered by the social upheaval in England. What is unique about the initial stage of the literary fairy-tale revival in England is that the *form itself* was part of the controversial subject matter of the larger Condition of England Debate. The shifting attitudes toward children, whose imaginations were gradually declared more innocent than sinful, allowed for greater use of works of fancy to educate and amuse them. Even so, despite changing attitudes, German, French, and Danish works of fantasy had first to pave the way for the resurgence of the literary fairy tale and the defense of the imagination in cultural products for children.

As we know, close to two centuries of British educators, writers, and publishers debated the merits of fairy tales and they were found—at least by the conservative camp, or what would be called the "moral majority" today— useless and dangerous for the moral education of young and old alike. Writers like Mrs Trimmer and Mrs Mortimer argued at the end of the eighteenth century that fairy tales made children depraved and turned them against the sacred institutions of society. Their arguments continued to be influential at the beginning of the nineteenth century, although in a somewhat modified form. For instance, one of the champions of the anti-fairy-tale school, Mrs Sherwood, wrote the following in her book *The Governess, or The Little Female Academy* (1820):

Instruction when conveyed through the medium of some beautiful story or pleasant tale, more easily insinuates itself into the youthful mind than any thing of a drier nature; yet the greatest care is necessary that the kind of instruction thus conveyed should be perfectly agreeable to the Christian dispensation. Fairy-tales therefore are in general an improper medium of instruction because it would be absurd in such tales to introduce Christian principles as motives of action. . . . On this account such tales should be very sparingly used, it being extremely difficult, if not impossible, from the reason I have specified, to render them really useful.

One way to oppose the rigid upholders of the Puritan law and order school was to import fairy tales from France, Germany, and Scandinavia and to translate them as exotic works of art. This mode of counterattack by the defenders of fairy tales gained momentum at the beginning of the nineteenth century. In 1804 Benjamin Tabart began to publish a series of popular tales which eventually led to his book *Popular Fairy Tales* (1818) containing selections from *Mother Goose*, *The Arabian Nights*, *Robin Hood*, and Madame D'Aulnoy's tales. In 1818 Friedrich de la Motte Fouqué's *Undine* was published and gained acceptance because of its obvious Christian message about the pagan water nymph who leads a virtuous life once she gains a human soul. In 1823, John Harris, an enterprising publisher, who had already produced *Mother Bunch's Fairy Tales* in 1802, edited an important volume entitled *The Court of Oberon; or, The Temple of Fairies*, which contained tales from Perrault, D'Aulnoy, and *The Arabian Nights*. Coincidentally, this book appeared in the same year that the most important publication to stimulate an awakened interest in fairy tales for children *and* adults was issued, namely *German Popular Stories*, Edgar Taylor's translation of a selection from *Kinder- und Hausmärchen* by the brothers Grimm with illustrations by the gifted artist George Cruikshank. Taylor made an explicit reference to the debate concerning fairy tales in his introduction, in which he aligned himself with the "enemies of the Enlightenment":

The popular tales of England have been too much neglected. They are nearly discarded from the libraries of childhood. Philosophy is made the companion of the nursery: we have lisping chemists and leading-string mathematicians; this is the age of reason, not of imagination; and the loveliest dreams of fairy innocence are considered as vain and frivolous. Much might be urged against this rigid and philosophic (or rather unphilosophic) exclusion of works of fancy and fiction. Our imagination is surely as susceptible of improvement by exercise, as our judgement or our memory; and so long as such fictions only are presented to the young mind as do not interfere with the important department of moral education, a beneficial effect must be produced by the pleasurable employment of a faculty in which so much of our happiness in every period of life consists.

The publication of *German Popular Stories* acted as a challenge to the anti-fairy-tale movement in Britain, and its favorable reception led to a second edition in 1826 and a new wave of translations. For instance, Thomas Carlyle published two volumes entitled *German Romances*, which included his translations of fairy tales by Musäus, Tieck, Chamisso, and Hoffmann in 1827. Also his unique book *Sartor Resartus* (1831) was based to a certain extent on Goethe's *Das Märchen*. Various English periodicals carried the translated tales of Otmar, Chamisso, Hoffmann, Tieck, Novalis, and Hauff in the 1830s, and new translations of the Grimm brothers' tales appeared in 1839, 1846, 1849, and 1855. In addition to the significant impact of the German tales, the arrival in 1846 of Hans Christian Andersen's *Wonderful Stories for Children*, translated by Mary Howitt, was a momentous occasion. His unusual tales, which combined fantasy with a moral impulse in line with traditional Christian standards, guaranteed the legitimacy of the literary fairy tale for middle-class audiences. From this point on, the fairy tale flowered in many different forms and colors and expanded its social discourse to cover such different topics as proper comportment for children, free will, social exploitation, political justice, and authoritarian government. The 1840s also saw the translation of the *Arabian Nights* (1840) by Edwin Lane; Felix Summerly's *Home Treasury* (1841–9), which included such works as *Little Red Riding Hood*, *Beauty and the Beast*, and *Jack and the Beanstalk*; Ambrose Merton's *The Old Story Books of England* (1845); and Anthony Montalba's *Fairy Tales of All Nations* (1849).

The gradual recognition and acceptance of the fairy tale by the middle classes, which had heretofore condemned the genre as frivolous and pernicious, did not mean that the Puritan outlook of the bourgeoisie had undergone a radical change, however. Indeed, to a certain extent, one can talk about a "cooption" of "the enemies of the Enlightenment." That is, middle-class writers, educators, publishers, and parents began to realize that the rigid, didactic training and literature used to rear their children was dulling their senses and creativity. Both children and adults needed more fanciful works to stimulate their imagination and keep them productive in the social and cultural spheres of British society. Emphasis was now placed on fairy-tale reading and storytelling as *recreation*—a period of time and a place in which the young could recuperate from instruction and training and re-create themselves, so to speak, without the social pressure calculated to make every second morally and economically profitable. The stimulation of the imagination became just as important as the cultivation of reason for moral improvement. Although many tedious books of fairy tales with didactic lessons were published, such as Alfred Crowquill's *Crowquill's Fairy Book* (1840) and Mrs Alfred Gatty's *The Fairy Godmothers* (1851), various English writers began to explore the potential of the fairy tale as a form of literary communication that might convey both individual and social protest and personal conceptions of alternative, if not utopian, worlds. To write a fairy tale was considered by many writers a social symbolical act that could have implications for the education of children and the future of society.

In the period between 1840 and 1880 the general trend among the more prominent fairy-tale writers was to use the fairy-tale form in innovative ways to raise social consciousness about the disparities among the different social classes and the problems faced by the oppressed due to the industrial revolution. Numerous writers took a philanthropic view of the poor and underprivileged and sought to voice a concern about the cruel exploitation and deprivation of the young. It was almost as though the fairy tales were to instill a spirit of moral protest in the readers—and, as I mentioned, the Victorian writers always had two implied ideal readers in mind: the middle-class parent *and* child—so that they would take a noble and ethical stand against forces of intolerance and authoritarianism. For instance, John Ruskin's *King of the Golden River* (1841) (pp. 13–36 below) depicted two cruel brothers who almost destroy their younger brother Gluck because of their greed and dictatorial ways. Moreover, they threaten the laws of nature, reminding one of the cruel materialism of the industrial revolution. However, due to Gluck's innocence and compassion, he does not succumb to the brutality of his brothers and is eventually helped by the King of the Golden River to re-create an idyllic realm. Similarly, Francis Edward Paget wrote *The Hope of the Katzekopfs* in 1844 to decry the selfishness of a spoiled prince and convey a sense of self-discipline through the lessons taught by a fairy, an imp, and the old man Discipline. William Makepeace Thackeray composed *The Rose and the Ring* (1855), a delightful discourse on rightful and moral rule in which the humble Prince Giglio and Princess Rosalba regain their kingdoms from power-hungry and materialistic usurpers. Frances Browne also made a significant contribution to the fairy-tale genre with the publication of *Granny's Wonderful Chair* in 1856. Here the wonderful chair provides the framework for a group of connected tales told to the young girl Snowflower, whose virtuous and modest behavior parallels the conduct of the protagonists in the tales. Though poor and orphaned at the beginning of the book, Snowflower's diligence is rewarded at the end. The progression in *Granny's Wonderful Chair* enables the reader to watch Snowflower learn and grow to be the "ideal" Victorian girl. Such is also the case in Charles Kingsley's *The Water Babies* (1863), except that here the model is a boy. To be exact it is Tom, a chimney sweep, who leaves his body behind him to become a water baby in the sea. There he (with others as well) undergoes various adventures and learns all about rewards and punishments for his behavior, especially from Mrs Bedonebyasyoudid. In the end he realizes that he must take the initiative in being good, for people always tend to reciprocate in kind.

Almost all the fairy tales of the 1840s and 1850s use allegorical forms to make a statement about Christian goodness in contrast to the greed and materialism that are apparently the most dangerous vices in English society. The moralistic tendency is most apparent in such works as Catherine Sinclair's "Uncle David's Nonsensical Story about Giants and Fairies" in *Holiday House* (1839), Clara de Chatelain's *The Silver Swan* (1847), Mark Lemon's *The Enchanted Doll* (1849) Alfred Crowquill's *The Giant Hands* (1856), and Mary and Elizabeth Kirby's *The Talking Bird* (1856). In each case the use of the fairy-tale form as a fanciful mode to delight readers is justified because of the seriousness of the subject matter. Consequently, the fairy tale at mid-century was a manifesto for itself and a social manifesto at the same time. The compulsion felt by writers to rationalize their preference for using the fairy tale to express their opinions about religion, education, and progress often undercut their aesthetic experiments. Nevertheless, even the boring allegorical fairy tales were an improvement on the stern, didactic tales of realism which English children had been obliged to read during the first part of the nineteenth century.

Underlying the efforts of the Victorian fairy-tale writers was also a psychological urge to recapture and retain childhood as a paradisiacal realm of innocence. This psychological drive was often mixed with a utopian belief that a more just society could be established on earth. U. C. Knoepflmacher makes the point in his essay "The Balancing of Child and Adult" (1983) that the Victorian writers' "regressive capacity can never bring about a total annihilation of the adult's self-awareness":

> Torn between the opposing demands of innocence and experience, the author who resorts to the wishful, magical thinking of the child nonetheless feels compelled, in varying degrees, to hold on to the grown-up's circumscribed notions about reality. In the better works of fantasy of the period, this dramatic tension between the adult and childhood selves becomes rich and elastic: conflict and harmony, friction and reconciliation, realism and wonder, are allowed to interpenetrate and co-exist.

Knoepflmacher asserts that the regressive tendency balanced by self-awareness was a major feature of most Victorian fantasies. And, certainly, if we consider the three most important writers and defenders of fairy tales from 1840 to 1880, Charles Dickens, Lewis Carroll, and George MacDonald, it is apparent that their quest for a new fairy-tale form stemmed from a psychological rejection and rebellion against the "norms" of English society. If the industrial revolution had turned England upside down on the path toward progress, then these writers believed that English society had to be revolutionized once more to regain a sense of free play and human compassion. The remarkable achievement of Dickens, Carroll, and MacDonald lies in their artistic capacity to blend their regressive urges with progressive social concerns, without succumbing to overt didacticism.

In his essay "Frauds on Fairies" (1853) published in *Household Words*, Dickens took issue with George Cruikshank and any other writers who might seek to abuse the fairy tale by attaching explicit moral or ethical messages to it. Dickens argued:

> in an utilitarian age, of all other times, it is a matter of grave importance that fairy tales should be respected. Our English red tape is too magnificently red even to be employed in the tying up of such trifles, but everyone who has considered the subject knows full well that a nation without fancy, without some romance, never did, never can, never will, hold a great place under the sun.

Dickens himself tended to incorporate fairy-tale motifs and plots primarily in his novels and particularly in his *Christmas Books* (1843–5). It is almost as though he did not want to tarnish the childlike innocence of the tales that he read as a young boy—tales which incidentally filled him with hope during his difficult childhood—by replacing them with new ones. But Dickens did use the fairy tale to make political and social statements, as in *Prince Bull* (1855) and *The Thousand and One Humbugs* (1855), and his regressive longings for the innocent bliss of fairyland are made most evident in his essay *A Christmas Tree* (1850):

> Good for Christmas time is the ruddy color of the clôak, in which—the tree making a forest of itself for her to trip through, with her basket—Little Red Riding-Hood comes to me one Christmas Eve, to give me information of the cruelty and treachery of that dissembling Wolf who ate her grandmother, without making any impression on his appetite, and then ate her, after making that ferocious joke about his teeth. She was my first love. I felt that if I could have married Little Red Riding-Hood, I should have known perfect bliss. But, it was not to be.

What was to be was Dickens' adult quest for fairy bliss in his novels, and it is not by chance that one of the last works he wrote toward the end of his life was "The Magic Fishbone" (pp. 89–99 below), part of a collection of humorous stories for children entitled *Holiday Romance* (1868). Here Dickens parodied a helpless king as a salaried worker, who is accustomed to understanding everything with his reason. He becomes totally confused by the actions of his daughter Alicia, who receives a magic fishbone from a strange and brazen fairy named Grandmarina. Alicia does *not* use the fishbone when one would expect her to. Only when the king reveals to her that he can no longer provide for the family does Alicia make use of the magic fishbone. Suddenly Grandmarina arrives to bring about a comical ending in which the most preposterous changes occur. Nothing can be grasped through logic, and this is exactly Dickens' point: his droll tale—narrated from the viewpoint of a child—depends on the unusual deployment of fairy-tale motifs to question the conventional standards of society and to demonstrate that there is strength and soundness in the creativity of the young. The patriarchal figure of authority is at a loss to rule and provide, and the reversal of circumstances points to a need for change in social relations. The realm of genuine happiness that is glimpsed at the end of Dickens' fairy tale is a wish-fulfillment that he himself shared with many Victorians who were dissatisfied with social conditions in English society.

Like Dickens, Carroll fought tenaciously to keep the child alive in himself and in his fiction as a critic of the absurd rules and regulations of the adult Victorian world. In *Alice's Adventures in Wonderland* (1865) and *Through the Looking Glass* (1871) Carroll made one of the most radical statements on behalf of the fairy tale and the child's perspective by conceiving a fantastic plot without an ostensible moral purpose. The questioning spirit of the child is celebrated in the Alice books, and Carroll continually returned to the realm of fantasy in his remarkable fairy tale "Bruno's Revenge" (1867) (pp. 73–87 below), which eventually served as the basis for his Sylvie and Bruno books (1889, 1893). The endeavor to reconcile the fairy world with the world of reality never meant compromising the imagination for Carroll. If anything, reason was to serve the imagination, to allow vital dreams of pleasure to take shape in a world that was threatening to turn those dreams into mere advertisements for better homes and better living, according to the plans of British industrial and urban leaders.

Carroll's deep-seated belief in the necessity of keeping alive the power of the imagination in children was shared by George MacDonald. In fact, after he had completed *Alice's Adventures in Wonderland* he sent the manuscript to the MacDonald family, who warmly encouraged him to have his fantastic narrative published. Though MacDonald himself was not as "radical" as Carroll in his own fairy tales, he was nonetheless just as pioneering in his endeavors to lend new shape and substance to the fairy-tale genre. In 1867 he published *Dealings with the Fairies*, which contained "The Light Princess," "The Giant's Heart," "The Shadows," "Cross Purposes," and "The Golden Key." Thereafter he continued to write fairy tales for children's magazines and included some in his novels. In fact, he wrote two compelling fairy-tale novels, *The Princess and the Goblin* (1872) and *The Princess and Curdie* (1883), which became classics in his own day. MacDonald stressed the aesthetic reversal of traditional fairy-tale schemes and motifs and social transformation in all his fairy tales. For instance, his most popular work, "The Light Princess," is a witty parody of *Sleeping Beauty* which stimulates serious reflection about social behavior and power through comical and unexpected changes in the traditional fairy-tale form and content. Here, a bumbling king and queen give birth to a daughter after many years of sterility, and because they insult one of the fairy godmothers their daughter is cursed with a lack of gravity. Thus, she can only fly around the court, and her hilarious behavior upsets the absurd conventions of the kingdom. But she is also potentially destructive, because she has no sense of balance and tends to seek to gratify her whims with little concern for other people. Only when she sees a humble prince about to die for her own pleasure does she develop human compassion and gain the gravity necessary for mature social interaction. MacDonald often turned the world upside-down and inside-out in his fairy tales, to demonstrate that society as it existed was based on false and artificial values. He purposely portrayed characters on quests to discover a divine spark within themselves, and self-discovery was always linked to a greater appreciation of other human beings and nature, as in the case of "The Day Boy and the Night Girl" (1882) (pp. 175–208 below). Domination is opposed by compassion. Magic is power used to attain self-awareness and sensitivity toward others. Fairy-tale writing itself becomes a means by which one can find the golden key for establishing harmony with the world—a utopian world, to be sure, that opens our eyes to the ossification of a society blind to its own faults and injustices.

The creation of fairy-tale worlds by British writers moved in two basic directions from 1860 until the turn of the century: conventionalism and utopianism. The majority of writers such as Dinah Mulock Craik (*The Fairy Book*, 1863), Annie Keary (*Little Wanderlin*, 1865), Tom Hood, (*Fairy Realm*, 1865, verse renditions of Perrault's prose tales), Harriet Parr (*Holme Lee's Fairy Tales*, 1868), Edward Knatchbull-Hugessen (*Moonshine*, 1871 and *Friends and Foes from Fairy Land*, 1886), Jean Ingelow (*The Little Wonder-Horn*, 1872), Mrs Molesworth (*The Tapestry Room*, 1879 and *Christmas-Tree Land*, 1884), Anne Isabella Ritchie (*Five Old Friends and a Young Prince*, 1868 and *Bluebeard's Keys*, 1874), Christina Rossetti (*Speaking Likenesses*, 1874), Lucy Lane Clifford (*Anyhow Stories*, 1882), Harriet Childe Pemberton (*Fairy Tales for Every Day*, 1882), Andrew Lang (*The Princess Nobody*, 1884 and *The Gold of Fairnilee*, 1888), Herbert Inman (*The One-Eyed Griffin and Other Fairy Tales*, 1897), and Edith Nesbit (*The Book of Dragons*, 1900) conceived plots conventionally to reconcile themselves and their readers to the status quo of Victorian society. Their imaginative worlds could be called exercises in complicity with the traditional opponents of fairy tales, for there is rarely a hint of social criticism and subversion in their works. It is almost as if the wings of the fairies had been clipped, for the "little people" do not represent a real threat to the established Victorian norms. Magic and nonsense are not liberating forces. After a brief period of disturbance, the fairies, brownies, elves, or other extraordinary creatures generally enable the protagonists to integrate themselves into a prescribed social order. If the fairies create mischief that makes the protagonists and readers think critically about their situation, they ultimately do this in the name of sobriety. Perseverance, good sense, and diligence are championed as virtues that must be acquired through trials in magical realms to prove they will become mature "solid citizens."

Yet, even in the works of the conventional writers, there seems to be a longing to maintain a connection to the fairy realm. Some of them, like Ingelow, Molesworth, and Nesbit, even broke with convention at times. Respect was paid to those spirits of the imagination, the fairies, who reinvigorated British cultural life in the nineteenth century after years of banishment. Indeed, the return of the fairies became a permanent one, for writers of all kinds of persuasions discovered that they could be used to maintain a discourse about subjects germane to their heart. Unfortunately, by the end of the century such publishers as Raphael Tuck and Routledge could make standard commodities out of the fairy tales—mainly the classical European tales—and published thousands of toy books and picture books to earn grand profits from what used to be considered pernicious items for sons and daughters of the middle classes.

Fairy tales for profit and fairy tales of conventionality were disregarded by English writers of the utopian direction. Their tales reveal a profound belief in the power of the imagination as a potent force that can be used to question the value of existing social relations. There is also a moral impulse in this second direction. However, it does not lead to reconciliation with the status quo—rather, rebellion against convention and conformity. Fairy-tale protagonists are sent on quests which change them as the world around them also changes. The fairies and other magical creatures inspire and compel the protagonists to alter their lives and pursue utopian dreams. In the works of MacDonald, Carroll, Mary De Morgan, Juliana Horatia Ewing, Oscar Wilde, Rudyard Kipling, Kenneth Grahame, Evelyn Sharp, and Laurence Housman the creation of fairy-tale worlds allows the writers to deal symbolically with social taboos and to suggest alternatives to common English practice, particularly in the spheres of child rearing and role-playing. In many instances the alternatives do not lead to a "happy end," or, if happiness is achieved, it is in stark contrast to the "happy" way of life in late Victorian and Edwardian England. In Humphrey Carpenter's critical study of the golden age of children's literature, *Secret Gardens* (1985), he makes the point that fantasy literature and fairy tales of the late nineteenth century stem from a deep dissatisfaction with the socio-political realities of England.

> While it was not overtly "realistic" and purported to have nothing to say about the "real" world, in this fantastic strain of writing may be found some profound observations about human character and contemporary society, and (strikingly often) about religion. It dealt largely with utopias, and

posited the existence of Arcadian societies remote from the nature and concerns of the everyday world; yet in doing this it was commentary, often satirically and critically, on real life.

Clearly there are signs in the works of Carroll, MacDonald, Wilde, Ewing, De Morgan, Grahame, Sharp, Housman, Nesbit, and even Molesworth that they identified with the "enemies of the Enlightenment." In a period when first Christian socialism and later the Fabian movement had a widespread effect, these writers instilled a utopian spirit into the fairy-tale discourse that endowed the genre with a vigorous and unique quality of social criticism which was to be developed even further by later writers of faerie works such as A. A. Milne, J. R. R. Tolkien, C. S. Lewis, and T. H. White. This endowment in itself was the major accomplishment of the utopian fairy-tale writers. But there were other qualities and features that they contributed to the development of the literary fairy tale as genre which deserve our attention.

To begin with, there is a strong feminine, if not feminist, influence in the writing of *both* male and female writers. In contrast to the *Kunstmärchen* tradition in Germany and folklore in general, which were stamped by patriarchal concerns, British writers created strong women characters and placed great emphasis on the fusion of female and male qualities and equality between men and women. For instance, in most of MacDonald's tales, particularly "The Day Boy and the Night Girl" (pp. 175–208 below), "Cross Purposes," and "Little Daylight," the male and female protagonists come to realize their mutual dependency. Their so-called masculine and feminine qualities are not genetically determined but are relative and assume their own particular value in given circumstances. What is often understood as masculine is feminine in MacDonald's tales. Gender has no specificity—rather, both male and female can develop courage, honesty, intelligence, compassion, etc. The most important goal in MacDonald's fairy tales lies beyond the limits set by society. The worth of an individual is indicated by his or her willingness to explore nature and to change according to the divine insights they gain. Magic is nothing else but the realization of the divine creative powers one possesses within oneself. Here MacDonald differed from many of the traditional Victorian writers by insisting on self-determination for women.

MacDonald was not alone in this conviction. Mary De Morgan, Juliana Horatia Ewing, Mary Louisa Molesworth, Evelyn Sharp, and Edith Nesbit all depicted female protagonists coming into their own and playing unusually strong roles in determining their own destinies. Princess Ursula's refusal to conform to the wishes of her ministers in De Morgan's "A Toy Princess" (1877) (pp. 163–174 below) celebrates the indomitable will of a young woman who is determined to run her life according to her needs rather than serve the royal court like a puppet. In Ewing's "The Ogre Courting" (1871) (pp. 127–33 below) Managing Molly, a clever peasant's daughter, maintains her independence while making a fool out of a brutal male oppressor. Mrs Molesworth's Princess Auréole in "Story of a King's Daughter" (1884) (pp. 263–84 below) uses another technique to tame the brute in man: she sets an example of compassion which eventually induces Prince Halbert to learn to feel for the sufferings of his fellow creatures. Princess Auréole uses her courage and imagination to get *her* way and *her* man in the end, just as Firefly in Sharp's "The Spell of the Magician's Daughter" (1902) (pp. 369–72 below) shows remarkable fortitude and creativity in disenchanting a country and captivating a young prince. Similarly the Princess in Nesbit's "The Last of the Dragons" (*c.* 1900) (pp. 351–8 below) acts in a very "unladylike" way by taking the initiative and defeating the last of the dragons with love.

In all of these tales—as well as in other works, such as Christina Rossetti's fascinating poem *The Goblin Market*—there is an intense quest for the female self. In contrast to such fairy tales as "Cinderella" (1868) by Anne Isabella Ritchie and "All my Doing" (1882) by Harriet Childe-Pemberton (pp. 209–48 below), which are fascinating examples of female self-deprecation, the narratives by De Morgan, Ewing, Molesworth, Sharp, and Nesbit allow for women's voices and needs to be heard. The narrative strategies of these tales strongly suggest that utopia will not be just another men's world. What is significant about the "feminist" utopian tales is not so much the strength shown by the female protagonists, but the manner in which they expose oppression and hypocrisy. Here, the social critique is both implicit and explicit as it pertains to Victorian society. The new "feminine quality" in these tales is part of the general re-utilization of the traditional fairy-tale motifs and topoi by utopian writers to express the need for a new type of government and society. All the formal aesthetic changes made in the tales are connected to an insistence that the substance of life be transformed, otherwise there will be alienation, petrification, and death. This is certainly the danger in De Morgan's "Toy Princess," and it is the reason why she also questioned and rejected arbitrary authority in such other tales as "The Necklace of Princess Fiormonde," "The Heart of Princess Joan," and "Three Clever Kings."

Male writers expressed their utopian inclinations in fairy tales by depicting English society as one which stifled and confined the creative energies of compassionate young protagonists. Both in his tales and his illustrations Laurence Housman portrayed Victorian society symbolically, as a rigid enclosure. In such tales as "The Rooted Lover" (pp. 317–26 below), "The Bound Princess," "The White Doe," and "A Chinese Fairy-Tale," Housman's protagonists reject material gains to pursue love and beauty. The aesthetic composition of the fairy tale and the noble actions of his characters are contrasted to the vulgar materialism of late Victorian society. Such a view of British society was shared by Oscar Wilde, who developed his critique of greed and hypocrisy in his two collections of fairy tales, *The Happy Prince and Other Tales* (1888) and *The House of Pomegranates* (1891). In particular, "The Happy Prince" (pp. 285–94 below) is a sad commentary on how isolated the ruling class had become from the majority of English people by the end of the century. Like many utopian writers of this period, Wilde felt that social relations had become reified, and he disparaged the philanthropic movement of the upper classes as mere ornamental patchwork. If British society was to reform itself substantially, then not only had it to undergo a spiritual reformation, but class domination and the destructive effects of industrialization had also to be brought to an end.

To oppose class domination and the crass exploitation of the "little people" became the underlying bond of many utopian fairy-tale writers toward the end of the nineteenth century. The unique quality of the individual tales often depended on the non-conformist message and the "non-sensical" play with words, plots, and motifs. These made sense once the reader realized that the writers were endeavoring to subvert those so-called sensible standards which appeared to fulfill the needs of the people but actually deceived them. For example, a fairy tale such as Kenneth Grahame's "The Reluctant Dragon" (1898) (pp. 327–49 below) plays with the expectations of the readers and refuses to meet them because Grahame was more interested in fostering human compassion than in human deception. His tale reveals how the aggressive instincts of people can be manipulated and can lead to a false sense of chauvinism because of stereotyping—in this case, of knights and dragons. Kipling, too, in "The Potted Princess" (1893) (pp. 307–16 below) composed an interesting tale that experimented with audience expectations and deception. In the process it allows for the rise of a lowly prince and the transformation of a young boy into a tale teller. The theme of coming into one's own is closely tied to the rejection of the materialistic and artificial standards set by society.

The German Romantic writer Novalis, who had a great influence on MacDonald, once remarked, "Mensch werden ist eine Kunst"—to become a human being is an art. This remark could have been Kipling's motto for his tale, and it certainly could have been the unwritten slogan of the utopian fairy-tale writers by the end of the nineteenth century. The fairy tale itself exhibited possibilities for the young to transform themselves and society into those Arcadian dreams conceived in childhood that the writers did not want to leave behind them. The artwork of the fairy tale assumed a religious quality in its apparent denial of the material world.

It is not by chance that many of the late Victorian fairy-tale writers took a resolute stand against materialism. The industrial revolution had transformed an agrarian population into an urban one. Compelled to work and live according to a profit motive and competitive market conditions, people became accustomed to think instrumentally about gain and exploitation. Both in the middle and lower classes it became necessary to compete with and exploit others to achieve success and a modicum of comfort. Here, the Christian Church relied on philanthropy as a means to rationalize the material values of a society that had abandoned the essence of Christian humanism. This is why the Christian minister George MacDonald—and the same might be said of Lewis Carroll—distanced himself from the practices of the Anglican and Congregational Churches. Most of his works, particularly his two fairy-tale novels *The Princess and the Goblin* and *The Princess and Curdie*, decry the lust for money in all social classes and the abandonment of Christian values based on human compassion.

Toward the end of the nineteenth century there was a growing tendency among writers to support the ideas of Christian and Fabian socialism. This tendency also marked the rise of utopian literature which was connected to the fairy tale and indicated the writers' deep dissatisfaction with the way Great Britain had been drastically changed by the industrial revolution. William Morris' *News from Nowhere* (1891) and H. G. Wells' *The Time Machine* (1895) illustrate the criticism of those Victorian writers who feared that the machine age would destroy human creativity and integrity. Though Great Britain was at its height as Empire, there was also a strong sentiment among utopian writers that the Empire had sold its soul to attain power and was using its power to maintain a system of domination and exploitation.

It is interesting to note that many of the late Victorian fairy-tale writers held similar political views and worked in the same milieux in an effort to create a *different* English society. As is well known, MacDonald was a good friend of Ruskin and Carroll and shared many of the social convictions of Dickens and Morris, whom he also knew. Morris was very much influenced by Ruskin, and in turn his ideas attracted Mary De Morgan, Laurence Housman, and Walter Crane, who illustrated numerous fairy books. Kipling heard the tales of De Morgan as a child and was a great admirer of Juliana Horatia Ewing. Wilde studied with both Ruskin and Walter Pater and developed his own anarchical brand of socialism which he expressed in his essay "The Soul of Man under Socialism" (1889), written at the same time as his fairy tales. Crane illustrated *The Happy Prince and Other Tales* as well as *Christmas-Tree Land* by Mary Louisa Molesworth. Evelyn Sharp, Laurence Housman, and Kenneth Grahame belonged to the coterie of writers around *The Yellow Book* founded by John Lane, who wanted to establish a new aesthetics while at the same time retaining respect for traditional craftsmanship. Grahame was greatly influenced by Frederick James Furnivall, an active member of the Christian Socialist movement, who introduced him to the works of Ruskin and Morris. Sharp went on to become one of the leading members of the women's suffragette movement and a socialist. At times she had contact with Laurence Housman, who also declared himself a socialist pacifist and became active in the political and cultural struggles of the early twentieth century. Nesbit was one of the founders of the Fabian Society with her husband Hubert Bland, and she became close to George Bernard Shaw, H. G. Wells, and numerous other members of the Fabian movement.

The social and political views of the fairy-tale writers and the cultural climate of late Victorian society make it evident that they felt the future of Britain and the young was at stake in their literary production. Such investment in their work enables us to understand why the literary fairy tale finally became a viable genre in Britain. The revolt of the fairies in the early part of the nineteenth century and their reintegration into English literature occurred at a time when British society was undergoing momentous social and political changes. The Puritan ban on fairy-tale literature that had existed since the late seventeenth century was gradually lifted because the rational discourse of the Enlightenment did not allow sufficient means to voice doubts and protest about conditions in England during the industrial revolution. Though many of the new fairy tales were contradictory, they opened up possibilities for children and adults to formulate innovative views about socialization, religious training, authority, sex roles, and art. For many late Victorian authors, the writing of a fairy tale meant a process of creating an *other world*, from which vantage point they could survey conditions in the real world and compare them to their ideal projections. The personal impetus for writing fairy tales was simultaneously a social one for the Victorians. This social impetus has kept their tales alive and stimulating for us today, for the aesthetics of these fairy tales stems from an experimental spirit and social conscience that raises questions which twentieth-century reality has yet to answer. The "enemies of the Enlightenment" are still very much with us, and though they are often packaged as commodities and made to appear harmless, they will continue to touch a utopian chord in every reader who remains open to their call for change.

I

CATHERINE SINCLAIR

Uncle David's Nonsensical Story
about Giants and Fairies
(1839)

ATHERINE SINCLAIR (1800–64) was born and educated in Edinburgh, Scotland. At the age of 14 she began working as secretary for her father, Sir John Sinclair, a wealthy philanthropist, who also achieved notoriety as a redoubtable politician. While assisting her father, Sinclair decided to embark on a career as writer and published a conventional moralistic novel for children, *Charlie Seymour; or The Good Aunt and the Bad Aunt* in 1832. After her father's death in 1835, she remained heavily involved in philanthropic activities while pursuing her writing career by publishing two novels for adults: *Modern Accomplishments* (1836) and *Modern Society* (1837). Her major work, however, was *Holiday House* (1839), which was intended for young readers and attracted attention by the manner in which she portrayed the careless, if not wild, behavior of two children without punishing them. After the publication of this work, Sinclair wrote other books for children such as *Frank Vansittart; or The Model Schoolboys* (1853) and *Picture Letters for Children* (1861–4) as well as novels and histories for adults, but she never produced another innovative work equal in quality to *Holiday House*.

"Uncle David's Nonsensical Story about Giants and Fairies" is purposely set as the central chapter in *Holiday House* because it provides an example of moderation for Laura and Harry, the two mischievous youngsters who are good at heart but are always causing trouble. They have been abandoned by their father (after the death of their mother) and left under the care of their Uncle David and Grandma Harriet Graham, who gently supervise their upbringing. Uncle David's story represents the manner in which Sinclair sought to educate children: not by deadening the imagination with rigid discipline, but by cultivating the imagination so that children would be able to make their own moral decisions. In her preface to *Holiday House*, she issued a "romantic" proclamation in defense of the fairy tale and fantasy literature:

In this age of wonderful inventions, the very mind of youth seems in danger of becoming a machine; and while every effort is used to stuff the memory, like a cricket-ball, with well-known facts and ready-made opinions, no room is left for the vigour of natural feeling, the glow of natural genius, and the ardour of natural enthusiasm. It was a remark of Sir Walter Scott's many years ago, to the author herself, that in the rising generation there would be no poets, wits, or orators, because all play of imagination is now carefully discouraged, and books written for young persons are generally a mere dry record of facts, unenlivened by any appeal to the heart, or any excitement to fancy.

Her fairy tale, told by Uncle David to Laura and Harry, is thus an appeal to children through the imagination to develop a moral sensibility.

UNCLE DAVID'S
NONSENSICAL STORY ABOUT
GIANTS AND FAIRIES

Pie-crust and pastry-crust, that was the wall;
The windows were made of black-puddings and white,
And slated with pancakes—you ne'er saw the like!

N THE DAYS OF yore, children were not all such clever, good sensible people as they are now! Lessons were then considered rather a plague—sugar-plums were still in demand—holidays continued yet in fashion—and toys were not then made to teach mathematics, nor story-books to give instruction in chemistry and navigation. These were very strange times, and there existed at that period, a very idle, greedy, naughty boy, such as we never hear of in the present day. His papa and mama were—no matter who,—and he lived, no matter where. His name was Master No-book, and he seemed to think his eyes were made for nothing but to stare out of the windows, and his mouth for no other purpose but to eat. This young gentleman hated lessons like mustard, both of which brought tears into his eyes, and during school-hours, he sat gazing at his books, pretending to be busy, while his mind wandered away to wish impatiently for dinner, and to consider where he could get the nicest pies, pastry, ices, and jellies, while he smacked his lips at the very thoughts of them. I think he must have been first cousin to Peter Grey, but that is not perfectly certain.

Whenever Master No-book spoke, it was always to ask for something, and you might continually hear him say, in a whining tone of voice, "Papa! may I take this piece of cake? Aunt Sarah! will you give me an apple? Mama! do send me the whole of that plum-pudding!" Indeed, very frequently when he did not get permission to gormandize, this naughty glutton helped himself without leave. Even his dreams were like his waking hours, for he had often a horrible nightmare about lessons, thinking he was smothered with Greek Lexicons, or pelted out of the school with a shower of English Grammars, while one night he fancied himself sitting down to devour an enormous plum-cake, and that all on a sudden it became transformed into a Latin Dictionary!

One afternoon, Master No-book, having played truant all day from school, was lolling on his mama's best sofa in the drawing-room, with his leather boots tucked up on the satin cushions, and nothing to do, but to suck a few oranges, and nothing to think of but how much sugar to put upon them, when suddenly an event took place which filled him with astonishment.

A sound of soft music stole into the room, becoming louder and louder the longer he listened, till at length, in a few moments afterwards, a large hole burst open in the wall of his room, and there stepped into his presence two magnificent fairies, just arrived from their castles in the air, to pay him a visit. They had travelled all the way on purpose to have some conversation with Master No-book, and immediately introduced themselves in a very ceremonious manner.

The fairy Do-nothing was gorgeously dressed with a wreath of flaming gas round her head, a robe of gold tissue, a necklace of rubies, and a bouquet in her hand, of glittering diamonds. Her cheeks were rouged to the very eyes,—her teeth were set in gold, and her hair was of a most brilliant purple; in short, so fine and fashionable-looking a fairy never was seen in a drawing-room before.

The fairy Teach-all, who followed next, was simply dressed in white muslin, with bunches of natural flowers in her light brown hair, and she carried in her hand a few neat small books, which Master No-book looked at with a shudder of aversion.

The two fairies now informed him, that they very often invited large parties of children to spend some time at their palaces, but as they lived in quite an opposite direction, it was necessary for their young guests to choose which it would be best to visit first; therefore now they had come to inquire of Master No-book, whom he thought it would be most agreeable to accompany on the present occasion.

"In my house," said the fairy Teach-all, speaking with a very sweet smile, and a soft, pleasing voice, "you shall be taught to find pleasure in every sort of exertion, for I delight in activity and diligence. My young friends rise at seven every morning, and amuse themselves with working in a beautiful garden of flowers,—rearing whatever fruit they wish to eat,—visiting among the poor,—associating pleasantly together,—studying the arts and sciences,—and learning to know the world in which they live, and to fulfil the purposes for which they have been brought into it. In short, all our amusements tend to some useful object, either for our own improvement or the good of others, and you will grow wiser, better, and happier every day you remain in the Palace of Knowledge."

"But in Castle Needless, where I live," interrupted the fairy Do-nothing, rudely pushing her companion aside, with an angry contemptuous look, "we never think of exerting ourselves for anything. You may put your head in your pocket, and your hands in your sides as long as you choose to stay. No one is ever even asked a question, that he may be spared the trouble of answering. We lead the most fashionable life imaginable, for nobody speaks to anybody! Each of my visitors is quite an exclusive, and sits with his back to as many of the company as possible, in the most comfortable arm-chair that can be contrived. There, if you are only so good as to take the trouble of wishing for anything, it is yours, without even turning an eye round to look where it comes from. Dresses are provided of the most magnificent kind, which go on of themselves, without your having the smallest annoyance with either buttons or strings,—games which you can play without an effort of thought,—and dishes dressed by a French cook, smoking hot under your nose, from morning till night,—while any rain we have, is either made of cherry brandy, lemonade, or lavender water,—and in winter it generally snows iced-punch for an hour during the forenoon."

Nobody need be told which fairy Master No-book preferred; and quite charmed at his own good fortune in receiving so agreeable an invitation, he eagerly gave his hand to the splendid new acquaintance who promised him so much pleasure and ease, and gladly proceeded, in a carriage lined with velvet, stuffed with downy pillows, and drawn by milk-white swans, to that magnificent residence Castle Needless, which was lighted by a thousand windows during the day, and by a million of lamps every night.

Here Master No-book enjoyed a constant holiday and a constant feast, while a beautiful lady covered with jewels was ready to tell him stories from morning till night, and servants waited to pick up his playthings if they fell, or to draw out his purse or his pocket-handkerchief when he wished to use them.

Thus Master No-book lay dozing for hours and days on rich embroidered cushions, never stirring from his place, but admiring the view of trees covered with the richest burned almonds, grottoes of sugar-candy, a jet d'eau of champagne, a wide sea which tasted of sugar instead of salt, and a bright clear pond, filled with gold-fish, that let themselves be caught whenever he pleased. Nothing could be more complete, and yet, very strange to say, Master No-book did not seem particularly happy! This appears exceedingly unreasonable, when so much trouble was taken to please him; but the truth is, that every day he became more fretful and peevish. No sweetmeats were worth the trouble of eating, nothing was pleasant to play at, and in the end he wished it were possible to sleep all day, as well as all night.

Not a hundred miles from the fairy Do-nothing's palace, there lived a most cruel monster called the giant Snap-'em-up, who looked, when he stood up, like the tall steeple of a great church, raising his head so high, that he could peep over the loftiest mountains, and was obliged to climb up a ladder to comb his own hair.

Every morning regularly, this prodigiously great giant walked round the world before breakfast for an appetite, after which, he made tea in a large lake, used the sea as a slop-basin, and boiled his kettle on Mount Vesuvius. He lived in great style, and his dinners were most magnificent, consisting very often of an elephant roasted whole, ostrich patties, a tiger smothered in onions, stewed lions, and whale soup; but for a side-dish his greatest favourite consisted of little boys, as fat as possible, fried in crumbs of bread, with plenty of pepper and salt.

No children were so well fed, or in such good condition for eating as those in the fairy Do-nothing's garden, who was a very particular friend of the giant Snap-'em-up's, and who sometimes laughingly said she would give him a license, and call her own garden his "preserve," because she allowed him to help himself, whenever he pleased, to as many of her visitors as he chose, without taking the trouble even to count them, and in return for such extreme civility, the giant very frequently invited her to dinner.

Snap-'em-up's favourite sport was, to see how many brace of little boys he could bag in a morning; so in passing along the streets, he peeped into all the drawing-rooms without having occasion to get upon tiptoe, and picked up every young gentleman who was idly looking out of the windows, and even a few occasionally who were playing truant from school, but busy children seemed always somehow quite out of his reach.

One day, when Master No-book felt even more lazy, more idle, and more miserable than ever, he lay beside a perfect mountain of toys and cakes, wondering what to wish for next, and hating the very sight of everything and everybody. At last he gave so loud a yawn of weariness and disgust, that his jaw very nearly fell out of joint, and then he sighed so deeply, that the giant Snap-'em-up heard the sound as he passed along the road after breakfast, and instantly stepped into the garden, with his glass at his eye, to see what was the matter. Immediately on observing a large, fat, over-grown boy, as round as a dumpling, lying on a bed of roses, he gave a cry of delight, followed by a gigantic peal of laughter, which was heard three miles off, and picking up Master No-book between his finger and his thumb, with a pinch that very nearly broke his ribs, he carried him rapidly towards his own castle, while the fairy Do-nothing laughingly shook her head as he passed, saying, "That little man does me great credit!—he has only been fed for a week, and is as fat already as a prize ox! What a dainty morsel he will be! When do you dine to-day, in case I should have time to look in upon you?"

On reaching home, the giant immediately hung up Master No-book by the hair of his head, on a prodigious hook in the larder, having first taken some large lumps of nasty suet, forcing them down his throat to make him become still fatter, and then stirring the fire, that he might be almost melted with heat, to make his liver grow larger. On a shelf quite near, Master No-book perceived the dead bodies of six other boys, whom he remembered to have seen fattening in the fairy Do-nothing's garden, while he recollected how some of them had rejoiced at thoughts of leading a long, useless, idle life, with no one to please but themselves.

The enormous cook now seized hold of Master No-book, brandishing her knife, with an aspect of horrible determination, intending to kill him, while he took the trouble of screaming and kicking in the most desperate manner, when the giant turned gravely round and said, that as pigs were considered a much greater dainty when whipped to death than killed in any other way, he meant to see whether children might not be improved by it also; therefore she might leave that great hog of a boy till he had time to try the experiment, especially as his own appetite would be improved by the exercise. This was a dreadful prospect for the unhappy prisoner; but meantime it prolonged his life a few hours, as he was immediately hung up again in the larder, and left to himself. There, in torture of mind and body,—like a fish upon a hook, the wretched boy began at last to reflect seriously upon his former ways, and to consider what a happy home he might have had, if he could only have been satisfied with business and pleasure succeeding each other, like day and night, while lessons might have come in, as a pleasant sauce to his play-hours, and his play-hours as a sauce to his lessons.

In the midst of many reflections, which were all very sensible, though rather too late, Master No-book's attention became attracted by the sound of many voices laughing, talking, and singing, which caused him to turn his eyes in a new direction, when, for the first time, he observed that the fairy Teach-all's garden lay upon a beautiful sloping bank not far off. There a crowd of merry, noisy, rosy-cheeked boys, were busily employed, and seemed happier than the day was long; while poor Master No-book watched them during his own miserable hours, envying the enjoyment with which they raked the flower borders, gathered the fruit, carried baskets of vegetables to the poor, worked with carpenter's tools, drew pictures, shot with bows and arrows, played at cricket, and then sat in the sunny arbours learning their tasks, or talking agreeably together, till at length, a dinner-bell having been rung, the whole party sat merrily down with hearty appetites, and cheerful good-humour, to an entertainment of plain roast meat and pudding, where the fairy Teach-all presided herself, and helped her guests moderately, to as much as was good for each.

Large tears rolled down the cheeks of Master No-book while watching this scene; and remembering that if he had known what was best for him, he might have been as happy as the happiest of these excellent boys, instead of suffering ennui and weariness, as he had done at the fairy Do-nothing's, ending in a miserable death; but his attention was soon after most alarmingly roused by hearing the giant Snap-'em-up again in conversation with his cook, who said, that if he wished for a good large dish of scolloped children at dinner, it would be necessary to catch a few more, as those he had already provided would scarcely be a mouthful.

As the giant kept very fashionable hours, and always waited dinner for himself till nine o'clock, there was still plenty of time; so, with a loud grumble about the trouble, he seized a large basket in his hand, and set off at a rapid pace towards the fairy Teach-all's garden. It was very seldom that Snap-'em-up ventured to think of foraging in this direction, as he had never once succeeded in carrying off a single captive from the enclosure, it was so well fortified and so bravely defended; but on this occasion, being desperately hungry, he felt as bold as a lion, and walked, with outstretched hands, straight towards the fairy Teach-all's dinner-table, taking such prodigious strides, that he seemed almost as if he would trample on himself.

A cry of consternation arose the instant this tremendous giant appeared; and as usual on such occasions, when he had made the same attempt before, a dreadful battle took place. Fifty active little boys bravely flew upon the enemy, armed with their dinner knives, and looked like a nest of hornets, stinging him in every direction, till he roared with pain, and would have run away, but the fairy Teach-all, seeing his intention, rushed forward with the carving knife, and brandishing it high over her head, she most courageously stabbed him to the heart!

If a great mountain had fallen to the earth, it would have seemed like nothing in comparison of the giant Snap-'em-up, who crushed two or three houses to powder beneath him, and upset several fine monuments that were to have made people remembered for ever; but all this would have seemed scarcely worth mentioning, had it not been for a still greater event which occurred on the occasion, no less than the death of the fairy Do-nothing, who had been indolently looking on at this great battle, without taking the trouble to interfere, or even to care who was victorious, but being also lazy about running away, when the giant fell, his sword came with so violent a stroke on her head, that she instantly expired.

Thus, luckily for the whole world, the fairy Teach-all got possession of immense property, which she proceeded without delay to make the best use of in her power.

In the first place, however, she lost no time in liberating Master No-book from his hook in the larder, and gave him a lecture on activity, moderation, and good conduct, which he never afterwards forgot; and it was astonishing to see the change that took place immediately in his whole thoughts and actions. From this very hour, Master No-book became the most diligent, active, happy boy in the fairy Teach-all's garden; and on returning home a month afterwards, he astonished all the masters at school by his extraordinary reformation. The most difficult lessons were a pleasure to him,—he scarcely ever stirred without a book in his hand,—never lay on a sofa again,—would scarcely even sit on a chair with a back to it, but preferred a three-legged stool,—detested holidays,—never thought any exertion a trouble,—preferred climbing over the top of a hill to creeping round the bottom,—always ate the plainest food in very small quantities,—joined a Temperance Society!—and never tasted a morsel till he had worked very hard and got an appetite.

Not long after this, an old uncle, who had formerly been ashamed of Master No-book's indolence and gluttony, became so pleased at the wonderful change, that, on his death, he left him a magnificent estate, desiring that he should take his name; therefore, instead of being any longer one of the No-book family, he is now called Sir Timothy Bluestocking,—a pattern to the whole country round, for the good he does to every one, and especially for his extraordinary activity, appearing as if he could do twenty things at once. Though generally very good natured and agreeable, Sir Timothy is occasionally observed in a violent passion, laying about him with his walking-stick in the most terrific manner, and beating little boys within an inch of their lives; but on inquiry, it invariably appears that he has found them out to be lazy, idle, or greedy, for all the industrious boys in the parish are sent to get employment from him, while he assures them that they are far happier breaking stones on the road, than if they were sitting idly in a drawing-room with nothing to do. Sir Timothy cares very little for poetry in general; but the following are his favourite verses, which he has placed over the chimney-piece at a school that he built for the poor, and every scholar is obliged, the very day he begins his education, to learn them:

> Some people complain they have nothing to do,
> And time passes slowly away;
> They saunter about with no object in view,
> And long for the end of the day.
>
> In vain are the trifles and toys they desire,
> For nothing they truly enjoy;
> Of trifles, and toys, and amusements they tire,
> For want of some useful employ.
>
> Although for transgression the ground was accursed,
> Yet gratefully man must allow,
> 'Twas really a blessing which doom'd him at first,
> To live by the sweat of his brow.
>
> NURSERY RHYMES

"Thank you a hundred times over, uncle David!" said Harry, when the story was finished. "I shall take care not to be found hanging any day, on a hook in the larder! Certainly, Frank, you must have spent a month with the good fairy; and

I hope she will some day invite me to be made a scholar of too, for Laura and I still belong to the No-book family."

"It is very important, Harry, to choose the best course from the beginning," observed Lady Harriet. "Good or bad habits grow stronger and stronger every minute, as if an additional string were tied on daily, to keep us in the road where we walked the day before; so those who mistake the path of duty at first, find hourly increasing difficulty in turning round."

"But, grandmama!" said Frank, "you have put up some finger-posts to direct us right; and whenever I see 'no passage this way,' we shall all wheel about directly."

"As Mrs. Crabtree has not tapped at the door yet, I shall describe the progress of a wise, and a foolish man, to see which Harry and you would prefer copying," replied Lady Harriet, smiling. "The fool begins, when he is young, with hating lessons, lying long in bed, and spending all his money on trash. Any books he will consent to read are never about what is true or important; but he wastes all his time and thoughts on silly stories that never could have happened. Thus he neglects to learn what was done and thought by all the great and good men who really lived in former times, while even his Bible, if he has one, grows dusty on the shelf. After so bad a beginning, he grows up with no useful or interesting knowledge; therefore his whole talk is to describe his own horses, his own dogs, his own guns, and his own exploits; boasting of what a high wall his horse can leap over, the number of little birds he can shoot in a day, and how many bottles of wine he can swallow without tumbling under the table. Thus, 'glorying in his shame,' he thinks himself a most wonderful person, not knowing that men are born to do much better things than merely to find selfish pleasure and amusement for themselves. Presently he grows old, gouty, and infirm—no longer able to do such prodigious achievements; therefore now his great delight is, to sit with his feet upon the fender, at a club all day, telling what a famous rider, shooter, and drinker, he was long ago; but nobody cares to hear such old stories; therefore he is called a 'proser,' and every person avoids him. It is no wonder a man talks about himself, if he has never read or thought about any one else. But at length his precious time has all been wasted, and his last hour comes, during which he can have nothing to look back upon but a life of folly and guilt. He sees no one around who loves him, or will weep over his grave; and when he looks forward, it is towards an eternal world which he has never prepared to enter, and of which he knows nothing."

"What a terrible picture, grandmama!" said Frank, rather gravely. "I hope there are not many people like that, or it would be very sad to meet with them. Now pray let us have a pleasanter description of the sort of persons you would like Harry and me to become."

"The first foundation of all is, as you already know, Frank, to pray that you may be put in the right course and kept in it, for of ourselves we are so sinful and weak that we can do no good thing. Then feeling a full trust in the Divine assistance, you must begin and end every day with studying your Bible, not merely reading it, but carefully endeavouring to understand and obey what it contains. Our leisure should be bestowed on reading of wiser and better people than ourselves, which will keep us humble while it instructs our understandings, and thus we shall be fitted to associate with persons whose society is even better than books. Christians who are enlightened and sanctified in the knowledge of all good things, will show us an example of carefully using our time, which is the most valuable of all earthly possessions. If we waste our money we may perhaps get more—if we lose our health it may be restored—but time squandered on folly, must hereafter be answered for, and can never be regained. Whatever be your station in life, waste none of your thoughts upon fancying how much better you might have acted in some other person's place, but see what duties belong to that station in which you live, and do what that requires with activity and diligence. When we are called to give an account of our stewardship, let us not have to confess at the last that we wasted our one talent, because we wished to have been trusted with ten; but let us prepare to render up what was given to us, with joy and thankfulness, perfectly satisfied that the best place in life is where God appoints, and where He will guide us to a safe and peaceful end."

"Yes!" added Major Graham. "You have two eyes in your minds as well as in your bodies. With one of these we see all that is good or agreeable in our lot—with the other we see all that is unpleasant or disappointing, and you may generally choose which eye to keep open. Some of my friends always peevishly look at the troubles and vexations they endure, but they might turn them into good, by considering that every circumstance is sent from the same hand, with the same merciful purpose—to make us better now and happier hereafter."

"Well! my dear children," said Lady Harriet, "it is time now for retiring to Bedfordshire; so good night."

"If you please, grandmama! not yet," asked Harry, anxiously. "Give us five minutes longer!"

"And then in the morning you will want to remain five minutes more in bed. That is the way people learn to keep such dreadfully late hours at last, Harry! I knew one very rich old gentleman formerly, who always wished to sit up a little later every night, and to get up a little later in the morning, till at length, he ended by hiring a set of servants to rise at nine in the evening, as he did himself, and to remain in bed all day."

"People should regulate their sleep very conscientiously," added Major Graham, "so as to waste as little time as possible; and our good king George III set us the example, for he remarked, that six hours in the night were quite enough for a man, seven hours for a woman, and eight for a fool. Or perhaps, Harry, you might like to live by Sir William Jones' rule:

> 'Six hours to read, to soothing slumber seven,
> Ten to the world allot—and all to Heaven.' "

2

JOHN RUSKIN

The King of the Golden River

or

The Black Brothers

(1841)

OHN RUSKIN (1819–1900) was the only son of John James and Margaret Ruskin, a wealthy couple, who provided him with an excellent private education at home and the experience of travel abroad to attain a wide knowledge of art and architecture. By the time Ruskin was 25, he had published *Modern Painters* (1834) and went on to become one of the foremost art and social critics of the Victorian period. Not only did he champion the experiments of modern painters and architects, but he also wrote pioneering studies of art in the Renaissance period. In time, Ruskin became a strident, if not somewhat eccentric, socialist. He attacked the greed and materialism of British society in such works as *The Political Economy of Art* (1857) and played a major role at the Working Men's College in London and also at the University of Oxford in introducing unconventional Christian socialist ideas to courses dealing with the appreciation and use of art.

Ruskin's interest in fairy tales stems from his early exposure to the 1823 translation by Edgar Taylor of the tales from Grimm, and later, in 1868, he wrote an introduction to the reissue of the book, *German Popular Stories*. Ruskin was a staunch opponent of explicit moralism in fairy tales, and he praised the Grimms' tales for possessing "true historical value;—historical at least in so far as it has naturally arisen out of the mind of a people under special circumstances, and risen not without meaning, nor removed altogether from their sphere of religious faith." According to Ruskin the power of the traditional fairy tales resides in their capacity "to animate the material world with inextinguishable life, to fortify children against the glacial cold of selfish science," and to prepare them to behold "the mystery of the fates that happen alike to the evil and the good." These principles are evidently at work in his own literary fairy tale *The King of the Golden River*, written first for his fiancée Euphemia Chalmers Gray in 1841 and published in 1851 with the illustrations of Richard Doyle. The tale was based on the brothers Grimm's "The Water of Life" and directed against the greed and exploitation that, he believed, was infecting Victorian society. Though it was the only tale he ever wrote for young readers, it gradually became a classic, and its appeal through the years can be attributed to the manner in which Ruskin combined his personal utopian longings with a social condemnation of cruelty and injustice.

THE KING OF THE GOLDEN RIVER

or

THE BLACK BROTHERS

N A SECLUDED and mountainous part of Stiria there was, in old time, a valley of the most surprising and luxuriant fertility. It was surrounded, on all sides, by steep and rocky mountains, rising into peaks, which were always covered with snow, and from which a number of torrents descended in constant cataracts. One of these fell westward, over the face of a crag so high, that, when the sun had set to everything else, and all below was darkness, his beams still shone full upon this waterfall, so that it looked like a shower of gold. It was, therefore, called by the people of the neighbourhood, the Golden River. It was strange that none of these streams fell into the valley itself. They all descended on the other side of the mountains, and wound away through broad plains and by populous cities. But the clouds were drawn so constantly to the snowy hills, and rested so softly in the circular hollow, that in time of drought and heat, when all the country round was burnt up, there was still rain in the little valley; and its crops were so heavy, and its hay so high, and its apples so red, and its grapes so blue, and its wine so rich, and its honey so sweet, that it was a marvel to everyone who beheld it, and was commonly called the Treasure Valley.

The whole of this little valley belonged to three brothers, called Schwartz, Hans, and Gluck. Schwartz and Hans, the two elder brothers, were very ugly men, with over-hanging eyebrows and small dull eyes, which were always half shut, so that you couldn't see into *them*, and always fancied they saw very far into *you*. They lived by farming the Treasure Valley, and very good farmers they were. They killed everything that did not pay for its eating. They shot the blackbirds, because they pecked the fruit; and killed the hedgehogs, lest they should suck the cows; they poisoned the crickets for eating the crumbs in the kitchen; and smothered the cicadas, which used to sing all summer in the lime trees. They worked their servants without any wages, till they would not work any more, and then quarrelled with them, and turned them out of doors without paying them. It would have been very odd, if with such a farm, and such a system of farming, they hadn't got very rich; and very rich they *did* get. They generally contrived to keep their corn by them till it was very dear, and then sell it for twice its value; they had heaps of gold lying about on their floors, yet it was never known that they had given so much as a penny or a crust in charity; they never went to mass; grumbled perpetually at paying tithes; and were, in a word, of so cruel and grinding a temper, as to receive from all those with whom they had any dealings, the nick-name of the "Black Brothers."

The youngest brother, Gluck, was as completely opposed, in both appearance and character, to his seniors as could possibly be imagined or desired. He was not above twelve years old, fair, blue-eyed, and kind in temper to every living thing. He did not, of course, agree particularly well with his brothers, or rather, they did not agree with *him*. He was usually appointed to the honourable office of turnspit, when there was anything to roast, which was not often; for, to do the brothers justice, they were hardly less sparing upon themselves than upon other people. At other times he used to clean the shoes, floors, and sometimes the plates, occasionally getting what was left on them, by way of encouragement, and a wholesome quantity of dry blows, by way of education.

Things went on in this manner for a long time. At last came a very wet summer, and everything went wrong in the country around. The hay had hardly been got in, when the haystacks were floated bodily down to the sea by an inundation; the vines were cut to pieces with the hail; the corn was all killed by a black blight; only in the Treasure Valley, as usual, all was safe. As it had rain when there was rain nowhere else, so it had sun when there was sun nowhere else. Everybody came to buy corn at the farm, and went away pouring maledictions on the Black Brothers. They asked what they liked, and got it, except from the poor people, who could only beg, and several of whom were starved at their very door, without the slightest regard or notice.

It was drawing towards winter, and very cold weather, when one day the two elder brothers had gone out, with their usual warning to little Gluck, who was left to mind the roast, that he was to let nobody in, and give nothing out. Gluck sat down quite close to the fire, for it was raining very hard, and the kitchen walls were by no means dry or comfortable looking. He turned and turned, and the roast got nice and brown. "What a pity," thought Gluck, "my brothers never ask anybody to dinner. I'm sure, when they've got such a nice piece of mutton as this, and nobody else has got so much as a piece of dry bread, it would do their hearts good to have somebody to eat it with them."

Just as he spoke, there came a double knock at the house door, yet heavy and dull, as though the knocker had been tied up—more like a puff than a knock.

"It must be the wind," said Gluck; "nobody else would venture to knock double knocks at our door."

No; it wasn't the wind: there it came again very hard, and what was particularly astounding, the knocker seemed to be in a hurry, and not to be in the least afraid of the consequences. Gluck went to the window, opened it, and put his head out to see who it was.

It was the most extraordinary looking little gentleman he had ever seen in his life. He had a very large nose, slightly brass-coloured; his cheeks were very round, and very red, and might have warranted a supposition that he had been blowing a refractory fire for the last eight-and-forty hours; his eyes twinkled merrily through long silky eyelashes, his moustaches curled twice round like a

corkscrew on each side of his mouth, and his hair, of a curious mixed pepper-
and-salt colour, descended far over his shoulders. He was about four-feet-six in
height, and wore a conical pointed cap of nearly the same altitude, decorated
with a black feather some three feet long. His doublet was prolonged behind
into something resembling a violent exaggeration of what is now termed a
"swallow tail," but was much obscured by the swelling folds of an enormous
black, glossy-looking cloak, which must have been very much too long in calm

weather, as the wind, whistling round the old house, carried it clear out from the wearer's shoulders to about four times his own length.

Gluck was so perfectly paralyzed by the singular appearance of his visitor, that he remained fixed without uttering a word, until the old gentleman, having performed another, and a more energetic concerto on the knocker, turned round to look after his fly-away cloak. In so doing he caught sight of Gluck's little yellow head jammed in the window, with its mouth and eyes very wide open indeed.

'Hollo!" said the little gentleman, "that's not the way to answer the door: I'm wet, let me in."

To do the little gentleman justice, he *was* wet. His feather hung down between his legs like a beaten puppy's tail, dripping like an umbrella; and from the ends of his moustaches the water was running into his waistcoast pockets, and out again like a mill stream.

"I beg pardon, sir," said Gluck, "I'm very sorry, but I really can't."

"Can't what?" said the old gentleman.

"I can't let you in, sir,—I can't indeed; my brothers would beat me to death, sir, if I thought of such a thing. What do you want, sir!"

"Want?" said the old gentleman, petulantly. "I want fire, and shelter; and there's your great fire there blazing, crackling, and dancing on the walls, with nobody to feel it. Let me in, I say; I only want to warm myself."

Gluck had had his head, by this time, so long out of the window, that he began to feel it was really unpleasantly cold, and when he turned, and saw the beautiful fire rustling and roaring, and throwing long bright tongues up the chimney, as if it were licking its chops at the savoury smell of the leg of mutton, his heart melted within him that it should be burning away for nothing. "He does look *very* wet," said little Gluck; "I'll just let him in for a quarter of an hour." Round he went to the door, and opened it; and as the little gentleman walked in, there came a gust of wind through the house, that made the old chimneys totter.

"That's a good boy," said the little gentleman. "Never mind your brothers. I'll talk to them."

"Pray, sir, don't do any such thing," said Gluck. "I can't let you stay till they come; they'd be the death of me."

"Dear me," said the old gentleman, "I'm very sorry to hear that. How long may I stay?"

"Only till the mutton's done, sir," replied Gluck, "and it's very brown."

Then the old gentleman walked into the kitchen, and sat himself down on the hob, with the top of his cap accommodated up the chimney, for it was a great deal too high for the roof.

"You'll soon dry there, sir," said Gluck, and sat down again to turn the mutton. But the old gentleman did *not* dry there, but went on drip, drip, dripping among the cinders, and the fire fizzed, and sputtered, and began to look very black, and uncomfortable: never was such a cloak; every fold in it ran like a gutter.

"I beg pardon, sir," said Gluck at length, after watching the water spreading in long, quicksilverlike streams over the floor for a quarter of an hour; "mayn't I take your cloak?"

"No, thank you," said the old gentleman.

"Your cap, sir?"

"I am all right, thank you," said the old gentleman rather gruffly.

"But,—sir,—I'm very sorry," said Gluck, hesitantly; "but—really, sir,— you're—putting the fire out."

"It'll take longer to do the mutton, then," replied his visitor drily.

Gluck was very much puzzled by the behaviour of his guest; it was such a strange mixture of coolness and humility. He turned away at the string meditatively for another five minutes.

"That mutton looks very nice," said the old gentleman at length. "Can't you give me a little bit?"

"Impossible, sir," said Gluck.

"I'm very hungry," continued the old gentleman: "I've had nothing to eat yesterday, nor to-day. They surely couldn't miss a bit from the knuckle!"

He spoke in so very melancholy a tone, that it quite melted Gluck's heart. "They promised me one slice to-day, sir," said he; "I can give you that, but not a bit more."

"That's a good boy," said the old gentleman again.

Then Gluck warmed a plate, and sharpened a knife. "I don't care if I do get beaten for it," thought he. Just as he had cut a large slice out of the mutton, there came a tremendous rap at the door. The old gentleman jumped off the hob, as if it had suddenly become inconveniently warm. Gluck fitted the slice into the mutton again, with desperate efforts at exactitude, and ran to open the door.

"What did you keep us waiting in the rain for?" said Schwartz, as he walked in, throwing his umbrella in Gluck's face. "Ay! what for, indeed, you little vagabond?" said Hans, administering an educational box on the ear, as he followed his brother into the kitchen.

"Bless my soul!" said Schwartz when he opened the door.

"Amen," said the little gentleman, who had taken his cap off, and was standing in the middle of the kitchen, bowing with the utmost possible velocity.

"Who's that?" said Schwartz, catching up a rolling-pin, and turning to Gluck with a fierce frown.

"I don't know, indeed, brother," said Gluck in great terror.

"How did he get in?" roared Schwartz.

"My dear brother," said Gluck, deprecatingly, "he was so *very* wet!"

The rolling-pin was descending on Gluck's head; but, at the instant, the old gentleman interposed his conical cap, on which it crashed with a shock that shook the water out of it all over the room. What was very odd, the rolling-pin no sooner touched the cap, than it flew out of Schwartz's hand, spinning like a straw in a high wind, and fell into the corner at the further end of the room.

"Who are you, sir?" demanded Schwartz, turning upon him.

"What's your business?" snarled Hans.

"I'm a poor old man, sir," the little gentleman began very modestly, "and I saw your fire through the window, and begged shelter for a quarter of an hour."

"Have the goodness to walk out again, then," said Schwartz. "We've quite enough water in our kitchen, without making it a drying-house."

"It is a cold day to turn an old man out in, sir; look at my grey hairs." They hung down to his shoulders, as I told you before.

"Ay!" said Hans, "there are enough of them to keep you warm. Walk!"

"I'm very, very hungry, sir; couldn't you spare me a bit of bread before I go?"

"Bread, indeed!" said Schwartz; "do you suppose we've nothing to do with our bread but to give it to such red-nosed fellows as you?"

"Why don't you sell your feather?" said Hans, sneeringly. "Out with you!"

"A little bit," said the old gentleman.

"Be off!" said Schwartz.

"Pray, gentlemen—"

"Off, and be hanged!" cried Hans, seizing him by the collar. But he had no sooner touched the old gentleman's collar, than away he went after the rolling-pin, spinning round and round, till he fell into the corner on the top of it. Then Schwartz was very angry, and ran at the old gentleman to turn him out; but he also had hardly touched him, when away he went after Hans and the rolling-pin, and hit his head against the wall as he tumbled into the corner. And so there they lay, all three.

Then the old gentleman spun himself round with velocity in the opposite direction; continued to spin until his long cloak was all wound neatly about him; clapped his cap on his head, very much on one side (for it could not stand upright without going through the ceiling), gave an additional twist to his corkscrew moustaches, and replied with perfect coolness: "Gentlemen, I wish you a very good morning. At twelve o'clock to-night I'll call again; after such a refusal of hospitality as I have just experienced, you will not be surprised if that visit is the last I ever pay you."

"If ever I catch you here again," muttered Schwartz, coming, half frightened, out of the corner—but, before he could finish his sentence, the old gentleman had shut the house door behind him with a great bang: and there drove past the window, at the same instant, a wreath of ragged cloud, that whirled and rolled away down the valley in all manner of shapes; turning over and over in the air, and melting away at last in a gush of rain.

"A very pretty business, indeed, Mr Gluck!" said Schwartz. "Dish the mutton, sir. If ever I catch you at such a trick again—bless me, why, the mutton's been cut!"

"You promised me one slice, brother, you know," said Gluck.

"Oh! and you were cutting it hot, I suppose, and going to catch all the gravy. It'll be long before I promise you such a thing again. Leave the room, sir; and have the kindness to wait in the coal-cellar till I call you."

Gluck left the room melancholy enough. The brothers ate as much mutton as they could, locked the rest in the cupboard, and proceeded to get very drunk after dinner.

Such a night as it was! Howling wind, and rushing rain, without intermission. The brothers had just sense enough left to put up all the shutters, and double bar the door, before they went to bed. They usually slept in the same room. As the clock struck twelve, they were both awakened by a tremendous crash. Their door burst open with a violence that shook the house from top to bottom.

"What's that?" cried Schwartz, starting up in his bed.

"Only I," said the little gentleman.

The two brothers sat up on their bolster, and stared into the darkness. The room was full of water, and by a misty moonbeam, which found its way through a hole in the shutter, they could see in the midst of it an enormous foam globe, spinning round, and bobbing up and down like a cork, on which, as on a most luxurious cushion, reclined the little old gentleman, cap and all. There was plenty of room for it now, for the roof was off.

"Sorry to incommode you," said their visitor, ironically. "I'm afraid your beds are dampish; perhaps you had better go to your brother's room: I've left the ceiling on, there."

They required no second admonition, but rushed into Gluck's room, wet through, and in an agony of terror.

"You'll find my card on the kitchen table," the old gentleman called after them. "Remember, the *last* visit."

"Pray Heaven it may!" said Schwartz, shuddering. And the foam globe disappeared.

Dawn came at last, and the two brothers looked out of Gluck's little window in the morning. The Treasure Valley was one mass of ruin and desolation. The inundation had swept away trees, crops, and cattle, and left in their stead a waste of red sand and grey mud. The two brothers crept shivering and horror-struck into the kitchen. The water had gutted the whole first floor; corn, money, almost every movable thing had been swept away, and there was left only a small white card on the kitchen table. On it, in large, breezy, long-legged letters, were engraved the words:

South West Wind Esquire.

CHAPTER II

South West Wind, Esquire, was as good as his word. After the momentous visit above related, he entered the Treasure Valley no more; and, what was worse, he had so much influence with his relations, the Wet Winds in general, and used it so effectually, that they all adopted a similar line of conduct. So no rain fell in the valley from one year's end to another. Though everything remained green and flourishing in the plains below, the inheritance of the Three Brothers was a desert. What had once been the richest soil in the kingdom, became a shifting heap of red sand; and the brothers, unable longer to contend with the adverse skies, abandoned their valueless patrimony in despair, to seek some means of gaining a livelihood among the cities and people of the plains. All their money was gone, and they had nothing left but some curious old-fashioned pieces of gold plate, the last remnants of their ill-gotten wealth.

"Suppose we turn goldsmiths?" said Schwartz to Hans, as they entered the large city. "It is a good knave's trade; we can put a great deal of copper into the gold, without any one's finding it out."

The thought was agreed to be a very good one; they hired a furnace, and turned goldsmiths. But two slight circumstances affected their trade: the first, that people did not approve of the coppered gold; the second, that the two elder brothers, whenever they had sold anything, used to leave little Gluck to mind the furnace, and go and drink out the money in the ale-house next door. So they melted all their gold, without making money enough to buy more, and were at last reduced to one large drinking mug, which an uncle of his had given to little Gluck, and which he was very fond of, and would not have parted with for the world; though he never drank anything out of it but milk and water. The mug was a very odd mug to look at. The handle was formed of two wreaths of flowing gold hair, so finely spun that it looked more like silk than metal, and these wreaths descended into, and mixed with, a beard and whiskers of the same exquisite workmanship, which surrounded and decorated a very fierce little face of the reddest gold imaginable, right in the front of the mug, with a pair of eyes in it which seemed to command its whole circumference. It was impossible to drink out of the mug without being subjected to an intense gaze out of the side of these eyes; and Schwartz positively averred, that once, after emptying it, full of Rhenish, seventeen times, he had seen them wink! When it came to the mug's turn to be made into spoons, it half broke poor little Gluck's heart; but the brothers only laughed at him, tossed the mug into the melting-pot, and staggered out to the ale-house: leaving him, as usual, to pour the gold into bars, when it was all ready.

When they were gone, Gluck took a farewell look at his old friend in the melting-pot. The flowing hair was all gone; nothing remained but the red nose, and the sparkling eyes, which looked more malicious than ever. "And no wonder," thought Gluck, "after being treated in that way." He sauntered disconsolately to the window, and sat himself down to catch the fresh evening air, and escape the hot breath of the furnace. Now this window commanded a direct view of the range of mountains, which, as I told you before, overhung the Treasure Valley, and more especially of the peak from which fell the Golden River. It was just at the close of the day, and when Gluck sat down at the window, he saw the rocks of the mountain tops, all crimson, and purple with the sunset; and there were bright tongues of fiery cloud burning and quivering about them; and the river, brighter than all, fell, in a waving column of pure gold, from precipice to precipice, with the double arch of a broad purple rainbow stretched across it, flushing and fading alternately in the wreaths of spray.

"Ah!" said Gluck aloud, after he had looked at it for a while, "if that river were really all gold, what a nice thing it would be."

"No it wouldn't, Gluck," said a clear metallic voice, close at his ear.

"Bless me! what's that?" exclaimed Gluck, jumping up. There was nobody there. He looked round the room, and under the table, and a great many times behind him, but there was certainly nobody there, and he sat down again at the window. This time he didn't speak, but he couldn't help thinking again that it would be very convenient if the river were really all gold.

"Not at all, my boy," said the same voice, louder than before.

"Bless me!" said Gluck again, "what *is* that?" He looked again into all the corners and cupboards, and then began turning round, and round, as fast as he could in the middle of the room, thinking there was somebody behind him, when the same voice struck again on his ear. It was singing now very merrily, "Lala-lira-la;" no words, only a soft running effervescent melody, something like that of a kettle on the boil. Gluck looked out of the window. No, it was certainly in the house. Upstairs, and downstairs. No, it was certainly in that very room, coming in quicker time, and clearer notes, every moment. "Lala-lira-la." All at once it struck Gluck that it sounded louder near the furnace. He ran to the opening, and looked in: yes, he saw right, it seemed to be coming, not only out of the furnace, but out of the pot. He uncovered it, and ran back in a great fright, for the pot was certainly singing! He stood in the farthest corner of the room, with his hands up, and his mouth open, for a minute or two, when the singing stopped, and the voice became clear, and pronunciative.

"Hollo!" said the voice.

Gluck made no answer.

"Hollo! Gluck, my boy," said the pot again.

Gluck summoned all his energies, walked straight up to the crucible, drew it out of the furnace, and looked in. The gold was all melted, and its surface as smooth and polished as a river; but instead of reflecting little Gluck's head, as he looked in, he saw meeting his glance from beneath the gold the red nose and sharp eyes of his old friend of the mug, a thousand times redder and sharper than ever he had seen them in his life.

"Come, Gluck, my boy," said the voice out of the pot again, "I'm all right; pour me out."

But Gluck was too much astonished to do anything of the kind.

"Pour me out, I say," said the voice rather gruffly.

Still Gluck couldn't move.

"*Will* you pour me out?" said the voice passionately, "I'm too hot."

By a violent effort, Gluck recovered the use of his limbs, took hold of the crucible, and sloped it so as to pour out the gold. But instead of a liquid stream, there came out, first, a pair of pretty little yellow legs, then some coat tails, then a pair of arms stuck a-kimbo, and, finally, the well-known head of his friend the mug; all which articles, uniting as they rolled out, stood up energetically on the floor, in the shape of a little golden dwarf, about a foot and a half high.

"That's right!" said the dwarf, stretching out first his legs, and then his arms, and then shaking his head up and down, and as far round as it would go, for five minutes, without stopping; apparently with the view of ascertaining if he were quite correctly put together, while Gluck stood contemplating him in speechless amazement. He was dressed in a slashed doublet of spun gold, so fine in its texture, that the prismatic colours gleamed over it, as if on a surface of mother of pearl; and, over this brilliant doublet, his hair and beard fell full halfway to the ground, in waving curls, so exquisitely delicate, that Gluck could hardly tell where they ended; they seemed to melt into air. The features of the face, however, were by no means finished with the same delicacy; they

were rather coarse, slightly inclining to coppery in complexion, and indicative, in expression, of a very pertinacious and intractable disposition in their small proprietor. When the dwarf had finished his self-examination, he turned his small sharp eyes full on Gluck, and stared at him deliberately for a minute or two. "No, it wouldn't, Gluck, my boy," said the little man.

This was certainly rather an abrupt and unconnected mode of commencing conversation. It might indeed be supposed to refer to the course of Gluck's thoughts, which had first produced the dwarf's observations out of the pot; but whatever it referred to, Gluck had no inclination to dispute the dictum.

"Wouldn't it, sir?" said Gluck, very mildly and submissively indeed.

"No," said the dwarf, conclusively, "No, it wouldn't." And with that, the dwarf pulled his cap hard over his brows, and took two turns, of three feet long, up and down the room, lifting his legs up very high, and setting them down very hard. This pause gave time for Gluck to collect his thoughts a little, and, seeing no great reason to view his diminutive visitor with dread, and feeling his curiosity overcome his amazement, he ventured on a question of peculiar delicacy.

"Pray, sir," said Gluck, rather hesitatingly, "were you my mug?"

On which the little man turned sharp round, walked straight up to Gluck, and drew himself up to his full height. "I," said the little man, "am the King of the Golden River." Whereupon he turned about again, and took two more turns, some six feet long, in order to allow time for the consternation which this announcement produced in his auditor to evaporate. After which, he again walked up to Gluck and stood still, as if expecting some comment on his communication.

Gluck determined to say something at all events.

"I hope your Majesty is very well," said Gluck.

"Listen!" said the little man, deigning to reply to this polite inquiry. "I am the King of what you mortals call the Golden River. The shape you saw me in was owing to the malice of a stronger king, for whose enchantments you have this instant freed me. What I have seen of you, and your conduct to your wicked brothers, renders me willing to serve you; therefore, attend to what I tell you. Whoever shall climb to the top of that mountain from which you see the Golden River issue, and shall cast into the stream at its source three drops of holy water, for him, and for him only, the river shall turn to gold. But no one failing in his first, can succeed in a second attempt; and if anyone shall cast unholy water into the river, it will overwhelm him, and he will become a black stone." So saying, the King of the Golden River turned away and deliberately walked into the centre of the hottest flame of the furnace. His figure became red, white, transparent, dazzling,—a blaze of intense light—rose, trembled, and disappeared. The King of the Golden River had evaporated.

"Oh!" cried poor Gluck, running to look up the chimney after him; "oh dear, dear, dear me! My mug! my mug! my mug!"

CHAPTER III

The King of the Golden River had hardly made the extraordinary exit related in the last chapter, before Hans and Schwartz came roaring into the house, very savagely drunk. The discovery of the total loss of their last piece of plate had the effect of sobering them just enough to enable them to stand over Gluck, beating him very steadily for a quarter of an hour; at the expiration of which period they dropped into a couple of chairs, and requested to know what he had got to say for himself. Gluck told them his story, of which, of course, they did not believe a word. They beat him again, till their arms were tired, and staggered to bed. In the morning, however, the steadiness with which he adhered to his story obtained him some degree of credence; the immediate consequence of which was, that the two brothers, after wrangling a long time on the knotty question, which of them should try his fortune first, drew their swords and began fighting. The noise of the fray alarmed the neighbours, who, finding they could not pacify the combatants, sent for the constable.

Hans, on hearing this, contrived to escape, and hid himself; but Schwartz was taken before the magistrate, fined for breaking the peace, and, having drunk out his last penny the evening before, was thrown into prison till he should pay.

When Hans heard this, he was much delighted, and determined to set out immediately for the Golden River. How to get the holy water was the question. He went to the priest, but the priest could not give any holy water to so abandoned a character. So Hans went to vespers in the evening for the first time in his life, and, under pretence of crossing himself, stole a cupful, and returned home in triumph.

Next morning he got up before the sun rose, put the holy water into a strong flask, and two bottles of wine and some meat in a basket, slung them over his back, took his alpine staff in his hand, and set off for the mountains.

On his way out of the town he had to pass the prison, and as he looked in at the windows, whom should he see but Schwartz himself peeping out of the bars, and looking very disconsolate.

"Good morning, brother," said Hans; "have you any message for the King of the Golden River?"

Schwartz gnashed his teeth with rage, and shook the bars with all his strength; but Hans only laughed at him, and advising him to make himself comfortable till he came back again, shouldered his basket, shook the bottle of holy water in Schwartz's face till it frothed again, and marched off in the highest spirits in the world.

It was, indeed, a morning that might have made any one happy, even with no Golden River to seek for. Level lines of dewy mist lay stretched along the valley, out of which rose the massy mountains—their lower cliffs in pale grey shadow, hardly distinguishable from the floating vapour, but gradually ascending till they caught the sunlight, which ran in sharp touches of ruddy colour along the angular crags, and pierced, in long level rays, through their fringes of spear-like pine. Far above, shot up red splintered masses of castellated rock, jagged and shivered into myriads of fantastic forms, with here and there a streak of sunlit snow, traced down their chasms like a line of forked lightning; and, far beyond, and far above all these, fainter than the morning cloud, but purer and changeless, slept, in the blue sky, the utmost peaks of the eternal snow.

The Golden River, which sprang from one of the lower and snowless elevations, was now nearly in shadow; all but the uppermost jets of spray, which rose like slow smoke above the undulating line of the cataract, and floated away in feeble wreaths upon the morning wind.

On this object, and on this alone, Hans' eyes and thoughts were fixed; forgetting the distance he had to traverse, he set off at an imprudent rate of walking, which greatly exhausted him before he had scaled the first range of the green and low hills. He was, moreover, surprised, on surmounting them, to find that a large glacier, of whose existence, notwithstanding his previous knowledge of the mountains, he had been absolutely ignorant, lay between him and the source of the Golden River. He entered on it with the boldness of a practised mountaineer; yet he thought he had never traversed so strange or so dangerous a glacier in his life. The ice was excessively slippery, and out of all its chasms came wild sounds of gushing water; not monotonous or low, but changeful and loud, rising occasionally into drifting passages of wild melody, then breaking off into short melancholy tones, or sudden shrieks, resembling those of human voices in distress or pain. The ice was broken into thousands of confused shapes, but none, Hans thought, like the ordinary forms of splintered ice. There seemed a curious *expression* about all their outlines—a perpetual resemblance to living features, distorted and scornful. Myriads of deceitful shadows, and lurid lights, played and floated about and through the pale blue pinnacles, dazzling and confusing the sight of the traveller; while his ears grew dull and his head giddy with the constant gush and roar of the concealed waters. These painful circumstances increased upon him as he advanced; the ice crashed and yawned into fresh chasms at his feet, tottering spires nodded around him, and fell thundering across his path; and though he had repeatedly faced these dangers on the most terrific glaciers, and in the wildest weather, it was with a new and oppressive feeling of panic terror that he leaped the last chasm, and flung himself, exhausted and shuddering, on the firm turf of the mountain.

He had been compelled to abandon his basket of food, which became a perilous incumbrance on the glacier, and had now no means of refreshing himself but by breaking off and eating some of the pieces of ice. This, however, relieved his thirst; an hour's repose recruited his hardy frame, and with the indomitable spirit of avarice, he resumed his laborious journey.

His way now lay straight up a ridge of bare red rocks, without a blade of grass to ease the foot, or a projecting angle to afford an inch of shade from the south sun. It was past noon, and the rays beat intensely upon the steep path, while the whole atmosphere was motionless, and penetrated with heat. Intense thirst was soon added to the bodily fatigue with which Hans was now afflicted; glance

after glance he cast on the flask of water which hung at his belt. "Three drops are enough," at last thought he; "I may, at least, cool my lips with it."

He opened the flask, and was raising it to his lips, when his eye fell on an object lying on the rock beside him; he thought it moved. It was a small dog, apparently in the last agony of death from thirst. Its tongue was out, its jaws dry, its limbs extended lifelessly, and a swarm of black ants were crawling about its lips and throat. Its eye moved to the bottle which Hans held in his hand. He raised it, drank, spurned the animal with his foot, and passed on. And he did not know how it was, but he thought that a strange shadow had suddenly come across the blue sky.

The path became steeper and more rugged every moment; and the high hill air, instead of refreshing him, seemed to throw his blood into a fever. The noise of the hill cataracts sounded like mockery in his ears; they were all distant, and his thirst increased every moment. Another hour passed, and he again looked down to the flask at his side; it was half empty; but there was much more than three drops in it. He stopped to open it, and again, as he did so, something moved in the path above him. It was a fair child, stretched nearly lifeless on the rock, its breast heaving with thirst, its eyes closed, and its lips parched and burning. Hans eyed it deliberately, drank, and passed on. And a dark grey cloud came over the sun, and long, snake-like shadows crept up along the mountain sides. Hans struggled on. The sun was sinking, but its descent seemed to bring no coolness; the leaden weight of the dead air pressed upon his brow and heart, but the goal was near. He saw the cataract of the Golden River springing from the hill-side, scarcely five hundred feet above him. He paused for a moment to breathe, and sprang on to complete his task.

At this instant a faint cry fell on his ear. He turned, and saw a grey-haired old man extended on the rocks. His eyes were sunk, his features deadly pale, and gathered into an expression of despair. "Water!" he stretched his arms to Hans, and cried feebly, "Water! I am dying."

"I have none," replied Hans; "thou hast had thy share of life." He strode over the prostrate body, and darted on. And a flash of blue lightning rose out of the East, shaped like a sword; it shook thrice over the whole heaven, and left it dark with one heavy, impenetrable shade. The sun was setting; it plunged towards the horizon like a red-hot ball.

The roar of the Golden River rose on Hans' ear. He stood at the brink of the chasm through which it ran. Its waves were filled with the red glory of the sunset: they shook their crests like tongues of fire, and flashes of bloody light gleamed along their foam. Their sound came mightier and mightier on his senses; his brain grew giddy with the prolonged thunder. Shuddering he drew the flask from his girdle, and hurled it into the centre of the torrent. As he did so, an icy chill shot through his limbs: he staggered, shrieked, and fell. The waters closed over his cry. And the moaning of the river rose wildly into the night, as it gushed over **The Black Stone**.

CHAPTER IV

Poor little Gluck waited very anxiously alone in the house for Hans' return. Finding he did not come back, he was terribly frightened, and went and told Schwartz in the prison all that had happened. Then Schwartz was very much pleased, and said that Hans must certainly have been turned into a black stone, and he should have all the gold to himself. But Gluck was very sorry, and cried all night. When he got up in the morning there was no bread in the house, nor any money; so Gluck went and hired himself to another goldsmith, and he worked so hard, and so neatly, and so long every day, that he soon got money enough together to pay his brother's fine, and he went and gave it all to Schwartz, and Schwartz got out of prison. Then Schwartz was quite pleased, and said he should have some of the gold of the river. But Gluck only begged he would go and see what had become of Hans.

Now when Schwartz had heard that Hans had stolen the holy water, he thought to himself that such a proceeding might not be considered altogether correct by the King of the Golden River, and determined to manage matters better. So he took some more of Gluck's money, and went to a bad priest, who gave him some holy water very readily for it. Then Schwartz was sure it was all quite right. So Schwartz got up early in the morning before the sun rose, and took some bread and wine in a basket, and put his holy water in a flask, and set off for the mountains. Like his brother, he was much surprised at the sight of the glacier, and had great difficulty in crossing it, even after leaving his basket behind him. The day was cloudless, but not bright: there was a heavy purple haze hanging over the sky, and the hills looked lowering and gloomy. And as Schwartz climbed the steep rock path, the thirst came upon him, as it had upon his brother, until he lifted his flask to his lips to drink. Then he saw the fair child lying near him on the rocks, and it cried to him, and moaned for water.

"Water indeed," said Schwartz; "I haven't half enough for myself," and passed on. And as he went he thought the sunbeams grew more dim, and he saw a low bank of black cloud rising out of the West; and, when he had climbed for another hour the thirst overcame him again, and he would have drunk. Then he saw the old man lying before him on the path, and heard him cry out for water. "Water, indeed," said Schwartz, "I haven't half enough for myself," and on he went.

Then again the light seemed to fade from before his eyes, and he looked up, and, behold, a mist, of the colour of blood, had come over the sun; and the bank of black cloud had risen very high, and its edges were tossing and tumbling like

the waves of the angry sea. And they cast long shadows, which flickered over Schwartz's path.

Then Schwartz climbed for another hour, and again his thirst returned; and as he lifted his flask to his lips, he thought he saw his brother Hans lying exhausted on the path before him, and, as he gazed, the figure stretched its arms to him, and cried for water. "Ha, ha," laughed Schwartz, "are you there? remember the prison bars, my boy. Water, indeed! do you suppose I carried it all the way up here for *you!*" And he strode over the figure; yet, as he passed, he thought he saw a strange expression of mockery about its lips. And, when he had gone a few yards farther, he looked back; but the figure was not there.

And a sudden horror came over Schwartz, he knew not why; but the thirst for gold prevailed over his fear, and he rushed on. And the bank of black cloud rose to the zenith, and out of it came bursts of spiry lightning, and waves of darkness seemed to heave and float between their flashes over the whole heavens. And the sky where the sun was setting was all level, and like a lake of blood; and a strong wind came out of that sky, tearing its crimson clouds into fragments, and scattering them far into the darkness. And when Schwartz stood by the brink of the Golden River, its waves were black, like thunder clouds, but their foam was like fire; and the roar of the waters below, and the thunder above, met, as he cast the flask into the stream. And, as he did so, the lightning glared into his eyes, and the earth gave way beneath him, and the waters closed over his cry. And the moaning of the river rose wildly into the night, as it gushed over the **Two Black Stones**.

CHAPTER V

When Gluck found that Schwartz did not come back he was very sorry, and did not know what to do. He had no money, and was obliged to go and hire himself again to the goldsmith, who worked him very hard, and gave him very little money. So, after a month or two, Gluck grew tired, and made up his mind to go and try his fortune with the Golden River. "The little king looked very kind," thought he. "I don't think he will turn me into a black stone." So he went to the priest, and the priest gave him some holy water as soon as he asked for it. Then Gluck took some bread in his basket, and the bottle of water, and set off very early for the mountains.

If the glacier had occasioned a great deal of fatigue to his brothers, it was twenty times worse for him, who was neither so strong nor so practised on the mountains. He had several very bad falls, lost his basket and bread, and was very much frightened at the strange noises under the ice. He lay a long time to rest on the grass, after he had got over, and began to climb the hill just in the hottest part of the day. When he had climbed for an hour, he got dreadfully thirsty, and was going to drink like his brothers, when he saw an old man coming down the path above him, looking very feeble, and leaning on a staff. "My son," said the old man, "I am faint with thirst, give me some of that water." Then Gluck looked at him, and when he saw that he was pale and weary, he gave him the water; "Only pray don't drink it all," said Gluck. But the old man drank a great deal, and gave him back the bottle two-thirds empty. Then he bade him good speed, and Gluck went on again merrily. And the path became easier to his feet, and two or three blades of grass appeared upon it, and some grasshoppers began singing on the bank beside it; and Gluck thought he had never heard such merry singing.

Then he went on for another hour, and the thirst increased on him so that he thought he should be forced to drink. But, as he raised the flask, he saw a little child lying panting by the roadside, and it cried out piteously for water. Then Gluck struggled with himself, and determined to bear the thirst a little longer; and he put the bottle to the child's lips, and it drank it all but a few drops. Then it smiled on him, and got up, and ran down the hill; and Gluck looked after it, till it became as small as a little star, and then turned and began climbing again. And then there were all kinds of sweet flowers growing on the rocks, bright green moss, with pale pink starry flowers, and soft belled gentians, more blue than the sky at its deepest, and pure white transparent lilies. And crimson and purple butterflies darted hither and thither, and the sky sent down such pure light, that Gluck had never felt so happy in his life.

Yet, when he had climbed for another hour, his thirst became intolerable again; and, when he looked at his bottle, he saw that there were only five or six drops left in it, and he could not venture to drink. And, as he was hanging the flask to his belt again, he saw a little dog lying on the rocks, gasping for breath—just as Hans had seen it on the day of his ascent. And Gluck stopped and looked at it, and then at the Golden River, not five hundred yards above him; and he thought of the dwarf's words, "that no one could succeed, except in his first attempt"; and he tried to pass the dog, but it whined piteously, and Gluck stopped again. "Poor beastie," said Gluck, "it'll be dead when I come down again, if I don't help it." Then he looked closer and closer at it, and its eye turned on him so mournfully, that he could not stand it. "Confound the King and his gold too," said Gluck; and he opened the flask, and poured all the water into the dog's mouth.

The dog sprang up and stood on its hind legs. Its tail disappeared, its ears became long, longer, silky, golden; its nose became very red, its eyes became very twinkling; in three seconds the dog was gone, and before Gluck stood his old acquaintance, the King of the Golden River.

"Thank you," said the monarch; "but don't be frightened, it's all right"; for Gluck showed manifest symptoms of consternation at this unlooked-for reply to his last observation. "Why didn't you come before," continued the dwarf, "instead of sending me those rascally brothers of yours, for me to have the trouble of turning into stones? Very hard stones they make too."

"Oh dear me!" said Gluck, "have you really been so cruel?"

"Cruel!" said the dwarf, "they poured unholy water into my stream: do you suppose I'm going to allow that?"

"Why," said Gluck, "I am sure, sir—your majesty, I mean—they got the water out of the church font."

"Very probably," replied the dwarf; "but," and his countenance grew stern as he spoke, "the water which has been refused to the cry of the weary and dying, is unholy, though it had been blessed by every saint in heaven; and the water which is found in the vessel of mercy is holy, though it had been defiled with corpses."

So saying, the dwarf stooped and plucked a lily that grew at his feet. On its white leaves there hung three drops of clear dew. And the dwarf shook them into the flask which Gluck held in his hand. "Cast these into the river," he said, "and descend on the other side of the mountains into the Treasure Valley. And so good speed."

As he spoke, the figure of the dwarf became indistinct. The playing colours of his robe formed themselves into a prismatic mist of dewy light; he stood for an instant veiled with them as with the belt of a broad rainbow. The colours grew faint, the mist rose into the air; the monarch had evaporated.

And Gluck climbed to the brink of the Golden River, and its waves were as clear as crystal, and as brilliant as the sun. And, when he cast the three drops of dew into the stream, there opened where they fell a small circular whirlpool, into which the waters descended with a musical noise.

Gluck stood watching it for some time, very much disappointed, because not only the river was not turned into gold, but its waters seemed much diminished in quantity. Yet he obeyed his friend the dwarf, and descended the other side of the mountains towards the Treasure Valley; and, as he went, he thought he heard the noise of water working its way under the ground. And, when he came in sight of the Treasure Valley, behold, a river, like the Golden River, was springing from a new cleft of the rocks above it, and was flowing in innumerable streams among the dry heaps of red sand.

And as Gluck gazed, fresh grass sprang beside the new streams, and creeping plants grew, and climbed among the moistening soil. Young flowers opened suddenly along the river sides, as stars leap out when twilight is deepening, and thickets of myrtle, and tendrils of vine, cast lengthening shadows over the valley as they grew. And thus the Treasure Valley became a garden again, and the inheritance, which had been lost by cruelty, was regained by love.

And Gluck went, and dwelt in the valley, and the poor were never driven from his door: so that his barns became full of corn, and his house of treasure. And, for him, the river had, according to the dwarf's promise, become a River of Gold.

And, to this day, the inhabitants of the valley point out the place where the three drops of holy dew were cast into the stream, and trace the course of the Golden River under the ground, until it emerges in the Treasure Valley. And at the top of the cataract of the Golden River, are still to be seen two **Black Stones**, round which the waters howl mournfully every day at sunset; and these stones are still called by the people of the valley **The Black Brothers**.

3
GEORGE CRUIKSHANK

Cinderella and the Glass Slipper
(1854)

EORGE CRUIKSHANK (1792–1878) was one of the foremost book illustrators of the nineteenth century. Trained by his father, Isaac Cruikshank, an artist and caricaturist, his artistic skills developed early, and by 1823 Cruikshank established a name for himself with highly original illustrations in the first English translation, by Edgar Taylor, of the fairy tales by the brothers Grimm. Not only did he create illustrations for books, but he also worked for leading magazines and journals in London. He formed a close relationship with Charles Dickens in the 1830s, and provided the illustrations for Dickens' *Sketches by Boz* (1836–7) and *Oliver Twist* (1838). His humorous, if not scurrilous, drawings had always appealed to Dickens, but, Cruikshank's work was soon to assume more serious and grave contours which led to the rupture of his friendship with Dickens. Cruikshank had been an eccentric and a heavy drinker at the time he met Dickens, but when his father died of alcoholism, Cruikshank feared he was heading down the same path and began reforming himself. By 1847 he had become one of the major champions of abstinence and published a highly popular book entitled *The Bottle*, which pictured the degradation of a family due to drinking. He followed this book with a sequel, *The Drunkard's Children*, in 1848, and it seemed that everything he drew or wrote from then on had to impart a message of teetotalism.

In 1853 Cruikshank began to publish a series of traditional fairy tales, which he revised to introduce the topic of drinking and its evils. For instance, his first tale, *Hop O' My Thumb*, depicts Hop's father as a count, who loses all his money through drinking. By reforming himself with the help of Hop, the father manages to regain his former stature. Such doctrinaire use of fairy tales to promote the cause of abstinence and to preach correct behavior drew the ire of Dickens, who criticized Cruikshank's work in *Fraud on the Fairies* (1853), which contained a mock version of *Cinderella* and teetotalism. Cruikshank responded with his serious rendition of *Cinderella and the Glass Slipper* (1854), which associated virtue and success with self-denial and abstinence. Cruikshank also changed *Jack and the Beanstalk* (1854) into a tale that preached against the alcoholism of the giant, and *Puss in Boots* (1864) was revised to show that the hero was entitled to take over the ogre's castle because the ogre was a drunkard. Cruikshank thus answered Dickens' charges not only by continuing to rewrite the traditional tales in support of teetotalism but also by publishing an essay in *George Cruikshank's Magazine* (1854) and a separate pamphlet. Eventually, he added the essay entitled "To Parents, Guardians, and all Persons Intrusted with the Care of Children" to his book publication of the four fairy tales, which was called *George Cruikshank's Fairy Library* (1865). Despite the remarkable illustrations in the book, Cruikshank's fairy tales never enjoyed the success he hoped they might have, but they do remain fascinating museum-pieces of moralism.

CINDERELLA AND THE
GLASS SLIPPER

HERE ONCE LIVED a gentleman of a high family, who was very rich, and who had a very amiable and handsome wife, and a most beautiful little daughter, so much so, that every one used to say upon seeing her, "Oh! what a lovely little girl! Oh, what a sweet little creature!" but although the little girl heard all these praises, they never made her proud or vain, for her disposition was even better than her looks. She was, indeed, one of those natures which cannot be spoiled by any praise or indulgence; but she was also well taught. Her mother was as good and as sensible as she was handsome; but, poor lady! her health was delicate, and although her husband, who loved her dearly, had all the first physicians in the town, and did all he could to save her life, yet she gradually declined and died,—regretted by every one who knew her, and deeply mourned for by her husband and her daughter.

After a few years his lady friends advised him to marry again; telling him that he should do so, not only for his own comfort, but more particularly for the sake of his little daughter; and that, although the love and care of her natural mother could never be replaced, yet that in a step-mother she would have many advantages, and probably a kind and loving relative. Feeling that this advice was good, and being acquainted with a widow who had two daughters, he thought it would be a proper and desirable match, as the lady's daughters would be excellent companions to his own darling child: and he therefore soon married.

It is the nature of woman to love children, because the Almighty has appointed her to bring them up; and when little boys or girls are placed at an early age under the charge of a step-mother, it is very rarely that they feel the loss of their own mother: but there are exceptions, and it was so, unfortunately, in this case; for Cinderella's step-mother was proud, selfish, and extravagant, and these bad qualities led her to be unjust and cruel.

The marriage was celebrated with great pomp, and the guests entertained

with great liberality, and for some time all seemed to go on very pleasantly. But the lady was so fond of company, that she was constantly giving grand and expensive parties; and being very greedy after money, and very fond of playing at cards, she became quite a gambler, and this with the hope of winning other people's money. But in this she was mistaken, for, amongst the many fine persons who visited the house, many of them were cheats—characters quite as bad as any common thieves, although they belong to what is called good society, and in time she not only was cheated out of nearly all her own money, but her husband's also; for he was an easy, good-natured man, and always gave her what money she required, until at last all his property was gone, and he was so much in debt that he was put into prison.

In consequence of this change of fortune, the lady was obliged to discharge all the servants; but as the house and furniture had been settled upon her at her marriage, she kept that, and, by pinching and contriving in various ways, she managed, with a little property she had left of her own, to keep up appearances. And now began the cruel conduct towards poor Cinderella, whom she compelled to do all the rough, hard, dirty work of the kitchen and scullery, whilst she and her daughters did all the light and clean work required for the best rooms.

It is a very unpleasant thing to speak ill of ladies, but the truth must be told; and in this case we are sorry to say that the lady in question came to have a very bad temper, and behaved in a very cruel manner to Cinderella—scolding her without any cause; and it is very painful to add that the young ladies were so influenced by their mother's example, that they also behaved very unkindly to their step-sister. But Cinderella was of such a kind and amiable disposition that she did all this drudgery and bore all this unkindness without murmuring; her only grief was for her poor father, who was in prison; and this so depressed her spirits that, after she had done all the housework, instead of sitting at the door or the window with her needle, or going into the garden, she would crouch in the corner of the large fireplace and sit amongst the ashes and cinders; and thus it was that she got the nickname of "Cinderella."

At this time, the King's son happening to come of age, his Majesty ordered a grand ball and banquet to be given in honour of the occasion, and directed that all the ladies in those parts should be invited, in order that the Prince, who was a fine, noble, handsome fellow, should choose a wife out from amongst them. Poor Cinderella, who was unknown, or looked upon as a poor, dirty drudge, was, of course, not invited, but her two step-sisters were; and they were more than delighted, and set to work with their mother to arrange and settle about their dresses. Such consultations about fashion, and trimmings, and muslin, and silks, and satins and laces, and ribbons, and braid, and bodices, and flowers, and trains, and dresses, and feathers, and jewels, and ornaments, and shoes, and

buckles, and sashes, and slippers, and all sorts of finery! Such cutting, and contriving, and working, that the day before the ball was to take place the mamma, who was not very strong, was so fatigued, that she was laid up in bed, and then the young ladies did not know what to do for some one to help them; but they were not long without assistance, for Cinderella's kind heart immediately prompted her to offer her services, which were readily accepted, as the girls knew that Cinderella had excellent taste, and was clever in every way. But they said: "What shall we do for a hair-dresser? Oh! what shall we do? We can never go to the ball unless we have a hair-dresser." Well might they say so, for their hair had got dreadfully tangled and out of order, in consequence of their having fallen into such idle habits that they did not comb and brush their hair night and morning, as they ought to have done.

Now, on account of so many ladies going to the grand Royal fête, all the hair-dressers in the country were in great request; so much so, that they raised their charges to a most extraordinary price, and thus it was only the rich who could afford to hire them; and even then many of the poor hair-dressers and their assistants were so fatigued that they fainted away whilst dressing the ladies' hair, so that the ladies and their maids had to recover them with their smelling bottles and other restoratives.

But Cinderella bade her sisters rest easy about their hair, assuring them that she could dress it to their satisfaction; and so she did,—a dear, good-natured, darling girl as she was. Cinderella exerted herself to the uttermost, and helped to dress and trim them up, even so as to astonish themselves. But, oh! there was such a looking in the glass!—such a twisting, and turning, and pulling, and breaking of staylaces, and trying on, and taking off, and putting on again!— such bursts, too, of ill-temper, when they thought anything was not done exactly as they wanted, would have tried anybody's patience. But dear Cinderella did all she could to soothe them, and to please them; and at last she pretty well succeeded, for they seemed to be quite satisfied as they took a last look at themselves in the glass. They then went and showed themselves to their mother, who was in her bedroom, and who declared that her dear girls looked beautiful, and wished that there were two Princes to captivate instead of one! As they had no carriage of their own, they had hired one of a gentleman who lived in the town, and who was so good as to lend out carriages upon hire to folks who did not keep their own; and having dressed up the driver, and a poor man who did their gardening, in some of the old livery suits, they stepped into the coach, and were driven off to the palace.

Poor Cinderella followed them with her eyes as long as they were in sight, and then, when she could see them no longer, her beautiful eyes filled with tears, and she then wished, for the first time, that *she* also had been going to the ball; and, turning from the door, went and took her usual place in the chimney corner.

Now you must know that Cinderella had a godmother, who was a dwarf, and who used to come to see her sometimes, and she came into the kitchen just as Cinderella had taken her seat in the chimney-corner. The little old lady sat down upon a small log of wood on the opposite side, and said,

"Why, Cindy, my darling, you have been crying?"

"Yes," she replied, with a sweet smile, "I did shed a few tears when I saw my sisters going to the Royal Ball, and I did think that I might have gone also, and I thought that I should like, above all things, to go, but the thought of my poor father came into my mind, and I now feel that I should not like to go and enjoy myself, and be merry, whilst my poor father is pining in prison."

"Well, that is spoken like a good, dutiful, feeling daughter. I like your sentiments, and approve of your conduct. Nevertheless, I think you ought to go to the ball as well as your sisters, and, what is more, you *shall* go."

Cinderella smiled to hear her godmother say she should go, knowing that she had neither dress nor coach to go in. And so she told her godmother (which was the truth) that she would rather not go.

"But," said the little lady, "if I wish you to go, to oblige me, particularly when I tell you that, by so doing, you will make friends at Court, and be able to set your father free from prison, I suppose you will not offer any objection."

"Certainly not," said Cinderella.

Her godmother then desired her to do everything she told her, and not to ask any questions. Cinderella was always obedient when it was to do good. The dwarf then said:

"Run into the garden and fetch me a pumpkin."

Cinderella brought in immediately the largest she could find. The dwarf then took a knife, and having cut a large round hole on each side, scooped out the middle, and placed it upon the ground, with some of the stem upon which the pumpkin grows. She then took five mushrooms, which were lying upon the dresser, and fastened four of them, by means of the tendrils, to the side of the pumpkin, like wheels; and the fifth she placed in the front, as if for a coach-box. She then told her goddaughter to fetch her the mouse-trap, in which she found six white mice; and having taken a little ball of thread out of her little pocket, she took the mice, one by one, and fastened the thread round their throats, and placed them one behind the other, like a team of horses.

"Now, child!" she said, "run into the garden again, and behind the water-butt, in a flower-pot, you will find six green lizards,—bring them here."

She did so; and the dwarf, placing a little bit of straw in the right claw of each, placed two behind the pumpkin, one on each side, and the other two in front of the mice.

"Now," said the little woman, "we want a coachman; and if there is a rat in the trap, we'll mount him on the box for a driver."

The trap was brought—there were two in it—and the dwarf, selecting the largest and the fattest, and with the longest tail and whiskers, placed him sitting upright upon the mushroom in the front of the pumpkin; and then, putting the end of the threads in one of his claws, and a long blade of straw in the other, she told Cinderella to open the kitchen door that led into the road. Then, taking up her little walking-stick in her hand, she waved it three times over the pumpkin, saying:

"Heigh ho! presto!—go!" and away went the mice, with the pumpkin rolling after them, and the lizards running upon their hind legs, out of the door into the road, followed by the dwarf, who again waved her tiny stick three times, exclaiming:

> "Now, pumpkin, mushrooms, rat, and mice, and lizards, all
> Change! to a coach-and-six, with servants strong and tall,
> To take my darling daughter to the Royal Ball."

Whilst the dwarf was harnessing the mice to the pumpkin, placing the lizards by the side, and putting the rat upon the mushroom, Cinderella was much amused; and when she saw it all move across the kitchen floor, like a little coach and horses, and go out into the road, she was more than surprised: but, when she saw the pumpkin turn into a real coach, and the rat into a real coachman, with a long pig-tail and large moustaches, the mice into milk-white steeds, and the green lizards into tall footmen with their green and gold liveries, she was struck with wonder and astonishment, which was increased, if possible, still more, when, after her godmother had gently touched her with her little cane, or wand, she found all her dingy, rough-working dress changed, in an instant, into one of the most beautiful dresses that can be imagined; her stomacher studded with diamonds, and her neck and arms encircled with the most costly jewels!

Her godmother then took from her tiny pocket a pair of beautiful glass shoes or slippers, and bade Cinderella put them on. Now the soles and lining of these slippers were made of an elastic material, and covered on the outside with delicate spun glass. They were exceedingly small, but Cinderella put them on without difficulty. Her godmother then conducted her to the coach, telling her, as she entered and took her seat upon a beautiful, soft, amber-coloured cushion, to be sure to leave the palace before the clock struck Twelve, and that if she disobeyed or neglected this injunction, the charm would be broken, and she and everything else about her would change back again to their former condition.

Cinderella promised to attend to this, and the coach drove on towards the King's palace, Cinderella wondering more and more at the strange things which had happened, and beginning to think—what she had never suspected

before—that her little dwarf godmother was a fairy. And so, indeed she was; for none else could have done such wonderful things!

When the coach arrived at the outer gate of the palace, the guards, porters, and attendants thought some grand Princess had arrived; for such a splendid equipage and such a beautiful lady had never been seen before. The young Prince, upon hearing this, hastened to the inner gate, and assisted Cinderella to alight. He was at once struck with her beauty and sweet expression, and fell deeply in love with her the moment he beheld her. He then conducted her to the presence chamber, where the King and Queen were seated on a throne, and introduced her to his Royal parents, who were amazed at the dazzling beauty of the young lady, and the novelty and splendour of her dress, and each secretly wished that their son would choose her for a bride. It was not only the King and Queen and the Prince who were amazed at the appearance of dear Cinderella, but the whole of the company assembled, including her two step-sisters, who had not the slightest idea that it was Cinderella, and all kept on exclaiming, as the Prince led her out to dance: "Oh, how handsome she is! Oh, how beautiful! What grace! what elegance! What a charming creature! What a beautiful dress! What splendid jewels!" Her appearance, indeed, created quite a sensation, and her modest demeanour, together with the sweetness of her expression, charmed everyone who beheld her. The Prince, by his marked attention, showed at once upon whom his choice had fallen; and, as he conversed with her, he felt his attachment increase, for he found her mind and disposition were as charming as her person was beautiful.

At the banquet, she was placed on the left of the Queen, who treated her with the greatest kindness, as well as the King also. The Prince, of course, was unremitting in his attentions, and everything was done that was possible to make Cinderella happy and comfortable. She felt it; when, suddenly, the thought of her poor father crossed her mind, and she inwardly prayed that her godmother's promise of her being able to assist him out of his troubles might be realised. She then thought of her godmother's warning to leave before the hour of *Twelve*; and, watching the opportunity when the ladies retired, she hastened to the court-yard and was on the road home long before the clock had struck the midnight hour.

When the company re-assembled, the Prince immediately sought for Cinderella, and as she was not to be found in any of the rooms, he flew to the gate to inquire if her carriage was there; but finding that she had departed he became quite distracted, for he had hoped to have found out who she was and where she lived. He instantly despatched messengers on horseback after the carriage, with a polite and earnest request that the lady would return for a short time; but they could nowhere find the carriage, although they had gone several miles in the direction which the coach had taken.

The Prince, in his distress, consulted the King as to what course he should pursue. The King, seeing the painful state of the Prince's mind, immediately had it announced by his chamberlains that a similar entertainment would be given the following evening; and being a kind and feeling King, and wishing to save his subjects from any increased expense for dress, they were given to understand that it was his Majesty's desire that the company should all appear in the same dresses that they wore that evening, in order, as he said, that he might recognise them again.

The reason for giving another ball was, as you may guess, the expectation that the charming young Princess would come again, and that then the Prince would ascertain who she was, and take an opportunity of declaring his love and requesting her hand in marriage.

When Cinderella arrived at her father's house she found her godmother standing at the garden gate, who told her to make haste into the kitchen. As she went in, she found herself in her working dress again, and as she took her seat once more amongst the cinders, she tried to collect her thoughts upon the extraordinary and wonderful events that had occurred during the evening. One thing was certain: the noble, manly bearing of the handsome young Prince, together with the intelligence of his mind, had made a great impression upon her. As Cinderella was entering the house, the thought struck her, "What will godmother do with the coach and horses?" and she was not surprised to see them gradually diminish until they returned to their original size, and followed the dwarf into the garden. What the Fairy did with them Cinderella nor anyone else ever knew to this day; but she supposed they were placed in a little out-house, with plenty of provender. In a short time after Cinderella had come home, her sisters arrived; and, as she was lighting their candles in the parlour, they gave her an account of the grand entertainment and the grand company, but, above all, of the beautiful Princess (for she could be nothing else, they said) who had been the great attraction of the evening, and with whom the Prince had surely fallen in love; that she had gone off, nobody knew where, and that the King was to give another grand fête the following evening, and that they and everybody who was there had been again invited. Cinderella could have told the greater part of this herself, but she only smiled and said, "Indeed!" and "Dear me!" and so on.

Early the next morning, by break of day, the hair-dressers were in request again, and again they raised their charges! It is recorded that it was a most extraordinary sight, such as had never been witnessed before, to see these hair-dressers flying about from house to house, and some that had to go a distance riding on horseback. They had been refreshed, of course, by a good night's rest, and at first they got on pretty well, but towards evening they became quite exhausted, and were constantly swooning and fainting away.

Cinderella had again to help her sisters to dress and to arrange their hair, and saw them depart again, but not with the same feelings as before, for her godmother had been with her in the morning, and told her she should go again to the palace. The Fairy kept her word, and soon after the sisters' carriage had left the door, she came into the kitchen, changed Cinderella's dress to one even more beautiful than the first, if that were possible, had the coach, as before, ready to convey her to the ball, bade her depart, giving her the same strict injunction to be sure and leave before the clock struck TWELVE.

The Prince had given orders to his pages to let him know instantly if they saw the beautiful Princess's carriage approaching; and when he heard that it was really driving into the court-yard, he flew down to receive Cinderella again, and again he conducted her, with a light heart and a smiling face, to the presence of his Royal parents, who were again delighted to see their beautiful visitor. She again became the principal object of attraction and conversation, and the Prince took the first opportunity to declare himself her admirer, and to ask her to become his bride. Her reply was that she must consult her father and friends; and he was about to beg that he might be allowed to pay his respects to them immediately, when the clock began to strike the hour of *Twelve!* She started up, and hastily quitted the apartment. The Prince, determined not to lose sight of her this time, followed Cinderella, for the purpose of escorting her home; but as he hurried after her, his attention was attracted by one of her beautiful glass slippers, which had slipped off her foot in her haste to gain the outer gate. As he stooped to pick up the glass slipper, Cinderella turned into one of the passages, and he lost sight of her. When she got as far as the court-yard, the palace clock struck the last stroke of *Twelve!* Instantly her dress was changed into her kitchen garb, and, as she passed the outer gate, the grand coach and all were again changed to pumpkin, mushrooms, rat, mice, and lizards.

The Prince, who had taken a wrong turning in the passages in pursuit of Cinderella, was, however, at the gate soon after she had passed, and inquired of the guards if they had seen the beautiful Princess pass, and which way the carriage had gone; but they all declared that no one, except a scullery maid, had passed out, and, upon looking for her coach, it was nowhere to be seen. The Prince ordered them to go and seek it in every direction; and he, even in his ball-dress, mounted a horse and dashed down the road the Princess had been seen to come.

Poor Cinderella arrived at home quite out of breath. The garden gate was open, but no godmother was there; she saw the pumpkin coach roll in, and the gate shut after it, and had just time to get inside the kitchen-door as the Prince galloped furiously past; and, after a time, she saw him gallop back towards the palace, with her heart beating quite as fast as the Prince's horse was galloping. She then returned to her chimney-corner again, but this time with no

desponding feelings: yet she wondered how it would all end. The Prince loved her, and she loved the Prince: that was all so far clear and settled; but how was it possible that a Royal Prince should marry such a poor girl as she was? In the midst of these thoughts her sisters returned, and they again described the doings at the palace and the re-appearance of the charming Princess, to all which Cinderella said, as before, "Indeed!" "Dear me!" and so on.

On the following morning, at an early hour, the town was aroused by the blowing of trumpets, and, upon the people coming out to know the occasion of it, they found two of the Royal herald trumpeters, with a Chamberlain, guards, and an attendant carrying a crimson velvet cushion, upon which was placed a glass slipper. When the trumpeters had blown a flourish, the Chamberlain read a proclamation, to the effect that the Royal Prince requested all the single ladies should try on this glass slipper, and declared that whomsoever it might fit he would make his bride. Oh! then immediately followed such a trying on—such efforts to squeeze in their dear little feet; but no! not one could get the glass slipper on, not even half-way; some could not get their toes in,—for the more they tried, the more it seemed to shrink,—and the Chamberlain requested that they would not use it too roughly, lest they should break the spun-glass covering.

The Chamberlain and attendants had gone nearly all over the town, and were growing weary, when they turned to where Cinderella lived, which was a little out of the road. The sisters were standing at the kitchen door, the mother at her bedroom window, for she was still unable to leave her room, and poor Cinderella in her dingy dress was peeping over her sisters' shoulders. The Chamberlain came forward, requesting the sisters to try on the slipper,— which they did to their uttermost, at the same time feeling that it was of very little use; after several unsuccessful efforts, they gave back the slipper, but the Chamberlain, having caught sight of Cinderella sitting in her old corner, requested that she also would try on the glass slipper; but the sisters set up a loud laugh, and said the idea was ridiculous! and would not allow any such thing; but the Chamberlain said his orders were imperative that *all* should try it on,—besides which, although it was a dark corner where Cinderella was, he saw enough to convince him that those beautiful long ringlets belonged to a beautiful face and person. He then requested Cinderella to take a seat. Just before this the dwarf had come in, and had privately handed the other glass slipper to Cinderella, which she had put into her pocket. However, she now stepped forward, took her seat, placed her foot upon the cushion, and the slipper slipped on in an instant, with the greatest ease. The sisters could scarcely believe their eyes; the Chamberlain and the attendants were surprised and startled; but they were all much more so when Cinderella quietly drew forth from her pocket the fellow glass slipper.

When the Chamberlain saw that Cinderella was the lady of whom he was in search, he informed her that, in case he should be successful in finding the lady whom the slipper would fit, he had a message to her from the Queen, to beg that she would be so obliging as to come to her at the palace without delay. Cinderella looked at her godmother to know what reply she should make. The dwarf said, "Please to signify to the Queen that my goddaughter will attend upon her Majesty immediately."

The Chamberlain then dispatched a messenger in all haste to the Prince, to inform him that the lady had been found who could put on the glass slipper, and who had also the fellow to it, and that she would soon be at the palace, agreeably to the request of the Queen. He then most respectfully informed Cinderella that he awaited her ladyship's pleasure to accompany her with the guard.

As soon as the sisters had recovered from the amazement into which this discovery had thrown them, they burst into tears and said: "Why, Cinderella, are you, indeed, the beautiful lady whom we saw at the palace? Oh, pray forgive us for all the rudeness and unkindness which we have been guilty of towards you!"

Cinderella's tender heart was touched at the repentant words of her step-sisters, and she also, bursting into tears, threw her arms around their necks, and, kissing them one after the other, said:

"Dear sisters, never say another word about it; I hope these strange changes will be the means of making us all the happier."

The two girls then ran up to their mother's room to tell her the wonderful news. Meanwhile, the Fairy retired into Cinderella's bedroom, followed by her goddaughter, and then, changing Cinderella's old, shabby, kitchen attire into an elegant morning dress, in which she looked even more charming, if possible, than she did in her full dress, told her to prepare to meet her father, to whom she had that day restored all his estates and property, and whom she expected there in a few minutes. Accordingly, almost before she had done speaking, a great shouting was heard. Her father had arrived; and when the people of the neighbourhood saw their worthy friend again, they welcomed him home with loud huzzas! for he was a great favourite with all the people in the town and country round about.

Cinderella rushed out to welcome him; and great was the joy of both father and daughter at this unexpected but pleasant meeting. He then went up to see his wife—it was an affectionate meeting. He was also glad to see her daughters, and they were glad to see him. At this moment the Chamberlain sent to remind Cinderella that the Queen would be then expecting her. A little explanation sufficed to make Cinderella's father not only acquainted with the extraordinary circumstances, but also to give him the greatest satisfaction at the prospect of his daughter's elevation and happiness; and he determined at once to accompany her to the palace. The Fairy had brought round Cinderella's grand coach to the door, into which she and her goddaughter both entered; whilst the father mounted the horse upon which he had returned home; and, with the herald, trumpeters, and Chamberlain in front, and the father followed by the guards in the rear, they proceeded towards the Royal palace, accompanied by a large concourse of people, who were in a state of great excitement, and kept on shouting until the cavalcade reached the palace, at the gates of which the Prince was waiting to receive Cinderella, which he did with great delight. He was somewhat surprised at the appearance of the dwarf; but when Cinderella informed him that she was her godmother and her best friend, he saluted the little lady with great respect, and conducted them both to the Queen, his mother. Cinderella had also presented her father to the Prince, whom he welcomed most cordially, desiring his page in waiting to conduct him to his own apartments, where he soon joined him to say that the King, his father, wished to have an interview. They accordingly repaired to the Royal library, where they found his Majesty, attended by his Chancellor and other law officers. The King was delighted to find an old friend in the person of Cinderella's father, who, as may be supposed, readily gave his consent to the marriage of his daughter to the Prince; and the lawyers having drawn up the marriage-contract, they all repaired to the Queen's apartments, to have it signed by Cinderella, the Royal Prince, and the other parties.

The Queen had been in conversation with the dwarf, and was so much pleased with her wit and good sense, that she introduced her to the King's especial notice, who received Cinderella's godmother with great condescension and affability. It was determined that the marriage should take place as soon as the necessary preparations could be made. "That is," his Majesty jocosely said, "if it met with the approbation of the young people." The Prince smilingly replied, that they would be guided by his Majesty's pleasure.

The King, who was in the highest flow of spirits, declared that there should be extraordinary grand doings to celebrate this wedding; and, amongst other things, ordered that there should be running "fountains of wine" in the court-yards of the palace, and also in the streets. Upon which Cinderella's godmother, who had been conversing with the King, begged that his Majesty would not carry out that part of the arrangements.

"Why not?" said the King; "it is the custom upon all great festive occasions, and the people would be disappointed were it omitted at a Royal wedding."

"It is true," replied the dwarf, "that the people look for such things, but although there is much boisterous mirth created by the drink around these wine fountains, yet your Majesty is aware that this same drink leads also to quarrels, brutal fights, and violent deaths."

"Well, I fear it is so," the King replied; "but this misconduct and violence is only committed by those who take *too much*, and not by those who take it in moderation."

"The history of the use of strong drink," the dwarf said, "is marked on every page by *excess, which follows, as a matter of course, from the very nature of its composition*, and is always accompanied by ill-health, misery, and crime."

"Well, but," said the King, "what is to be done? Are not these things intended by Providence for our use?"

"With all deference to your Majesty," said the dwarf in reply, "most assuredly not; for such is the POWER of the CREATOR that, if it had been necessary for man to take stimulating drinks, the ALMIGHTY could have given them to him *free from all intoxicating qualities*, as He has done with all solids and liquids necessary and fit for the support of man's life; and as He never intended that any man should be intoxicated, and as He knows that all men cannot take these drinks alike, *such is His goodness and mercy*, THAT HE WOULD HAVE SENT THEM TO US WITHOUT THE INTOXICATING PRINCIPLE; and when people talk of these intoxicating drinks, that do so much deadly mischief, being *sent* to us by the ALMIGHTY, we might as well say that He sends us gunpowder, because man converts certain materials into such a deadly composition. And as *to moderation*, pardon me, your Majesty, but so long as your Majesty continues to take even half a glass of wine a-day, so long will the drinking customs of society be considered respectable and be kept up; and it thus follows, as a necessary consequence, that thousands of your Majesty's subjects will be constantly falling by *excess* into *vice, wretchedness*, and *crime*; and as to people not being able to do without stimulating drinks, I beg your Majesty to look at Cinderella, who never has taken any in all her life, and who never will."

"My dear little lady," exclaimed the King, good-humouredly, "your arguments have convinced me: there shall be no more fountains of wine in my dominions." And he immediately gave orders that all the wine, beer, and spirits in the place should be collected together and piled upon the top of a rocky mound in the vicinity of the palace, and made a great bonfire of on the night of the wedding;—which was accordingly done, and a splendid blaze it made!

An early day was then fixed for the wedding, which was solemnised in the cathedral with great pomp and splendour, all the great people in the country being present, including, of course, Cinderella's father and her step-mother. The King and Queen were seated upon a throne near the altar. Many beautiful young ladies attended Cinderella as bridemaids, amongst whom were her two step-sisters. The bride's dress was of the richest white satin, ornamented with bouquets of orange-blossoms; a large white lace veil covered her head; her brow was encircled with a wreath of orange-blossoms, mixed with diamonds, whose sparkles seemed dimmed by the brightness of her beautiful blue eyes; and her long, waving, and clustering ringlets shadowed the rosy blush of her lovely face.

A number of beautiful little girls, dressed in white, carrying baskets containing flowers, preceded Cinderella and the Royal Prince, her handsome bridegroom, and strewed their path with flowers as they approached the altar.

After the marriage there was a magnificent banquet, and festivities upon the grandest scale were kept up for several days. And they all lived to a great age in happiness and comfort.

4

ALFRED CROWQUILL

Heinrich; or,
The Love of Gold

(1860)

LFRED CROWQUILL (pseudonym of Alfred Henry Forrester, 1804–72) was born and educated in London. After studying law he began working with his older brother, who was also a novelist, in business. However, Crowquill felt drawn to journalism and art, and during the 1820s he wrote for various newspapers and studied drawing and engraving. In 1828 he provided the illustrations for his brother's book *Absurdities* and soon earned a fine reputation as illustrator. By 1840 he was a regular contributor of illustrations, mostly designs on wood, to Bentley's *Miscelleny* and later to *Punch* and the *Illustrated London News*. In 1843 he designed some unusual pictures for Albert R. Smith's *The Beauty and the Beast*, which was a comic spoof on the traditional tale. Most of Crowquill's best illustrative work for adults was in the form of parody and often highly fantastic. However, his work for children was much more serious. Indeed, Crowquill's fairy-tale writings and illustrations for children were often didactic allegories. Such works as *Tales of Magic and Meaning* (1856) and *Fairy Footsteps; or Lessons from Legends* (1860), though artfully crafted, contain overbearing moral messages. Typical of his work was *The Giant Hands* (1856), in which a little wood-cutter's son sets out into the world to help his widowed mother. His diligence and industry are rewarded by magical giant hands that enable him to succeed in everything he does. In contrast to *The Giant Hands*, Crowquill's tale "Heinrich; or, The Love of Gold," which was published in *Fairy Footsteps*, depicts what occurs when the protagonist abandons his soul and integrity for money. Both plots amount to the same thing, namely the fairy tale with moral purpose, and "Heinrich; or, The Love of Gold" is a good example of the way in which many Victorian writers endeavored to tame the fantasy of the literary fairy tale with Christian teaching.

HEINRICH; OR,
THE LOVE OF GOLD

EINRICH WAS A stonemason, and he worked very hard at his business; not from a positive love of his art, nor a natural tendency to industry—not a bit of it; he grumbled perseveringly, and his mallet struck his cold chisel savagely; for he always felt that he was an injured man, and that fortune had not done its best for him. So he worked hard that he might hold up his head with the best of people.

"For," said he to himself, "am I not as good flesh and blood as any nobleman? And why should not he work as well as I? He, forsooth, rolls by in his coach, on stuffed cushions, and looks down upon a poor devil like me as if I were dirt. He enjoys all the luxuries of life, with a fine lady for a wife, with large feathers on her head, whilst I stand chipping in this bleak stone-pit all day; and if I should marry, would have to go home to squalling children and a hard-working wife, who would hardly have time to arrange her hair under her mob cap by the time I got home, where, tired out with my day's work, I should scarcely seem to close my eyes before it would be morning again, and labour again. What's the use of living when you do away with all life's pleasures that you may live? Psha! A poor man's life is a cheat and a delusion."

As all this discontent and envy of every one else was passing through the mind of Heinrich he kept on striking savagely at his work, which, though rude in character, possessed much talent. It was a large, nondescript figure, of colossal size, intended as an ornament, or corbel as it was termed, for the neighbouring convent then building. It had been found too large a mass to take into his own little workshop; so he had worked upon it where it had fallen when blasted from its native rock.

It was curious to observe how the mason's mind had worked upon the expression of the grotesque demon. The scowl of discontent that contracted its brows embodied that which laboured at his heart; the fierce look of its eyes were full of envy, and the corners of its mouth dropped with the disdain that Heinrich felt for his more fortunate fellow-creatures. In fact, it was all his ugly thoughts turned into stone.

On the day that I introduce him he had amused himself by putting the finishing touches to his frightful piece of work, which had occupied him till the sun began to decline. At last he rested from his labour, and seated himself at some distance from the figure, to see if any trifling alteration might benefit it, before he sent for the builder to fetch it away. After lighting his pipe, he leant back against the rock, and shutting one eye, gazed silently upon the stone demon.

The stone-pit in which he sat was a marvellously lone spot. Its rugged sides took the most fantastic forms. It was pierced here and there with yawning gloomy caverns, whose shadowy depths sent a chill to the heart. The pines waved their funereal arms all around the quarry, ever and anon breaking the stillness by scattering their hard cones, that rattled as they fell, to the stony bed beneath.

It was only once in the day that the sun had a chance of peeping into this solemn workshop, and that was when it came in a line with the road made for the work-people through the fallen pines. Just before going to rest, a few last, struggling rays would run down this road, and, peeping over the edge, illumine the opposite rocky side for a few minutes, then leave it to look more gloomy than ever.

There sat Heinrich, nearly as sombre as his own workshop, and there he sat until the sun peeped over behind him. The sun was ruddy red, and made the demon corbel glow again in all its beams.

"Not so bad, that effect," said Heinrich, as he watched the rays play about the exaggerated features of his ecclesiastical beauty. " 'Pon my word," continued he, "it gives it quite a life-like effect." As he spoke he approached a few steps towards the figure, and then made three or four wonderful bounds backwards, and fell his length among the rather rough pieces of rock. He did not lie long, for he regained his feet with astonishing agility, and stood with his eyes fixed upon the figure with a gaze full of terror.

What did he see? Why, that the figure had raised one of its scaly arms, and was shading its stony eyes from the sun's rays with its paw.

"Heinrich, my good master," at last, after many curious efforts, said the demon, "you have finished me, I believe; but you have left so much confounded dust in my mouth, that I feel great difficulty in giving utterance to what I wish to say to you. It cannot be supposed that after being so long in your company as I have been, that I do not feel some gratitude towards you; your soliloquies I have attended to with the greatest care, and I find that you are discontented with your situation, and wish to rise in the world, and be equal to the great of the land. Now, as you have very kindly provided for me in the church, I think I ought to give you something in return. If you will collect your scattered senses, so that you may be able to understand and recollect what I tell you, I will give you a hint, by following out which you may become all that you desire. This rocky pit, out of which you have chiselled me, has, for many years, been the resort of witches and knomes. Here they hold their midnight meetings, with only the moon to look on; and funny scenes I have seen enacted, and wonderful secrets have I listened to, I assure you. At first I was, as you know, but a block of stone, when you came and picked me out of a mass of rubbish, and commenced the fashioning of me into shape. When you chiselled my eyes I saw, for I had been stone-blind before; and what a wonderful world did I see, full of flowers and trees; for, I assure you, I imagined this pit was the world. Then the day was so beautiful and bright! But the first one came to an end, and I trembled, for I feared that I was to become blind again; but the moon rose in all her splendour, and dissipated my fears, and I saw the first night.

"All kinds of strange sights perplexed me: first came forms of beauty, sliding down the bright rays of the moon into the midst of the pit. These were soon joined by others more fantastic, if possible, than my own, that emerged from every nook and corner, dancing about in curious circles, but not a voice did I hear.

"The next day brought you to your work, and you chiselled my rather large ears, and for the first time I heard. That day appeared very short to me, for I was amused with your grumbling soliloquies. But what was my astonishment and delight, when the nightly gathering took place, to find myself the listener to secrets only known to the fairy world, of the paths to hidden riches in the bowels of the earth, and how to dig them from the stony clutch of the cavern knomes. Ah, ah! what do you say to that, good master of mine?"

Heinrich started as the stone image raised his voice with what might be called a very respectable laugh as he uttered his last sentence.

"Say to it?" said he, eagerly; "why, that as I have been the making of you, the least you can do is to be the making of me."

"Come, that's honestly said," answered the knome, "and it is really what I intend to do, or I should not have troubled myself with this long preamble; although, I confess, I do like to hear myself talk. Well, then, to continue my revelations, I have discovered that in nearly all these ravines lie heaps of gold— glittering heaps—that only want the seeking to be found; and the seeker must not flag, he must give up all objects but this one, or the riches within his reach sink back again into the recesses of the earth, like spilt water; for the gold knomes are a proud and jealous tribe, and their worshippers must be their worshippers only. Now, if I mistake not, I have heard you whisper to your-self the name of some one that you love. What is this love? Is it not some human foolishness that prompts a man to become a slave for life for some-thing that very seldom lasts for a year, nay, sometimes not for a month? Is it not so?"

"Well," replied Heinrich, with rather a bashful air, considering that he was a full-grown stonemason, with a very reasonable beard for his age; "well, I confess that I have a kindness for a young woman in our village, indeed, almost an engagement; but I have been prudent enough not to make it a positive one, and if you thought that I ought not, I will not; but what has that got to do with my success as a gold-digger? Would not the thoughts of her bright eyes make me—"

"Nonsense, man," interrupted the stone adviser, "all this poetry must be thrown overboard; you must stand alone, work alone, and become rich alone, and when you are so do as you like; but while you are at business you must stick to business. If the young woman cares about you, she'll wait; if she does not, all the better for you. I fear, though," continued he, "that you are too soft-hearted to set about this arduous task; come nearer to me, and I will fit you for your mission."

Heinrich drew nearer to the wonderful figure, which, when he was within arm's length, placed its stony hand upon his breast. A chill, almost of death, quivered through his frame, and he stood transfixed to the spot. After a moment of awful stillness, the figure again addressed him.

"You now," said he, "have a heart partaking of my impenetrable nature, which will serve you better than it could have done in its original state. But I must hasten to finish my lesson, for I can only speak whilst the sun's rays remain upon me. The knomes spoke of their cunning hidings of their treasures; you will find them in the sands of the rivulets that wash the mountain's foot, and masses are hidden in their very bowels that would enrich you in one night. Seek, then, and you shall find; and when you have possessed yourself of enough, come and stand beneath the shadows of the convent church, of which I shall soon become a part, when the moon is at the full. Seek me, and say *that you have enough*, and the stone-like hardness of your heart shall be removed, and open to all the enjoyments of the world, which your gold will so easily procure you. And I would further advise you to—to—"

At this point of its speech the last ray of sun glided off the forehead of the figure, and it became dumb.

Heinrich looked for a moment, expecting yet another word; but he only saw the work of his hands as it was before the glowing light had illumined it. He started from his reverie, and hurried on his homeward path; but no sleep visited his eyelids. That night he feared to sleep lest he might forget the corbel's instructions.

The early daylight found him the first man in the stone-pit, for he was nervously anxious to look upon his handiwork in broad daylight. He walked up to it, and around it, in hopes that he might hear "some more last words." Not a sound met his ears but the chattering and chirping of the birds.

There stood that provoking figure, with a most expressive look in its quaint features, as if enjoying Heinrich's embarrassment and wonder.

"Surely," thought Heinrich, "I did not go home last night and dream that this tormenting corbel had a long talk to me! But dream or no dream, I shall follow out the sense of its instructions, for, in all ways, it jumps with my humour."

So saying, or thinking, he turned upon his heel, and looking up the precipitous road, beheld the rumbling carriage approaching that was to bear his charming figure to its destination. Upon its arrival he watched, with some curiosity, the workmen throw his friend upon his back, and bind him with strong cords, to all which treatment he showed no signs of resentment. Nor did he answer any of their jibes and jests at his grotesque appearance, which, from the expression of his face, he seemed so well able to do.

They soon departed on their way. Heinrich did not follow them, but waited only until they had gone out of sight, when he gathered up his tools and prepared to go on his quest of riches.

He knew well that it would not do for him to linger about the neighbourhood in pursuit of his new avocation, so he resolved to seek his fortune in a valley not far distant, that offered all the advantages pointed out by his stone adviser, as well as at once sever all those relations which would impede him in his progress to the fulfilment of his wishes. This resolve once taken, the night found him many miles from his native home.

*

Months rolled on, and the lost Heinrich was forgotten; but he was toiling with an unceasing industry in the beds of the mountain streams, and truly, as he had been told, did he reap a golden harvest.

His beard and hair had grown in wild luxuriance, completely altering his appearance, whilst his patched garb gave him a character of extreme poverty; this rather delighted him, as it misled the people as to his real condition when he ventured into their villages for provision, the only time he was seen by his fellow-man, his habitation being in the wildest ravines, under the shelter of the trees, or, as the season grew colder, some cavern, not much larger or better than the den of the wild wolf. But he felt no privation; his life was one scene of delightful excitement, as the gold separated itself from the sand, and glittered in his hands; he felt himself as one to be envied, above all others, not to be pitied; his life of luxury and enjoyment was to come.

Suddenly, in the midst of all this self-gratulation and triumph, the sands refused, from some cause, to yield him a single grain. In vain he toiled; it was but the yellow sand that rewarded him. A mortal fear came over him, and he rushed to the cavern in which he had stored the gold that was the produce of some many toilsome months. He dreaded to find that he had been in a waking dream, and that all his treasure was imaginary. No! there it was; but what a small prize! So thought Heinrich, as he clutched it; for what was it to the load his imagination and his hopes had painted, when cheered by his first success!

He sat down in despair; his brows were knit, and his fierce eyes glared through his tangled hair, as the small space of daylight illumined the mouth of the cavern. There he sat and watched in moody silence; for disappointed avarice was gnawing at his heart; but he saw not that daylight faded into twilight, and twilight gave place to the darkness of night. All outward things were to him as nothing.

The night wore on, but his eyes closed not; he still looked into the darkness. Suddenly he thought he heard voices whispering in his close vicinity. He started, and his heart burst into a sudden flutter, like an alarmed bird. He placed his hand upon his gold. He turned his head and beheld, with fear and astonishment, a figure approaching towards him from one of the avenues of the cavern. It bore in its hand a flambeau, which gave out a fitful, lambent flame, that played over its glittering form, which seemed composed of one sparkling mass of gold.

Heinrich started to his feet and attempted to fly.

"Stay, gold-seeker!" exclaimed the figure, in a voice of command; "I have come for you, and you must accompany me to my palace below. You have been knocking at the door long enough, so I have resolved at last to let you in. Come! Oh, never mind that handful of gold!" continued he, as he saw Heinrich put out his hand to secure his treasure, before he followed him; "you will have enough and to spare where you are going, and you will be quite welcome on certain conditions."

Heinrich reluctantly did as he was bidden, and followed his mysterious guide, who led him through caverns of stalactite that glittered like diamonds. Here and there he saw rich veins of gold, meandering through the mass in most tempting abundance. At last they arrived at a golden mound, which rose almost to the ceiling of a vast cavern, the sides of which were supported by rude columns of the same rich material. Here the guide stopped, and turning to Heinrich, said:

"Here is the heart of the earth, which, by its pulsations, sends the rich, golden blood through the veins of the universal world. It is to such as you only can I discover it, for you have sacrificed, at its shrine, love, friendship, peace of mind, and all that is supposed to make life lovely. I have watched you through the long day, and the dreary night, and seen you give up, without a sigh, these cherished things, one by one, that they might not interfere with your devotion for the one great object. Your novitiate is past, and I admit you to this grand secret as one of my slaves; for none rules here but myself.

"Whenever you wish it, you can retreat from this cavern, with all that you have worked for. You will then only be able to see the price you pay for the possession of that which you so much desire."

A laugh played over his face as he said this, and thrust his golden torch into a crevice of the rock.

"The time," continued he, "will not hang heavily on your hands, for we take no note of it here, as nothing marks the day from the night, nor the vesper hour from the hour of revel; so, set to, Heinrich, and fill that capacious measure of thine, called greediness. You are free to begin, and free to leave off."

And so Heinrich did set to work, and with a glorious prospect to begin with.

★

Time had marched on, and marked his way by the changes which he left in his path.

He had placed a beautifully picturesque convent amidst the deeply wooded recesses of a valley, whose richly ornamented spires pointed like pious fingers to heaven. The woods, the water, and the luxuriant grain-laden hills spoke of peace and abundance around the holy place. For a moment only the last rays of the sun sparkled upon the gilded vanes, and then came the gray twilight, which soon yielded to the bright lustre of a harvest moon.

The glare from the lighted shrines within spread over the painted windows of its chapel, as the devout worshippers assembled to offer up their evening orisons, and the grand voice of the giant organ pealed through the valley with melodious harmony.

A figure, bending with age, crept through the trees and emerged into the moonlight; but it did not seek the door of the chapel; with uncertain foot it wandered around the building, as seeking for something lost.

The pious prayers were over, the lights faded from the windows of the chapel, and the last notes of the organ died in the echoes of the valley, as the happy peasantry departed for their homes.

Again appeared that wandering figure, in the broad moonlight; and as it turned towards the bright orb, it showed a pale face as monumental marble, and a flowing beard of silver.

It seemed to scan every pinnacle and window of the holy building with untiring scrutiny, ever and anon stopping, as if its search had been successful; and then, after a moment's hesitation, proceeded again on its way.

At length it paused, and gazed up at the quaint features which ornamented the deeply overhanging cornice of the chapel. Immoveable as the carved figures above its head, it stood for a long time; then, spreading out its arms, exclaimed—

"Enough! enough! enough!"

One of the figures, upon this summons, unfolded its stony arms, and spread them above the head of the speaker.

"Heinrich," said he; for it was Heinrich who stood in that bright moonlight, beneath the figure of the corbel that he had chiselled so long ago in the pine pit, "Heinrich, you have been long coming."

"Long! It is not very long since I parted with you in the stone quarry," said Heinrich; "yet, short or long as the time may be, I am full weary of it, and come to you for the fulfilment of your promise; for the stony heart you gave me then grows heavy, and I would fain be quit of it, and resume the one I possessed, which will enable me to have the full enjoyment of the riches I have amassed."

"You had much better retain the one you have got, my friend," replied the figure. "It is less likely to give you pain, or disturb you about other people's affairs."

"Good figure, your promise!" said Heinrich, imploringly. "I will run the risk; for curious, half-defined visions of happiness neglected, flit through my mind, which vanish as I attempt to fix them. Restore me to myself, then, good figure, or I have no happiness."

"Rash Heinrich! have your will," replied the monster, grinning down from his height upon the suppliant. As he spoke he waved his arm, and Heinrich sprang, with a convulsive start, from the ground.

And well he might; for all that he had forgotten rushed like a stream of light through his mind; his home, his friends, his love, all sprang up, as in reality, before him, from the oblivion in which his avarice had buried them. After a confused moment he looked up again.

"Thanks, thanks!" said he, almost convulsively; "now tell me of my loved Ada; is she living?"

"Heinrich," answered the voice from above, "she now lies two paces from you, beneath that white stone on which is engraven her history. Look, and you will see that she was a faithful wife to a man who loved her, and an affectionate mother to the children who placed that memorial over her."

"Dead! and so young!" sighed Heinrich.

"So young? Why, man, you forget that time has rolled on unheeded by you, since your occupation did not allow you to take note of him. Your love died at a good old age. I can read the figures from here, even by this light. A good

seventy, as I am a true corbel to the mother Church," laughed the figure.

"And my friends?" inquired Heinrich.

"Swallowed up by the same devourer. They lie around you at peace, after their duties had been well performed as good citizens," said the figure. "Look, then, to yourself, Heinrich, that you may leave as good an epitaph, although your time is full scant for doing it."

"My time scant?" said Heinrich, "why, all the remainder of my span I have appropriated for enjoyment."

"Just so," replied the figure; "but, do you know, that since I have been attached to this church I have found myself mighty prone to preach, and your folly gives me an excellent opportunity to indulge myself in the desire. Listen, then, my friend. You have filled up your span of life very nearly to the end by one great gratification, leaving yourself little or no room for the fulfilment of the desires for which you have sacrificed so large a portion of it. You are too late. Your beard is silvered, and your body bent. You have no taste left for luxurious viands, no sight to distinguish beauty from ugliness; and to begin your charity now, would be like the waste of treasure which the mariner throws overboard to save his craft from sinking. No, no; you have gathered it into a heap, here let it lie. You need none of it to assist you on the remainder of your pilgrimage, and it would be too trite an observation to say that you cannot take it with you. It is too late. You have postponed your enjoyment of life until life is yours no longer. And now you would fain turn back upon your path; but it is a path that closes behind you, and you must pass on. Go, then, the few steps allotted to you further, for I will speak no more."

Heinrich uttered no word, but passed like a shadow from amidst the tombs of the cemetery.

A few days after, a venerable hermit took up his abode in the valley, and ministered to the wants of the simple people about him. He refused all remuneration from them, and lived upon the simplest herbs. After some years he died, much to their grief. When they missed him they entered his cave, and found him extended before a figure which he had chiselled out of the solid rock. It had a strange expression in its face, and pointed with its finger to the words "Too late," engraven under it.

5
LEWIS CARROLL

Bruno's Revenge
(1867)

EWIS CARROLL (pseudonym of Charles Lutwidge Dodgson, 1832–98) was raised in a parsonage and revealed an aptitude for mathematics at an early age. Given his desire to learn and early achievements, his parents sent him to Rugby School in 1846 and then to Christ Church, Oxford, to obtain a formal education. In 1855 he was appointed sublibrarian of Christ Church and eventually became a lecturer of mathematics. Aside from his teaching duties, which Carroll took most seriously, he developed an interest in photography, attended the theater in London on a frequent basis, and began publishing comic poetry and prose. In 1861 he was ordained a deacon, but he never desired to become a priest nor to leave Oxford. He became close friends with the four children of Henry George Liddell, Dean of Christ Church, often taking them on outings and sharing his stories with them. In 1864 he wrote and illustrated "Alice's Adventures Under Ground" as a Christmas gift for Alice Liddell. An expanded version with illustrations by John Tenniel was published under the title *Alice's Adventures in Wonderland* the year after, and he followed this famous book with a sequel entitled *Through the Looking Glass, and What Alice Found There* (1871). Carroll concentrated on his photography in the 1870s and also published one more significant work of nonsense literature, *The Hunting of the Snark* (1876). Throughout his life his interest in nonsense and the fantastic was matched by his work in logic. For example, he invented a number of games such as *Doublets a Word Puzzle* (1879) and *The Game of Logic* (1886) while also publishing textbooks on mathematics. His last major literary work, ostensibly for young readers, was the Sylvie and Bruno books (1889, 1893), based on stories and fragments he had written during the past twenty years.

Carroll's contribution to children's literature and the literary fairy tale is immense, for his Alice books served to liberate the fairy tale from moralism and encouraged young readers to think for themselves and question the accepted norms of the adult world. Though *Sylvie and Bruno* is the least successful of Carroll's fantasy works, it does contain memorable incidents and chapters that hark back to his Alice books. The plot is based on the adventures of two fairy children, Sylvie and Bruno, whose antics and struggles are observed by the adult narrator, a man, who enters their world either by dreaming or experiencing an eerie state. In the real world the narrator is occupied by the endeavors of a close friend who wants to marry the beautiful daughter of an earl. As the narrator moves from the real to the fantastic and back, he comments on religion, manners, and morality, and such digressions weigh down the book. However, this is not the case with "Bruno's Revenge," first published in *Aunt Judy's Magazine* (1867), which he later made into one of the major episodes of the book. Unfortunately, Carroll revised the tale for the book and it lost much of its playful irony. In its original form, "Bruno's Revenge" reveals Carroll at his best as an experimental writer of fairy tales, and thus the version of 1867 is printed here.

BRUNO'S REVENGE

T WAS A VERY hot afternoon—too hot to go for a walk or do anything—or else it wouldn't have happened, I believe.

In the first place, I want to know why fairies should always be teaching *us* to do our duty, and lecturing *us* when we go wrong, and we should never teach *them* anything? You can't mean to say that fairies are never greedy, or selfish, or cross, or deceitful, because that would be nonsense, you know. Well then, don't you agree with me that they might be all the better for a little scolding and punishing now and then?

I really don't see why it shouldn't be tried, and I'm almost sure (only *please* don't repeat this loud in the woods) that if you could only catch a fairy, and put it in the corner, and give it nothing but bread and water for a day or two, you'd find it quite an improved character—it would take down its conceit a little, at all events.

The next question is, what is the best time for seeing fairies? I believe I can tell you all about that.

The first rule is, that it must be a *very* hot day—that we may consider as settled: and you must be just a *little* sleepy—but not too sleepy to keep your eyes open, mind. Well, and you ought to feel a little—what one may call "fairyish"—the Scotch call it "eerie," and perhaps that's a prettier word; if you don't know what it means, I'm afraid I can hardly explain it; you must wait till you meet a fairy, and then you'll know.

And the last rule is, that the crickets shouldn't be chirping. I can't stop to explain that rule just now—you must take it on trust for the present.

So, if all these things happen together, you've a good chance of seeing a fairy—or at least a much better chance than if they didn't.

The one I'm going to tell you about was a real, naughty little fairy. Properly speaking, there were two of them, and one was naughty and one was good; but perhaps you would have found that out for yourself.

Now we really *are* going to begin the story.

It was Tuesday afternoon, about half past three—it's always best to be particular as to dates—and I had wandered down into the wood by the lake, partly because I had nothing to do, and that seemed to be a good place to do it in, and partly (as I said at first) because it was too hot to be comfortable anywhere, except under trees.

The first thing I noticed, as I went lazily along through an open place in the wood, was a large beetle lying struggling on its back, and I went down directly on one knee to help the poor thing on its feet again. In some things, you know, you can't be quite sure what an insect would like: for instance, I never could quite settle, supposing I were a moth, whether I would rather be kept out of the candle, or be allowed to fly straight in and get burnt—or again, supposing I were a spider, I'm not sure if I should be *quite* pleased to have my web torn down, and the fly let loose—but I felt quite certain that, if I were a beetle and had rolled over on my back, I should always be glad to be helped up again.

So, as I was saying, I had gone down on one knee, and was just reaching out a little stick to turn the beetle over, when I saw a sight that made me draw back hastily and hold my breath, for fear of making any noise and frightening the little creature away.

Not that she looked as if she would be easily frightened: she seemed so good and gentle that I'm sure she would never expect that anyone could wish to hurt her. She was only a few inches high, and was dressed in green, so that you really would hardly have noticed her among the long grass; and she was so delicate and graceful that she quite seemed to belong to the place, almost as if she were one of the flowers. I may tell you, besides, that she had no wings (I don't believe in fairies with wings), and that she had quantities of long brown hair and large, earnest brown eyes, and then I shall have done all I can to give you an idea of what she was like.

Sylvie (I found out her name afterwards) had knelt down, just as I was doing, to help the beetle; but it needed more than a little stick for *her* to get it on its legs again; it was as much as she could do, with both arms, to roll the heavy thing over; and all the while she was talking to it, half scolding and half comforting, as a nurse might do with a child that had fallen down.

"There, there! You needn't cry so much about it; you're not killed yet—though if you were, you couldn't cry, you know, and so it's a general rule against crying, my dear! And how did you come to tumble over? But I can see well enough how it was—I needn't ask you that—walking over sand-pits with your chin in the air, as usual. Of course if you go among sand-pits like that, you must expect to tumble; you should look."

The beetle murmured something that sounded like "I *did* look," and Sylvie went on again:

"But I know you didn't! You never do! You always walk with your chin up—you're so dreadfully conceited. Well, let's see how many legs are broken this time. Why, none of them, I declare! though that's certainly more than you deserve. And what's the good of having six legs, my dear, if you can only kick them all about in the air when you tumble? Legs are meant to walk with, you know. Now don't be cross about it, and don't begin putting out your wings yet; I've some more to say. Go down to the frog that lives behind that buttercup—give him my compliments—Sylvie's compliments—can you say 'compliments'?"

The beetle tried and, I suppose, succeeded.

"Yes, that's right. And tell him he's to give you some of that salve I left with him yesterday. And you'd better get him to rub it in for you; he's got rather cold hands, but you mustn't mind that."

I think the beetle must have shuddered at this idea, for Sylvie went on in a graver tone: "Now you needn't pretend to be so particular as all that, as if you were too grand to be rubbed by a frog. The fact is, you ought to be very much obliged to him. Suppose you could get nobody but a toad to do it, how would you like that?"

There was a little pause, and then Sylvie added: "Now you may go. Be a good beetle, and don't keep your chin in the air." And then began one of those performances of humming and whizzing and restless banging about, such as a beetle indulges in when it has decided on flying, but hasn't quite made up its mind which way to go. At last, in one of its awkward zigzags, it managed to fly right into my face, and by the time I had recovered from the shock, the little fairy was gone.

I looked about in all directions for the little creature, but there was no trace of her—and my "eerie" feeling was quite gone off, and the crickets were chirping again merrily—so I knew she was really gone.

And now I've got time to tell you the rule about the crickets. They always leave off chirping when a fairy goes by—because a fairy's a kind of queen over them, I suppose—at all events it's a much grander thing than a cricket—so whenever you're walking out, and the crickets suddenly leave off chirping, you may be sure that either they see a fairy, or else they're frightened at your coming so near.

I walked on sadly enough, you may be sure. However I comforted myself with thinking: "It's been a very wonderful afternoon, so far—I'll just go quietly on and look about me, and I shouldn't wonder if I come across another fairy somewhere."

Peering about in this way, I happened to notice a plant with rounded leaves, and with queer little holes cut out in the middle of several of them. "Ah! The leaf-cutter bee," I carelessly remarked—you know I am very learned in natural history (for instance, I can always tell kittens from chickens at one glance)—

and I was passing on, when a sudden thought made me stoop down and examine the leaves more carefully.

Then a little thrill of delight ran through me—for I noticed that the holes were all arranged so as to form letters; there were three leaves side by side, with B, R, and U marked on them, and after some search I found two more, which contained an N and an O.

By this time the "eerie" feeling had all come back again, and I suddenly observed that no crickets were chirping; so I felt quite sure that "Bruno" was a fairy, and that he was somewhere very near.

And so indeed he was—so near that I had very nearly walked over him without seeing him; which would have been dreadful, always supposing that fairies *can* be walked over—my own belief is that they are something of the nature of will-o'-the wisps, and there's no walking over *them*.

Think of any pretty little boy you know, rather fat, with rosy cheeks, large dark eyes, and tangled brown hair, and then fancy him made small enough to go comfortably into a coffee-cup, and you'll have a very fair idea of what the little creature was like.

"What's your name, little fellow?" I began, in as soft a voice as I could manage. And, by the way, that's another of the curious things in life that I never could quite understand—why we always begin by asking little children their names; is it because we fancy there isn't quite enough of them, and a name will help to make them a little bigger? You never thought of asking a real large man his name, now, did you? But, however that may be, I felt it quite necessary to know *his* name; so, as he didn't answer my question, I asked it again a little louder. "What's your name, my little man?"

"What's yours?" he said, without looking up.

"My name's Lewis Carroll," I said, quite gently, for he was much too small to be angry with for answering so uncivilly.

"Duke of Anything?" he asked, just looking at me for a moment, and then going on with his work.

"Not Duke at all," I said, a little ashamed of having to confess it.

"You're big enough to be two Dukes," said the little creature; "I suppose you're Sir Something, then?"

"No," I said, feeling more and more ashamed. "I haven't got any title."

The fairy seemed to think that in that case I really wasn't worth the trouble of talking to, for he quietly went on digging, and tearing the flowers to pieces as fast as he got them out of the ground.

After a few minutes I tried again. "*Please* tell me what your name is."

"B'uno," the little fellow answered, very readily; "why didn't you say 'please' before?"

"That's something like what we used to be taught in the nursery," I thought to myself, looking back through the long years (about a hundred and fifty of them) to the time when I used to be a little child myself. And here an idea came into my head, and I asked him: "Aren't you one of the fairies that teach children to be good?"

"Well, we have to do that sometimes," said Bruno, "and a d'eadful bother it is." As he said this he savagely tore a heartsease in two, and trampled on the pieces.

"What *are* you doing there, Bruno?" I said.

"Spoiling Sylvie's garden," was all the answer Bruno would give at first. But, as he went on tearing up the flowers, he muttered to himself: "The nasty c'oss thing—wouldn't let me go and play this morning, though I wanted to ever so much—said I must finish my lessons first—lessons, indeed!—I'll vex her finely, though!"

"Oh, Bruno, you shouldn't do that," I cried. "Don't you know that's revenge? And revenge is a wicked, cruel, dangerous thing!"

"River-edge?" said Bruno. "What a funny word! I suppose you call it c'ooel and dangerous because if you went too far and tumbled in, you'd get d'owned."

"No, not river-edge," I explained; "rev-enge" (saying the word very slowly and distinctly). But I couldn't help thinking that Bruno's explanation did very well for either word.

"Oh!" said Bruno, opening his eyes very wide, but without attempting to repeat the word.

"Come! Try and pronounce it, Bruno!" I said cheerfully. "Rev-enge, rev-enge."

But Bruno only tossed his little head, and said he couldn't; that his mouth wasn't the right shape for words of that kind. And the more I laughed the more sulky the little fellow got about it.

"Well, never mind, little man!" I said. "Shall I help you with the job you've got there?"

"Yes, please," Bruno said, quite pacified. "Only I wish I could think of something to vex her more than this. You don't know how hard it is to make her ang'y!"

"Now listen to me, Bruno, and I'll teach you quite a splendid kind of revenge!"

"Something that'll vex her finely?" Bruno asked with gleaming eyes.

"Something that'll vex her finely. First, we'll get up all the weeds in her garden. See, there are a good many at this end—quite hiding the flowers."

"But *that* won't vex her," said Bruno, looking rather puzzled.

"After that," I said, without noticing the remark, "we'll water this highest bed—up here. You see, it's getting quite dry and dusty."

Bruno looked at me inquisitively, but he said nothing this time.

"Then after that," I went on, "the walks want sweeping a bit; and I think you might cut down that tall nettle—it's so close to the garden that it's quite in the way—"

"What *are* you talking about?" Bruno impatiently interrupted me. "All that won't vex her a bit!"

"Won't it?" I said innocently. "Then, after that, suppose we put in some of these coloured pebbles—just to mark the divisions between the different kinds of flowers, you know. That'll have a very pretty effect."

Bruno turned round and had another good stare at me. At last there came an odd little twinkle in his eye, and he said, with quite a new meaning in his voice: "Very well—let's put 'em in rows—all the 'ed together, and all the blue together."

"That'll do capitally," I said; "and then—what kind of flowers does Sylvie like best in her garden?"

Bruno had to put his thumb in his mouth and consider a little before he could answer. "Violets," he said at last.

"There's a beautiful bed of violets down by the lake—"

"Oh, let's fetch 'em!" cried Bruno, giving a little skip into the air. "Here! Catch hold of my hand, and I'll help you along. The g'ass is rather thick down that way."

I couldn't help laughing at his having so entirely forgotten what a big

creature he was talking to. "No, not yet, Bruno," I said; "we must consider what's the right thing to do first. You see, we've got quite a business before us."

"Yes, let's consider," said Bruno, putting his thumb into his mouth again, and sitting down upon a dead mouse.

"What do you keep that mouse for?" I said. "You should bury it, or throw it into the lake."

"Why, it's to measure with!" cried Bruno. "How ever would you do a garden without one? We make each bed th'ee mouses and a half long, and two mouses wide."

I stopped him, as he was dragging it off by the tail to show me how it was used, for I was half afraid the "eerie" feeling might go off before we had finished the garden, and in that case I should see no more of him or Sylvie. "I think the best way will be for *you* to weed the beds, while *I* sort out these pebbles, ready to mark the walks with."

"That's it!" cried Bruno. "And I'll tell you about the caterpillars while we work."

"Ah, let's hear about the caterpillars," I said, as I drew the pebbles together into a heap, and began dividing them into colours.

And Bruno went on in a low, rapid tone, more as if he were talking to himself. "Yesterday I saw two little caterpillars, when I was sitting by the b'ook, just where you go into the wood. They were quite g'een, and they had yellow eyes, and they didn't see *me*. And one of them had got a moth's wing to carry—a g'eat b'own moth's wing, you know, all d'y, with feathers. So he couldn't want it to eat, I should think—perhaps he meant to make a cloak for the winter?"

"Perhaps," I said, for Bruno had twisted up the last word into a sort of question, and was looking at me for an answer.

One word was quite enough for the little fellow, and he went on merrily: "Well, and so he didn't want the other caterpillar to see the moth's wing, you know—so what must he do but t'y to carry it with all his left legs, and he t'ied to walk on the other set. Of course he toppled over after that."

"After what?" I said, catching at the last word, for, to tell the truth, I hadn't been attending much.

"He toppled over," Bruno repeated, very gravely, "and if *you* ever saw a caterpillar topple over, you'd know it's a serious thing, and not sit g'inning like that—and I shan't tell you any more."

"Indeed and indeed, Bruno, I didn't mean to grin. See, I'm quite grave again now."

But Bruno only folded his arms, and said: "Don't tell *me*. I see a little twinkle in one of your eyes—just like the moon."

"Am *I* like the moon, Bruno?" I asked.

"Your face is large and round like the moon," Bruno answered, looking at me thoughtfully. "It doesn't shine quite so b'ight—but it's cleaner."

I couldn't help smiling at this. "You know I wash *my* face, Bruno. The moon never does that."

"Oh, doesn't she though!" cried Bruno; and he leant forwards and added in a solemn whisper: "The moon's face gets dirtier and dirtier every night, till it's black all ac'oss. And then, when it's dirty all over, *so*"—he passed his hand across his own rosy cheeks as he spoke—"then she washes it."

"And then it's all clean again, isn't it?"

"Not all in a moment," said Bruno. "What a deal of teaching you want! She washes it little by little—only she begins at the other edge."

By this time he was sitting quietly on the dead mouse with his arms folded, and the weeding wasn't getting on a bit; so I was obliged to say: "Work first and pleasure afterwards—no more talking till that bed's finished."

After that we had a few minutes of silence, while I sorted out the pebbles, and amused myself with watching Bruno's plan of gardening. It was quite a new plan to me: he always measured each bed before he weeded it, as if he was afraid the weeding would make it shrink; and once, when it came out longer than he wished, he set to work to thump the mouse with his tiny fist, crying out: "There now! It's all 'ong again! Why don't you keep your tail st'aight when I tell you!"

"I'll tell you what I'll do," Bruno said in a half-whisper, as we worked: "I'll get you an invitation to the king's dinner-party. I know one of the head-vraiters."

I couldn't help laughing at this idea. "Do the waiters invite the guests?" I asked.

"Oh, not *to sit down*!" Bruno hastily replied. "But to help, you know. You'd like that, wouldn't you? To hand about plates, and so on."

"Well, but that's not so nice as sitting at the table, is it?"

"Of course it isn't," Bruno said, in a tone as if he rather pitied my ignorance; "but if you're not even Sir Anything, you can't expect to be allowed to sit at the table, you know."

I said, as meekly as I could, that I didn't expect it, but it was the only way of going to a dinner-party that I really enjoyed. And Bruno tossed his head, and said, in a rather offended tone, that I might do as I pleased—there were many he knew that would give their ears to go.

"Have you ever been yourself, Bruno?"

"They invited me once last year," Bruno said, very gravely. "It was to wash up the soup-plates—no, the cheese-plates, I mean—that was g'and enough. But the g'andest thing of all was, *I* fetched the Duke of Dandelion a glass of cider!"

"That *was* grand!" I said, biting my lip to keep myself from laughing.

"Wasn't it?" said Bruno, very earnestly. "You know it isn't everyone that's had such an honour as *that*!"

This set me thinking of the various queer things we call "an honour" in this world, which, after all, haven't a bit more honour in them than what the dear little Bruno enjoyed (by the way, I hope you're beginning to like him a little, naughty as he was?) when he took the Duke of Dandelion a glass of cider.

I don't know how long I might have dreamed on in this way, if Bruno hadn't suddenly roused me. "Oh, come here quick!" he cried, in a state of the wildest excitement. "Catch hold of his other horn! I can't hold him more than a minute!"

He was struggling desperately with a great snail, clinging to one of its horns, and nearly breaking his poor little back in his efforts to drag it over a blade of grass.

I saw we should have no more gardening if I let this sort of thing go on, so I quietly took the snail away, and put it on a bank where he couldn't reach it. "We'll hunt it afterwards, Bruno," I said, "if you really want to catch it. But what's the use of it when you've got it?"

"What's the use of a fox when you've got it?" said Bruno. "I know you big things hunt foxes."

I tried to think of some good reason why "big things" should hunt foxes, and he shouldn't hunt snails, but none came into my head; so I said at last: "Well, I suppose one's as good as the other. I'll go snail-hunting myself some day."

"I should think you wouldn't be so silly," said Bruno, "as to go snail-hunting all by yourself. Why, you'd never get the snail along, if you hadn't somebody to hold on to his other horn!"

"Of course I shan't go alone," I said quite gravely. "By the way, is that the best kind to hunt, or do you recommend the ones without shells?"

"Oh no, we never hunt the ones without shells," Bruno said, with a little shudder at the thought of it. "They're always so c'oss about it; and then, if you tumble over them, they're ever so sticky!"

By this time we had nearly finished the garden. I had fetched some violets, and Bruno was just helping me to put in the last, when he suddenly stopped and said, "I'm tired."

"Rest, then," I said. "I can go on without you."

Bruno needed no second invitation: he at once began arranging the dead mouse as a kind of sofa. "And I'll sing you a little song," he said, as he rolled it about.

"Do," said I. "There's nothing I should like better."

"Which song will you choose?" Bruno said, as he dragged the mouse into a place where he could get a good view of me. " 'Ting, ting, ting' is the nicest."

There was no resisting such a strong hint as this: however, I pretended to think about it for a moment, and then said: "Well, I like 'Ting, ting, ting' best of all."

"That shows you're a good judge of music," Bruno said, with a pleased look. "How many bluebells would you like?" And he put his thumb into his mouth to help me to consider.

As there was only one bluebell within easy reach, I said very gravely that I thought one would do *this* time, and I picked it and gave it to him. Bruno ran his hand once or twice up and down the flowers, like a musician trying an instrument, producing a most delicious, delicate tinkling as he did so. I had never heard flower-music before—I don't think one can, unless one's in the "eerie" state—and I don't know quite how to give you an idea of what it was like, except by saying that it sounded like a peal of bells a thousand miles off. When he had satisfied himself that the flowers were in tune, he seated himself on the dead mouse (he never seemed really comfortable anywhere else), and, looking up at me with a merry twinkle in his eyes, he began. By the way, the tune was rather a curious one, and you might like to try it for yourself, so here are the notes:

Rise, oh, rise! The daylight dies:
    The owls are hooting, ting, ting, ting!
Wake, oh, wake! Beside the lake
    The elves are fluting, ting, ting, ting!
Welcoming our fairy king,
    We sing, sing, sing.

He sang the first four lines briskly and merrily, making the bluebells chime in time with the music; but the last two he sang quite slowly and gently, and merely waved the flowers backwards and forwards above his head. And when he had finished the first verse, he left off to explain. "The name of our fairy king is Obberwon"—he meant "Oberon," I believe—"and he lives over the lake—*there*—and now and then he comes in a little boat—and then we go and meet him—and then we sing this song, you know."

"And then you go and dine with him?" I said mischievously.

"You shouldn't talk," Bruno hastily said; "it interrupts the song so."

I said I wouldn't do it again.

"I never talk myself when I'm singing," he went on, very gravely; "so you shouldn't either." Then he tuned the bluebells once more, and sang:

"Hear, oh, hear! From far and near
   A music stealing, ting, ting, ting!
Fairy bells adown the dells
   Are merrily pealing, ting, ting, ting!
Welcoming our fairy king
   We ring, ring, ring.

"See, oh, see! On every tree
   What lamps are shining, ting, ting, ting!
They are eyes of fiery flies
   To light our dining, ting, ting, ting!
Welcoming our fairy king
   They swing, swing, swing.

"Haste, oh haste! to take and taste
   The dainties waiting, ting, ting, ting!
Honey-dew is stored—"

"Hush, Bruno!" I interrupted, in a warning whisper. "She's coming!"

Bruno checked his song only just in time for Sylvie not to hear him, and then, catching sight of her as she slowly made her way through the long grass, he suddenly rushed out headlong at her like a little bull, shouting: "Look the other way! Look the other way!"

"Which way?" Sylvie asked, in rather a frightened tone, as she looked round in all directions to see where the danger could be.

"*That* way!" said Bruno, carefully turning her round with her face to the wood. "Now, walk backwards—walk gently—don't be f'ightened: you shan't t'ip!"

But Sylvie did "t'ip" notwithstanding: in fact he led her, in his hurry, across so many little sticks and stones, that it was really a wonder the poor child could keep on her feet at all. But he was far too much excited to think of what he was doing.

I silently pointed out to Bruno the best place to lead her to, so as to get a view of the whole garden at once: it was a little rising ground, about the height of a potato; and, when they had mounted it, I drew back into the shade, that Sylvie mightn't see me.

I heard Bruno cry out triumphantly "*Now* you may look!" and then followed a great clapping of hands, but it was all done by Bruno himself. Sylvie was quite silent—she only stood and gazed with her hands clasped tightly together, and I was half afraid she didn't like it after all.

Bruno too was watching her anxiously, and when she jumped down off the mound, and began wandering up and down the little walks, he cautiously followed her about, evidently anxious that she should form her own opinion of it all, without any hint from him. And when at last she drew a long breath, and gave her verdict—in a hurried whisper, and without the slightest regard to grammar—"It's the loveliest thing as I never saw in all my life before!" the little fellow looked as well pleased as if it had been given by all the judges and juries in England put together.

"And did you really do it all by yourself, Bruno?" said Sylvie. "And all for me?"

"I was helped a bit," Bruno began, with a merry little laugh at her surprise. "We've been at it all the afternoon—I thought you'd like—" and here the poor little fellow's lip began to quiver, and all in a moment he burst out crying, and running up to Sylvie he flung his arms passionately round her neck, and hid his face on her shoulder.

There was a little quiver in Sylvie's voice too as she whispered: "Why, what's the matter, darling?" and tried to lift up his head and kiss him.

But Bruno only clung to her, sobbing, and wouldn't be comforted till he had confessed all. "I t'ied—to spoil your garden—first—but—I'll never— never—" and then came another burst of tears, which drowned the rest of the sentence. At last he got out the words, "I liked—putting in the flowers—for *you*, Sylvie—and I never was so happy before—" and the rosy little face came up at last to be kissed, all wet with tears as it was.

Sylvie was crying too by this time, and she said nothing but "Bruno, dear!" and "*I* never was so happy before—" though why two children who had never been so happy before should both be crying, was a great mystery to me.

I felt very happy too, but of course I didn't cry: "big things" never do, you know—we leave all that to the fairies. Only I think it must have been raining a little just then, for I found a drop or two on my cheeks.

After that they went through the whole garden again, flower by flower, as if it were a long sentence they were spelling out, with kisses for commas, and a great hug by way of a full-stop when they got to the end.

"Do you know, that was my river-edge, Sylvie?" Bruno began, looking solemnly at her.

Sylvie laughed merrily. "What *do* you mean?" she said; and she pushed back her heavy brown hair with both hands, and looked at him with dancing eyes in which the big tear-drops were still glittering.

Bruno drew in a long breath, and made up his mouth for a great effort. "I mean rev-enge," he said; "now you under'tand." And he looked so happy and proud at having said the word right at last, that I quite envied him. I rather think Sylvie didn't "under'tand" at all; but she gave him a little kiss on each cheek, which seemed to do just as well.

So they wandered off lovingly together, in among the buttercups, each with an arm twined round the other, whispering and laughing as they went, and never so much as once looked back at poor me. Yes, once, just before I quite lost sight of them, Bruno half turned his head, and nodded me a saucy little good-bye over one shoulder. And that was all the thanks I got for *my* trouble.

I know you're sorry the story's come to an end—aren't you?—so I'll just tell you one thing more. The very last thing I saw of them was this—Sylvie was stooping down with her arms round Bruno's neck, and saying coaxingly in his ear: "Do you know, Bruno, I've quite forgotten that hard word—do say it once more. Come! Only this once, dear!"

But Bruno wouldn't try it again.

6

CHARLES DICKENS

The Magic Fishbone
(1868)

HARLES DICKENS (1812–70) was greatly influenced by his reading of fairy tales during his youth, especially *The Arabian Nights*, *The Tales of the Genii*, *Aesop's Fables*, and individual tales such as *Little Red Riding Hood* from the collections of Charles Perrault and the Brothers Grimm. Indeed, two scholarly studies, *Dickens and the Fairy Tale* by Michael Kotzin and *Dickens and the Invisible World* by Harry Stone, have documented how crucial Dickens' early exposure to fairy tales was for the development of his later works such as *Dombey and Son*, *David Copperfield*, and *Great Expectations*. Aside from these novels, Dickens used fairy-tale motifs, patterns, and themes in his *Christmas Books* (1843–8), ghost stories, and other works. His strong attachment to the fairy tale reflected his rebellion against the stifling pedantry and narrow-minded, religious training which he experienced during his youth. Dickens came to associate the fairyland realm with freedom of the imagination, tolerance, and hope. Thus, it was not coincidence that, in 1853, he became involved in an acrimonious debate with his friend George Cruikshank. In "Fraud on the Fairies" printed in *Household Words* he argued that traditional fairy tales were pure and innocent and should not be revised in a doctrinaire way. This position did not stop Dickens himself from employing traditional fairy-tale motifs in extraordinary ways in his novels. Nor did it prevent him, toward the end of his life, from writing his own unusual fairy tales which broke traditional fairy-tale conventions.

"The Magic Fishbone" was one of the series of tales entitled *Holiday Romance* which was published in the magazines *All the Year Round* and *Our Young Folks* in 1868, two years before his death. The stories in *Holiday Romance* were supposedly written by children on holiday to show adults how the world should be. Dickens created childlike narrators aged from "half-past-six" to nine to play ingenuously and imaginatively with four different genres: the adventure story, the fairy tale, the pirate story, and the domestic romance. In "The Magic Fishbone," Alice Rainbird, "aged seven," tells a tale that conveys Dickens' own childlike faith in the power of magic to bring about changes in the pedestrian bourgeois life. His reversal of traditional fairy-tale motifs and use of nonsense do not destroy the "free spirit" of the fairy tale as is the case in Cruikshank's doctrinaire revisions. Rather, they reinforce the aspects of innocence and hope which Dickens felt were necessary in all true fairy tales.

THE MAGIC FISHBONE

ROMANCE.   FROM THE PEN OF MISS ALICE RAINBIRD*

 HERE WAS ONCE a King, and he had a Queen, and he was the manliest of his sex, and she was the loveliest of hers. The King was, in his private profession, Under Government. The Queen's father had been a medical man out of town.

They had nineteen children, and were always having more. Seventeen of these children took care of the baby, and Alicia, the eldest, took care of them all. Their ages varied from seven years to seven months.

Let us now resume our story.

One day the King was going to the Office, when he stopped at the fishmonger's to buy a pound and a half of salmon not too near the tail, which the Queen (who was a careful housekeeper) had requested him to send home. Mr Pickles, the fishmonger, said, "Certainly, sir, is there any other article, good morning."

The King went on towards the Office in a melancholy mood, for Quarter Day was such a long way off, and several of the dear children were growing out of their clothes. He had not proceeded far, when Mr Pickles's errand-boy came running after him, and said, "Sir, you didn't notice the old lady in our shop."

"What old lady?" inquired the King. "I saw none."

Now, the King had not seen any old lady, because this old lady had been invisible to him, though visible to Mr Pickles's boy. Probably because he messed and splashed the water about to that degree, and flopped the pairs of soles down in that violent manner, that, if she had not been visible to him, he would have spoilt her clothes.

Just then the old lady came trotting up. She was dresed in shot-silk of the richest quality, smelling of dried lavender.

"King Watkins the First, I believe?" said the old lady.

"Watkins," replied the King, "is my name."

"Papa, if I am not mistaken, of the beautiful Princess Alicia?" said the old lady.

*Aged Seven.

"And of eighteen other darlings," replied the King.

"Listen. You are going to the Office," said the old lady.

It instantly flashed upon the King that she must be a Fairy, or how could she know that?

"You are right," said the old lady, answering his thoughts, "I am the Good Fairy Grandmarina. Attend. When you return home to dinner, politely invite the Princess Alicia to have some of the salmon you bought just now."

"It may disagree with her," said the King.

The old lady became so very angry at this absurd idea, that the King was quite alarmed, and humbly begged her pardon.

"We hear a great deal too much about this thing disagreeing and that thing disagreeing," said the old lady, with the greatest contempt it was possible to express. "Don't be greedy. I think you want it all yourself."

The King hung his head under this reproof, and said he wouldn't talk about things disagreeing, any more.

"Be good then," said the Fairy Grandmarina, "and don't! When the beautiful Princess Alicia consents to partake of the salmon—as I think she will—you will find she will leave a fish-bone on her plate. Tell her to dry it, and to rub it, and to polish it till it shines like mother-of-pearl, and to take care of it as a present from me."

"Is that all?" asked the King.

"Don't be impatient, sir," returned the Fairy Grandmarina, scolding him severely. "Don't catch people short, before they have done speaking. Just the way with you grown-up persons. You are always doing it."

The King again hung his head, and said he wouldn't do so any more.

"Be good then," said the Fairy Grandmarina, "and don't! Tell the Princess Alicia, with my love, that the fish-bone is a magic present which can only be used once; but that it will bring her, that once, whatever she wishes for, PROVIDED SHE WISHES FOR IT AT THE RIGHT TIME. That is the message. Take care of it."

The King was beginning, "Might I ask the reason—?" when the Fairy became absolutely furious.

"*Will* you be good, sir?" she exclaimed, stamping her foot on the ground. "The reason for this, and the reason for that, indeed! You are always wanting the reason. No reason. There! Hoity toity me! I am sick of your grown-up reasons."

The King was extremely frightened by the old lady's flying into such a passion, and said he was very sorry to have offended her, and he wouldn't ask for reasons any more.

"Be good then," said the old lady, "and don't!"

With those words, Grandmarina vanished, and the King went on and on and on, till he came to the Office. There he wrote and wrote and wrote, till it was time to go home again. Then he politely invited the Princess Alicia, as the Fairy had directed him, to partake of the salmon. And when she had enjoyed it very much, he saw the fish-bone on her plate, as the Fairy had told him he would, and he delivered the Fairy's message, and the Princess Alicia took care to dry the bone, and to rub it, and to polish it till it shone like mother-of-pearl.

And so when the Queen was going to get up in the morning, she said, "O dear me, dear me, my head, my head!" And then she fainted away.

The Princess Alicia, who happened to be looking in at the chamber door, asking about breakfast, was very much alarmed when she saw her Royal Mamma in this state, and she rang the bell for Peggy,—which was the name of the Lord Chamberlain. But remembering where the smelling-bottle was, she climbed on a chair and got it, and after that she climbed on another chair by the bedside and held the smelling-bottle to the Queen's nose, and after that she jumped down and got some water, and after that she jumped up again and wetted the Queen's forehead, and, in short, when the Lord Chamberlain came in, that dear old woman said to the little Princess, "What a Trot you are! I couldn't have done it better myself!"

But that was not the worst of the Queen's illness. O no! She was very ill indeed, for a long time. The Princess Alicia kept the seventeen young Princes and Princesses quiet, and dressed and undressed and danced the baby, and made the kettle boil, and heated the soup, and swept the hearth, and poured out the medicine, and nursed the Queen, and did all that ever she could, and was as busy busy busy, as busy could be. For there were not many servants at that Palace, for three reasons; because the King was short on money, because a rise in his office never seemed to come, and because quarter-day was so far off that it looked almost as far off and as little as one of the stars.

But on the morning when the Queen fainted away, where was the magic fish-bone? Why, there it was in the Princess Alicia's pocket. She had almost taken it out to bring the Queen to life again, when she put it back, and looked for the smelling bottle.

After the Queen had come out of her swoon that morning, and was dozing, the Princess Alicia hurried up-stairs to tell a most particular secret to a most particularly confidential friend of hers, who was a Duchess. People did suppose her to be a Doll, but she was really a Duchess, though nobody knew it except the Princess.

This most particular secret was the secret about the magic fish-bone, the history of which was well known to the Duchess, because the Princess told her everything. The Princess kneeled down by the bed on which the Duchess was lying, full dressed and wide-awake, and whispered the secret to her. The Duchess smiled and nodded. People might have supposed that she never smiled and nodded, but she often did, though nobody knew it except the Princess.

Then the Princess Alicia hurried down stairs again, to keep watch in the Queen's room. She often kept watch by herself in the Queen's room; but every evening, while the illness lasted, she sat there watching with the King. And every evening the King sat looking at her with a cross look, wondering why she never brought out the magic fish-bone. As often as she noticed this, she ran up stairs, whispered the secret to the Duchess over again, and said to the Duchess besides, "They think we children never have a reason or a meaning!" And the Duchess, though the most fashionable Duchess that ever was heard of, winked her eye.

"Alicia," said the King, one evening when she wished him Good Night.

"Yes, Papa."

"What is become of the magic fish-bone?"

"In my pocket, Papa."

"I thought you had lost it?"

"O no, Papa!"

"Or forgotten it?"

"No, indeed, Papa!"

And so another time the dreadful little snapping pug-dog next door made a rush at one of the young Princes as he stood on the steps coming home from school, and terrified him out of his wits, and he put his hand through a pane of glass, and bled bled bled. When the seventeen other young Princes and Princesses saw him bleed bleed bleed, they were terrified out of their wits too, and screamed themselves black in their seventeen faces all at once. But the Princess Alicia put her hands over all their seventeen mouths, one after another, and persuaded them to be quiet because of the sick Queen. And then she put the wounded Prince's hand in a basin of fresh cold water, while they stared with their twice seventeen are thirty-four put down four and carry three eyes, and then she looked in the hand for bits of glass, and there were fortunately no bits of glass there. And then she said to two chubby-legged Princes who were sturdy though small, "Bring me in the Royal rag-bag; I must snip and stitch and cut and contrive." So those two young Princes tugged at the Royal rag-bag and lugged it in, and the Princess Alicia sat down on the floor with a large pair of scissors and a needle and thread, and snipped and stitched and cut and contrived, and made a bandage and put it on, and it fitted beautifully, and so when it was all done she saw the King her Papa looking on by the door.

"Alicia."

"Yes, Papa."

"What have you been doing?"

"Snipping, stitching, cutting and contriving, Papa."

"Where is the magic fish-bone?"

"In my pocket, Papa."

"I thought you had lost it?"

"O no, Papa!"

"Or forgotten it?"

"No, indeed, Papa!"

After that, she ran up stairs to the Duchess and told her what had passed, and told her the secret over again, and the Duchess shook her flaxen curls and laughed with her rosy lips.

Well! and so another time the baby fell under the grate. The seventeen young Princes and Princesses were used to it, for they were almost always falling under the grate or down the stairs, but the baby was not used to it yet, and it gave him a swelled face and a black eye. The way the poor little darling came to tumble was, that he slid out of the Princess Alicia's lap just as she was sitting, in a great coarse apron that quite smothered her, in front of the kitchen fire, beginning to peel the turnips for the broth for dinner; and the way she came to be doing that was, that the King's cook had run away that morning with her own true love, who was a very tall but very tipsy soldier. Then, the seventeen young Princes and Princesses, who cried at everything that happened, cried and roared. But the Princess Alicia (who couldn't help crying a little herself) quietly called to them to be still, on account of not throwing back the Queen up stairs, who was fast getting well, and said, "Hold your tongues you wicked little monkeys, every one of you, while I examine baby!" Then she examined baby, and found that he hadn't broken anything, and she held cold iron to his poor dear eye, and smoothed his poor dear face, and he presently fell asleep in her arms. Then she said to the seventeen Princes and Princesses, "I am afraid to lay him down yet, lest he should wake and feel pain, be good and you shall all be cooks." They jumped for joy when they heard that, and began making themselves cooks' caps out of old newspapers. So to one she gave the salt-box, and to one she gave the barley, and to one she gave the herbs, and to one she gave the turnips, and to one she gave the carrots, and to one she gave the onions, and to one she gave the spice-box, till they were all cooks, and all running about at work, she sitting in the middle, smothered in the great coarse apron, nursing baby. By and by the broth was done, and the baby woke up, smiling like an angel, and was trusted to the sedatest Princess to hold, while the other Princes and Princesses were squeezed into a far-off corner to look at the Princess Alicia turning out the saucepan-full of broth, for fear (as they were always getting into trouble) they should get splashed and scalded. When the broth came tumbling out, steaming beautifully, and smelling like a nosegay good to eat, they clapped their hands. That made the baby clap his hands; and that, and his looking as if he had a comic toothache, made all the Princes and Princesses laugh. So the Princess Alicia said, "Laugh and be good, and after dinner we will make a nest on the floor in a corner, and he shall sit in his nest and see a dance of eighteen cooks." That delighted the young Princes and Princesses, and they ate up all the broth, and washed up all the plates and dishes, and cleared away, and pushed the table into a corner, and then they in their cooks' caps, and the Princess Alicia in the smothering coarse apron that belonged to the cook that had run away with her own true love that was the very tall but very tipsy soldier, danced a dance of eighteen cooks before the angelic baby, who forgot his swelled face and his black eye, and crowed with joy.

And so then, once more the Princess Alicia saw King Watkins the First, her father, standing in the doorway looking on, and he said: "What have you been doing Alicia?"

"Cooking and contriving, Papa."

"What else have you been doing, Alicia?"

"Keeping the children light-hearted, Papa."

"Where is the magic fish-bone, Alicia?"

"In my pocket, Papa."

"I thought you had lost it?"

"O no, Papa."

"Or forgotten it?"

"No, indeed, Papa."

The King then sighed so heavily, and seemed so low-spirited, and sat down so miserably, leaning his head upon his hand, and his elbow upon the kitchen table pushed away in the corner, that the seventeen Princes and Princesses crept softly out of the kitchen, and left him alone with the Princess Alicia and the angelic baby.

"What is the matter, Papa?"

"I am dreadfully poor, my child."

"Have you no money at all, Papa?"

"None, my child."

"Is there no way left of getting any, Papa?"

"No way," said the King. "I have tried very hard, and I have tried all ways."

When she heard those last words, the Princess Alicia began to put her hand into the pocket where she kept the magic fish-bone.

"Papa," said she, "when we have tried very hard, and tried all ways, we must have done our very very best?"

"No doubt, Alicia."

"When we have done our very very best, Papa, and that is not enough, then I think the right time must have come for asking help of others." This was the very secret connected with the magic fish-bone, which she had found out for herself from the good fairy Grandmarina's words, and which she had so often whispered to her beautiful and fashionable friend the Duchess.

So she took out of her pocket the magic fish-bone that had been dried and rubbed and polished till it shone like mother-of-pearl, and she gave it one little kiss and wished it was quarter-day. And immediately it *was* quarter-day, and the King's quarter's salary came rattling down the chimney, and bounced into the middle of the floor.

But this was not half of what happened, no not a quarter, for immediately afterwards the good fairy Grandmarina came riding in, in a carriage and four (Peacocks), with Mr Pickles's boy up behind, dressed in silver and gold, with a cocked-hat, powdered hair, pink silk stockings, a jewelled cane, and a nosegay. Down jumped Mr Pickles's boy with his cocked-hat in his hand and wonderfully polite (being entirely changed by enchantment), and handed Grandmarina out, and there she stood, in her rich shot-silk smelling of dried lavender, fanning herself with a sparkling fan.

"Alicia, my dear," said this charming old Fairy, "how do you do, I hope I see you pretty well, give me a kiss."

The Princess Alicia embraced her, and then Grandmarina turned to the King, and said rather sharply: "Are you good?"

The King said he hoped so.

"I suppose you know the reason, *now*, why my god-Daughter here," kissing the Princess again, "did not apply to the fish-bone sooner?" said the Fairy.

The King made her a shy bow.

"Ah! But you didn't *then*!" said the Fairy.

The King made her a shyer bow.

"Any more reasons to ask for?" said the Fairy.

The King said no, and he was very sorry.

"Be good then," said the Fairy, "and live happy ever afterwards."

Then, Grandmarina waved her fan, and the Queen came in most splendidly dressed, and the seventeen young Princes and Princesses, no longer grown out of their clothes, came in, newly fitted out from top to toe, with tucks in everything to admit of its being let out. After that, the Fairy tapped the Princess Alicia with her fan, and the smothering coarse apron flew away, and she appeared exquisitely dressed, like a little Bride, with a wreath of orange-flowers, and a silver veil. After that, the kitchen dresser changed of itself into a wardrobe, made of beautiful woods and gold and looking-glass, which was full of dresses of all sorts, all for her and all exactly fitting her. After that, the angelic baby came in, running alone, with his face and eye not a bit the worse but much the better. Then, Grandmarina begged to be introduced to the Duchess, and when the Duchess was brought down many compliments passed between them.

A little whispering took place between the Fairy and the Duchess, and then the Fairy said out loud, "Yes, I thought she would have told you." Grandmarina then turned to the King and Queen, and said, "We are going in search of Prince Certainpersonio. The pleasure of your company is requested at church in half an hour precisely." So she and the Princess Alicia got into the carriage, and Mr Pickles's boy handed in the Duchess who sat by herself on the opposite seat, and then Mr Pickles's boy put up the steps and got up behind, and the Peacocks flew away with their tails spread.

Prince Certainpersonio was sitting by himself, eating barley-sugar and waiting to be ninety. When he saw the Peacocks followed by the carriage, coming in at the window, it immediately occurred to him that something uncommon was going to happen.

"Prince," said Grandmarina, "I bring you your Bride."

The moment the Fairy said those words, Prince Certainpersonio's face left off being sticky, and his jacket and corduroys changed to peach-bloom velvet, and his hair curled, and a cap and feather flew in like a bird and settled on his head. He got into the carriage by the Fairy's invitation, and there he renewed his acquaintance with the Duchess whom he had seen before.

In the church were the Prince's relations and friends, and the Princess Alicia's relations and friends, and the seventeen Prince and Princesses, and the baby, and a crowd of the neighbours. The marriage was beautiful beyond expression. The Duchess was bridesmaid, and beheld the ceremony from the pulpit where she was supported by the cushion of the desk.

Grandmarina gave a magnificent wedding feast afterwards, in which there was everything and more to eat, and everything and more to drink. The wedding cake was delicately ornamented with white satin ribbons, frosted silver and white lilies, and was forty-two yards round.

When Grandmarina had drunk her love to the young couple, and Prince Certainpersonio had made a speech, and everybody had cried Hip Hip Hip Hurrah! Grandmarina announced to the King and Queen that in future there would be eight quarter-days in every year, except in leap-year, when there would be ten. She then turned to Certainpersonio and Alicia, and said, "My dears, you will have thirty-five children, and they will all be good and beautiful. Seventeen of your children will be boys, and eighteen will be girls. The hair of the whole of your children will curl naturally. They will never have the measles, and will have recovered from the whooping-cough before being born."

On hearing such good news, everybody cried out, "Hip Hip Hip Hurrah!" again.

"It only remains," said Grandmarina in conclusion, "to make an end of the fish-bone."

So she took it from the hand of the Princess Alicia, and it instantly flew down the throat of the dreadful little snapping pug-dog next door and choked him, and he expired in convulsions.

7

ANNE ISABELLA RITCHIE

Cinderella
(1868)

NNE ISABELLA RITCHIE (née Thackeray, 1837–1919) was the daughter of William Makepeace Thackeray and was greatly influenced by her father's writings. Educated at home and also in Paris, she benefited from a dual cultural heritage. She was encouraged by her father to start writing at an early age, and in 1863 she published a novel, *The Story of Elizabeth*, which received favorable reviews. Subsequently she wrote five more novels that were moderately successful; however, her most important literary work was in the field of biography. Not only did she write the "Biographical Introductions" to her father's *Complete Works* (1898), but she also wrote lively and stimulating studies of other writers: *Madame de Sévigné* (1881), *A Book of Sibyls: Mrs. Barbauld, Mrs. Opie, Miss Edgeworth, Miss Austen* (1883), *Records of Tennyson, Ruskin and Robert and Elizabeth Browning* (1892), and *Chapters from some Memoirs* (1894).

In her fairy-tale writings she endeavored to imitate both her father and Madame D'Aulnoy, whose tales she introduced in 1895 with the publication of *The Fairy Tales of Madame D'Aulnoy*. Her own "modern" tales were published in *Five Old Friends and a Young Prince* (1868) and *Bluebeard's Keys and Other Stories* (1874). Ritchie revised such tales as *Little Red Riding Hood, Beauty and the Beast, Sleeping Beauty, Jack and the Beanstalk*, and *Riquet à la Houppe* to comment on "proper" manners in Victorian society. "Cinderella," which appeared in *Five Old Friends*, contains features that can be found in all her tales: a realistic setting, careful depiction of contemporary mores and customs, concern for problems besetting women, and overt moralism. Although Ritchie was inventive in creating realistic plots based on traditional fairy tales, she often lost touch with the magic of the originals.

CINDERELLA

T IS, HAPPILY, not only in fairy tales that things sometimes fall out as one could wish, that anxieties are allayed, mistakes explained away, friends reconciled; that people inherit large fortunes, or are found out in their nefarious schemes; that long-lost children are discovered disguised in soot, that vessels come safely sailing into port after the storm; and that young folks who have been faithful to one another are married off at last. Some of these young couples are not only happily married, but they also begin life in pleasant palaces tastefully decorated, and with all the latest improvements; with convenient cupboards, bath-rooms, back staircases, speaking-tubes, lifts from one story to another, hot and cold water laid on; while outside lie well-kept parks, and gardens, and flower-beds; and from the muslin-veiled windows they can see the sheep browsing; the long shadowy grass, deer starting across the sunny glades, swans floating on the rivers, and sailing through the lilies and tall lithe reeds. There are fruit-gardens, too, where great purple plums are sunning on the walls, and cucumbers lying asleep among their cool dark leaves. There are glass-houses where heavy dropping bunches of grapes are hanging, so that one need only open one's mouth for them to fall into it all ready cooked and sweetened. Sometimes, in addition to all these good things, the young couple possess all the gracious gifts of youth, beauty, gay and amiable dispositions. Some one said, the other day, that it seemed as if Fate scarcely knew what she was doing, when she lavished with such profusion every gift and delight upon one pair of heads, while others were left bald, shorn, unheeded, dishevelled, forgotten, dishonoured. And yet the world would be almost too sad to bear, if one did not sometimes see happiness somewhere. One would scarcely believe in its possible existence, if there was nobody young, fortunate, prosperous, delighted; nobody to think of with satisfaction, and to envy a little. The sight of great happiness and prosperity is like listening to harmonious music, or looking at beautiful pictures, at certain times of one's life. It seems to suggest possibilities, it sets sad folks longing; but while they are wishing, still, may be, a little reproachfully, they realize the existence of what perhaps they had doubted before. Fate has been hard to them, but there *is* compensation even in this life, they tell themselves. Which of us knows when his turn may come? Happiness is a fact: it does lie within some people's grasp. To this or that young fairy couple, age, trial, and trouble may be in store; but now at least the present is golden; the innocent delights and triumphs of youth and nature are theirs.

I could not help moralizing a little in this way, when we were staying with young Lulworth and his wife the other day, coming direct from the struggling dull atmosphere of home to the golden placidity of Lulworth farm. They drove us over to Cliffe Court—another oasis, so it seemed to me, in the arid plains of life. Cliffe Court is a charming, cheerful, Italian-looking house, standing on a hill in the midst of a fiery furnace of geraniums and flower-beds. "It belongs to young Sir Charles Richardson. He is six-and-twenty, and the handsomest man in the county," said Frank.

"Oh, no, Frank; you are joking, surely," said Cecilia; and then she stared, and then blushed in her odd way. She still stared sometimes when she was shy, as she used to do before she married.

So much of her former habits Cecilia had also retained, that as the clock struck eight every morning a great punctual breakfast-bell used to ring in the outer hall. The dining-room casement was wide open upon the beds of roses, the tea was made, Cecilia in her crisp white morning dress, and with all her wavy bronze hair curling about her face, was waiting to pour it out, the eggs were boiled, the bacon was frizzling hot upon the plate to a moment; there was no law allowed, not a minute's grace for anybody, no matter how lazy. They had been married a little more than two years, and were quite established in their country home. I wish I could perform some incantation like those of my friends the fairies, and conjure up the old farm bodily with a magic wave of my pen, or by drawing a triangle with a circle through it upon the paper—as the enchanters do.

The most remarkable things about the farm were its curious and beautiful old chimneys—indeed the whole county of Sussex is celebrated for them, and the meanest little cottages have noble-looking stacks all ornamented, carved and weather-beaten. There were gables also, and stony mullioned windows, and ancient steps with rusty rings hanging to them, affixed there to fasten the bridles of horses that would have run away several hundred years ago, if this precaution had not been taken. And then there were storehouses and ricks and barns, all piled with the abundance of the harvest. The farmyard was alive with young fowls and cocks and hens; and guinea-hens, those gentle little dowagers, went about glistening in silver and grey, and Cecilia's geese came clamouring to meet her. I can see it all as I think about it. The old walls are all carved and ornamented, sometimes by art and work of man's hand, sometimes by time and lovely little natural mosses. House-leeks grow in clumps upon the thatch, a pretty girl is peeping through a lattice window, a door is open while a rush of sweet morning scent comes through the shining oaken passage from the herb-garden and orchard behind. Cows with their soft brown eyes and cautious tread are passing on their way to a field across the road. A white horse waiting by his stable-door shakes his head and whinnies.

Frank and Cecilia took us for a walk after breakfast the first morning we came. We were taken to the stables first and the cow-houses, and then we passed out through a gate into a field, and crossing the field we got into a copse which skirted it, and so by many a lovely little winding path into the woods. Young Lulworth took our delight and admiration as a personal compliment. It was all Lulworth property as far as we could see. I thought it must be strangely delightful to be the possessor of such beautiful hills, mist, sunshine and shadow, violet tones, song of birds, and shimmer of foliage; but Frank, I believe, looked at his future prospects from a material point of view. "You see it ain't the poetic part of it which pays," he said. But he appreciated it nevertheless, for Cecilia came out of the woods that morning, all decked out with great convolvulus leaves, changed to gold, which Frank had gathered as we went along and given to her. This year all the leaves were turning to such beautiful colours that people remarked upon it, and said they never remembered such a glowing autumn; even the year when Frank came to Dorlicote was not to compare to it. Browns and russet, and bright amber and gold flecks, berries, red leaves, a lovely blaze and glitter in the woods along the lanes and beyond the fields and copses. All the hills were melting with lovely colour in the clear warm autumn air, and the little nut-wood paths seemed like Aladdin's wonderful gardens, where precious stones hung to the trees; there was a twinkle and crisp shimmer, yellow leaves and golden light, yellow light and golden leaves, red hawthorn, convolvulus-berries, holly-berries beginning to glow, and heaped-up clustering purple blackberries. The sloe-berries, or snowy blackthorn fruit, with their soft gloom of colour, were over, and this was the last feast of the year. On the trees the apples hung red and bright, the pears seemed ready to drop from their branches and walls, the wheat was stacked, the sky looked violet behind the yellow ricks. A blackbird was singing like a ripple of water, somebody said. It is hard to refrain from writing of all these lovely things, though it almost is an impertinence to attempt to set them down on paper in long lists, like one of Messrs Rippon and Burton's circulars. As we were walking along the high-road on our way back to the farm, we passed a long pale melancholy-looking man riding a big horse, with a little sweet-faced creature about sixteen who was cantering beside him.

He took off his hat, the little girl kissed her hand as they passed, nodding a gay triumphant nod, and then we watched them down the hill, and disappearing at the end of the lane.

"I am quite glad to see Ella Ashford out riding with her father again," said Lulworth, holding the garden gate open for us to pass in.

"Mrs Ashford called here a day or two ago with her daughter," said Cecilia. "They're going to stay at the Ravenhill, she told me. I thought Colonel Ashford was gone too. I suppose he is come back."

"Of course he is," said Frank, "since we have just seen him with Ella, and of course his wife is away for the same reason."

"The child has grown very thin," said H.

"She has a difficult temper," said Cecilia—who, once she got an idea into her soft, silly head, did not easily get rid of it again. "She is a great anxiety to poor Mrs Ashford. She is very different, she tells me, to Julia and Lisette Garnier, her own daughters."

"I knew them when they were children," said H. "We used to see a great deal of Mrs Ashford when she was first a widow, and I went to her second wedding."

We were at Paris one year—ten years before the time I am writing of—and Mrs Garnier lived over us, in a tiny little apartment. She was very poor, and very grandly dressed, and she used to come rustling in to see us. Rustling is hardly the word, she was much too graceful and womanly a person to rustle; her long silk gowns used to ripple, and wave, and flow away as she came and went; and her beautiful eyes used to fill with tears as she drank her tea and confided her troubles to us. H. never liked her; but I must confess to a very kindly feeling for the poor, gentle, beautiful, forlorn young creature, so passionately lamenting the loss she had sustained in Major-General Garnier. He had left her very badly off, although she was well connected, and Lady Jane Peppercorne, her cousin, had offered her and her two little girls a home at Ravenhill, she used to tell us in her *éploré* manner. I do not know why she never availed herself of the offer. She said once that she would not be doing justice to her precious little ones, to whom she devoted herself with the assistance of an experienced attendant. My impression is, that the little ones used to scrub one another's little ugly faces, and plait one another's little light Chinese-looking tails, while the experienced attendant laced and dressed and adorned and scented and powdered their mamma. She really was a beautiful young woman, and would have looked quite charming if she had left herself alone for a single instant, but she was always posing. She had dark bright eyes; she had a lovely little arched mouth; and hands so white, so soft, so covered with rings, that one felt that it was indeed a privilege when she said, "Oh, *how* do you do?" and extended two or three gentle confiding fingers. At first she went nowhere except to church, and to walk in the retired paths of the Parc de Monçeau, although she took in *Galignani* and used to read the lists of arrivals. But by degrees she began to— chiefly to please me, she said—go out a little, to make a few acquaintances. One day I was walking with her down the Champs Elysées, when she suddenly started and looked up at a tall, melancholy-looking gentleman who was passing, and who stared at her very hard; and soon after that it was that she began telling me she had determined to make an effort for her children's sake, and to go a little more into society. She wanted me to take her to Madame de Girouette's, where she heard I was going one evening, and where she believed she should meet an old friend of hers, whom she particularly wished to see again. Would I help her? Would I be so *very* good? Of course I was ready to do anything I could. She came punctual to her time, all grey moire and black lace; a remise was sent for, and we set off, jogging along the crowded streets, with our two lamps lighted, and a surly man, in a red waistcoat and an oilskin hat, to drive us to the Rue de Lille. All the way there, Mrs Garnier was strange, silent, nervous, excited. Her eyes were like two shining craters, I thought, when we arrived, and as we climbed up the interminable flights of stairs. I guessed which was the old friend in a minute: a tall, well-looking, sick-looking man with a grey moustache, standing by himself in a corner.

I spent a curious evening, distracted between Madame de Girouette's small talk, to which I was supposed to be listening, and Mrs Garnier's murmured conversation with her old friend in the corner, to which I was vainly endeavouring not to attend.

"My dear, imagine a *bouillon*, surmounted with little tiny flutings all round the bottom, and then three *ruches*, alternating with three little *volants*, with great *choux* at regular intervals; over this a tunic, caught up at the side by a *jardinière*, a *ceinture à la Bébé*."

"When you left us I was a child, weak, foolish, easily frightened and influenced. It nearly broke my heart. Look me in the face, if you can, and tell me you do not believe me," I heard Mrs Garnier murmuring in a low thrilling whisper. She did not mean me to hear it, but she was too absorbed in what she was saying to think of all the people round about her.

"Ah, Lydia, what does it matter now?" the friend answered in a sad voice, which touched me somehow. "We have both been wrecked in our ventures, and life has not much left for either of us now."

"It is cut *en biais*," Madame de Girouette went on; "the pieces which are taken out at one end are let in at the other: the effect is quite charming, and the economy is immense."

"For you, you married the person you loved," Lydia Garnier was answering; "for me, out of the wreck, I have at least my children, and a remembrance, and a friend—is it so? Ah, Henry, have I not at least a friend?"

"Everybody wants one," said Madame de Girouette, concluding her conversation, "and they cannot be made fast enough to supply the demand. I am promised mine to wear to-morrow at the opening of the salon, but I am afraid that you have no chance. How the poor thing is over-worked—her magazin is crowded—I believe she will leave it all in charge of her première demoiselle, and retire to her campagne as soon as the season is over."

"And you will come and see me, will you not," said the widow, as we went away, looking up at her friend. I do not know to this day if she was acting. I believe, to do her justice, that she was only acting what she really felt, as many of us do at times.

I took Mrs Garnier home as I had agreed. I did not ask any questions. I met Colonel Ashford on the stairs next day, and I was not surprised when, about a week after, Mrs Garnier flitted into the drawing-room early one morning, and sinking down at my feet in a careless attitude, seized my hand, and said that she had come for counsel, for advice. . . . She had had an offer from a person whom she respected, Colonel Ashford, whom I might have remarked that night at Madame de Girouette's; would I—would I give her my candid opinion; for her children's sake, did I not think it would be well to think seriously?" . . .

"And for your own, too, my dear," said I. "Colonel Ashford is in Parliament, he is very well off. I believe you will be making an excellent marriage. Accept him by all means."

"Dear friend, since this is your real heart-felt opinion, I value your judgment too highly not to act by its dictates. Once, years ago, there was thought of this between me and Henry. I will now confide to you, my heart has never failed from its early devotion. A cruel fate separated us. I married. He married. We are brought together as by a miracle, but our three children will never know the loss of their parents' love," etc. etc. Glance, hand pressure, etc.—tears, etc. then a long, soft, irritating kiss. I felt for the first time in my life inclined to box her ears.

The little Garniers certainly gained by the bargain, and the colonel sat down to write home to his little daughter, and tell her the news.

Poor little Ella, I wonder what sort of anxieties Mrs Ashford had caused to her before she had been Ella's father's wife a year. Miss Ashford made the best of it. She was a cheery, happy little creature, looking at everything from the sunny side, adoring her father, running wild out of doors, but with an odd turn for house-keeping, and order and method at home. Indeed, for the last two years, ever since she was twelve years old, she had kept her father's house. Languid, gentle, easily impressed, Colonel Ashford was quite curiously influenced by this little daughter. She could make him come and go, and like and dislike. I think it was Ella who sent him into Parliament: she could not bear Sir Rainham

Richardson, their next neighbour, to be an M.P., and an oracle, while her father was only a retired colonel. Her ways and her sayings were a strange and pretty mixture of childishness and precociousness. She would be ordering dinner, seeing that the fires were alight in the study and dining-room, writing notes to save her father trouble (Colonel Ashford hated trouble), in her cramped, crooked, girlish hand; the next minute she was perhaps flying, agile-footed, round and round the old hall, skipping up and down the oak stairs, laughing out like a child as she played with her puppy, and dangled a little ball of string under his black nose. Puff, with a youthful bark, would seize the ball and go scuttling down the corridors with his prize, while Ella pursued him with her quick flying feet. She could sing charmingly, with a clear, true, piping voice, like a bird's, and she used to dance to her own singing in the prettiest way imaginable. Her dancing was really remarkable: she had the most beautiful feet and hands, and as she seesawed in time, still singing and moving in rhythm, any one seeing her could not fail to have been struck by the weird-like little accomplishment. Some girls have a passion for dancing—boys have a hundred other ways and means of giving vent to their activity and exercising their youthful limbs, and putting out their eager young strength; but girls have no such chances; they are condemned to walk through life for the most part quietly, soberly, putting a curb on the life and vitality which is in them. They long to throw it out, they would like to have wings to fly like a bird, and so they dance sometimes with all their hearts, and might, and energy. People rarely talk of the poetry of dancing, but there is something in it of the real inspiration of art. The music plays, the heart beats time, the movements flow as naturally as the branches of a tree go waving in the wind. . . .

One day a naughty boy, who had run away, for a lark, from his tutor and his schoolroom at Cliffe, hard by, and who was hiding in a ditch, happened to see Ella alone in a field. She was looking up at the sky and down at the pretty scarlet and white pimpernels, and listening to the birds; suddenly she felt so strong and so light, and as if she *must* jump about a little, she was so happy; and so she did, shaking her pretty golden mane, waving her poppies high over head, and singing higher and higher, like one of the larks that were floating in mid air. The naughty boy was much frightened, and firmly believed that he had seen a fairy.

"She was all in white," he said afterwards, in an aggrieved tone of voice. "She'd no hat, or anything; she bounded six foot into the air. You never saw anything like it."

Master Richardson's guilty conscience had something to do with his alarm. When his friend made a few facetious inquiries he answered quite sulkily,— "Black pudden? she offered me no pudden or anything else. I only wish you had been there, that's all, then you'd believe a fellow when he says a thing, instead of always chaffing."

Ella gave up her dancing after the new wife came to Ash Place. It was all so different; she was not allowed any more to run out into the fields alone. She supposed it was very nice having two young companions like Lisette and Julia, and at first, in her kindly way, the child did the honours of her own home, showed them the way which led to her rabbits, her most secret bird's nest, the old ivy-grown smugglers' hole in the hollow. Lisette and Julia went trotting about in their frill trowsers and Chinese tails of hair, examining everything, making their calculations, saying nothing, taking it all in (poor little Ella was rather puzzled, and could not make them out). Meantime her new mother was gracefully wandering over the house on her husband's arm, and standing in attitudes, admiring the view from the windows, and asking gentle little indifferent questions, to all of which Colonel Ashford replied unsuspectingly enough.

"And so you give the child an allowance? Is she not very young for one? And is this Ella's room? how prettily it is furnished."

"She did it all herself," said her father, smiling. "Look at her rocking-horse, and her dolls' house, and her tidy little arrangements."

The house-keeping books were in a little pile on the table; a very suspicious-looking doll was lying on the bed, so were a pile of towels, half marked, but neatly folded; there was a bird singing in a cage, a squirrel, a little aged dog—Puff's grandmother—asleep on a cushion, some sea-anemones in a glass, gaping with their horrid mouths, strings of birds' eggs were suspended, and whips were hanging up on the walls. There was a great bunch of flowers in the window, and a long daisy-chain fastened up in festoons round the glass; and then on the toilette-table there were one or two valuable trinkets set out in their little cases.

"Dear me," said Mrs Ashford, "is it not a pity to leave such temptation in the way of the servants? Little careless thing—had I not better keep them for her, Henry? they are very beautiful." And Mrs Ashford softly collected Ella's treasures in her long white hands.

'Ella has some very valuable things," Colonel Ashford said. "She keeps them locked up in a strong box, I believe; yes, there it is in the corner."

"It had much better come into my closet," Mrs Ashford said. "Oh, how heavy! Come here, strong-arm, and help me." Colonel Ashford obediently took up the box as he was bid.

"And I think I may as well finish marking the dusters," said Mrs Ashford, looking round the room as she collected them all in her apron. "The books, of course, are now my duty. I think Ella will not be sorry to be relieved of her cares. Do you know, dear, I think I am glad, for her sake, that you married me, as well as for my own. I think she has had too much put upon her, is a little too decided, too *prononcée* for one so young. One would not wish to see her grow up before the time. Let them remain young and careless while they can, Henry."

So when Ella came back to mark the dusters that she had been hemming, because Mrs Milton was in a hurry for them and the housemaid had hurt her eye, they were gone, and so were her neat little books that she had taken such pride in, and had been winding up before she gave them to Mrs Ashford to keep in future; so was her pretty coral necklace that she wore of an evening; and her pearls with the diamond clasp; and her beautiful clear carbuncle brooch that she was so fond of, and her little gold clasp bracelet. Although Eliza and Susan had lived with them all her life long, *they* had never taken her things, poor Ella thought, a little bitterly. "Quite unsuitable, at your age, dearest," Mrs Ashford murmured, kissing her fondly.

And Ella never got them back any more. Many and many other things there were she never got back, poor child. Ah me! treasures dearer to her than the pretty coral necklace and the gold clasp bracelet—liberty, confidence—the tender atmosphere of admiring love in which she had always lived, the first place in her father's heart. That should never be hers again some one had determined.

The only excuse for Mrs Ashford is that she was very much in love with her husband, and so selfishly attached to him that she grudged the very care and devotion which little Ella had spent upon her father all these years past. Every fresh proof of thought and depth of feeling in such a childish little creature hurt and vexed the other woman. Ella must be taught her place, this lady determined, not in so many words. Alas! if we could always set our evil thoughts and schemes to words, it would perhaps be well with us, and better far than drifting, unconscious, and unwarned, into nameless evil, unowned to oneself, scarcely recognized.

And so the years went by. Julia and Lisette grew up into two great tall fashionable bouncing young ladies; they pierced their ears, turned up their pigtails, and dressed very elegantly. Lisette used to wear a coral necklace, Julia was partial to a clear carbuncle brooch her mother gave her. Little Ella, too, grew up like a little green plant springing up through the mild spring rains and the summer sunshine, taller and prettier and sadder every year. And yet perhaps it was as well after all that early in life she had to learn to be content with a very little share of its bounties; she might have been spoilt and over-indulged if things had gone on as they began, if nothing had ever thwarted her, and if all her life she had had her own way. She was a bright smiling little thing for all her worries, with a sweet little face; indeed her beauty was so remarkable, and her manner so simple and charming, that Julia and Lisette, who were a year or two her elders, used to complain to their mother nobody ever noticed them when Ella was by. Lady Jane Peppercorne, their own cousin, was always noticing her, and actually gave her a potato off her own plate the other day.

"I fear she is a very forward, designing girl. I shall not think of taking her out in London this year," Mrs Ashford said, with some asperity; "nor shall I allow her to appear at our croquet party next week. She is far too young to be brought out."

So Ella was desired to remain in her own room on this occasion. She nearly cried, poor little thing, but what could she do; her father was away, and when he came back Mrs Ashford would be sure to explain everything to him. Mrs Ashford had explained life to him in so strangely ingenious a manner that he had got to see it in a very topsy-turvy fashion. Some things she had explained away altogether, some she had distorted and twisted, poor little Ella had been explained and explained, until there was scarcely anything of her left at all. Poor child, she sometimes used to think she had not a single friend in the world, but she would chide herself for such fancies: it must be fancy. Her father loved her as much as ever, but he was engrossed by business, and it was not to be expected he should show what he felt before Julia and Lisette, who might be hurt. And then Ella would put all her drawers in order, or sew a seam, or go out and pull up a bedful of weeds to chase such morbid fancies out of her mind.

Lady Jane Peppercorne, of whom mention has been already made, had two houses, one in Onslow Square, another at Hampstead. She was very rich, she had never married, and was consequently far more sentimental than ladies of her standing usually are. She was a flighty old lady, and lived sometimes at one house, sometimes at the other, sometimes at hotels here and there, as the fancy seized her. She was very kind as well as flighty, and was constantly doing generous things, and trying to help anyone who seemed to be in trouble or who appeared to wish for anything she had it in her power to grant.

So when Mrs Ashford said,—"Oh, Lady Jane, pity me! My husband says he cannot afford to take me to town this year. I should so like to go, for the dear girls' sake of course—" Lady Jane gave a little grunt, and said,—"I will lend you my house in Onslow Square, if you like—that is, if you keep my room ready for me in case I want to come up at any time. But I daresay you won't care for such an unfashionable quarter of the world."

"Oh, Lady Jane, how exceedingly kind, how very delightful and unexpected!" cried Mrs Ashford, who had been hoping for it all the time, and who hastened to communicate the news to Lisette and Julia.

"I shall want a regular outfit, mamma," said Julia, who was fond of dress. "Perhaps we shall meet young Mr Richardson in town."

"I shall be snapped up directly by some one, I expect," said Lisette, who was very vain, and thought herself irresistible.

"Am I to come too?" asked Ella, timidly, from the other end of the room, looking up from her sewing.

"I do not know," replied her stepmother, curtly, and Ella sighed a little wistfully, and went on stitching.

"At what age shall you let me come out?" she presently asked, shyly.

"When you are fit to be trusted in the world, and have cured your unruly temper," said Mrs Ashford. Ella's eyes filled with tears, and she blushed up; but her father came into the room, and she smiled through her tears, and thought to herself that since her temper was so bad, she had better begin to rule it that very instant. . . . When Mrs Ashford began to explain to her husband, however, how much better it would be for Ella to remain in the country, the child's wistful glance met his, and for once he insisted that she should not be left behind.

It is a bright May morning after a night of rain, and although this is London and not the country any more, Onslow Square looks bright and clean. Lady Jane has had the house smartly done up: clean chintz, striped blinds, a balcony full of mignonette. She has kept two little rooms for herself and her maid, but all the rest of the house is at the Ashfords' disposal. Everybody is satisfied, and Ella is enchanted with her little room upstairs. Mrs Ashford is making lists of visits and dinner-parties and milliners' addresses; Lisette is looking out of a window at some carriages which are passing; the children and nurses are sitting under the trees in the square; Julia is looking at herself in the glass and practising her court curtseys; and Ella is in the back room arranging a great heap of books in a bookcase. "I should so like to go to the Palace, mamma," she says, looking up with a smudgy face, for the books were all dirty and covered with dust. "Do you think there will be room for me?"

Ella had no proper pride, as it is called, and always used to take it for granted she was wanted, and that some accident prevented her from going with the others. "I am sorry there is no room for you, Ella," said Mrs Ashford, in her deep voice; "I have asked Mr Richardson to come with us, and if he fails, I promised to call for the Countess Bricabrac. Pray, if you do not care for walking in the square this afternoon, see that my maid puts my things properly away in the cupboards, as well as Julia's and Lisette's, and help her to fold the dresses, because it is impossible for one person to manage these long trains unassisted."

"Very well," said Ella, cheerfully. "I hope you will have a pleasant day. How nice it must be to be going."

"I wish you would learn not to wish for everything and anything that you happen to hear about, Ella," said Mrs Ashford. "And, by the way, if you find any visitors coming, go away, for I cannot allow you to be seen in this dirty state."

"There's a ring," said Ella, gathering some of the books together. "Good-by."

Young Mr Richardson, who was announced immediately after, passed a pretty maid-servant, carrying a great pile of folios, upon the stairs. She looked so little fitted for the task that he involuntarily stopped and said, "Can I assist you?" The little maid smiled and shook her head, without speaking. "What a charming little creature!" thought Mr Richardson. He came to say that he and his friend, Jack Prettyman, were going to ride down together, and would join the ladies at the Palace.

"We are to pick Colonel Ashford up at his club," Mrs Ashford said, "and Madame de Bricabrac. I shall count upon you then." And the young ladies waved him gracious *au revoirs* from the balcony.

"Oh! don't you like white waistcoats, Julia?" said Lisette, as she watched him down the street.

They are gone. Ella went up to help with the dresses, but presently the maid said in her rude way that she must go down to dinner, and she could not have anybody messing the things about while she was away. Carter hated having a "spy" set over her, as she called Miss Ashford. The poor little spy went back to the drawing-room. She was too melancholy and out of spirits to dress herself and go out. Her face was still smudgy, and she had cried a little over Lisette's pink tarlatane. Her heart sank down, down, down. She did so long for a little fun and delight, and laughter and happiness. She knew her father would say, "Where is Ella?" and her mother would answer, "Oh, I really cannot account for Ella's fancies. She was sulky this morning again. I cannot manage her strange tempers."

The poor child chanced to see her shabby face and frock and tear-stained cheeks in one of the tall glasses over the gilt tables. It was very silly, but the woebegone little face touched her so; she was so sorry for it that all of a sudden she burst out sob, sob, sob, crying. "Oh, how nice it must be to be loved and cherished, and very happy," she thought. "Oh, I could be so good if they would only love me." She could not bear to think more directly of her father's change of feeling. She sat down on the floor, as she had a way of doing, all in a little heap, staring at the empty grate. The fire had burnt out, and no one had thought of relighting it. For a few minutes her tears overflowed, and she cried and cried in two rivulets down her black little face. She thought how forlorn she was, what a dull life she led, how alone she lived—such a rush of regret and misery overpowered her, that she hid her face in her hands, unconscious of anything else but her own sadness. ...

She did not hear the bell ring, nor a carriage stop, nor Lady Jane's footsteps. That lady came across the room and stood looking at her. "Why, my dear little creature, what is the matter?" said Lady Jane at last. "Crying? don't you know it is very naughty to cry, no matter how bad things are? Are they all gone—are you all alone?"

Ella jumped up quite startled, blushed, wiped her tears in a smudge. "I thought nobody would see me cry," she said, "for they are all gone to the Crystal Palace."

And did they leave you behind quite by yourself?" the old lady asked.

"They were so sorry they had no room for me," said good-natured little Ella. She could not bear to hear people blamed. "They had promised Madame de Bricabrac."

"Is that all?" said Lady Jane, in her kind imperious way. "Why, I have driven in from Hampstead on purpose to go there too. There's a great flower-show to-day, and you know I am a first-rate gardener. I've brought up a great hamper of things. Put on your bonnet, wash your face, and come along directly. I've plenty of room. Who is that talking in that rude way?" for at that instant Carter called out with a sniff from the drawing-room door, without looking in,—

"Now then, Miss Ella, you can come and help me fold them dresses. I'm in a hurry."

Carter was much discomposed when, instead of her victim, Lady Jane appeared, irate, dignified.

"Go upstairs directly, and do not forget yourself again," said the old lady.

"Oh, I think I ought to go and fold up the dresses," said Ella, hesitating, flushing, blushing, and looking more than grateful. "How very very kind of you to think of me. I'm afraid they wouldn't—I'm afraid I've no bonnet. Oh, thank you, I—but—"

"Nonsense, child," said Lady Jane; "my maid shall help that woman. Here," ringing the bell violently, to the footman, "what have you done with the hamper I brought up? let me see it unpacked here immediately. Can't trust those people, my dear—always see to everything myself."

All sorts of delicious things, scents, colours, spring-flowers and vegetables came out of the hamper in delightful confusion. It was a hamper full of treasures—sweet, bright, delicious-tasted—asparagus, daffodillies, bluebells, salads, cauliflowers, hot-house flowers, cowslips from the fields, azaleas. Ella's natty little fingers arranged them all about the room in plates and in vases so perfectly and so quickly, that old Lady Jane cried out in admiration,—

"Why, you would be a first-rate girl, if you didn't cry. Here, you John, get some bowls and trays for the vegetables, green pease, strawberries; and oh, here's a cucumber and a nice little early pumpkin. I had it forced, my dear. Your stepmother tells me she is passionately fond of pumpkins. Here, John, take all this down to the cook; tell her to put it in a cool larder, and order the carriage and horses round directly. Now then," to Ella, briskly, "go and put your things on, and come along with me. *I'll* make matters straight. I always do. There, go directly. I can't have the horses kept. Raton, my coachman, is terrible if he is kept waiting—frightens me to death by his driving when he is put out."

Ella did not hesitate a moment longer; she rushed upstairs; her little feet flew as they used to do formerly. She came down in a minute, panting, rapturous, with shining hair and a bright face, in her very best Sunday frock, cloak, and hat. Shabby enough they were, but she was too happy, too excited, to think about the deficiencies in her toilet.

"Dear me, this will never do, I see," said the old lady, looking at her disapprovingly; but she smiled so kindly as she spoke, that Ella was not a bit frightened.

"Indeed, I have no other," she said.

"John," cried the old lady, "where is my maid? Desire her to come and speak to me directly. Now then, sir!"

All her servants knew her ways much too well not to fly at her commands. A maid appeared as if by magic.

"Now, Batter, be quick; get that blue and silver bournous of mine from the box upstairs—it will look very nice; and a pair of grey kid gloves, Batter; and let me see, my dear, you wouldn't look well in a brocade. No, that grey satin skirt, Batter; her own white bodice will do, and we can buy a bonnet as we go along. Now, quick; am I to be kept waiting all day?"

Ella in a moment found herself transformed somehow into the most magnificent lady she had seen for many a day. It was like a dream, she could hardly believe it; she saw herself move majestically, sweeping in silken robes across the very same pier-glass, where a few minutes before she had looked at the wretched little melancholy creature, crying with a dirty face, and watched the sad tears flowing....

"Now then—now then," cried Lady Jane, who was always saying "Now then," and urging people on—"where's my page—are the outriders there? They are all workhouse boys, my dear; they came to me as thin and starved as church mice, and then I fatten them up and get 'em situations. I always go with outriders. One's obliged to keep up a certain dignity in these Chartist days—universal reform—suffrage—vote by ballot. I've no patience with Mr Gladstone, and it all rests with us to keep ourselves well aloof. Get in, get in! Drive to Sydenham, if you please."

Lady Jane's manners entirely changed when she spoke to Raton. And it is a fact that coachmen from their tall boxes rule with a very high hand, and most ladies tremble before them. Raton looked very alarming in his wig, with his shoebuckles and great red face.

What a fairy tale it was! There was little Ella sitting in this lovely chariot, galloping down the Brompton Road, with all the little boys cheering and hurrahing; and the little outriders clattering on ahead, and the old lady sitting bolt upright as pleased as Punch. She really *had* been going to Sydenham; but I think if she had not, she would have set off instantly, if she thought she would make anybody happy by so doing. They stopped at a shop in the Brompton Road—the wondering shop-woman came out.

"A white bonnet, if you please," said Lady Jane. "That will do very well. Here, child, put it on, and mind you don't crease the strings." And then away and away they went once more through the town, the squares, over the bridges. They saw the ships and steamers coming down the silver Thames, but the carriage never stopped: the outriders paid the tolls and clattered on ahead. They rolled along pleasant country lanes and fields, villas and country houses, road-side inns, and pedestrians, and crawling carts and carriages. At the end of three-quarters of an hour, during which it seemed to Ella as if the whole gay *cortège* had been flying through the air, they suddenly stopped at last, at the great gates of a Crystal Palace blazing in the sun, and standing on a hill. A crowd was looking on. All sorts of grand people were driving up in their carriages; splendid ladies were passing in. Two gentlemen in white waistcoats were dismounting from their horses just as Ella and Lady Jane were arriving. They rushed up to the carriage-door, and helped them to the ground.

"And pray, sir, who are you?" said Lady Jane, as soon as she was safely deposited on her two little flat feet with the funny old-fashioned shoes.

The young man coloured up and bowed. "You don't remember me, Lady Jane," he said. "Charles Richardson—I have had the honour of meeting you at Ash Place, and at Cliffe, my uncle's house. This is my friend Mr Prettyman."

"This is Mr Richardson, my dear Ella, and that is Mr Prettyman. Tell them to come back in a couple of hours" (to the page), "and desire Raton to see that the horses have a feed. Now then—yes—give her your arm, and you are going to take me?—very well," to the other white waistcoat; and so they went into the Palace.

What are the young princes like now-a-days? Do they wear diamond aigrettes, swords at their sides, top-boots, and little short cloaks over one shoulder? The only approach to romance that I can see, is the flower in their button-hole, and the nice little moustaches and curly beards in which they delight. But all the same besides the flower in the button, there is also, I think, a possible flower of sentiment still growing in the soft hearts of princes in these days, as in the old days long, long ago.

Charles Richardson was a short ugly little man, very gentlemanlike, and well-dressed. He was the next heir to a baronetcy; he had a pale face and a snub nose, and such a fine estate in prospect—Cliffe Court its name was—that I do not wonder at Miss Lisette's admiration for him. As for Ella, she thought how kind he had been on the stairs that morning; she thought what a bright genial smile he had. How charming he looked, she said to herself; no never, never had she dreamt of any one so nice. She was quite—more than satisfied, no prince in romance would have seemed to her what this one was, there actually walking beside her. As for Richardson himself, it was a case of love at first sight. He had seen many thousand young ladies in the last few years, but not one of them to compare with this sweet-faced, ingenuous, tender, bright little creature. He offered her his arm, and led her along.

Ella observed that he said a few words to his friend; she little guessed their purport. "You go first," he whispered, "and if you see the Ashfords get out of the way. I should have to walk with those girls, and my heart is here transfixed for ever." . . . "Where have I seen you before?" he went on, talking to Ella, as they roamed through the beautiful courts and gardens, among fountains and flowers, and rare objects of art. "Forgive me for asking you, but I must have met you somewhere long ago, and have never forgotten you. I am haunted by your face." Ella was too much ashamed to tell him where and how it was they had met that very morning. She remembered him perfectly, but she thought he would rush away and leave her, if she told him that the untidy little scrub upon the stairs had been herself. And she was so happy: music playing, flowers blooming, the great wonderful fairy Palace flashing over head; the kind, clever, delightful young man to escort her; the gay company, the glitter, the perfume, the statues, the interesting figures of Indians, the dear, dear, kind Lady Jane to look to for sympathy and for good-humoured little nods of encouragement. She had *never* been so happy; she had never known what a wonder the Palace might be. Her heart was so full. It was all so lovely, so inconceivably beautiful and delightful, that she was nearly tipsy with delight; her head turned for an instant, and she clung to young Richardson's protecting arm.

"Are you faint—are you ill?" he said, anxiously.

"Oh, no!" said Ella, "it's only that everything is so beautiful; it is almost more than I can bear. I—I am not often so happy; oh, it is so charming! I do not think anything could be so delightful in all the world." She looked herself so charming and unconscious as she spoke, looking up with her beautiful face out of her white bonnet, that the young fellow felt as if he *must* propose to her, then and there, off-hand on the very spot; and at the instant he looked up passionately—O horror!—he caught sight of the Ashfords, mother, daughters, Madame de Bricabrac, all in a row, coming right down upon them.

"Prettyman, this way to the right," cried little Richardson, desperately; and Prettyman, who was a good-natured fellow, said, "This way, please, Lady Jane; there's some people we want to avoid over there."

★

"I'm *sure* it was," Lisette said. "I knew the colour of his waistcoat. Who could he have been walking with, I wonder?"

"Some lady of rank, evidently," said Julia. "I think they went up into the gallery in search of us."

"Let us go into the gallery, dears," said Mrs Ashford, and away they trudged.

★

The young men and their companions had gone into the Tropics, and meanwhile were sitting under a spreading palm-tree, eating pink ices; while the music played and played more delightfully, and all the air was full of flowers and waltzes, of delight, of sentiment. To young Richardson the whole Palace was Ella in everything, in every sound, and flower and fountain; to Ella, young Richardson seemed an enormous giant, and his kind little twinkling eyes were shining all round her.

Poor dear! she was so little used to being happy, her happiness almost overpowered her.

"Are you going to the ball at Guildhall to-morrow?" Mr Richardson was saying to his unknown princess. "How shall I ever meet you again? will you not tell me your name? But—"

"I wonder what o'clock it is, and where your mother can be, Ella," said Lady Jane; "it's very odd we have not met."

★

"I can't imagine where they can have hid themselves," said Julia, very crossly, from the gallery overhead.

"I'm so tired, and I'm ready to drop," said Miss Lisette.

"Oh, let us sit," groaned Madame de Bricabrac. "I can walk no more; what does it matter if we do not find your friends?"

"If we take our places at the door," said Lisette, "we shall be sure to catch them as they pass."

★

"Perhaps I may be able to go to the ball," said the princess, doubtfully. "I—I don't know." Lady Jane made believe not to be listening. The voices in the gallery passed on. Lady Jane having finished her ice, pulled out her little watch, and gave a scream of terror. "Heavens! my time is up," she said. "Raton will frighten me out of my wits, driving home. Come, child, come—come—come. Make haste—thank these gentlemen for their escort," and she went skurrying along, a funny little active figure, followed by the breathless young people. They got to the door at last, where Raton was waiting, looking very ferocious. "Oh, good-by," said Ella. "Thank you so much," as Richardson helped her into the chariot.

"And you will not forget me?" he said, in a low voice. "I shall not need any name to remember you by."

"My name is Ella," she answered, blushing, and driving off; and then Ella flung her arms round Lady Jane, and began to cry again, and said, "Oh, I have been so happy! so happy! How good, good of you to make me so happy! Oh, thank you, dear Lady Jane!"

The others came back an hour after them, looking extremely cross, and were much surprised to find Lady Jane in the drawing-room. "I am not going back till Wednesday," said the old lady. "I've several things to do in town. . . . Well, have you had a pleasant day?"

"Not at all," said Mrs Ashford, plaintively. "The colonel deserted us; we didn't find our young men till just as we were coming away. We are all very tired, and want some supper—some of your delicious fruit, Lady Jane."

"Oh, dear, how tired I am!" said Julia.

"Poor Richardson was in very bad spirits," said Lisette.

"What a place it is for losing one another," said old Lady Jane. "I took Ella there this afternoon, and though I looked about I couldn't see you anywhere."

"*Ella!*" cried the other girls, astonished; "was *she* there?" . . . But they were too much afraid of Lady Jane to object more openly.

That evening, after the others left the room, as Ella was pouring out the tea, she summoned up courage to ask whether she might go to the ball at Guildhall with the others next evening. "Pray, pray, please take me," she implored. Mrs Ashford looked up amazed at her audacity.

Poor little Ella! refused, scorned, snubbed, wounded, pained, and disappointed. She finished pouring out the tea in silence, while a few bitter scalding tears dropped from her eyes into the teacups. Colonel Ashford drank some of them, and asked for more sugar to put into his cup.

"There, never mind," he said, kindly. He felt vexed with his wife, and sorry for the child; but he was, as usual, too weak to interfere. "You know you are too young to go into the world, Ella. When your sisters are married, then *your* turn will come."

Alas! would it ever come? The day's delight had given her a longing for more; and now she felt the beautiful glittering vision was only a vision, and over already: the cloud-capped towers, the gorgeous palace; and the charming prince himself—was he a vision too? Ah! it was too sad to think of. Presently Lisette and Julia came back: they had been upstairs to see about their dresses.

"I shall wear my bird-of-paradise, and my yellow tarlatane," said Lisette; "gold and purple is such a lovely contrast."

"Gobert has sent me a lovely thing," said Julia; "tricolour flounces all the way up—she has so much taste."

Good old Lady Jane asked her maid next morning if any dress was being got ready for Miss Ella. Hearing that she was not going, and that no preparations were being made, she despatched Batter on a secret mission, and ordered her carriage at nine o'clock that evening. She went out herself soon after breakfast in a hired brougham, dispensing with the outriders for once. Ella was hard at work all day for her sisters: her little fingers quilled, fluted, frilled, pleated, pinned, tacked the trimmings on their dresses more dexterously than any dressmaker or maid-servant could do. She looked so pretty, so kind, and so tired, so wistful, as she came to help them to dress, that Lisette was quite touched, and said,—"Well, Ella, I shouldn't wonder if, after I am snapped up, you were to get hold of a husband some day. I daresay *some* people might think you nice-looking."

"Oh, do you think so really, Lisette?" said Ella, quite pleased; and then faltering, "Do you think ... Shall you see Mr Richardson?"

"Of course I shall," said Lisette. "He was talking great nonsense yesterday after we found him; saying that he had met with perfection at last—very devoted altogether; scarcely spoke to me at all; but that is the greatest proof of devotion, you know. I know what he meant very well. I shouldn't be at all surprised if he was to propose to-night. I don't know whether I shall have him. I'm always afraid of being thrown away," said Lisette, looking over her shoulder at her train.

Ella longed to send a message, a greeting of some sort, to Lisette's adorer. Oh, how she envied her; what would she not have given to be going too? ...

"What! are not you dressing, child?" said Lady Jane, coming into the room. "Are they again obliged to call for Madame de Bricabrac? I had looked up a pair of shoebuckles for you in case you went; but keep them all the same, they only want a little rubbing up."

"Oh, thank you; how pretty they are; how kind you are to me," said Ella, sadly. "I—I am not going." And she gulped down a great sob.

It was just dreadful not to go; the poor child had had a great draught of delight the day before, and she was aching and sickening for more, and longing with a passion of longing which is only known to very young people—she looked quite worn and pale, though she was struggling with her tears.

"Rub up your shoebuckles—that will distract you," said the old lady, kindly. "They are worth a great deal of money, though they are only paste; and if you peep in my room you will find a little pair of slippers to wear them with. I hope they will fit. I could hardly get any small enough for you." They were the loveliest little white satin slippers, with satin heels, all embroidered with glass beads; but small as they were, they were a little loose, only Ella took care not to say so, as she tried them on.

We all know what is coming, though little Ella had no idea of it. The ball was at Guildhall, one of the grandest and gayest that ever was given in the city of London. It was in honour of the beautiful young Princess, who had just landed on our shores. Princes, ambassadors, nobles, stars, orders and garters, and decorations, were to be present; all the grandest, gayest, richest, happiest people in the country, all the most beautiful ladies and jewels and flowers, were to be there to do homage to the peerless young bride. The Ashfords had no sooner started, than Lady Jane, who had been very mysterious all day, and never told anyone that she had been to the city to procure two enormous golden tickets which were up in her bedroom, now came, smiling very benevolently, into the drawing-room. Little Ella was standing out in the balcony with her pale face and all her hair tumbling down her back. She had been too busy to put it up, and now she was only thinking of the ball, and picturing the dear little ugly disappointed face of Prince Richardson, when he should look about everywhere for her in vain—while she was standing hopelessly gazing after the receding carriage.

"Well, my dear, have you rubbed up the shoebuckles? That is right," said the old lady. "Now come quick into my room and see some of my conjuring."

Conjuring! It was the most beautiful white net dress, frothed and frothed up to the waist, and looped up with long grasses. The conjuring was her own dear old pearl necklace with the diamond clasp and a diamond star for her hair. It was a bunch of grasses and delicate white azaleas for a headdress, and over all the froth a great veil of flowing white net. The child opened her violet eyes, gasped, screamed, and began dancing about the room like a mad thing, jumping, bounding, clapping her hands, all so softly and gaily, and yet so lightly, in such an ecstasy of delight, that Lady Jane felt she was more than rewarded.

★

"Ah! there she is at last!" cried Mr Richardson, who was turning carefully round and round with the energetic Lisette.

"What do you mean?" said Lisette.

Can you fancy her amazement when she looked round and saw Ella appearing in her snow and sunlight dress, looking so beautiful that everybody turned to wonder at her, and to admire? As for Ella, she saw no one, nothing; she was looking up and down, and right and left, for the kind little pale plain face which she wanted.

"Excuse me one minute, Miss Lisette," said Mr Richardson, leaving poor Lisette planted in the middle of the room, and rushing forward.

"Are you engaged," Ella heard a breathless voice saying in her ear, "for the next three, six, twenty dances? I am so delighted you have come! I thought you were never coming."

Julia had no partner at all, and was standing close by the entrance with her mother. They were both astounded at the apparition. Mrs Ashford came forward to make sure that her eyes were not deceiving her. Could it be—?

yes—no,—yes, it was Ella! She flicked her fan indignantly into an alderman's eye, and looked so fierce, that the child began to tremble.

"Please forgive me, mamma," said Ella, piteously.

"Forgive you! never," said Mrs Ashford, indignant. "What does all this mean, pray?" she continued. "Lady Jane, I really must—" and then she stopped, partly because she was so angry she could scarcely speak, and partly because she could not afford to quarrel with Lady Jane until the season was over.

"You really *must* forgive me, dear Lydia," said Lady Jane. "She wanted to come so much, I could not resist bringing her."

Weber's inspiring Last Waltz was being played; the people and music went waving to and fro like the waves of the sea, sudden sharp notes of exceeding sweetness sounded, and at the sound the figures all swayed in harmony. The feet kept unseen measure to the music; the harmonious rhythm thrilled and controlled them all. The music was like an enchantment, which kept them moving and swaying in circles and in delightful subjection. Lassitude, sadness, disappointment, Ella's alarm, all melted away for the time; pulses beat, and the dancers seesawed to the measure.

All that evening young Richardson danced with Ella and with no one else: they scarcely knew how the time went. It was a fairy world: they were flying and swimming in melody—the fairy hours went by to music, in light, in delightful companionship. Ella did not care for Mrs Ashford's darkening looks, for anything that might happen: she was so happy in the moment, she almost forgot to look for Lady Jane's sympathetic glance.

"You must meet me in the ladies' cloak-room punctually at half-past eleven," her patroness had whispered to her. "I cannot keep Raton, with his bad cough, out after twelve o'clock. Mind you are punctual, for I have promised not to keep him waiting."

"Yes, yes, dear Lady Jane," said Ella, and away she danced again to the music. And time went on, and Julia had no partners; and Colonel Ashford came up to his wife, saying,—"I'm so glad you arranged for Ella too," he said. "How nice she is looking! What is the matter with Julia; why don't she dance?" Tumty, tumty, tumty, went the instruments. And meanwhile Mr Richardson was saying,—"Your dancing puts me in mind of a fairy I once saw in a field at Cliffe long ago. Nobody would ever believe me, but I did see one."

"A fairy—what was she like?" asked Ella.

"She was very like you," said Mr Richardson, laughing. "I do believe it *was* you, and that was the time when I saw you before."

"No, it was not," said Ella, blushing, and feeling she ought to confess. "I will tell you," she said, "if you will promise to dance *one* more dance with me, after you know.—Only one."

"Then you, too, remember," he cried, eagerly. "One more dance?—twenty—for ever and ever. Ah, you must know, you must guess the feeling in my heart . . ."

"Listen first," said Ella, trembling very much and waltzing on very slowly. "It was only the other day—" The clock struck three-quarters.

"Ella, I am going," said Lady Jane, tapping her on the shoulder. "Come along, my dear—"

"One word!" cried Richardson, eagerly.

"You can stay with your mother if you like," the old lady went on, preoccupied—she was thinking of her coachman's ire—"but I advise you to come with me."

"Oh, pray, pray stay!" said young Richardson; "where is your mother? Let me go and ask her?"

"You had better go yourself, Ella," said old Lady Jane. "Will you give me your arm to the door, Mr Richardson?"

Ella went up to Mrs Ashford—she was bold with happiness to-night, and made her request. "Stay with me? certainly not, it is quite out of the question. You do me great honour," said the lady, laughing sarcastically. "Lady Jane brought you, Lady Jane must take you back," said the stepmother. "Follow your chaperone if you please, I have no room for you in my brougham. Go directly, Miss!" said Mrs Ashford, so savagely that the poor child was quite frightened, and set off running after the other two. She would have caught them up, but at that instant Lisette—who had at last secured a partner—came waltzing up in such a violent, angry way, that she bumped right up against the little flying maiden and nearly knocked her down. Ella gave a low cry of pain: they had trodden on her foot roughly—they had wounded her; her little satin slipper had come off. Poor Ella stooped and tried to pull at the slipper, but other couples came surging up, and she was alone, and frightened, and obliged to shuffle a little way out of the crowd before she could get it on. The poor little frightened thing thought she never should get through the crowd. She made the best of her way to the cloak-room: it seemed to her as if she had been hours getting there. At last she reached it, only to see, to her dismay, as she went in at one door the other two going out of another a long way off! She called, but they did not hear her, and at the same moment St Paul's great clock began slowly to strike twelve. "My cloak, my cloak, anything, please," she cried in great agitation and anxiety; and a stupid, bewildered maid hastily threw a shabby old shawl over her shoulders—it belonged to some assistant in the place. Little Ella, more and more frightened, pulled it up as she hurried along the blocked passages and corridors all lined with red and thronged with people. They all stared at her in surprise as she flew along. Presently her net tunic caught in a doorway and tore into a long ragged shred which trailed after her. In her agitation her comb fell out of her hair—she looked all scared and frightened—nobody would have recognized the beautiful triumphal princess of half an hour before. She heard the linkmen calling, "Peppercorne's carriage stops the way!" and she hurried faster and faster down the endless passages and steps, and at last, just as she got to the doorway—O horror! she saw the carriage and outriders going gleaming off in the moonlight, while every thing else looked black, dark, and terrible.

"Stop, stop, please stop!" cried little Ella, rushing out into the street through the amazed footmen and linkmen. "Stop! stop!" she cried, flying past Richardson himself, who could hardly believe his eyes. Raton only whipped his horses, and Ella saw them disappearing into gloom in the distance in a sort of agony of despair. She was excited beyond measure, and exaggerated all her feelings. What was to be done? Go back?—that was impossible; walk home?—she did not know her way. Was it fancy?—was not somebody following her? She felt quite desperate in the moonlight and darkness. At that instant it seemed to her like a fairy chariot coming to her rescue, when a cabman, who was slowly passing, stopped and said, "Cab, mum?"

"Yes! oh, yes! To Onslow Square," cried Ella, jumping in and shutting the door in delight and relief. She drove off just as the bewildered little Richardson, who had followed her, reached the spot. He came up in time only to see the cab drive off, and to pick up something which was lying shining on the pavement. It was one of the diamond buckles which had fallen from her shoe as she jumped in. This little diamond buckle might, perhaps, have led to her identification if young Richardson had not taken the precaution of ascertaining from old Lady Jane Ella's name and address.

He sent a servant next morning with a little parcel and a note to inquire whether one of the ladies had lost what was enclosed, and whether Colonel Ashford would see him at one o'clock on business.

"Dear me, what a pretty little buckle!" said Lisette, trying it on her large flat foot. "It looks very nice, don't it, Julia? I think I guess—don't you?—what he is coming for. I shall say 'No.'"

"It's too small for you. It would do better for me," said Julia, contemplating her own long slipper, embellished with the diamonds. "It is not ours. We must send it back, I suppose."

"A shoebuckle?" said Ella, coming in from the kitchen, where she had been superintending preserves in her little brown frock. "Let me see it. Oh, how glad I am; it is mine. Look here!" and she pulled the fellow out of her pocket. "Lady Jane gave them to me."

And so the prince arrived before luncheon, and was closeted with Colonel Ashford, who gladly gave his consent to what he wanted. And when Mrs Ashford began to explain things to him, as was her way, he did not listen to a single word she said. He was so absorbed wondering when Ella was coming into the room. He thought once he heard a little rustle on the stairs outside, and he jumped up and rushed to the door. It was Ella, sure enough, in her shabby little gown. Then he knew where and when he had seen her before.

"Ella, why did you run away from me last night?" he said. "You see I have followed you after all."

They were so good, so happy, so devoted to one another, that even Lisette and Julia relented. Dear little couple; good luck go with them, happiness, content and plenty. There was something quite touching in their youth, tenderness, and simplicity; and as they drove off in their carriage for the honeymoon, Lady Jane flung the very identical satin slipper after them which Ella should have lost at the ball.

8

JULIANA HORATIA EWING

The Ogre Courting
(1871)

ULIANA HORATIA EWING (née Gatty, 1841–85) was
exposed to literature at a very early age. Her mother,
Margaret Gatty, wrote books on natural history and
didactic stories of family life. Among her most important
works were *The Fairy Godmother and Other Tales* (1851),
Aunt Judy's Tales (1859), and *Aunt Judy's Letters* (1862).
She had a great influence on Juliana, who was considered
the most talented storyteller in the family and became her mother's most
important contributor to her journal, *Aunt Judy's Magazine*. In 1862 Juliana
published her first collection of tales, *Melchior's Dream*, and in 1866 she became
chief editor of *Aunt Judy's Magazine*. The following year she married Major
Alexander Ewing of the British Army Pay Department, and she accompanied
him to Canada for two years. Upon returning to England, Mrs Ewing published
The Brownies and Other Tales (1870) with illustrations by George Cruikshank.
This collection of amusing tales established her reputation as one of the major
writers for children in Victorian society, and she followed this publication with
many other significant works such as *Six to Sixteen* (1875) about the trials and
tribulations of an orphan girl and *Jackanapes* (1879) about an orphan boy who
grows up to become a bugler in the army and dies while saving a friend's life.

Nearly all Mrs Ewing's stories were first published in magazines, and in 1882
she collected various narratives for her book *Old-Fashioned Fairy Tales*. Unlike
her mother, Mrs Ewing dealt with moral issues in a subtle and often humorous
manner. Moreover, she wrote on behalf of children and did not seek to impose
adult authoritarian values on them. In her preface to *Old-Fashioned Fairy Tales*,
she discussed two principles that guided her writing of the tales:

First, that there are ideas and types, occurring in the myths of all countries,
which are common properties, to use which does not lay the teller of fairy
tales open to the charge of plagiarism. Such as the idea of the weak
outwitting the strong; the failure of man to choose wisely when he may have
his wish; or the desire of the sprites to exchange their careless and unfettered
existence for the pains and penalties of humanity, if they may thereby share

in the hopes of the human soul. Secondly, that in these household stories (the models for which were originally oral tradition) the thing most to be avoided is a discursive or descriptive style of writing. Brevity and epigram must ever be soul of their wit, and they should be written as tales that are told.

"The Ogre Courting," first published in *Aunt Judy's Magazine* in 1871 and included in *Old-Fashioned Fairy Tales*, is a good example of how Mrs Ewing followed her own principles. It recalls many of the traditional oral tales about the dumb giant or ogre and derives its effect from the succinct and comical style Mrs Ewing uses to show a clever woman making a fool out of a tyrant.

THE OGRE COURTING

N DAYS WHEN ogres were still the terror of certain districts, there was one who had long kept a whole neighbourhood in fear without any one daring to dispute his tyranny.

By thefts and exactions, by heavy ransoms from merchants too old and tough to be eaten, in one way and another, the Ogre had become very rich; and although those who knew could tell of huge cellars full of gold and jewels, and yards and barns groaning with the weight of stolen goods, the richer he grew the more anxious and covetous he became. Moreover, day by day, he added to his stores; for though (like most ogres) he was as stupid as he was strong, no one had ever been found, by force or fraud, to get the better of him.

What he took from the people was not their heaviest grievance. Even to be killed and eaten by him was not the chance they thought of most. A man can die but once; and if he is a sailor, a shark may eat him, which is not so much better than being devoured by an ogre. No, that was not the worst. The worst was this—he would keep getting married. And as he liked little wives, all the short women lived in fear and dread. And as his wives always died very soon, he was constantly courting fresh ones.

Some said he ate his wives; some said he tormented, and others, that he only worked them to death. Everybody knew it was not a desirable match, and yet there was not a father who dare refuse his daughter if she were asked for. The Ogre only cared for two things in a woman—he liked her to be little, and a good housewife.

Now it was when the Ogre had just lost his twenty-fourth wife (within the memory of man) that these two qualities were eminently united in the person of the smallest and most notable woman of the district, the daughter of a certain poor farmer. He was so poor that he could not afford properly to dower his daughter, who had in consequence remained single beyond her first youth. Everybody felt sure that Managing Molly must now be married to the Ogre.

The tall girls stretched themselves till they looked like maypoles, and said, "Poor thing!" The slatterns gossiped from house to house, the heels of their shoes clacking as they went, and cried that this was what came of being too thrifty.

And sure enough, in due time, the giant widower came to the farmer as he was in the field looking over his crops, and proposed for Molly there and then. The farmer was so much put out that he did not know what he said in reply, either when he was saying it, or afterwards, when his friends asked about it. But he remembered that the Ogre had invited himself to sup at the farm that day week.

Managing Molly did not distress herself at the news.

"Do what I bid you, and say as I say," said she to her father; "and if the Ogre does not change his mind, at any rate you shall not come empty-handed out of the business."

By his daughter's desire the farmer now procured a large number of hares, and a barrel of white wine, which expenses completely emptied his slender stocking, and on the day of the Ogre's visit, she made a delicious and savoury stew with the hares in the biggest pickling tub, and the wine-barrel was set on a bench near the table.

When the Ogre came, Molly served up the stew, and the Ogre sat down to sup, his head just touching the kitchen rafters. The stew was perfect, and there was plenty of it. For what Molly and her father ate was hardly to be counted in the tubful. The Ogre was very much pleased, and said politely:

"I'm afraid, my dear, that you have been put to great trouble and expense on my account. I have a large appetite, and like to sup well."

"Don't mention it, sir," said Molly. "The fewer rats the more corn. How do *you* cook them?"

"Not one of all the extravagant hussies I have had as wives ever cooked them at all," said the Ogre; and he thought to himself, "Such a stew out of rats! What frugality! What a housewife!"

When he broached the wine, he was no less pleased, for it was of the best.

"This, at any rate, must have cost you a great deal, neighbour," said he, drinking the farmer's health as Molly left the room.

"I don't know that rotten apples could be better used," said the farmer; "but I leave all that to Molly. Do you brew at home?"

"We give *our* rotten apples to the pigs," growled the Ogre. "But things will be better ordered when she is my wife."

The Ogre was now in great haste to conclude the match, and asked what dowry the farmer would give his daughter.

"I should never dream of giving a dowry with Molly," said the farmer, boldly. "Whoever gets her, gets dowry enough. On the contrary, I shall expect

a good round sum from the man who deprives me of her. Our wealthiest farmer is just widowed, and therefore sure to be in a hurry for marriage. He has an eye to the main chance, and would not grudge to pay well for such a wife, I'll warrant."

"I am no churl myself," said the Ogre, who was anxious to secure his thrifty bride at any price; and he named a large sum of money, thinking, "We shall live on rats henceforward, and the beef and mutton will soon cover the dowry."

"Double that, and we'll see," said the farmer, stoutly.

But the Ogre became angry, and cried: "What are you thinking of, man? Who is to hinder my carrying your lass off, without 'with your leave' or 'by your leave,' dowry or none?"

"How little you know her!" said the farmer. "She is so firm that she would be cut to pieces sooner than give you any benefit of her thrift, unless you dealt fairly in the matter."

"Well, well," said the Ogre, "let us meet each other." And he named a sum larger than he at first proposed, and less than the farmer had asked. This the farmer agreed to, as it was enough to make him prosperous for life.

"Bring it in a sack to-morrow morning," said he to the Ogre, "and then you can speak to Molly; she's gone to bed now."

The next morning, accordingly, the Ogre appeared, carrying the dowry in a sack, and Molly came to meet him.

"There are two things," said she, "I would ask of any lover of mine: a new farmhouse, built as I should direct, with a view to economy; and a feather-bed of fresh goose feathers, filled when the old woman plucks her geese. If I don't sleep well, I cannot work well."

"That is better than asking for finery," thought the Ogre; "and after all the house will be my own." So, to save the expense of labour, he built it himself, and worked hard, day after day, under Molly's orders, till winter came. Then it was finished.

"Now for the feather-bed," said Molly. "I'll sew up the ticking, and when the old woman plucks her geese, I'll let you know."

When it snows, they say the old woman up yonder is plucking her geese, and so at the first snowstorm Molly sent for the Ogre.

"Now you see the feathers falling," said she, "so fill the bed."

"How am I to catch them?" cried the Ogre.

"Stupid! don't you see them lying there in a heap?" cried Molly; "get a shovel, and set to work."

The Ogre accordingly carried in shovelfuls of snow to the bed, but as it melted as fast as he put it in, his labour never seemed done. Towards night the room got so cold that the snow would not melt, and now the bed was soon filled.

Molly hastily covered it with sheets and blankets, and said: "Pray rest here to-night, and tell me if the bed is not comfort itself. To-morrow we will be married."

So the tired Ogre lay down on the bed he had filled, but, do what he would, he could not get warm.

"The sheets must be damp," said he, and in the morning he woke with such horrible pains in his bones that he could hardly move, and half the bed had melted away. "It's no use," he groaned, "she's a very managing woman, but to sleep on such a bed would be the death of me." And he went off home as quickly as he could, before Managing Molly could call upon him to be married; for she was so managing that he was more than half afraid of her already.

When Molly found that he had gone, she sent the farmer after him.

"What does he want?" cried the Ogre, when they told him the farmer was at the door.

"He says the bride is waiting for you," was the reply.

"Tell him I'm too ill to be married," said the Ogre.

But the messenger soon returned:

"He says she wants to know what you will give her to make up for the disappointment."

"She's got the dowry, and the farm, and the feather-bed," groaned the Ogre; "what more does she want?"

But again the messenger returned:

"She says you've pressed the feather-bed flat, and she wants some more goose feathers."

"There are geese enough in the yard," yelled the Ogre. "Let him drive them home; and if he has another word to say, put him down to roast."

The farmer, who overheard this order, lost no time in taking his leave, and as he passed through the yard he drove home as fine a flock of geese as you will see on a common.

It is said that the Ogre never recovered from the effects of sleeping on the old woman's goose feathers, and was less powerful than before.

As for Managing Molly, being now well dowered, she had no lack of offers of marriage, and was soon mated to her mind.

9

JEAN INGELOW

The Prince's Dream
(1872)

EAN INGELOW (1820–97) was born in Boston, Lincolnshire, and remained there until the 1850s when she moved to London. She had a great fondness for the British seacoast and nature, which she described in her poems and stories. She achieved great success in 1863 with the publication of her first series of *Poems*, written for adults, and she produced additional volumes of verse which were well received by the public. She also became a notable writer for children and published such works as *Stories Told to a Child* (1865), *A Sister's Bye Hours* (1868), *Mopsa the Fairy* (1869), *Studies for Stones* (1870), and *The Little Wonder-Horn* (1872).

Ingelow's works often endeavor to recapture a lost paradise and are filled with idyllic landscapes. Her quest for an ideal realm was a reaction against the harsh living conditions that she encountered in London. In "The Prince's Dream," published in *The Little Wonder-Horn*, Ingelow presented her criticism of the unchristian ways of the real world and drew an interesting picture of a protagonist who learns of a better way of life but may not be able to realize it.

THE PRINCE'S DREAM

F WE MAY CREDIT the fable, there is a tower in the midst of a great Asiatic plain, wherein is confined a prince who was placed there in his earliest infancy, with many slaves and attendants, and all the luxuries that are compatible with imprisonment.

Whether he was brought there from some motive of state, whether to conceal him from enemies, or to deprive him of rights, has not transpired; but it is certain that up to the date of this little history he had never set his foot outside the walls of that high tower, and that of the vast world without he knew only the green plains which surrounded it; the flocks and the birds of that region were all his experience of living creatures, and all the men he saw outside were shepherds.

And yet he was not utterly deprived of change, for sometimes one of his attendants would be ordered away, and his place would be supplied by a new one. This fresh companion the prince would never weary of questioning, and letting him talk of cities, of ships, of forests, of merchandise, of kings; but though in turns they all tried to satisfy his curiosity, they could not succeed in conveying very distinct notions to his mind; partly because there was nothing in the tower to which they could compare the external world, partly because, having chiefly lived lives of seclusion and indolence in Eastern palaces, they knew it only by hearsay themselves.

At length, one day, a venerable man of a noble presence was brought to the tower, with soldiers to guard him and slaves to attend him. The prince was glad of his presence, though at first he seldom opened his lips, and it was manifest that confinement made him miserable. With restless feet he would wander from window to window of the stone tower, and mount from story to story; but mount as high as he would there was still nothing to be seen but the vast unvarying plain, clothed with scanty grass, and flooded with the glaring sunshine; flocks and herds, and shepherds, moved across it sometimes, but nothing else, not even a shadow, for there was no cloud in the sky to cast one.

The old man, however, always treated the prince with respect, and answered his questions with a great deal of patience, till at length he found a pleasure in satisfying his curiosity, which so much pleased the poor young prisoner, that, as a great condescension, he invited him to come out on the roof of the tower and drink sherbet with him in the cool of the evening, and tell him of the country beyond the desert, and what seas are like, and mountains, and towns.

"I have learnt much from my attendants, and know this world pretty well by hearsay," said the prince, as they reclined on the rich carpet which was spread on the roof.

The old man smiled, but did not answer; perhaps because he did not care to undeceive his young companion, perhaps because so many slaves were present, some of whom were serving them with fruit, and others burning rich odours on a little chafing-dish that stood between them.

"But there are some words that I never could attach any particular meaning to," proceeded the prince, as the slaves began to retire, "and three in particular that my attendants cannot satisfy me upon, or are reluctant to do so."

"What words are those, my prince?" asked the old man. The prince turned on his elbow to be sure that the last slave had descended the tower stairs, then replied—

"O man of much knowledge, the words are these—Labour, and Liberty, and Gold."

"Prince," said the old man, "I do not wonder that it has been hard to make thee understand the first, the nature of it, and the cause why most men are born to it; as for the second, it would be treason for thee and me to do more than whisper it here, and sigh for it when none are listening; but the third need hardly puzzle thee, thy hookah is bright with it; all thy jewels are set in it; gold is inlaid in the ivory of thy bath; thy cup and thy dish are of gold, and golden threads are wrought into thy raiment."

"That is true," replied the prince, "and if I had not seen and handled this gold, perhaps I might not find its merits so hard to understand; but I possess it in abundance, and it does not feed me, nor make music for me, nor fan me when the sun is hot, nor cause me to sleep when I am weary; therefore when my slaves have told me how merchants go out and brave the perilous wind and sea, and live in the unstable ships, and run risks from shipwreck and pirates, and when, having asked them why they have done this, they have answered, 'For gold,' I have found it hard to believe them; and when they have told me how men have lied, and robbed, and deceived; how they have murdered one another, and leagued together to depose kings, to oppress provinces, and all for gold; then I have said to myself, either my slaves have combined to make me believe that which is not, or this gold must be very different from the yellow stuff that this coin is made of, this coin which is of no use but to have a hole pierced through it and hang to my girdle, that it may tinkle when I walk."

"Notwithstanding," said the old man, "nothing can be done without gold; for look you, prince, it is better than bread, and fruit, and music, for it can buy them all, since all men love it, and have agreed to exchange it for whatever they may need."

"How so?" asked the prince.

"If a man has many loaves he cannot eat them all," answered the old man; "therefore he goes to his neighbour and says, 'I have bread and thou hast a coin of gold; let us change'; so he receives the gold and goes to another man, saying, 'Thou hast two houses and I have none; lend me one of thy houses to live in, and I will give thee my gold'; thus again they change, and he that has the gold says, 'I have food enough and goods enough, but I want a wife, I will go to the merchant and get a marriage gift for her father, and for it I will give him this gold.'"

"It is well," said the prince; "but in time of drought, if there is no bread in a city, can they make it of gold?"

"Not so," answered the old man, "but they must send their gold to a city where there is food, and bring that back instead of it."

"But if there was a famine all over the world," asked the prince, "what would they do then?"

"Why, then, and only then," said the old man, "they must starve, and the gold would be nought, for it can only be changed for that which *is*; it cannot make that which is not."

"And where do they get gold?" asked the prince; "is it the precious fruit of some rare tree, or have they whereby they can draw it down from the sky at sunset?"

"Some of it," said the old man, "they dig out of the ground."

Then he told the prince of ancient rivers running through terrible deserts, whose sands glitter with golden grains and are yellow in the fierce heat of the sun, and of dreary mines where the Indian slaves work in gangs tied together, never seeing the light of day; and lastly (for he was a man of much knowledge, and had travelled far), he told him of the valley of the Sacramento in the New World, and of those mountains where the people of Europe send their criminals, and where now their free men pour forth to gather gold, and dig for it as hard as if for life; sitting up by it at night lest any should take it from them, giving up houses and country, and wife and children, for the sake of a few feet of mud, whence they dig clay that glitters as they wash it; and how they sift it and rock it as patiently as if it were their own children in the cradle, and afterwards carry it in their bosoms, and forego on account of it safety and rest.

"But, prince," he proceeded, observing that the young man was absorbed in his narrative, "if you would pass your word to me never to betray me, I would procure for you a sight of the external world, and in a trance you should see those places where gold is dug, and traverse those regions forbidden to your mortal footsteps."

Upon this, the prince threw himself at the old man's feet, and promised heartily to observe the secrecy required, and entreated that, for however short a time, he might be suffered to see this wonderful world.

Then, if we may credit the story, the old man drew nearer to the chafing-dish which stood between them, and having fanned the dying embers in it, cast upon them a certain powder and some herbs, from whence as they burnt a peculiar smoke arose. As their vapours spread, he desired the prince to draw near and inhale them, and then (says the fable) when he should sleep he should find himself, in his dream, at whatever place he might desire, with this strange advantage, that he should see things in their truth and reality as well as in their outward shows.

So the prince, not without some fear, prepared to obey; but first he drank his sherbet, and handed over the golden cup to the old man by way of recompense; then he reclined beside the chafing-dish and inhaled the heavy perfume till he became overpowered with sleep, and sank down upon the carpet in a dream.

The prince knew not where he was, but a green country was floating before him, and he found himself standing in a marshy valley, where a few wretched cottages were scattered here and there with no means of communication. There was a river, but it had overflowed its banks and made the central land impassable, the fences had been broken down by it, and the fields of corn laid low; a few wretched peasants were wandering about there; they looked half clad and half starved. "A miserable valley indeed!" exclaimed the prince; but as he said it a man came down from the hills with a great bag of gold in his hand.

"This valley is mine," said he to the people; "I have bought it for gold. Now make banks that the river may not overflow, and I will give you gold; also make fences and plant fields, and cover in the roofs of your houses, and buy yourselves richer clothing." So the people did so, and as the gold got lower in the bag the valley grew fairer and greener, till the prince exclaimed, "O gold, I see your value now! O wonderful, beneficent gold!"

But presently the valley melted away like a mist, and the prince saw an army besieging a city; he heard a general haranguing his soldiers to urge them on, and the soldiers shouting and battering the walls; but shortly, when the city was well-nigh taken, he saw some men secretly throwing gold among the soldiers, so much of it that they threw down their arms to pick it up, and said that the walls were so strong that they could not throw them down. "O powerful gold!" thought the prince; "thou art stronger than the city walls!"

After that it seemed to himself that he was walking about in a desert

country, and in his dream he thought, "Now I know what labour is, for I have seen it, and its benefits; and I know what liberty is, for I have tasted it; I can wander where I will, and no man questions me; but gold is more strange to me than ever, for I have seen it buy both liberty and labour." Shortly after this he saw a great crowd digging upon a barren hill, and when he drew near he understood that he had reached the summit of his wishes, and that he was to see the place where the gold came from.

He came up and stood a long time watching the people as they toiled ready to faint in the sun, so great was the labour of digging up the gold.

He saw who had much and could not trust any one to help them to carry it, binding it in bundles over their shoulders, and bending and groaning under its weight; he saw others hide it in the ground, and watch the place clothed in rags, that none might suspect that they were rich; but some, on the contrary, who had dug up an unusual quantity, he saw dancing and singing, and vaunting their success, till robbers waylaid them when they slept, and rifled their bundles and carried their golden sand away.

"All these men are mad," thought the prince, "and this pernicious gold has made them so."

After this, as he wandered here and there, he saw groups of people smelting the gold under the shadow of the trees, and he observed that a dancing, quivering vapour rose up from it, which dazzled their eyes, and distorted everything that they looked at; arraying it also in different colours from the true one. He observed that this vapour from the gold caused all things to rock and reel before the eyes of those who looked through it, and also, by some strange affinity, it drew their hearts towards those who carried much gold on their persons, so that they called them good and beautiful; it also caused them to see darkness and dulness in the faces of those who carried none. "This," thought the prince, "is very strange;" but not being able to explain it, he went still further, and there he saw more people. Each of these had adorned himself with a broad golden girdle, and was sitting in the shade, while other men waited on them.

"What ails these people?" he inquired of one who was looking on, for he observed a peculiar air of weariness and dulness in their faces. He was answered that the girdles were very tight and heavy, and being bound over the regions of the heart, were supposed to impede its action, and prevent it from beating high, and also to chill the wearer, as, being of opaque material, the warm sunshine of the earth could not get through to warm him.

"Why, then, do they not break them asunder," exclaimed the prince, "and fling them away?"

"Break them asunder!" cried the man; "why, what a madman you must be; they are made of the purest gold!"

"Forgive my ignorance," replied the prince; "I am a stranger."

So he walked on, for feelings of delicacy prevented him from gazing any longer at the men with the golden girdles; but as he went he pondered on the misery he had seen, and thought to himself that this golden sand did more mischief than all the poisons of the apothecary; for it dazzled the eyes of some, it strained the hearts of others, it bowed down the heads of many to the earth with its weight; it was a sore labour to gather it, and when it was gathered, the robber might carry it away; it would be a good thing, he thought, if there were none of it.

After this he came to a place where were sitting some aged widows and some orphan children of the gold-diggers, who were helpless and destitute; they were weeping and bemoaning themselves, but stopped at the approach of a man, whose appearance attracted the prince, for he had a very great bundle of gold on his back, and yet it did not bow him down at all; his apparel was rich, but he had no girdle on, and his face was anything but sad.

"Sir," said the prince to him, "you have a great burden; you are fortunate to be able to stand under it."

"I could not do so," he replied, "only that as I go on I keep lightening it"; and as he passed each of the widows, he threw gold to her, and stooping down, hid pieces of it in the bosoms of the children.

"You have no girdle," said the prince.

"I once had one," answered the gold gatherer; "but it was so tight over my breast that my very heart grew cold under it, and almost ceased to beat. Having a great quantity of gold on my back, I felt almost at the last gasp; so I threw off my girdle, and being on the bank of a river, which I knew not how to cross, I was about to fling it in, I was so vexed! 'But no,' thought I, 'there are many people waiting here to cross besides myself. I will make my girdle into a bridge, and we will cross over on it.'"

"Turn your girdle into a bridge!" exclaimed the prince doubtfully, for he did not quite understand.

The man explained himself.

"And then, sir, after that," he continued, "I turned one half of my burden into bread, and gave it to these poor people. Since then I have not been oppressed by its weight, however heavy it may have been; for few men have a heavier one. In fact, I gather more from day to day."

As the man kept speaking, he scattered his gold right and left with a cheerful countenance, and the prince was about to reply, when suddenly a great trembling under his feet made him fall to the ground. The refining fires of the gold gatherers sprang up into flames, and then went out; night fell over everything on the earth, and nothing was visible in the sky but the stars of the southern cross, which were glittering above him.

"It is past midnight," thought the prince, "for the stars of the cross begin to bend."

He raised himself upon his elbow, and tried to pierce the darkness, but could not. At length a slender blue flame darted out, as from ashes in a chafing-dish, and by the light of it he saw the strange pattern of his carpet and the cushions lying about. He did not recognise them at first, but presently he knew that he was lying in his usual place, at the top of his tower.

"Wake up, prince," said the old man.

The prince sat up and sighed, and the old man inquired what he had seen.

"O man of much learning!" answered the prince, "I have seen that this is a wonderful world; I have seen the value of labour, and I know the uses of it; I have tasted the sweetness of liberty, and am grateful, though it was but in a dream; but as for that other word that was so great a mystery to me, I only know this, that it must remain a mystery for ever, since I am fain to believe that all men are bent on getting it; though, once gotten, it causeth them endless disquietude, only second to their discomfort that are without it. I am fain to believe that they can procure with it whatever they most desire, and yet that it cankers their hearts and dazzles their eyes; that it is their nature and their duty to gather it; and yet that, when once gathered, the best thing they can do is to scatter it!"

Alas! the prince visited this wonderful world no more; for the next morning, when he awoke, the old man was gone. He had taken with him the golden cup which the prince had given him. And the sentinel was also gone, none knew whither. Perhaps the old man had turned his golden cup into a golden key.

10

EDWARD H. KNATCHBULL-HUGESSEN

Charlie Among the Elves
(1871)

 DWARD H. KNATCHBULL-HUGESSEN, later Lord Brabourne (1829–93) was educated at Eton and Oxford. Soon after graduating from the university he entered politics as a Liberal Member of Parliament. In 1869 he published *Stories for My Children* and began writing fairy tales as a pastime. The result was a number of charming but mediocre books such as *Crackers for Christmas* (1870), *Moonshine* (1871), *Tales at Tea Time* (1872), and *Queer Folk* (1874) which had a fair amount of success with the public. At the same time he made great strides in his political career, serving as Under Secretary of the Home Office when Gladstone was Prime Minister. In 1880 he was raised to the peerage as Lord Brabourne and became more conservative in his political thinking.

From the beginning, Knatchbull-Hugessen's attitude toward fairy tales was more unconventional than his politics. In the introduction to one of his last books, *Friends and Foes from Fairy Land* (1886) he remarked:

> In the first place, so far as I am concerned, the tales are written only in the most leisurely of leisure moments, as a relaxation from heavier work; and, in the second place, I cannot think any time wasted which contributes to the amusement of the young. To my mind there is enough of dry, prosy matter stuffed into their poor brains in these dull times, and a little lighter food is as useful as it is welcome to them.

"Charlie Among the Elves," published in *Moonshine*, is one of Knatchbull-Hugessen's best tales in that it embraces a philosophic defense of the imagination and the importance of free play during childhood. Significant here also is the mood of nostalgia which was characteristic of the regressive psychological tendency among most Victorian fairy-tale writers. Like many, Knatchbull-Hugessen believed that lost childhood must somehow be regained in the future if life was to have meaning.

CHARLIE AMONG THE ELVES

NCE UPON A TIME there was a little Boy named Charlie. He was very fond of driving his hoop along the gravel-walks in his father's garden, and of trying how long he could keep it up; and as it was a good hoop, and he was an active Boy, he could do so as long as most boys of his own age. Indeed, sometimes he kept it going so long, and ran with it so far, that he got quite out of sight of his nursery-maid, Jane, and she would come puffing and blowing after him, rather angry at his proceedings.

His Mamma had given strict orders that Jane was not to let the little Boy out of her sight, for fear of any accident happening to him; and, as she was rather a particular lady, the maid generally took pains to obey her orders. But it was not always easy to do so; and, in fact, little boys with hoops run so fast, that no nursery-maid with ordinary self-respect, or a proper consciousness of her own position and dignity, can possibly keep up with them. And so it happened that, upon one occasion, Charlie ran quite out of Jane's sight, and still his hoop kept up, and on and on he ran. At last he came to where the gravel-walk ended in a green path, and the ground sloped rapidly downwards. On rushed the hoop as if it thought it was in for a good thing and had better make the most of it, and on rushed Charlie, first because he wanted to keep up his hoop as long as he could, and secondly because he couldn't help it. For when boys or girls try to run down a hill, their legs very soon begin to feel as if they didn't belong to their bodies, and go on and on in the most independent manner, until very often the bodies won't stand it any longer, and come toppling over on the heads, as if that was the only way of stopping their impertinent limbs from running quite away with them. This did not happen to Charlie, but he certainly went on a great deal faster and further than he had intended.

At the bottom of the hill there was a short length of flat green path, on each side of which were a number of gorse bushes scattered about, and the path ended at a strong iron-rail fence, beyond which was a large meadow, full of daisies and buttercups, which seemed the very place for cows to enjoy themselves to their hearts' content. The hoop bounded down to the bottom of the hill, with Charlie close behind it, and then it rushed on till it came against the rail fence, and then it gave a spring back and fell down upon the green path, and lay as still and quiet as hoops generally do if they are only left alone. On rushed Charlie after it, and was only a couple of yards from where it lay, when he found something coming across his face and eyes just like a cobweb. Apparently, too, it *was* a cobweb, or some delicate thing of the kind, which hung from gorse-bush to gorse-bush, all across the path, sparkling with the early dew, and touching the Boy's face with a cool and pleasant touch as he ran through it. But he did not run far through it; he put up his hands to brush it away, and thought he would have no trouble in doing so, but the case was quite different. Delicate as the web seemed, it turned out to be in reality a network of some strength, and, to his great surprise, he was quite checked by it.

But far greater was his surprise, when from the bushes on each side there ran suddenly out a number of little Beings, who surrounded him in a moment with cries of pleasure and triumph. "A mortal, a mortal!" they cried with one voice. "We've got him, we've got him! a real prize! draw the nets tighter and tighter!"

And before Charlie knew what was about to happen to him, the dewy nets were woven round and round his arms and legs, and body and head, and down he was pulled upon the ground in less than no time. He had only time, in fact, to see that his captors were elegant, graceful little creatures, fairy-like in form and general appearance, and dressed in light and fanciful costume—only time, I say, had Charlie to see as much as this, before his head swam, and his eyes grew heavy, and he seemed to fall into a deep sleep, and to forget everything that had happened. I do not know how long he slept, and in fact I do not think that it signifies very much; what I have to do is to tell you the wonderful things which happened afterwards.

When Charlie next became conscious of anything he was lying under an oak-tree, which grew, as oak-trees sometimes *do* grow, in a large green field or park. It was not the only oak-tree there—oh no! not by a good many—and there was nothing particular about it to distinguish it from other trees. It had a trunk and branches, and leaves, and even oak-apples, for anything I know, and it seemed very much like other oak-trees except in one respect. This difference consisted in its having a regular face, half-way up its stem, hair, eyes, nose, mouth, and beard; and as Charlie opened his eyes and looked up at it, an immense yawn, which the mouth was just giving, disclosed a set of teeth far beyond the average in size and whiteness. The face wore a kind and friendly look, and seemed almost to smile upon the Boy as he gazed up at it with some little fear and a great deal of astonishment.

"I never!" exclaimed Charlie, after he had stared steadily for a few moments. "Well! I never did!"

"Didn't you really," politely replied the face; "I am very glad to hear it, if it pleases you, but what is it that you never did?"

Charlie was still more astonished when he heard the voice, the tones of which were not disagreeable, though somewhat husky. After a moment's pause, however, he rejoined, "Why, I never saw a tree with a face, and a mouth that could speak."

"Roots and leaves!" cried the tree, creaking as he spoke in evident displeasure; "what do you mean by that? Why shouldn't trees speak as well as other people? I'm barked if I like such observations"; and the face frowned.

"I didn't mean any harm," said Charlie, "and I'm sure I'm very glad you *can* speak, Mr Oak, for perhaps you'll be able to tell me now where I am and what has happened, and you look so kind and pleasant that I'm sure you will if you can."

At these words the tree-face smiled, for trees, like human beings, like to be well spoken of, and are not insensible to civility and kindness.

"Well, my Boy," said he, "you're in very good quarters, be it where it may, and nothing has happened to you to which you need at all object. I don't know how much or how little I ought to tell you, but the fact is that you are at this moment in—"

At this instant, just as the oak-tree was going to tell Charlie that which he so much wanted to know, a hand was clapped quickly on his mouth, so that he couldn't utter another syllable, and a different voice exclaimed, rather angrily, "Little oaks should be seen, and not heard," upon which the oak was immediately silent and spoke no more.

Charlie looked up in great surprise at this interruption, but his surprise was increased when he perceived that the speaker was a little Being about a foot and a half in height, and dressed in green from top to toe. A slight figure he was, very well formed, and graceful in his movements, and with a cheerful expression of countenance. He held a small silver-headed cane in his hand, had a green "wide-awake" on his head, set rather on one side in a dandified manner, with the breast feather of a cock robin stuck jauntily in it for ornament. It was a tiny little hand which he had laid on the oak's mouth, and as he withdrew it, and turned round towards Charlie, the Boy saw that he wore a sparkling diamond ring of great beauty and brilliancy. As he looked good-natured, and had a smile on his face, Charlie felt encouraged to ask him for information upon certain points which were at that moment of considerable interest to him—namely, where he was, and how he had come there. But the little Being did not want to be spoken to, but as soon as he saw Charlie's eyes staring at him with unmistakeable wonder, he burst out laughing—a musical, silvery laugh it was, pleasant enough to hear, and Charlie was not the least bit afraid when he saw how cheerful the stranger seemed to be. Even less did he fear (if it is possible to be less afraid than the least bit) when the little man spoke up in a gay tone, and said, "Well, mortal child, you have had a good sleep, and now don't you want some breakfast?" and, without another word, he suddenly produced a bag of nuts and put them into Charlie's hand.

The Boy felt too hungry to doubt as to what he should do, so he at once put one of the nuts into his mouth. Oh, you can't think how delicious it was! Just fancy the good taste of sugar-candy, mince-pie, plum-pudding, and strawberries and cream all rolled into one, and then you may have some idea of the taste of these nuts. Charlie ate at least a dozen of them right off without stopping, and felt better and stronger at every nut. Then he sat upright, and was again going to question his new friend, when the latter exclaimed in the same cheery voice, "Now come and see the races!"

Charlie instantly got up, and walked quietly after the little gentleman, wondering what would happen next. Right through a yellow carpet of buttercups and daisies they walked, along a little track and Charlie couldn't imagine where he was or where he was going to. At last, all of a sudden, they came to a hollow place, on the flat of which was quite a smooth piece of turf, levelled with great care, and evidently laid out for a race-course. Posts marked the course out, and the posts were made of a white stuff, which Charlie could not at first make out, but which he afterwards discovered to be petrified blancmange. Then there was a grand stand composed entirely of sponge cake, whilst several private stands of burnt-almonds also ornamented the course, and the judge's stand was made entirely of sugar-candy.

But where were the horses and riders? Charlie had not long to wait. Several mice came cantering along, upon the back of each of which sat a very small frog; each frog had a cap of a different colour upon his head, and wore a proper jockey's dress, and it was beautiful to see how gracefully the mice-horses bore their riders. After they had cantered up and down opposite the grand stand, the jockeys ranged their steeds in line, and everybody seemed full of excitement. Perhaps you will ask who "everybody" was, and well you may, since I have not told you of anybody as yet excepting Charlie and the green Elf. Well, there were a quantity of other little green Elves—not so tall by a couple of inches or more as the first one, but all elegantly made, as far as Charlie could see, all with their green clothes well-fitting and nicely put on, and all apparently full of fun and as happy as possible. They were so anxious about the race that they didn't take much notice of Charlie, and he for his part thought more about the little mice-horses and their curious riders than anything else. And then he heard the little people talking about the start, and he found that the signal for the start was to be given by two Elves pulling at a regular Christmas cracker: when it went off with a "pop," the horses were to go off too. But the first cracker was damp and wouldn't go off at all, and there was something wrong about the second, for the end of it came out without its going off, and the Elf at the end fell backwards head over heels with the force of his own pulling, at which all his companions laughed heartily. However, the third cracker went off all right, and away dashed the little mice, whilst the Elves clapped their hands, and shouted out the name of their favourite mouse. "Now, Crumb-lover!" "Here comes Dainty-bit!" and at last a loud cry arose, "Nibble-cheese wins! Nibble-cheese wins!" and a mouse came racing past the winning-post with a little green frog with a white cap and a black sash, closely pressed by a cherry and black frog on

another mouse, whom he belaboured with a dry dandelion stalk, but who was fairly beaten by "Nibble-cheese."

Next came a hurdle-race of grasshoppers, which was the funniest and most ridiculous thing that Charlie had ever seen. The hurdles were made of dried daisy-stalks, and it was the greatest sport to see the grasshoppers jump. "Green-back" was the name of the winner, and he was as proud of his victory as any boy who ever won a race. Then came a wrestling match between two hedgehogs, which made Charlie roar with laughter. Over and over they rolled on the ground, the object of each being to push the other over a boundary-line which had been drawn in the grass. At last one of them got the better of the other, and all the lookers-on clapped their hands in approval. Charlie began to clap his hands too, but his friend the Elf told him not do so, or he would frighten the animals, upon which he left off.

Various other amusements followed, the like of which mortal children have seldom or ever witnessed. A hornpipe was danced by young rabbits, whose grave faces, whilst they twisted and twirled their legs about in the dance, convulsed Charlie with laughter; a sack-race, in which moles were the performers, next followed, and this seemed to please everybody very much, except the moles themselves, who appeared as if they had rather have been left in their holes.

At last the games seemed to be over as far as the animals were concerned, and Charlie began to wonder what would happen next, when one of the Elves suddenly exclaimed, "Let's have a mushroom match!" and in a moment the little people began to pelt each other with mushrooms, shrieking with laughter all the time, in which Charlie heartily joined.

Presently one of them cried out—"Stop, stop, that's not fair! somebody has thrown a fungus"; and then they began to talk very fast and abuse the Elf that had committed such a crime, as a punishment for which he was obliged to eat a slice of the fungus he had thrown, at which he made all kinds of queer faces, and seemed greatly to dislike it.

When the excitement to which this little occurrence gave rise was over, Charlie thought it was high time to inquire where he was, and what was to become of him. Accordingly, he accosted the Elf who had brought him to the races, and asked him the question which was uppermost in his head. "If you please, Sir, where am I, and mayn't I go home soon?"

To his surprise the Elf appeared either entirely to misunderstand his question, or at all events to be determined to take no notice of it, for the only answer which he returned appeared to have nothing whatever to do with the question.

"Reels and jigs!" he cried. "I quite agree with you, little mortal. There is nothing like dancing, and this is the very place for it!" So saying, he seized hold of the hand of the Elf nearest to him, and his example was immediately followed by all his companions, who, joining hands and forming several circles, began to dance round and round in the maddest manner, trampling down grass, daisies, and buttercups, and making those curious Fairy rings at which we have so often looked in the green meadows, and wondered how and why they came there.

This amusement continued for some little time, during which Charlie stood and watched the dancing Elves until his head grew quite giddy with their continually going round and round. All of a sudden they stopped, and the chief Elf exclaimed in his clear, pleasant voice, "It's getting late for this fun now; come to the grove and sing." Upon which off he set, the other Elves following, and Charlie, finding that he had nothing better to do, went with the rest.

Presently they came to a group of large trees, five or six in number, growing in the meadow, and affording a pleasant shelter from the sun to the sheep or cattle which might be pastured there. Underneath the trees was a regular carpet of Blue-bells, and a number of Lords and Ladies growing amongst them. When the Elf had arrived at this place, he gave a signal to his followers, who ranged themselves on either side of him, and after a little of the coughing and clearing of throats in which all singers think it necessary to indulge before beginning their songs, they struck up a melody which Charlie thought was the very sweetest music which he had ever heard in the whole course of his life; and thus ran the song of the Elves:

> "In the waning summer light,
>   Which the hearts of mortals love,
> 'Tis the hour for elfin sprite
>   Through the flow'ry mead to rove.
>
> "Mortal eyes the spot may scan,
>   Yet our forms they ne'er descry;
> Though so near the haunts of man,
>   Merrily our trade we ply.
>
> "Ever 'mid the fragrant flowers,
>   With the songster birds and bees,
> Practise we our magic powers,
>   Loving playmates such as these.
>
> "Shrink we from the crowded town
>   And the din of noisy street,
> Where would harsher voices drown
>   Elfin music pure and sweet.
>
> "Shrink we from the busy throng
>   And the scenes of mortal life,

> Where, enthralled by passions strong,
>   Men engage in endless strife.
>
> "Endless strife for gold or fame,
>   (Empty bubbles to content!)
> Let them strive: but all the same
>   Elfin life is different.
>
> "Elfin life in mead and glen,
>   Ever joyous, ever free;
> Better than the life of men
>   In its quiet purity.
>
> "Heav'n on Elves has kindly smiled,
>   Smiled on Elves and elfin art;
> Let us to this mortal child
>   Of our bliss a share impart."

And as Charlie listened to these words, a soft, soothing feeling seemed to steal gently over him, and he felt just as if he was asleep and yet awake—asleep enough to be resting and enjoying his rest, and awake enough to understand perfectly well all that was going on.

Very strange things they were which went on, I can tell you. When the little Elves had done singing, they sat down under the trees, and some of them drew forth certain musical instruments, which Charlie could never exactly describe, but from which proceeded the most exquisitely delicious music that ever delighted mortal ears. And as the Elves played, curious results followed. All the Lords and Ladies came out of their green cloaks, ranged themselves opposite to each other, bowed, asked each other to dance, just as if they were real people at a ball, and *did* dance, as gracefully as you could have wished to see them. They waltzed, they galoped, they went through the "Lancers" without a mistake, and had besides several dances of their own, which Charlie had never seen or heard of before, but which he thought remarkably pretty.

When they had all danced for some time, the music began to be played slower and slower; and as it nearly came to a stop, the little Lords and Ladies all went back into their homes, and nestled up warmly in their green cloaks as comfortably as possible. Then the Elves began to play at riddles, and asked each other the funniest questions in the world, only the answers were still funnier, and Charlie could not make head or tail of them.

"Why does the sun shine?" asked one Elf of another.

"Because there's no lamp big enough to light the world without him," was the answer.

"How many stars are there?" shouted one.

"Twice as many as half," said another.

"What flower does the calf like best?"

"The cow's-lips."

"Why is our grove like a king's court?"

"Because there are lots of Lords and Ladies in it."

"Which is the stupidest tree?"

"The sloe-tree."

All these questions and answers passed merrily round the elfin circle, till at last one Elf turned round and said quite sharply to Charlie, "Why is a green linnet like a rhinoceros?"

"It isn't a bit like," said Charlie.

"No more it is!" cried the Elf; "but how in the world did you find that out, mortal child?" and they all burst into screams of laughter, and rolled about under the trees as merry a party as you could wish to see.

At last, when they were quite tired of laughing, the chief Elf cried out suddenly, "Now let us tell some stories!" Upon which another Elf began directly:

"Once there was a grasshopper so big that he knocked down the sheep and cows when he ran against them." And a second Elf chimed in as fast as possible—"Once there was a man so tall that he could wade through the deepest sea without the water coming up to his waistcoat!"

"Oh, you stupid creatures!" said the chief Elf, "I didn't mean those kind of stories, but real, good, amusing little tales, such as mortal fathers tell when they take their little girls one on each knee, and draw their chairs up near the fire, and the boys sit on the rug at their feet and listen. Now then, Flit-by-night, tell us one of your best at once!"

Flit-by-night was a delicately formed little Elf with a pleasant face, and a merry twinkle in his eye withal; and when he was thus called upon by his chief, he turned head over heels directly to show his respect for him, and then crossed his legs, folded his arms, and thus began his story:

"Once there was a Boy who didn't believe in Fairies. He had read the wise writings of some *very* grave and clever people who had written reviews upon Fairy-tale books and had said they were all nonsense, and that the age of Fairies and Ogres was past and gone. The Boy believed these wise writers, and in his childhood there was no romance, no pleasant fancies flitted through his young brain, but everything was plain and plodding and matter-of-fact, and he was quite a man-boy, with none of the sparkling nonsense life of merry childhood about him. The dear Fairies saw and pitied him, but they could do nothing with him. If they came in the night and teased him with a dream, from which he woke up with a frightened start, he only muttered to himself that he had eaten too much plum-pudding the evening before, and must not do so again; if they slyly put a drop of magic ache-powder in his ear, and gave him the ear-ache, he always remembered he had sat in some draught or other lately, and laid it all to *that;* and even the pretty little Fairy rings in the green meadows he explained in some knowing way, as proceeding from some natural cause, and having nothing in the world to do with the Fairy race. This, as you may imagine, was very provoking to the merry Fairies; for, like mortal people, they like to be thought something of, and don't at all approve of being neglected and scorned. So they determined to teach this Boy to *be* a Boy if they could, and not to be such a grave old philosopher before he was even in trousers. Philosophers, you know, are terrible people to deal with in society; and if the world were governed by them, it would soon be a place hardly fit to live in, for Elves or mortals either. But philosophers not in trousers are things not to be endured, and the sooner they give up the trade the better.

"So the Fairies set their wits to work to show this Boy that there were Fairies, and they played him every trick you can imagine. For some time it was of no use: if they suddenly pinched his feet, he declared it was corns; if they whispered to him as he walked in the woods, he said it was the wind blowing through the leaves of the trees; and when they tore in half in the night the pincushion in his room, he told everybody that it was a mouse, and set a trap next evening. Unfortunately, too, the trap happened to catch a mouse, which confirmed him all the more in his disbelief. So the Fairies were quite in despair of teaching him by common means the lesson they had intended, and they determined to try something rather more unusual.

"One evening the Boy had sauntered out just after tea, and was walking towards the gravel-walk at the end of the lawn, when a very small figure, clad entirely in green, walked quietly before him from one bush into another. The Boy stopped short: another figure followed, another and another. The Boy thought to himself very gravely for a minute, and then said out aloud, 'Oh! I see: toads—green toads.' At that moment something struck him a sharp blow on the forehead; it was like the blow of a pea from a peashooter, and, as he looked up and down in astonishment, he felt several more of the same blows.

" 'Hallo!' he cried out, 'how suddenly it has come on to hail!' and at that moment he cast his eyes down, and as the blows continued he perceived that they came not from hail or from peas, but from large, round, white sugar-plums.

"This surprised him very much, and he stepped on for a yard or two, still thinking the matter might be explained somehow in a natural way, when all of a sudden out jumped the little green figures, and began to pelt him so furiously that he hardly knew whether to stand still or run away. A chocolate drop hit him full on the nose; he closed his eye just in time to save it from being nearly put out by a burnt almond, and a large bit of 'toffy' went bang into his mouth.

Then, and then only, did he perceive that he was actually standing within the circle of a Fairy ring, and it flashed across his mind like lightning that these were Fairies, and that the stories he had always disbelieved were true after all. He stood still, dumb with amazement; and whilst his face was still tingling with the blows of the sugar-plums and other sweet bullets, a low, clear voice sang to him—though he could not distinguish the singer—

> " 'Boy that doubts the Fairy race,
>   Tempt no more their magic spleen;
> Never more avert thy face
>   From the mystic Fairy Green.
>
> " 'Fairy legends list and learn,
>   Fairy fantasies enjoy,
> Unbelieving science spurn,
>   Be—while still you can—a boy.'

"And as he listened his heart grew lighter, and his spirit bounded within him with a pleasure which he had never felt before. He threw up his arms in the air, and cried out aloud, 'Then there really *are* Fairies! Oh dear, kind little Fairies! how happy I am to make friends with you, and to know that you *do* exist!' And in a moment the Boy seemed to feel a new being altogether, and all his old, dull, heavy, matter-of-fact ways were charmed out of him by the Fairy magic. He stood still in the Fairy ring, and the merry little creatures around him smiled sweet smiles upon him, and kissed their hands to him as they slowly and gracefully glided back into the bushes and faded away from his sight and hearing.

"But the memory of that evening never, never faded from the Boy's heart. He was a changed Boy from that hour. True, he did not forget to work when there was work to be done, but at other times he was ever merry and light-hearted, and it seemed as if some of the loving cheerfulness of the little Elves had settled in his heart, never to be rooted out again in his journey through the world. It held by him after he grew up to be a man; people used to say that he sometimes talked a great deal of nonsense and was always ready for a laugh and a joke; but if they had known the truth, they would have said that it was the pleasant spirit of the Fairies still resting upon him, and lighting up his life with a glow unknown to mortals of a duller and heavier disposition."

Here Flit-by-night stopped, and all the Elves clapped their hands in approbation of his story, to which Charlie had listened with deep attention. Then the chief Elf turned round to another of his friends and said "Tickling Tim, now it is your turn."

Tickling Tim was an Elf with a long face and a quaint expression of dry fun upon his countenance; he made but little pause or hesitation when he was accosted, but sat bolt upright in his place and began at once in a very grave voice.

"Once there was a cabbage bigger than all the cabbages about him. He was a very proud vegetable, and turned up his leaves at all the other cabbages, despising cauliflowers and broccoli, sneering at green peas and French beans, and ranking parsnips and onions as the lowest of the low. In fact he claimed to be King of the cabbages, and no one dared to contradict him. At last one day a respectable asparagus, whom he had grossly insulted by allusions to his leafless condition, telling him that he must be little better than a pauper to walk about without a great coat, demanded the reason of his fancying himself so much better than all the other fellows in the garden.

"Curling up his outside leaf in a contemptuous manner, the cabbage replied, 'It is only through my kindness, contemptible weed, that I condescend to reply to you; but the fact is, that besides the claim to superiority which my size and general appearance give me, I can show you at once that I possess a title to dignity which is shared by no other vegetable around me.' And, opening his leaves, the haughty cabbage displayed a large snail comfortably located in his very heart, and directed the attention of the asparagus to this, which he termed a Royal visitor.

"The asparagus wagged his head with a knowing look. 'Humph,' said he, 'to show me this may be a proof of your kindness, but in my opinion it does not say much for your goodness of heart, and I think you will live to rue the hour when you admitted such a visitor.'

"With these words he went quietly back to his bed, and left his proud neighbour to himself. The cabbage continued to puff and swell with pride, and to hold his head very high. No one was good enough to speak to him, and in fact honest vegetables of proper feeling soon ceased to wish for his society. He found, however, that in the midst of his glory, he was afflicted with occasional pains and strange twinges, which were anything but comfortable. For some time he could not understand the cause, until at last it suddenly flashed across him that these new feelings might proceed from his noble and precious visitor. However, he folded his leaves the more closely around him, and bore everything cheerfully for the sake of presenting a good appearance to the world.

"So things went on, and days rolled by, until one fine morning the gardener entered the cabbage row, knife in hand, and began to inspect the vegetables. He came up to the proud cabbage, and, after looking at him for a moment or two, remarked, 'Here's a good big one, but I doubt he's all right.' And then, stooping down, he opened the leaves and looked carefully into the heart.

"'Ah,' said he, 'it is just as I thought; them nasty snails has eat the heart right out—the cabbage ain't fit for the pigs!' These words, pronounced in a tone easily audible by every vegetable in the neighbourhood, filled the proud cabbage with feelings of the deepest humiliation and dismay. What, then, had his cherished visitor wrought him this evil? Had he, whom he had entertained as a friend, and of whose visit he had been so proud, all the time occupied himself in eating into his vitals, and destroying his very existence? How would he be disgraced and lowered in the eyes of all his neighbours! Never more could he hold up his head among cabbages! His reputation was lost for ever! Small time for meditation, however, had the miserable wretch, for, seizing him in one hand, the gardener, with his knife in the other, cut out the heart of the unfortunate cabbage, threw it on the ground, and only afforded him a melancholy satisfaction by making an end of the snail by setting the heel of his boot upon it with a force sufficient to have smashed twenty of such creatures into fragments; he then calmly cut off the rest of the cabbage, which he presently flung into the pig-sty, leaving a miserable barren stalk as the only relic of the haughty but ill-fated vegetable. Thus, brother Elves, we may learn from the fate of this cabbage that to cherish pride in our hearts is to entertain therein a dangerous guest, who may prove a very snail to our happiness, and eventually destroy us from off the face of the earth!"

Tickling Tim had scarcely finished his tale, which he did in the same grave manner as that with which he had begun it, than several elfin voices shouted loudly, "Oh, what a serious story! don't let's have any more of them!" and they all jumped up as if eager for a new amusement. At last one called out, "Come and chaff the nightingales!" and off they set at once to the edge of the shrubbery, where the nightingales were singing as sweetly as usual. They stopped to listen, and presently a nightingale began to sing close to them, and thus ran the song:

> "How pleasant it is in the sweet moon-light
>   To warble low notes to the beautiful moon;
> With melody sweet to enliven the night,
>   And make mortals regret the sun rises so soon!"

Scarcely had the nightingale sang these notes, which Charlie somehow or other perfectly understood, than one of the Elves, imitating the bird in the most wonderful manner, sang as follows:

> "How stupid it is in the chill, damp night
>   To warble dull ditties both foolish and old;
> To open their windows weak mortals t' invite,
>   Whence they probably catch a detestable cold."

The nightingale stopped its song for a moment when it heard this rival songster, but, as if careless of the interruption, or not having properly understood it, he presently began again:

> "On the branches I hop, which are near to the ground,
>   Where my mate guards her eggs in the snug little nest,
> And I make the whole grove with my warbling resound,
>   My song is the music which mortals love best."

To which the Elf immediately rejoined:

> "The cat will catch birds which hop near to the ground.
>   And a foot stamp on mate, eggs, and snug little nest;
> The noise which you make restless sleepers confound,
>   And both you and your din most devoutly detest."

At this the nightingale grew very angry, stopped singing, and began to make a little chattering noise, like one stone being struck upon another, which nightingales always do when they are interrupted or suspect an enemy near. This was just what the Elves wanted, and they all went into fits of laughter.

Suddenly one of them cried out, "Oh, here comes the old white owl! Let's have some fun with her!" and one of them ran up to some dead roses which were lying on the ground underneath a rose-tree, and touched two or three of them, which immediately took the form of mice, and began to run along the ground. Down pounced the old owl, and found to her surprise that she had only caught a dead rose in her claws, so she mounted in the air again, vexed and surprised, muttering that she must be getting terribly old and blind to have made such a stupid mistake. She never for a moment suspected the Elves, who were delighted at the trick, and seemed in such a mischievous humour that Charlie thought he should hardly be surprised at anything which they did now.

However, after they had laughed enough, one or two of the little creatures began to yawn, for all the world like a child whose bedtime is near, but whose nursery-maid doesn't come, and when Charlie saw this he somehow or other began to yawn too; and as he opened his mouth very wide for a regular good yawn, the little Elves seemed to fade gradually away from before his eyes, their voices became more and more indistinct, their laughter was no longer to be heard, and a strange feeling stole over the little Boy's senses, as if he hardly knew whether what had happened had *really* happened, or whether he had only been listening to an amusing story.

And as he yawned again and opened his eyes wide, there he was in his own little cot, and his own dear Mamma was bending over him with a sweet loving smile—such a smile as touches a chord of tenderness in one's heart ever after through life when one calls it to mind.

"Charlie, my darling," she said, "you have had a nice long sleep, and now my little Boy may get up and have a run in the garden with Jane before dinner."

Charlie couldn't understand it. Surely he *had* been out in the garden with Jane, for there it was he had met with the Elves and had such strange adventures. He didn't know what to make of it, and looked up at his Mamma with a curiously puzzled expression of countenance. "Where are the Elves gone to?" he asked; and his Mamma smiled again as she replied,—

"I don't know, my Boy, unless they have flown back to dream-land. My darling has been dreaming!"

So Charlie said no more, for he knew very well that when grown-up people take such fancies into their head, it is of no use trying to persuade them to the contrary. But for all that he was certain that he had been into the elfin country and seen all the strange things of which I have told you; and no doubt the Elves had managed by their magic that his Mamma should think he had been all the time safely in bed at home.

II

MARY DE MORGAN

A Toy Princess
(1877)

ARY DE MORGAN (1850–1907) was the youngest daughter of August De Morgan, a renowned professor of mathematics at University College London, and Sophia Feind, a gifted writer. Due to her parents' large circle of friends and their interest in the arts and literature, De Morgan came into contact with Sir Edward Burne-Jones, Dante Gabriel Rossetti, and William Morris, and she herself displayed an early interest in writing and painting. When her father died in 1871, she began to share a house with her older brother William, a talented novelist and illustrator. Located in Chelsea, their house became a center for most of the famous artists and writers of their day.

In 1873 De Morgan published her first book with a friend entitled *Six by Two*, a collection of realistic stories for older girls, but the narratives were too didactic, even for her own taste. It was first through telling her original fairy tales to the children of her friends—one of the youngsters was Rudyard Kipling—that De Morgan realized she had more potential as a fairy-tale writer. By 1877 she was ready to publish her first collection of tales entitled *On a Pincushion and Other Tales* with woodcuts by her brother William. Though sometimes too moralistic, De Morgan succeeded in such stories as "The Seeds of Love" and "A Toy Princess" to use symbols in a subtle manner to reflect social issues of concern in Victorian society. Her next volume, *The Necklace of Princess Fiorimonde* (1880), contained some of her very best tales such as "The Wanderings of Arasmon," "The Heart of Princess Joan," "The Bread of Discomfort," and "The Three Clever Kings." As in the tales by George MacDonald, De Morgan emphasized human compassion and the utopian quest. Her protagonists are often discontent with their decadent surroundings, and they seek more meaningful lives rather than compromise their integrity for money or power. These same themes are also stressed in *The Windfairies and Other Tales* (1900). Like her other stories, they were first told and retold to children and adults before she set them down on paper. This mode of preparation accounts for the fine cadence and rhythm of her tales, which are often embued with a mysterious quality. Though she set most of the tales in the distant past, it is apparent, as in the case of "A Toy Princess," that she was concerned in addressing social, if not political, problems in Victorian England. Not only does De Morgan critique the insipid attitudes of mindless rulers in "A Toy Princess," but she also argues for greater independence for women. Confident and strong-willed herself, De Morgan never married and dedicated her time to working with artists and children. When her health began to fail at the beginning of the century, she moved to Egypt and directed a reformatory for children in Cairo, where she eventually died on May 17, 1907.

A TOY PRINCESS

ORE THAN A thousand years ago, in a country quite on the other side of the world, it fell out that the people all grew so very polite that they hardly ever spoke to each other. And they never said more than was quite necessary, as "Just so," "Yes indeed," "Thank you," and "If you please." And it was thought to be the rudest thing in the world for any one to say they liked or disliked, or loved or hated, or were happy or miserable. No one ever laughed aloud, and if any one had been seen to cry they would at once have been avoided by their friends.

The King of this country married a Princess from a neighbouring land, who was very good and beautiful, but the people in her own home were as unlike her husband's people as it was possible to be. They laughed and talked, and were noisy and merry when they were happy, and cried and lamented if they were sad. In fact, whatever they felt they showed at once, and the Princess was just like them.

So when she came to her new home, she could not at all understand her subjects, or make out why there was no shouting and cheering to welcome her, and why every one was so distant and formal. After a time, when she found they never changed, but were always the same, just as stiff and quiet, she wept, and began to pine for her own old home.

Every day she grew thinner and paler. The courtiers were much too polite to notice how ill their young Queen looked, but she knew it herself, and she believed she was going to die.

Now she had a fairy godmother, named Taboret, whom she loved dearly, and who was always kind to her. When she knew her end was drawing near she sent for her godmother, and when she came had a long talk with her quite alone.

No one knew what was said, and soon afterwards a little Princess was born, and the Queen died. Of course all the courtiers were sorry for the poor Queen's death, but it would have been thought rude to say so. So, although there was a grand funeral, and the court put on mourning, everything else went on much as it had done before.

The little baby was christened Ursula, and given to some court ladies to be taken charge of. Poor little Princess! *She* cried hard enough, and nothing could stop her.

All her ladies were frightened, and said that they had not heard such a dreadful noise for a long time. But, till she was about two years old, nothing could stop her crying when she was cold or hungry, or crowing when she was pleased.

After that she began to understand a little what was meant when her nurses told her, in cold, polite tones, that she was being naughty, and she grew much quieter.

She was a pretty little girl, with a round baby face and big merry blue eyes; but as she grew older, her eyes grew less and less merry and bright, and her fat little face grew thin and pale. She was not allowed to play with any other children, lest she might learn bad manners; and she was not taught any games or given any toys. So she passed most of her time, when she was not at her lessons, looking out of the window at the birds flying against the clear blue sky; and sometimes she would give a sad little sigh when her ladies were not listening.

One day the old fairy Taboret made herself invisible, and flew over to the King's palace to see how things were going on there. She went straight up to the nursery, where she found poor little Ursula sitting by the window, with her head leaning on her hand.

It was a very grand room, but there were no toys or dolls about, and when the fairy saw this, she frowned to herself and shook her head.

"Your Royal Highness's dinner is now ready," said the head nurse to Ursula.

"I don't want any dinner," said Ursula, without turning her head.

"I think I have told your Royal Highness before that it is not polite to say you don't want anything, or that you don't like it," said the nurse. "We are waiting for your Royal Highness."

So the Princess got up and went to the dinner-table, and Taboret watched them all the time. When she saw how pale little Ursula was, and how little she ate, and that there was no talking or laughing allowed, she sighed and frowned even more than before, and then she flew back to her fairy home, where she sat for some hours in deep thought.

At last she rose, and went out to pay a visit to the largest shop in Fairyland.

It was a queer sort of shop. It was neither a grocer's, nor a draper's, nor a hatter's. Yet it contained sugar, and dresses, and hats. But the sugar was magic sugar, which transformed any liquid into which it was put; the dresses each had some special charm, and the hats were wishing-caps. It was, in fact, a shop where every sort of spell or charm was sold.

Into this shop Taboret flew; and as she was well known there as a good customer, the master of the shop came forward to meet her at once, and bowing, begged to know what he could get for her.

"I want," said Taboret, "a Princess."

"A Princess!" said the shopman, who was in reality an old wizard. "What size do you want it? I have one or two in stock."

"It must look now about six years old. But it must grow."

"I can make you one," said the wizard, "but it'll come rather expensive."

"I don't mind that," said Taboret. "See! I want it to look exactly like this," and so saying she took a portrait of Ursula out of her bosom and gave it to the old man, who examined it carefully.

"I'll get it for you," he said. "When will you want it?"

"As soon as possible," said Taboret. "By to-morrow evening if possible. How much will it cost?"

"It'll come to a good deal," said the wizard, thoughtfully. "I have such difficulty in getting these things properly made in these days. What sort of a voice is it to have?"

"It need not be at all talkative," said Taboret, "so that won't add much to the price. It need only say, 'If you please,' 'No, thank you,' 'Certainly,' and 'Just so.'"

"Well, under those circumstances," said the wizard, "I will do it for four cats' footfalls, two fishes' screams, and two swans' songs."

"It is too much," cried Taboret. "I'll give you the footfalls and the screams, but to ask for swans' songs!"

She did not really think it dear, but she always made a point of trying to beat tradesmen down.

"I can't do it for less," said the wizard, "and if you think it too much, you'd better try another shop."

"As I am really in a hurry for it, and cannot spend time in searching about, I suppose I must have it," said Taboret; "but I consider the price very high. When will it be ready?"

"By to-morrow evening."

"Very well, then, be sure it is ready for me by the time I call for it, and whatever you do, don't make it at all noisy or rough in its ways"; and Taboret swept out of the shop and returned to her home.

Next evening she returned and asked if her job was done.

"I will fetch it, and I am sure you will like it," said the wizard, leaving the shop as he spoke. Presently he came back, leading by the hand a pretty little girl of about six years old—a little girl so like the Princess Ursula that no one could have told them apart.

"Well," said Taboret, "it looks well enough. But are you sure that it's a good piece of workmanship, and won't give way anywhere?"

"It's as good a piece of work as ever was done," said the wizard, proudly, striking the child on the back as he spoke. "Look at it! Examine it all over, and see if you find a flaw anywhere. There's not one fairy in twenty who could tell it from the real thing, and no mortal could."

"It seems to be fairly made," said Taboret, approvingly, as she turned the little girl round. "Now I'll pay you and then will be off"; with which she raised her wand in the air and waved it three times, and there arose a series of strange sounds.

The first was a low tramping, the second shrill and piercing screams, the third voices of wonderful beauty, singing a very sorrowful song.

The wizard caught all the sounds and pocketed them at once, and Taboret, without ceremony, picked up the child, took her head downwards under her arm, and flew away.

At court that night the little Princess had been naughty, and had refused to go to bed. It was a long time before her ladies could get her into her crib, and when she was there, she did not really go to sleep, only lay still and pretended, till every one went away; then she got up and stole noiselessly to the window, and sat down on the window-seat all curled up in a little bunch, while she looked out wistfully at the moon. She was such a pretty soft thing, with all her warm bright hair falling over her shoulders, that it would have been hard for most people to be angry with her. She leaned her chin on her tiny white hands, and as she gazed out, the tears rose to her great blue eyes; but remembering that her ladies would call this naughty, she wiped them hastily away with her nightgown sleeve.

"Ah moon, pretty bright moon!" she said to herself, "I wonder if they let you cry when you want to. I think I'd like to go up there and live with you; I'm sure it would be nicer than being here."

"Would you like to go away with me?" said a voice close beside her; and looking up she saw a funny old woman in a red cloak, standing near to her. She was not frightened, for the old woman had a kind smile and bright black eyes, though her nose was hooked and her chin long.

"Where would you take me?" said the little Princess, sucking her thumb, and staring with all her might.

"I'd take you to the sea-shore, where you'd be able to play about on the sands, and where you'd have some little boys and girls to play with, and no one to tell you not to make a noise."

"I'll go," said Ursula, springing up at once.

"Come along," said the old woman, taking her tenderly in her arms and folding her in her warm red cloak. Then they rose up in the air, and flew out of the window, right away over the tops of the houses.

The night air was sharp, and Ursula soon fell asleep; but still they kept flying on, on, over hill and dale, for miles and miles, away from the palace, towards the sea.

Far away from the court and the palace, in a tiny fishing village, on the sea, was a little hut where a fisherman named Mark lived with his wife and three children. He was a poor man, and lived on the fish he caught in his little boat. The children, Oliver, Philip, and little Bell, were rosy-cheeked and bright-eyed. They played all day long on the shore, and shouted till they were hoarse. To this village the fairy bore the still sleeping Ursula, and gently placed her on the door-step of Mark's cottage; then she kissed her cheeks, and with one gust blew the door open, and disappeared before any one could come to see who it was.

The fisherman and his wife were sitting quietly within. She was making the children clothes, and he was mending his net, when without any noise the door opened and the cold night air blew in.

"Wife," said the fisherman, "just see who's at the door."

The wife got up and went to the door, and there lay Ursula, still sleeping soundly, in her little white nightdress.

The woman gave a little scream at sight of the child, and called to her husband.

"Husband, see, here's a little girl!" and so saying she lifted her in her arms, and carried her into the cottage. When she was brought into the warmth and light, Ursula awoke, and sitting up, stared about her in fright. She did not cry, as another child might have done, but she trembled very much, and was almost too frightened to speak.

Oddly enough, she had forgotten all about her strange flight through the air, and could remember nothing to tell the fisherman and his wife, but that she was the Princess Ursula; and, on hearing this, the good man and woman thought the poor little girl must be a trifle mad. However, when they examined her little nightdress, made of white fine linen and embroidery, with a crown worked in one corner, they agreed that she must belong to very grand people. They said it would be cruel to send the poor little thing away on such a cold night, and they must of course keep her till she was claimed. So the woman gave her some warm bread-and-milk, and put her to bed with their own little girl.

In the morning, when the court ladies came to wake Princess Ursula, they found her sleeping as usual in her little bed, and little did they think it was not she, but a toy Princess placed there in her stead. Indeed the ladies were much pleased; for when they said, "It is time for your Royal Highness to arise," she only answered, "Certainly," and let herself be dressed without another word. And as the time passed, and she was never naughty, and scarcely ever spoke, all said she was vastly improved, and she grew to be a great favourite.

The ladies all said that the young Princess bid fair to have the most elegant manners in the country, and the King smiled and noticed her with pleasure.

THE·TOY·PRINCESS

In the meantime, in the fisherman's cottage far away, the real Ursula grew tall and straight as an alder, and merry and light-hearted as a bird.

No one came to claim her, so the good fisherman and his wife kept her and brought her up among their own little ones. She played with them on the beach, and learned her lessons with them at school, and her old life had become like a dream she barely remembered.

But sometimes the mother would take out the little embroidered nightgown and show it to her, and wonder whence she came, and to whom she belonged.

"I don't care who I belong to," said Ursula; "they won't come and take me from you, and that's all I care about." So she grew tall and fair, and as she grew, the toy Princess, in her place at the court, grew too, and always was just like her, only that whereas Ursula's face was sunburnt and her cheeks red, the face of the toy Princess was pale, with only a very slight tint in her cheeks.

Years passed, and Ursula at the cottage was a tall young woman, and Ursula at the court was thought to be the most beautiful there, and every one admired her manners, though she never said anything but "If you please," "No, thank you," "Certainly," and "Just so."

The King was now an old man, and the fisherman Mark and his wife were grey-headed. Most of their fishing was now done by their eldest son Oliver, who was their great pride. Ursula waited on them, and cleaned the house, and did the needlework, and was so useful that they could not have done without her. The fairy Taboret had come to the cottage from time to time, unseen by anyone, to see Ursula, and always finding her healthy and merry, was pleased to think of how she had saved her from a dreadful life. But one evening when she paid them a visit, not having been there for some time, she saw something which made her pause and consider. Oliver and Ursula were standing together watching the waves, and Taboret stopped to hear what they said,—

"When we are married," said Oliver, softly, "we will live in that little cottage yonder, so that we can come and see them every day. But that will not be till little Bell is old enough to take your place, for how would my mother do without you?"

"And we had better not tell them," said Ursula, "that we mean to marry, or else the thought that they are preventing us will make them unhappy."

When Taboret heard this she became grave, and pondered for a long time. At last she flew back to the court to see how things were going on there. She found the King in the middle of a state council. On seeing this, she at once made herself visible, when the King begged her to be seated near him, as he was always glad of her help and advice.

"You find us," said his Majesty, "just about to resign our sceptre into younger and more vigorous hands; in fact, we think we are growing too old to reign, and mean to abdicate in favour of our dear daughter, who will reign in our stead."

"Before you do any such thing," said Taboret, "just let me have a little private conversation with you"; and she led the King into a corner, much to his surprise and alarm.

In about half an hour he returned to the council, looking very white, and with a dreadful expression on his face, whilst he held a handkerchief to his eyes.

"My lords," he faltered, "pray pardon our apparently extraordinary behaviour. We have just received a dreadful blow; we hear on authority, which we cannot doubt, that our dear, dear daughter"—here sobs choked his voice, and he was almost unable to proceed—"is—is—in fact, not our daughter at all, and only a *sham*." Here the King sank back in his chair, overpowered with grief, and the fairy Taboret, stepping to the front, told the courtiers the whole story; how she had stolen the real Princess, because she feared they were spoiling her, and how she had placed a toy Princess in her place. The courtiers looked from one to another in surprise, but it was evident they did not believe her.

"The Princess is a truly charming young lady," said the Prime Minister.

"Has your Majesty any reason to complain of her Royal Highness's conduct?" asked the old Chancellor.

"None whatever," sobbed the King; "she was ever an excellent daughter."

"Then I don't see," said the Chancellor, "what reason your Majesty can have for paying any attention to what this—this person says."

"If you don't believe me, you old idiots," cried Taboret, "call the Princess here, and I'll soon prove my words."

"By all means," cried they.

So the King commanded that her Royal Highness should be summoned.

In a few minutes she came, attended by her ladies. She said nothing, but then she never did speak till she was spoken to. So she entered, and stood in the middle of the room silently.

"We have desired that your presence be requested," the King was beginning, but Taboret without any ceremony advanced towards her, and struck her lightly on the head with her wand. In a moment the head rolled on the floor, leaving the body standing motionless as before, and showing that it was but an empty shell. "Just so," said the head, as it rolled towards the King, and he and the courtiers nearly swooned with fear.

When they were a little recovered, the King spoke again. "The fairy tells me," he said, "that there is somewhere a real Princess whom she wishes us to adopt as our daughter. And in the meantime let her Royal Highness be carefully placed in a cupboard, and a general mourning be proclaimed for this dire event."

So saying he glanced tenderly at the body and head, and turned weeping away.

So it was settled that Taboret was to fetch Princess Ursula, and the King and council were to be assembled to meet her.

That evening the fairy flew to Mark's cottage, and told them the truth about Ursula, and that they must part from her.

Loud were their lamentations, and great their grief, when they heard she must leave them. Poor Ursula herself sobbed bitterly.

"Never mind," she cried after a time, "if I am really a great Princess, I will have you all to live with me. I am sure the King, my father, will wish it, when he hears how good you have been to me."

On the appointed day, Taboret came for Ursula in a grand coach and four, and drove her away to the court. It was a long, long drive; and she stopped on the way and had the Princess dressed in a splendid white silk dress trimmed with gold, and put pearls round her neck and in her hair, that she might appear properly at court.

The King and all the council were assembled with great pomp, to greet their new Princess, and all looked grave and anxious. At last the door opened, and Taboret appeared, leading the young girl by the hand.

"That is your father!" said she to Ursula, pointing to the King; and on this, Ursula, needing no other bidding, ran at once to him, and putting her arms round his neck, gave him a sounding kiss.

His Majesty almost swooned, and all the courtiers shut their eyes and shivered.

"This is really!" said one.

"This is truly!" said another.

"What have I done?" cried Ursula, looking from one to another, and seeing that something was wrong, but not knowing what. "Have I kissed the *wrong person*?" On hearing which every one groaned.

"Come now," cried Taboret, "if you don't like her, I shall take her away to those who do. I'll give you a week, and then I'll come back and see how you're treating her. She's a great deal too good for any of you." So saying she flew away on her wand, leaving Ursula to get on with her new friends as best she might. But Ursula could not get on with them at all, as she soon began to see.

If she spoke or moved they looked shocked, and at last she was so frightened and troubled by them that she burst into tears, at which they were more shocked still.

"This is indeed a change after our sweet Princess," said one lady to another.

"Yes, indeed," was the answer, "when one remembers how even after her head was struck off she behaved so beautifully, and only said, 'Just so.'"

And all the ladies disliked poor Ursula, and soon showed her their dislike. Before the end of the week, when Taboret was to return, she had grown quite thin and pale, and seemed afraid of speaking above a whisper.

"Why, what is wrong?" cried Taboret, when she returned and saw how much poor Ursula had changed. "Don't you like being here? Aren't they kind to you?"

"Take me back, dear Taboret," cried Ursula, weeping. "Take me back to Oliver, and Philip, and Bell. As for these people, I *hate* them."

And she wept again.

Taboret only smiled and patted her head, and then went in to the King and courtiers.

"Now, how is it," she cried, "I find the Princess Ursula in tears? and I am sure you are making her unhappy. When you had that bit of wood-and-leather

Princess, you could behave well enough to it, but now that you have a real flesh-and-blood woman, you none of you care for her."

"Our late dear daughter——" began the King, when the fairy interrupted him.

"I do believe," she said, "that you would like to have the doll back again. Now I will give you your choice. Which will you have—my Princess Ursula, the real one, or your Princess Ursula, the sham?"

The King sank back into his chair. "I am not equal to this," he said: "summon the council, and let them settle it by vote." So the council were summoned, and the fairy explained to them why they were wanted.

"Let both Princesses be fetched," she said; and the toy Princess was brought in with great care from her cupboard, and her head stood on the table beside her, and the real Princess came in with her eyes still red from crying and her bosom heaving.

"I should think there could be no doubt which one would prefer," said the Prime Minister to the Chancellor.

"I should think not either," answered the Chancellor.

"Then vote," said Taboret; and they all voted, and every vote was for the sham Ursula, and not one for the real one. Taboret only laughed.

"You are a pack of sillies and idiots," she said, "but you shall have what you want"; and she picked up the head, and with a wave of her wand stuck it on to the body, and it moved round slowly and said, "Certainly," just in its old voice; and on hearing this, all the courtiers gave something as like a cheer as they thought polite, whilst the old King could not speak for joy.

"We will," he cried, "at once make our arrangements for abdicating and leaving the government in the hands of our dear daughter"; and on hearing this the courtiers all applauded again.

But Taboret laughed scornfully, and taking up the real Ursula in her arms, flew back with her to Mark's cottage.

In the evening the city was illuminated and there were great rejoicings at the recovery of the Princess, but Ursula remained in the cottage and married Oliver, and lived happily with him for the rest of her life.

12

GEORGE MACDONALD

The Day Boy and the Night Girl (1879)

EORGE MACDONALD (1824–1905) was raised in Aberdeenshire, Scotland, a farming region rich in folklore that was to influence his later writings. MacDonald studied at Aberdeen University between 1842 and 1845, and after receiving a master's degree he went to London, where he completed his studies at a theological seminary in 1851. After serving two years as minister at a small Congregationalist church outside London, he was dismissed because of his heretical views. MacDonald had always been drawn to German transcendentalism and mysticism—he admired Novalis and translated *Hymnen an die Nacht* in 1849—and he was convinced that all earthly creatures, including so-called heathens, could discover the essence of divinity in themselves by perceiving God's truth in nature. Thus, salvation could be attained by everyone, a notion which was not acceptable to the Congregational Church.

Nevertheless, MacDonald found another way to preach his views: he spent the remainder of his life giving public lectures and sermons and writing poems, novels, fairy tales, and religious essays. MacDonald was an indefatigable writer and brilliant orator, and through his books and lectures he was able to support a family of eleven children, often under adverse conditions. Indeed, he became one of the leading writers in the Victorian period, and among his fifty-one volumes were bestselling novels such as *David Elginbrod* (1863), *Alec Forbes of Howglen* (1865), *Robert Falconer* (1868), and *Malcolm* (1875). These works contained conventional plots in which Christian charity and philanthropy were emphasized. MacDonald was not an original thinker as writer of realistic novels. However, his fantasy works such as *Phantastes* (1858) and *Lilith* (1895) are marked by innovative compositional techniques and striking erotic features.

MacDonald's most significant narratives are undoubtedly his fairy tales, which were written for children and adults. He was one of the first British writers to experiment successfully with the traditional motifs and themes of well-known tales such as *Sleeping Beauty* and *Rapunzel*, by mocking them and developing new ideas of sexuality and love. He rebelled against the strict Victorian code of puritan upbringing by questioning traditional sex roles and creating young protagonists who share their dreams in pursuit of compassionate love and equal partnership. This is most evident in tales like "The Light Princess" (1863) and "Little Daylight" (1867) in which mutual recognition forms the basis for the love between the male and female protagonists. In other tales such as "The Golden Key" (1867) and "Cross Purposes" (1867) MacDonald sends his characters in search for their true selves beyond society, striking an Arcadian note. Social transgression and transcendence are necessary, according to MacDonald, because the societal conventions restrict self-development. This becomes evident in "The Day Boy and the Night Girl" (1879), in which the two protagonists must overcome the limits of their social conditioning to discover their identities. Self-discovery occurs through compassion and social interaction. In most of MacDonald's tales there is a composite hero, not a single one. That is, the triumph of the self is a union of the masculine and feminine, an erotic display of the utopian drive, that MacDonald allowed himself to express primarily in symbolic form.

THE DAY BOY AND THE
NIGHT GIRL

WATHO

HERE WAS ONCE A witch who desired to know everything. But the wiser a witch is, the harder she knocks her head against the wall when she comes to it. Her name was Watho, and she had a wolf in her mind. She cared for nothing in itself—only for knowing it. She was not naturally cruel, but the wolf had made her cruel.

She was tall and graceful, with a white skin, red hair, and black eyes, which had a red fire in them. She was straight and strong, but now and then would fall bent together, shudder, and sit for a moment with her head turned over her shoulder, as if the wolf had got out of her mind on to her back.

AURORA

This witch got two ladies to visit her. One of them belonged to the court, and her husband had been sent on a far and difficult embassy. The other was a young widow whose husband had lately died, and who had since lost her sight. Watho lodged them in different parts of her castle, and they did not know of each other's existence.

The castle stood on the side of a hill sloping gently down into a narrow valley, in which was a river, with a pebbly channel and a continual song. The garden went down to the bank of the river, enclosed by high walls, which crossed the river and there stopped. Each wall had a double row of battlements, and between the rows was a narrow walk.

In the topmost story of the castle the Lady Aurora occupied a spacious apartment of several large rooms looking southward. The windows projected oriel-wise over the garden below, and there was a splendid view from them both up and down and across the river. The opposite side of the valley was steep, but not very high. Far away snowpeaks were visible. These rooms Aurora seldom left, but their airy spaces, the brilliant landscape and sky, the plentiful sunlight, the musical instruments, books, pictures, curiosities, with the company of Watho, who made herself charming, precluded all dulness. She had venison and feathered game to eat, milk and pale sunny sparkling wine to drink.

She had hair of the yellow gold, waved and rippled; her skin was fair, not white like Watho's, and her eyes were of the blue of the heavens when bluest; her features were delicate but strong, her mouth large and finely curved, and haunted with smiles.

VESPER

Behind the castle the hill rose abruptly; the northeastern tower, indeed, was in contact with the rock and communicated with the interior of it. For in the rock was a series of chambers, known only to Watho and the one servant whom she trusted, called Falca. Some former owner had constructed these chambers after the tomb of an Egyptian king, and probably with the same design, for in the centre of one of them stood what could only be a sarcophagus, but that and others were walled off. The sides and roofs of them were carved in low relief, and curiously painted. Here the witch lodged the blind lady, whose name was Vesper. Her eyes were black, with long black lashes; her skin had a look of darkened silver, but was of purest tint and grain; her hair was black and fine and straight-flowing; her features were exquisitely formed, and if less beautiful yet more lovely from sadness; she always looked as if she wanted to lie down and not rise again. She did not know she was lodged in a tomb, though now and then she wondered she never touched a window. There were many couches, covered with richest silk, and soft as her own cheek, for her to lie upon; and the carpets were so thick, she might have cast herself down anywhere—as befitted a tomb. The place was dry and warm, and cunningly pierced for air, so that it was always fresh, and lacked only sunlight. There the witch fed her upon milk, and wine dark as a carbuncle, and pomegranates, and purple grapes, and birds that dwell in marshy places; and she played to her mournful tunes, and caused wailful violins to attend her, and told her sad tales, thus holding her ever in an atmosphere of sweet sorrow.

PHOTOGEN

Watho at length had her desire, for witches often get what they want: a splendid boy was born to the fair Aurora. Just as the sun rose, he opened his eyes. Watho carried him immediately to a distant part of the castle, and persuaded the mother that he never cried but once, dying the moment he was born. Overcome with grief, Aurora left the castle as soon as she was able, and Watho never invited her again.

And now the witch's care was, that the child should not know darkness. Persistently she trained him until at last he never slept during the day, and never woke during the night. She never let him see anything black, and even kept all dull colours out of his way. Never, if she could help it, would she let a shadow fall upon him, watching against shadows as if they had been live things that would hurt him. All day he basked in the full splendour of the sun, in the same large rooms his mother had occupied. Watho used him to the sun, until he could bear more of it than any dark-blooded African. In the hottest of every day, she stript him and laid him in it, that he might ripen like a peach; and the boy rejoiced in it, and would resist being dressed again. She brought all her knowledge to bear on making his muscles strong and elastic and swiftly responsive—that his soul, she said laughingly, might sit in every fibre, be all in every part, and awake the moment of call. His hair was of the red gold, but his eyes grew darker as he grew, until they were as black as Vesper's. He was the merriest of creatures, always laughing, always loving, for a moment raging, then laughing afresh. Watho called him Photogen.

NYCTERIS

Five or six months after the birth of Photogen, the dark lady also gave birth to a baby: in the windowless tomb of a blind mother, in the dead of night, under the feeble rays of a lamp in an alabaster globe, a girl came into the darkness with a wail. And just as she was born for the first time, Vesper was born for the second, and passed into a world as unknown to her as this was to her child—who would have to be born yet again before she could see her mother.

Watho called her Nycteris, and she grew as like Vesper as possible—in all but one particular. She had the same dark skin, dark eyelashes and brows, dark hair, and gentle sad look; but she had just the eyes of Aurora, the mother of Photogen, and if they grew darker as she grew older, it was only a darker blue. Watho, with the help of Falca, took the greatest possible care of her—in every way consistent with her plans, that is,—the main point in which was that she should never see any light but what came from the lamp. Hence her optic nerves, and indeed her whole apparatus for seeing, grew both larger and more sensitive; her eyes, indeed, stopped short only of being too large. Under her dark hair and forehead and eyebrows, they looked like two breaks in a cloudy night-sky, through which peeped the heaven where the stars and no clouds live. She was a sadly dainty little creature. No one in the world except those two was aware of the being of the little bat. Watho trained her to sleep during the day, and wake during the night. She taught her music, in which she was herself a proficient, and taught her scarcely anything else.

HOW PHOTOGEN GREW

The hollow in which the castle of Watho lay, was a cleft in a plain rather than a valley among hills, for at the top of its steep sides, both north and south, was a table-land, large and wide. It was covered with rich grass and flowers, with here and there a wood, the outlying colony of a great forest. These grassy plains were the finest hunting grounds in the world. Great herds of small, but fierce cattle, with humps and shaggy manes, roved about them, also antelopes and gnus, and the tiny roedeer, while the woods were swarming with wild creatures. The tables of the castle were mainly supplied from them. The chief of Watho's huntsmen was a fine fellow, and when Photogen began to outgrow the training she could give him, she handed him over to Fargu. He with a will set about teaching him all he knew. He got him pony after pony, larger and larger as he grew, every one less manageable than that which had preceded it, and advanced him from pony to horse, and from horse to horse, until he was equal to anything in that kind which the country produced. In similar fashion he trained him to the use of bow and arrow, substituting every three months a stronger bow and longer arrows; and soon he became, even on horseback, a wonderful archer. He was but fourteen when he killed his first bull, causing jubilation among the huntsmen, and indeed, through all the castle, for there too he was the favourite. Every day, almost as soon as the sun was up, he went out hunting, and would in general be out nearly the whole of the day. But Watho had laid upon Fargu just one commandment, namely, that Photogen should on no account, whatever the plea, be out until sundown, or so near it as to wake in him the desire of seeing what was going to happen; and this commandment Fargu was anxiously careful not to break; for although he would not have trembled had a whole herd of bulls come down upon him, charging at full speed across the level, and not an arrow left in his quiver, he was more than afraid of his mistress. When she looked at him in a certain way, he felt, he said, as if his heart turned to ashes in his breast, and what ran in his veins was no longer blood, but milk and water. So that, ere long, as Photogen grew older, Fargu began to tremble, for he found it steadily growing harder to restrain him. So full of life was he, as Fargu said to his mistress, much to her content, that he was more like a live thunderbolt than a human being. He did not know what fear was, and that not because he did not know danger; for he had had a severe laceration from the razor-like tusk of a boar—whose spine, however, he had severed with one blow of his hunting-knife, before Fargu could reach him with defence. When he would spur his horse into the midst of a herd of bulls, carrying only his bow and his short sword, or shoot an arrow into a herd, and go after it as if to reclaim it for a runaway shaft, arriving in time to follow it with a spear-thrust before the wounded animal knew which way to charge, Fargu thought with terror how it would be when he came to know the temptation of the huddle-spot leopards, and the knife-clawed lynxes, with which the forest was haunted. For the boy had been so steeped in the sun, from childhood so saturated with his influence, that he looked upon every danger from a sovereign height of courage. When, therefore, he was approaching his sixteenth year, Fargu ventured to beg Watho that she would lay her commands upon the youth himself, and release him from responsibility for him. One might as soon hold a tawny-maned lion as Photogen, he said. Watho called the youth, and in the presence of Fargu laid her command upon him never to be out when the rim of the sun should touch the horizon, accompanying the prohibition with hints of consequences, none the less awful than they were obscure. Photogen listened respectfully, but, knowing neither the taste of fear nor the temptation of the night, her words were but sounds to him.

HOW NYCTERIS GREW

The little education she intended Nycteris to have, Watho gave her by word of mouth. Not meaning she should have light enough to read by, to leave other reasons unmentioned, she never put a book in her hands. Nycteris, however, saw so much better than Watho imagined, that the light she gave her was quite sufficient, and she managed to coax Falca into teaching her the letters, after which she taught herself to read, and Falca now and then brought her a child's book. But her chief pleasure was in her instrument. Her very fingers loved it, and would wander about its keys like feeding sheep. She was not unhappy. She knew nothing of the world except the tomb in which she dwelt, and had some pleasure in everything she did. But she desired, nevertheless, something more or different. She did not know what it was, and the nearest she could come to expressing it to herself was—that she wanted more room. Watho and Falca would go from her beyond the shine of the lamp, and come again; therefore surely there must be more room somewhere. As often as she was left alone, she would fall to poring over the coloured bas-reliefs on the walls. These were intended to represent various of the powers of Nature under allegorical similitudes, and as nothing can be made that does not belong to the general scheme, she could not fail at least to imagine a flicker of relationship between some of them, and thus a shadow of the reality of things found its way to her.

There was one thing, however, which moved and taught her more than all the rest—the lamp, namely, that hung from the ceiling, which she always saw alight, though she never saw the flame, only the slight condensation towards the centre of the alabaster globe. And besides the operation of the light itself after its kind, the indefiniteness of the globe, and the softness of the light, giving her the feeling as if her eyes could go in and into its whiteness, were somehow also associated with the idea of space and room. She would sit for an hour together gazing up at the lamp, and her heart would swell as she gazed. She would wonder what had hurt her, when she found her face wet with tears, and then would wonder how she could have been hurt without knowing it. She never looked thus at the lamp except when she was alone.

THE LAMP

Watho having given orders, took it for granted they were obeyed, and that Falca was all night long with Nycteris, whose day it was. But Falca could not get into the habit of sleeping through the day, and would often leave her alone half the night. Then it seemed to Nycteris that the white lamp was watching over her. As it was never permitted to go out—while she was awake at least—Nycteris, except by shutting her eyes, knew less about darkness than she did about light. Also, the lamp being fixed high overhead, and in the centre of everything, she did not know much about shadows either. The few there were fell almost entirely on the floor, or kept like mice about the foot of the walls.

Once, when she was thus alone, there came the noise of a far-off rumbling: she had never before heard a sound of which she did not know the origin, and here therefore was a new sign of something beyond these chambers. Then came a trembling, then a shaking; the lamp dropped from the ceiling to the floor with a great crash, and she felt as if both her eyes were hard shut and both her hands over them. She concluded that it was the darkness that had made the rumbling and the shaking, and rushing into the room, had thrown down the lamp. She sat trembling. The noise and the shaking ceased, but the light did not return. The darkness had eaten it up!

Her lamp gone, the desire at once awoke to get out of her prison. She scarcely knew what *out* meant; out of one room into another, where there was not even a dividing door, only an open arch, was all she knew of the world. But suddenly she remembered that she had heard Falca speak of the lamp *going out*: this must be what she had meant? And if the lamp had gone out, where had it gone? Surely where Falca went, and like her it would come again. But she could not wait. The desire to go out grew irresistible. She must follow her beautiful lamp! She must find it! She must see what it was about!

Now there was a curtain covering a recess in the wall, where some of her toys and gymnastic things were kept; and from behind that curtain Watho and Falca always appeared, and behind it they vanished. How they came out of solid wall, she had not an idea, all up to the wall was open space, and all beyond it seemed wall; but clearly the first and only thing she could do, was to feel her way behind the curtain. It was so dark that a cat could not have caught the largest of mice. Nycteris could see better than any cat, but now her great eyes were not of the smallest use to her. As she went she trod upon a piece of the broken lamp. She had never worn shoes or stockings, and the fragment, though, being of soft alabaster, it did not cut, yet hurt her foot. She did not know what it was, but as it had not been there before the darkness came, she suspected that it had to do with the lamp. She kneeled therefore, and searched with her hands, and bringing two large pieces together, recognized the shape of the lamp. Therefore it flashed upon her that the lamp was dead, that this brokenness was the death of which she had read without understanding, that the darkness had killed the lamp. What then could Falca have meant when she spoke of the lamp *going out*? There was the lamp—dead indeed, and so changed that she would never have taken it for a lamp but for the shape! No, it was not the lamp any more now it was dead, for all that made it a lamp was gone, namely, the bright shining of it. Then it must be the shine, the light, that had gone out! That must be what Falca meant—and it must be somewhere in the other place in the wall. She started afresh after it, and groped her way to the curtain.

Now she had never in her life tried to get out, and did not know how; but instinctively she began to move her hands about over one of the walls behind the curtain, half expecting them to go into it, as she supposed Watho and Falca did. But the wall repelled her with inexorable hardness, and she turned to the one opposite. In so doing, she set her foot upon an ivory die, and as it met sharply the same spot the broken alabaster had already hurt, she fell forward with her outstretched hands against the wall. Something gave way, and she tumbled out of the cavern.

OUT

But alas! *out* was very much like *in*, for the same enemy, the darkness, was here also. The next moment, however, came a great gladness—a firefly, which had wandered in from the garden. She saw the tiny spark in the distance. With slow pulsing ebb and throb of light, it came pushing itself through the air, drawing nearer and nearer, with that motion which more resembles swimming than flying, and the light seemed the source of its own motion.

"My lamp! my lamp!" cried Nycteris. "It is the shiningness of my lamp, which the cruel darkness drove out. My good lamp has been waiting for me here all the time! It knew I would come after it, and waited to take me with it."

She followed the firefly, which, like herself, was seeking the way out. If it did not know the way, it was yet light; and, because all light is one, any light may serve to guide to more light. If she was mistaken in thinking it the spirit of her lamp, it was of the same spirit as her lamp—and had wings. The gold-green jet-boat, driven by light, went throbbing before her through a long narrow passage. Suddenly it rose higher, and the same moment Nycteris fell upon an ascending stair. She had never seen a stair before, and found going-up a curious sensation. Just as she reached what seemed the top, the firefly ceased to shine, and so disappeared. She was in utter darkness once more. But when we are following the light, even its extinction is a guide. If the firefly had gone on shining, Nycteris would have seen the stair turn, and would have gone up to Watho's bedroom; whereas now, feeling straight before her, she came to a latched door, which after a good deal of trying she managed to open—and stood in a maze of wondering perplexity, awe, and delight. What was it? Was it outside of her, or something taking place in her head? Before her was a very long and very narrow passage, broken up she could not tell how, and spreading out above and on all sides to an infinite height and breadth and distance—as if space itself were growing out of a trough. It was brighter than her rooms had ever been—brighter than if six alabaster lamps had been burning in them. There was a quantity of strange streaking and mottling about it, very different from the shapes on her walls. She was in a dream of pleasant perplexity, of delightful bewilderment. She could not tell whether she was upon her feet or drifting about like the firefly, driven by the pulses of an inward bliss. But she knew little as yet of her inheritance. Unconsciously, she took one step forward from the threshold, and the girl who had been from her very birth a troglodyte, stood in the ravishing glory of a southern night, lit by a perfect moon—not the moon of our northern clime, but the moon like silver glowing in a furnace—a moon one could see to be a globe—not far off, a mere flat disc on the face of the blue, but hanging down halfway, and looking as if one could see all round it by a mere bending of the neck.

"It is my lamp," she said, and stood dumb with parted lips. She looked and felt as if she had been standing there in silent ecstasy from the beginning.

"No, it is not my lamp," she said after a while; "it is the mother of all the lamps."

And with that she fell on her knees, and spread out her hands to the moon. She could not in the least have told what was in her mind, but the action was in reality just a begging of the moon to be what she was—that precise incredible splendour hung in the far-off roof, that very glory essential to the being of poor girls born and bred in caverns. It was a resurrection—nay, a birth itself, to Nycteris. What the vast blue sky, studded with tiny sparks like the heads of diamond nails could be; what the moon, looking so absolutely content with light—why, she knew less about them than you and I! but the greatest of atronomers might envy the rapture of such a first impression at the age of sixteen. Immeasurably imperfect it was, but false the impression could not be, for she saw with the eyes made for seeing, and saw indeed what many men are too wise to see.

As she knelt, something softly flapped her, embraced her, stroked her, fondled her. She rose to her feet, but saw nothing, did not know what it was. It was likest a woman's breath. For she knew nothing of the air even, had never breathed the still newborn freshness of the world. Her breath had come to her only through long passages and spirals in the rock. Still less did she know of the air alive with motion—of that thrice blessed thing, the wind of a summer night. It was like a spiritual wine, filling her whole being with an intoxication of purest joy. To breathe was a perfect existence. It seemed to her the light itself she drew into her lungs. Possessed by the power of the gorgeous night, she seemed at one and the same moment annihilated and glorified.

She was in the open passage or gallery that ran round the top of the garden walls, between the cleft battlements, but she did not once look down to see what lay beneath. Her soul was drawn to the vault above her with its lamp and its endless room. At last she burst into tears, and her heart was relieved, as the night itself is relieved by its lightning and rain.

And now she grew thoughtful. She must hoard this splendour! What a little ignorance her gaolers had made of her! Life was a mighty bliss, and they had scraped hers to the bare bone! They must not know that she knew. She must hide her knowledge—hide it even from her own eyes, keeping it close in her bosom, content to know that she had it, even when she could not brood on its presence, feasting her eyes with its glory. She turned from the vision, therefore, with a sigh of utter bliss, and with soft quiet steps and groping hands, stole back into the darkness of the rock. What was darkness or the laziness of Time's feet to one who had seen what she had that night seen? She was lifted above all weariness—above all wrong.

When Falca entered, she uttered a cry of terror. But Nycteris called to her not to be afraid, and told her how there had come a rumbling and a shaking, and the lamp had fallen. Then Falca went and told her mistress, and within an hour a new globe hung in the place of the old one. Nycteris thought it did not look so bright and clear as the former, but she made no lamentation over the change; she was far too rich to heed it. For now, prisoner as she knew herself, her heart was full of glory and gladness; at times she had to hold herself from jumping up, and going dancing and singing about the room. When she slept, instead of dull dreams, she had splendid visions. There were times, it is true, when she became restless, and impatient to look upon her riches, but when she would reason with herself, saying "What does it matter if I sit here for ages with my poor pale lamp, when out there a lamp is burning at which ten thousand little lamps are glowing with wonder?"

She never doubted she had looked upon the day and the sun, of which she had read; and always when she read of the day and the sun, she had the night and the moon in her mind; and when she read of the night and the moon, she thought only of the cave and the lamp that hung there.

THE GREAT LAMP

It was some time before she had a second opportunity of going out, for Falca since the fall of the lamp had been a little more careful, and seldom left her for long. But one night, having a little headache, Nycteris lay down upon her bed, and was lying with her eyes closed, when she heard Falca come to her, and felt she was bending over her. Disinclined to talk, she did not open her eyes, and lay quite still. Satisfied that she was asleep, Falca left her, moving so softly that her very caution made Nycteris open her eyes and look after her—just in time to see her vanish—through a picture, as it seemed, that hung on the wall a long way from the usual place of issue. She jumped up, her headache forgotten, and ran in the opposite direction; got out, groped her way to the stair, climbed, and reached the top of the wall.—Alas! the great room was not so light as the little one she had left! Why?—Sorrow of sorrows! the great lamp was gone! Had its globe fallen and its lovely light gone out upon great wings, a resplendent firefly, oaring itself through a yet grander and lovelier room? She looked down to see if it lay anywhere broken to pieces on the carpet below; but she could not even see the carpet. But surely nothing very dreadful could have happened—no rumbling or shaking; for there were all the little lamps shining brighter than before, not one of them looking as if any unusual matter had befallen. What if each of those little lamps was growing into a big lamp, and after being a big lamp for a while, had to go out and grow a bigger lamp still—out there, beyond this *out*?—Ah! here was the living thing that could not be seen, come to her again— bigger tonight with such loving kisses, and such liquid strokings of her cheeks and forehead, gently tossing her hair, and delicately toying with it! But it ceased, and all was still. Had it gone out? What would happen next? Perhaps the little lamps had not to grow great lamps, but to fall one by one and go out first?—With that, came from below a sweet scent, then another, and another. Ah, how delicious! Perhaps they were all coming to her only on their way out after the great lamp!—Then came the music of the river, which she had been too absorbed in the sky to note for the first time. What was it? Alas! alas! another sweet living thing on its way out. They were all marching slowly out in long lovely file, one after the other, each taking its leave of her as it passed! It must be so; here were more and more sweet sounds, following and fading! The whole of the *Out* was going out again; it was all going after the great lovely lamp! She would be left the only creature in the solitary day! Was there nobody to hang up a new lamp for the old one, and keep the creatures from going!—She crept back to her rock very sad. She tried to comfort herself by saying that anyhow there would be room out there; but as she said it she shuddered at the thought of *empty* room.

When next she succeeded in getting out, a half-moon hung in the east: a new lamp had come, she thought, and all would be well.

It would be endless to describe the phases of feeling through which Nycteris passed, more numerous and delicate than those of a thousand changing moons. A fresh bliss bloomed in her soul with every varying aspect of infinite nature. Ere long she began to suspect that the new moon was the old moon, gone out and come in again like herself; also that, unlike herself, it wasted and grew again; that it was indeed a live thing, subject like herself to caverns, and keepers and solitudes, escaping and shining when it could. Was it a prison like hers it was shut in and did it grow dark when the lamp left it? Where could be the way into it?—With that first she began to look below, as well as above and around her; and then first noted the tops of the trees between her and the floor. There were palms with their red-fingered hands full of fruit; eucalyptus trees crowded with little boxes of powder-puffs; oleanders with their half-caste roses; and orange trees with their clouds of young silver stars, and their aged balls of gold. Her eyes could see colours invisible to ours in the moonlight, and all these she could distinguish well, though at first she took them for the shapes and colours of the carpet of the great room. She longed to get down among them, now she saw they were real creatures, but she did not know how. She went along the whole length of the wall to the end that crossed the river, but found no way of going down. Above the river she stopped to gaze with awe upon the rushing water. She knew nothing of water but from what she drank and what she bathed in; and, as the moon shone on the dark, swift stream, singing lustily as it flowed, she did not doubt the river was alive, a swift rushing serpent of life, going— out?—whither? And then she wondered if what was brought into her rooms had been killed that she might drink it, and have her bath in it.

Once when she stepped out upon the wall, it was into the midst of a fierce wind. The trees were all roaring. Great clouds were rushing along the skies, and tumbling over the little lamps: the great lamp had not come yet. All was in tumult. The wind seized her garments and hair, and shook them as if it would tear them from her. What could she have done to make the gentle creature so angry? Or was this another creature altogether—of the same kind, but hugely bigger, and of a very different temper and behaviour? But the whole place was angry? Or was it that the creatures dwelling in it, the wind, and the trees, and the clouds, and the river, had all quarrelled, each with all the rest? Would the whole come to confusion and disorder? But, as she gazed wondering and disquieted, the moon, larger than ever she had seen her, came lifting herself above the horizon to look, broad and red, as if she, too, were swollen with anger that she had been roused from her rest by their noise, and compelled to hurry up to see what her children were about, thus rioting in her absence, lest they should rack the whole frame of things. And as she rose, the loud wind grew quieter and scolded less fiercely, the trees grew stiller and moaned with a lower complaint, and the clouds hunted and hurled themselves less wildly across the sky. And as if she were pleased that her children obeyed her very presence, the moon grew smaller as she ascended the heavenly stair; her puffed cheeks sank, her complexion grew clearer, and a sweet smile spread over her countenance, as peacefully she rose and rose. But there was treason and rebellion in her court; for, ere she reached the top of her great stairs, the clouds had assembled, forgetting their late wars, and very still they were as they laid their heads together and conspired. Then combining, and lying silently in wait until she came near, they threw themselves upon her, and swallowed her up. Down from the roof came spots of wet, faster and faster, and they wetted the cheeks of Nycteris; and what could they be but the tears of the moon, crying because her children were smothering her? Nycteris wept too, and not knowing what to think, stole back in dismay to her room.

The next time, she came out in fear and trembling. There was the moon still! away in the west—poor, indeed, and old, and looking dreadfully worn, as if all the wild beasts in the sky had been gnawing at her—but there she was, alive still, and able to shine!

THE SUNSET

Knowing nothing of darkness, or stars, or moon, Photogen spent his days in hunting. On a great white horse he swept over the grassy plains, glorying in the sun, fighting the wind, and killing the buffaloes.

One morning, when he happened to be on the ground a little earlier than usual, and before his attendants, he caught sight of an animal unknown to him, stealing from a hollow into which the sunrays had not yet reached. Like a swift shadow it sped over the grass, slinking south-ward to the forest. He gave chase, noted the body of a buffalo it had half eaten, and pursued it the harder. But with great leaps and bounds the creature shot farther and farther ahead of him, and vanished. Turning therefore defeated, he met Fargu, who had been following him as fast as his horse could carry him.

"What animal was that, Fargu?" he asked. "How he did run!"

Fargu answered he might be a leopard, but he rather thought from his pace and look that he was a young lion.

"What a coward he must be!" said Photogen.

"Don't be too sure of that," rejoined Fargu. "He is one of the creatures the sun makes uncomfortable. As soon as the sun is down, he will be brave enough."

He had scarcely said it, when he repented; nor did he regret it the less when he found that Photogen made no reply. But alas! said was said.

"Then," said Photogen to himself, "that contemptible beast is one of the terrors of sundown, of which Madame Watho spoke!"

He hunted all day, but not with his usual spirit. He did not ride so hard, and did not kill one buffalo. Fargu to his dismay observed also that he took every pretext for moving farther south, nearer to the forest. But all at once, the sun now sinking in the west, he seemed to change his mind, for he turned his horse's head, and rode home so fast that the rest could not keep him in sight. When they arrived, they found his horse in the stable, and concluded that he had gone into the castle. But he had in truth set out again by the back of it. Crossing the river a good way up the valley, he reascended to the ground they had left, and just before sunset reached the skirts of the forest.

The level orb shone straight in between the bare stems, and saying to himself he could not fail to find the beast, he rushed into the wood. But even as he entered, he turned, and looked to the west. The rim of the red was touching the horizon, all jagged with broken hills. "Now," said Photogen, "we shall see"; but he said it in the face of a darkness he had not proved. The moment the sun began to sink among the spikes and saw-edges, with a kind of sudden flap at his heart a fear inexplicable laid hold of the youth; and as he had never felt anything of the kind before, the very fear itself terrified him. As the sun sank, it rose like the shadow of the world, and grew deeper and darker. He could not even think what it might be, so utterly did it enfeeble him. When the last flaming scimitar-edge of the sun went out like a lamp, his horror seemed to blossom into very madness. Like the closing lids of an eye—for there was no twilight, and this night no moon—the terror and the darkness rushed together, and he knew them for one. He was no longer the man he had known, or rather thought himself. The courage he had had was in no sense his own— he had only had courage, not been courageous; it had left him, and he could scarcely stand—certainly not stand straight, for not one of his joints could he make stiff or keep from trembling. He was but a spark of the sun, in himself nothing.

The beast was behind him—stealing upon him! He turned. All was dark in the wood, but to his fancy the darkness here and there broke into pairs of green eyes, and he had not the power even to raise his bow-hand from his side. In the strength of despair he strove to rouse courage enough—not to fight—that he did not even desire—but to run. Courage to flee home was all he could ever imagine, and it would not come. But what he had not, was ignominiously given him. A cry in the wood, half a screech, half a growl, sent him running like a boar-wounded cur. It was not even himself that ran, it was the fear that had come alive in his legs; he did not know that they moved. But as he ran he grew able to run—gained courage at least to be a coward. The stars gave a little light. Over the grass he sped, and nothing followed him. "How fallen, how changed," from the youth who had climbed the hill as the sun went down! A mere contempt to himself, the self that contemned was a coward with the self it contemned! There lay the shapeless black of a buffalo, humped upon the grass: He made a wide circuit, and swept on like a shadow driven in the wind. For the wind had arisen, and added to his terror: it blew from behind him. He reached the brow of the valley, and shot down the steep descent like a falling star. Instantly the whole upper country behind him arose and pursued him! The wind came howling after him, filled with screams, shrieks, yells, roars, laughter, and chattering, as if all the animals of the forest were careering with it. In his ears was a trampling rush, the thunder of the hoofs of the cattle, in career from every quarter of the wide plains to the brow of the hill above him. He fled straight for the castle, scarcely with breath enough to pant.

As he reached the bottom of the valley, the moon peered up over its edge. He had never seen the moon before—except in the daytime, when he had taken her for a thin bright cloud. She was a fresh terror to him—so ghostly! so ghastly! so gruesome!—so knowing as she looked over the top of her garden wall upon the world outside! That was the night itself! the darkness alive—and after him! the horror of horrors coming down the sky to curdle his blood, and turn his brain to a cinder! He gave a sob, and made straight for the river, where it ran between the two walls, at the bottom of the garden. He plunged in, struggled through, clambered up the bank, and fell senseless on the grass.

THE GARDEN

Although Nycteris took care not to stay out long at a time, and used every precaution, she could hardly have escaped discovery so long, had it not been that the strange attacks to which Watho was subject had been more frequent of late, and had at last settled into an illness which kept her to her bed. But whether from an access of caution or from suspicion, Falca, having now to be much with her mistress both day and night, took it at length into her head to fasten the door as often as she went by her usual place of exit, so that one night, when Nycteris pushed, she found, to her surprise and dismay, that the wall pushed her again, and would not let her through; nor with all her searching could she discover wherein lay the cause of the change. Then first she felt the pressure of her prison-walls, and turning, half in despair, groped her way to the picture where she had once seen Falca disappear. There she soon found the spot by pressing upon which the wall yielded. It let her through into a sort of cellar, where was a glimmer of light from a sky whose blue was paled by the moon. From the cellar she got into a long passage, into which the moon was shining, and came to a door. She managed to open it, and, to her great joy found herself in *the other place*, not on the top of the wall, however, but in the garden she had longed to enter. Noiseless as a fluffy moth she flitted away into the covert of the trees and shrubs, her bare feet welcomed by the softest of carpets, which, by the very touch, her feet knew to be alive, whence it came that it was so sweet and friendly to them. A soft little wind was out among the trees, running now here, now there, like a child that had got its will. She went dancing over the grass, looking behind her at her shadow as she went. At first she had taken it for a little black creature that made game of her, but when she perceived that it was only where she kept the moon away, and that every tree, however great and grand a creature, had also one of these strange attendants, she soon learned not to mind it, and by and by it became the source of as much amusement to her, as to any kitten its tail. It was long before she was quite at home with the trees, however. At one time they seemed to disapprove of her; at another not even to know she was there, and to be altogether taken up with their own business. Suddenly, as she went from one to another of them, looking up with awe at the murmuring mystery of their branches and leaves, she spied one a little way off, which was very different from all the rest. It was white, and dark, and sparkling, and spread like a palm—a small slender palm, without much head; and it grew very fast, and sang as it grew. But it never grew any bigger, for just as fast as she could see it growing, it kept falling to pieces. When she got close to it, she discovered that it was a water-tree—made of just such water as she washed with—only it was alive of course, like the river—a different sort of water from that, doubtless, seeing the one crept swiftly along the floor, and the other shot straight up, and fell, and swallowed itself, and rose again. She put her feet into the marble basin, which was the flower-pot in which it grew. It was full of real water, living and cool—so nice, for the night was hot!

But the flowers! ah, the flowers! she was friends with them from the very first. What wonderful creatures they were!—and so kind and beautiful—always sending out such colours and such scents—red scent, and white scent, and yellow scent—for the other creatures! The one that was invisible and everywhere, took such a quantity of their scents, and carried it away! yet they did not seem to mind. It was their talk, to show they were alive, and not painted like those on the walls of her rooms, and on the carpets.

She wandered along down the garden, until she reached the river. Unable then to get any further—for she was a little afraid, and justly, of the swift watery serpent—she dropped on the grassy bank, dipped her feet in the water, and felt it running and pushing against them. For a long time she sat thus, and her bliss seemed complete, as she gazed at the river, and watched the broken picture of the great lamp overhead, moving up one side of the roof, to go down the other.

SOMETHING QUITE NEW

A beautiful moth brushed across the great blue eyes of Nycteris. She sprang to her feet to follow it—not in the spirit of the hunter, but of the lover. Her heart—like every heart, if only its fallen sides were cleared away—was an inexhaustible fountain of love: she loved everything she saw. But as she followed the moth, she caught sight of something lying on the bank of the river, and not yet having learned to be afraid of anything, ran straight to see what it was. Reaching it, she stood amazed. Another girl like herself! But what a strange-looking girl!—so curiously dressed too!—and not able to move! Was she dead? Filled suddenly with pity, she sat down, lifted Photogen's head, laid it on her lap and began stroking his face. Her warm hands brought him to himself. He opened his black eyes, out of which had gone all the fire, and looked up with a strange sound of fear, half moan, half gasp. But when he saw her face, he drew a deep breath, and lay motionless—gazing at her: those blue marvels above him, like a better sky, seemed to side with courage and assuage his terror, At length, in a trembling, awed voice, and a half whisper, he said, "Who are you?"

"I am Nycteris," she answered.

"You are a creature of the darkness, and love the night," he said, his fear beginning to move again.

"I may be a creature of the darkness," she replied. "I hardly know what you mean. But I do not love the night. I love the day—with all my heart; and I sleep all the night long."

"How can that be?" said Photogen, rising on his elbow, but dropping his head on her lap again the moment he saw the moon; "—how can it be," he repeated, "when I see your eyes there—wide awake?"

She only smiled and stroked him, for she did not understand him, and thought he did not know what he was saying.

"Was it a dream then?" resumed Photogen, rubbing his eyes. But with that his memory came clear, and he shuddered, and cried, "Oh, horrible! horrible! to be turned all at once into a coward! a shameful, contemptible, disgraceful coward! I am ashamed—ashamed—and *so* frightened! It is all so frightful!"

"What is so frightful?" asked Nycteris, with a smile like that of a mother to her child waked from a bad dream.

"All, all," he answered; "all this darkness and the roaring."

"My dear," said Nycteris, "there is no roaring. How sensitive you must be! What you hear is only the walking of the water, and the running about of the sweetest of all the creatures. She is invisible, and I call her Everywhere, for she goes through all the other creatures, and comforts them. Now she is amusing herself, and them too, with shaking them and kissing them, and blowing in their faces. Listen: do you call that roaring? You should hear her when she is rather angry though! I don't know why, but she is sometimes, and then she does roar a little."

"It is so horribly dark!" said Photogen, who, listening while she spoke, had satisfied himself that there was no roaring.

"Dark!" she echoed. "You should be in my room when an earthquake has killed my lamp. I do not understand. How *can* you call this dark? Let me see: yes, you have eyes, and big ones, bigger than Madame Watho's or Falca's—not so big as mine, I fancy—only I never saw mine. But then—oh, yes!—I know now what is the matter! You can't see with them, because they are so black. Darkness can't see, of course. Never mind: I will be your eyes, and teach you to see. Look here—at these lovely white things in the grass, with red sharp points all folded together into one. Oh, I love them so! I could sit looking at them all day, the darlings!"

Photogen looked close at the flowers, and thought he had seen something like them before, but could not make them out. As Nycteris had never seen an open daisy, so had he never seen a closed one.

Thus instinctively Nycteris tried to turn him away from his fear: and the beautiful creature's strange lovely talk helped not a little to make him forget it.

"You call it dark!" she said again, as if she could not get rid of the absurdity of the idea; "why, I could count every blade of the green hair—I suppose it is what the books call grass—within two yards of me! And just look at the great lamp! It is brighter than usual to-day, and I can't think why you should be frightened, or call it dark!"

As she spoke, she went on stroking his cheeks and hair, and trying to comfort him. But oh how miserable he was! and how plainly he looked it! He was on the point of saying that her great lamp was dreadful to him, looking like a witch, walking in the sleep of death; but he was not so ignorant as Nycteris, and knew even in the moonlight that she was a woman, though he had never seen one so young or so lovely before; and while she comforted his fear, her presence made him the more ashamed of it. Besides, not knowing her nature, he might annoy her, and make her leave him to his misery. He lay still therefore, hardly daring to move: all the little life he had seemed to come from her, and if he were to move, she might move: and if she were to leave him, he must weep like a child.

"How did you come here?" asked Nycteris, taking his face between her hands.

"Down the hill," he answered.

"Where do you sleep?" she asked.

He signed in the direction of the house. She gave a little laugh of delight.

"When you have learned not to be frightened, you will always be wanting to come out with me," she said.

She thought with herself she would ask her presently, when she had come to herself a little, how she had made her escape, for she must, of course, like herself, have got out of a cave, in which Watho and Falca had been keeping her.

"Look at the lovely colours," she went on, pointing to a rose-bush, on which

Photogen could not see a single flower. "They are far more beautiful—are they not?—than any of the colours upon your walls. And then they are alive, and smell so sweet!"

He wished she would not make him keep opening his eyes to look at things he could not see; and every other moment would start and grasp tight hold of her, as some fresh pang of terror shot into him.

"Come, come, dear!" said Nycteris, "you must not go on this way. You must be a brave girl, and—"

"A girl!" shouted Photogen, and started to his feet in wrath. "If you were a man, I should kill you."

"A man?" repeated Nycteris, "what is that? How could I be that? We are both girls—are we not?"

"No, I am not a girl," he answered; "—although," he added, changing his tone, and casting himself on the ground at her feet, "I have given you too good reason to call me one."

"Oh, I see!" returned Nycteris. "No, of course!—you can't be a girl: girls are not afraid—without reason. I understand now: it is because you are not a girl that you are so frightened."

Photogen twisted and writhed upon the grass.

"No, it is not," he said sulkily; "it is this horrible darkness that creeps into me, goes all through me, into the very marrow of my bones—that is what makes me behave like a girl. If only the sun would rise!"

"The sun! what is it?" cried Nycteris, now in her turn conceiving a vague fear.

Then Photogen broke into a rhapsody, in which he vainly sought to forget his.

"It is the soul, the life, the heart, the glory of the universe," he said. "The worlds dance like motes in his beams. The heart of man is strong and brave in his light, and when it departs his courage grows from him—goes with the sun, and he becomes such as you see me now."

"Then that is not the sun?" said Nycteris, thoughtfully, pointing up to the moon.

"That!" cried Photogen, with utter scorn; "I know nothing about *that*, except that it is ugly and horrible. At best it can be only the ghost of a dead sun. Yes, that is it! That is what makes it look so frightful."

"No," said Nycteris, after a long, thoughtful pause; you must be wrong there. I think the sun is the ghost of a dead moon, and that is how he is so much more splendid as you say.—Is there, then, another big room, where the sun lives in the roof?"

"I do not know what you mean," replied Photogen. "But you mean to be kind, I know, though you should not call a poor fellow in the dark a girl. If you will let me lie here, with my head in your lap, I should like to sleep. Will you watch me, and take care of me?"

"Yes, that I will," answered Nycteris, forgetting all her own danger.

So Photogen fell asleep.

THE SUN

There Nycteris sat, and there the youth lay all night long, in the heart of the great cone-shadow of the earth, like two Pharaohs in one Pyramid. Photogen slept, and slept; and Nycteris sat motionless lest she should wake him, and so betray him to his fear.

The moon rode high in the blue eternity; it was a very triumph of glorious night; the river ran babble-murmuring in deep soft syllables; the fountain kept rushing moon-ward, and blossoming momently to a great silvery flower, whose petals were for ever falling like snow, but with a continuous musical clash, into the bed of its exhaustion beneath; the wind woke, took a run among the trees, went to sleep, and woke again; the daisies slept on their feet at hers, but she did not know they slept; the roses might well seem awake, for their scent filled the air, but in truth they slept also, and the odour was that of their dreams; the oranges hung like gold lamps in the trees, and their silvery flowers were the souls of their yet unembodied children; the scent of the acacia blooms filled the air like the very odour of the moon herself.

At last, unused to the living air, and weary with sitting so still and so long, Nycteris grew drowsy. The air began to grow cool. It was getting near the time when she too was accustomed to sleep. She closed her eyes just a moment, and nodded—opened them suddenly wide, for she had promised to watch.

In that moment a change had come. The moon had got round, and was fronting her from the west, and she saw that her face was altered, that she had grown pale, as if she too were wan with fear, and from her lofty place espied a coming terror. The light seemed to be dissolving out of her; she was dying—she was going out! And yet everything around looked strangely clear—clearer than ever she had seen anything before; how could the lamp be shedding more light when she herself had less? Ah, that was just it! See how faint she looked! It was because the light was forsaking her, and spreading itself over the room, that she grew so thin and pale! She was giving up everything! She was melting away from the roof like a bit of sugar in water.

Nycteris was fast growing afraid, and sought refuge with the face upon her lap. How beautiful the creature was!—what to call it she could not think, for it had been angry when she called it what Watho called her. And, wonder upon wonders! now, even in the cold change that was passing upon the great room, the colour as of a red rose was rising in the wan cheek. What beautiful yellow hair it was that spread over her lap! What great huge breaths the creature took!

And what were those curious things it carried? She had seen them on her walls, she was sure.

Thus she talked to herself while the lamp grew paler and paler, and everything kept growing yet clearer. What could it mean? The lamp was dying—going out into the other place of which the creature in her lap had spoken, to be a sun! But why were the things growing clearer before it was yet a sun? That was the point. Was it her growing into a sun that did it? Yes! yes! it was coming death! She knew it, for it was coming upon her also! She felt it coming! What was she about to grow into? Something beautiful, like the creature in her lap? It might be! Anyhow, it must be death; for all her strength was going out of her, while all around her was growing so light she could not bear it? She must be blind soon! Would she be blind or dead first?

For the sun was rushing up behind her. Photogen woke, lifted his head from her lap, and sprang to his feet. His face was one radiant smile. His heart was full of daring—that of the hunter who will creep into the tiger's den. Nycteris gave a cry, covered her face with her hands, and pressed her eyelids close. Then blindly she stretched out her arms to Photogen, crying, "Oh, I am *so* frightened! What is this? It must be death! I don't wish to die yet. I love this room and the old lamp. I do not want the other place. This is terrible. I want to hide. I want to get into the sweet, soft, dark hands of all the other creatures. Ah me! ah me!"

"What is the matter with you, girl?" said Photogen, with the arrogance of all male creatures until they have been taught by the other kind. He stood looking down upon her over his bow, of which he was examining the string. "There is no fear of anything now, child! It is day. The sun is all but up. Look! he will be above the brow of yon hill in one moment more! Good-bye. Thank you for my night's lodging. I'm off. Don't be a goose. If ever I can do anything for you—and all that, you know!"

"Don't leave me; oh, don't leave me!" cried Nycteris. "I am dying! I am dying! I can't move. The light sucks all the strength out of me. And oh, I am *so* frightened!"

But already Photogen had splashed through the river, holding high his bow that it might not get wet. He rushed across the level, and strained up the opposing hill. Hearing no answer, Nycteris removed her hands. Photogen had reached the top, and the same moment the sunrays alighted upon him; the glory of the king of day crowded blazing upon the golden-haired youth. Radiant as Apollo, he stood in mighty strength, a flashing shape in the midst of flame. He fitted a glowing arrow to a gleaming bow. The arrow parted with a keen musical twang of the bowstring, and Photogen darting after it, vanished with a shout. Up shot Apollo himself, and from his quiver scattered astonishment and exultation. But the brain of poor Nycteris was pierced through and through. She fell down in utter darkness. All around her was a flaming furnace. In despair and feebleness and agony, she crept back, feeling her way with doubt and difficulty and enforced persistence to her cell. When at last the friendly darkness of her chamber folded her about with its cooling and consoling arms, she threw herself on her bed and fell fast asleep. And there she slept on, one alive in a tomb, while Photogen, above in the sun-glory, pursued the buffaloes on the lofty plain, thinking not once of her where she lay dark and forsaken, whose presence had been his refuge, her eyes and her hands his guardians through the night. He was in his glory and his pride; and the darkness and its disgrace had vanished for a time.

THE COWARD HERO

But no sooner had the sun reached the noonstead, than Photogen began to remember the past night in the shadow of that which was at hand, and to remember it with shame. He had proved himself—and not to himself only, but to a girl as well—a coward!—one bold in the daylight, while there was nothing to fear, but trembling like any slave when the night arrived. There was, there must be, something unfair in it! A spell had been cast upon him! He had eaten, he had drunk something that did not agree with courage! In any case he had been taken unprepared! How was he to know what the going down of the sun would be like? It was no wonder, he should have been surprised into terror, seeing it was what it was—in its very nature so terrible! Also, one could not see where danger might be coming from! You might be torn in pieces, carried off, or swallowed up, without even seeing where to strike a blow! Every possible excuse he caught at, eager as a self-lover to lighten his self-contempt. That day he astonished the huntsmen—terrified them with his reckless daring—all to prove to himself he was no coward. But nothing eased his shame. One thing only had hope in it—the resolve to encounter the dark in solemn earnest, now that he knew something of what it was. It was nobler to meet a recognized danger than to rush contemptuously into what seemed nothing—nobler still to encounter a nameless horror. He could conquer fear and wipe out disgrace together. For a marksman and swordsman like him, he said, one with his strength and courage, there was but danger. Defeat there was not. He knew the darkness now, and when it came he would meet it as fearless and cool as now he felt himself. And again he said, "We shall see!"

He stood under the boughs of a great beech as the sun was going down, far away over the jagged hills: before it was half down, he was trembling like one of the leaves behind him in the first sigh of the night-wind. The moment the last of the glowing disc vanished, he bounded away in terror to gain the valley, and his fear grew as he ran. Down the side of the hill, an abject creature, he went bounding and rolling and running; fell rather than plunged into the river, and came to himself, as before, lying on the grassy bank in the garden.

But when he opened his eyes, there were no girl-eyes looking down into his; there were only the stars in the waste of the sunless Night—the awful all-enemy he had again dared, but could not encounter. Perhaps the girl was not yet come out of the water! He would try to sleep, for he dared not move, and perhaps when he woke he would find his head on her lap, and the beautiful dark face, with its deep blue eyes, bending over him. But when he woke he found his head on the grass, and although he sprang up with all his courage, such as it was, restored, he did not set out for the chase with such an *élan* as the day before; and, despite the sun-glory in his heart and veins, his hunting was this day less eager; he ate little, and from the first was thoughtful even to sadness. A second time he was defeated and disgraced! Was his courage nothing more than the play of the sunlight on his brain? Was he a mere ball tossed between the light and the dark? Then what a poor contemptible creature he was! But a third chance lay before him. If he failed the third time, he dared not foreshadow what he must then think of himself! It was bad enough now—but then!

Alas! it went no better. The moment the sun was down, he fled as if from a legion of devils.

Seven times in all, he tried to face the coming night in the strength of the past day, and seven times he failed—failed with such increase of failure, with such a growing sense of ignominy, overwhelming at length all the sunny hours and joining night to night, that, what with misery, self-accusation, and loss of confidence, his daylight courage too began to fade, and at length, from exhaustion, from getting wet, and then lying out of doors all night, and night after night,—worst of all, from the consuming of the deathly fear, and the shame of shame, his sleep forsook him, and on the seventh morning, instead of going to the hunt, he crawled into the castle, and went to bed. The grand health, over which the witch had taken such pains, had yielded, and in an hour or two he was moaning and crying out in delirium.

AN EVIL NURSE

Watho was herself ill, as I have said, and was the worse tempered; and besides, it is a peculiarity of witches, that what works in others to sympathy, works in them to repulsion. Also, Watho had a poor, helpless, rudimentary spleen of a conscience left, just enough to make her uncomfortable, and therefore more wicked. So, when she heard that Photogen was ill, she was angry. Ill, indeed! after all she had done to saturate him with the life of the system, with the solar might itself! He was a wretched failure, the boy! And because he was *her* failure, she was annoyed with him, began to dislike him, grew to hate him. She looked on him as a painter might upon a picture, or a poet upon a poem, which he had only succeeded in getting into an irrecoverable mess. In the hearts of witches, love and hate lie close together, and often tumble over each other. And whether it was that her failure with Photogen foiled also her plans in regard to Nycteris, or that her illness made her yet more of a devil's wife, certainly Watho now got sick of the girl too, and hated to know her about the castle.

She was not too ill, however, to go to poor Photogen's room and torment him. She told him she hated him like a serpent, and hissed like one as she said it, looking very sharp in the nose and chin, and flat in the forehead. Photogen thought she meant to kill him, and hardly ventured to take anything brought him. She ordered every ray of light to be shut out of his room; but by means of this he got a little used to the darkness. She would take one of his arrows, and now tickle him with the feather end of it, now prick him with the point till the blood ran down. What she meant finally I cannot tell, but she brought Photogen speedily to the determination of making his escape from the castle: what he should do then he would think afterwards. Who could tell but he might find his mother somewhere beyond the forest! If it were not for the broad patches of darkness that divided day from day, he would fear nothing!

But now, as he lay helpless in the dark, ever and anon would come dawning through it the face of the lovely creature who on that first awful night nursed him so sweetly: was he never to see her again? If she was as he had concluded, the nymph of the river, why had she not reappeared? She might have taught him not to fear the night, for plainly she had no fear of it herself! But then, when the day came, she did seem frightened:—why was that, seeing there was nothing to be afraid of then? Perhaps one so much at home in the darkness, was correspondingly afraid of the light! Then his selfish joy at the rising of the sun, blinding him to her condition, had made him behave to her, in ill return for her kindness, as cruelly as Watho behaved to him! How sweet and dear and lovely she was! If there were wild beasts that came out only at night, and were afraid of the light, why should there not be girls too, made the same way—who could not endure the light, as he could not bear the darkness? If only he could find her again! Ah, how differently he would behave to her! But alas! perhaps the sun had killed her—melted her—burned her up!—dried her up—that was it, if she was the nymph of the river!

WATHO'S WOLF

From that dreadful morning Nycteris had never got to be herself again. The sudden light had been almost death to her: and now she lay in the dark with the memory of a terrific sharpness—a something she dared scarcely recall, lest the very thought of it should sting her beyond endurance. But this was as nothing to the pain which the recollection of the rudeness of the shining creature whom she had nursed through his fear caused her; for, the moment his suffering passed over to her, and he was free, the first use he made of his returning strength had been to scorn her! She wondered and wondered; it was all beyond her comprehension.

Before long, Watho was plotting evil against her. The witch was like a sick child weary of his toy: she would pull her to pieces, and see how she liked it. She would set her in the sun, and see her die, like a jelly from the salt ocean cast out on a hot rock. It would be a sight to soothe her wolf-pain. One day, therefore, a little before noon, while Nycteris was in her deepest sleep, she had a darkened litter brought to the door, and in that she made two of her men carry her to the plain above. There they took her out, laid her on the grass, and left her.

Watho watched it all from the top of her high tower, through her telescope; and scarcely was Nycteris left, when she saw her sit up, and the same moment cast herself down again with her face to the ground.

"She'll have a sunstroke," said Watho, "and that'll be the end of her."

Presently, tormented by a fly, a huge-humped buffalo, with great shaggy mane, came galloping along, straight for where she lay. At sight of the thing on the grass, he started, swerved yards aside, stopped dead, and then came slowly up, looking malicious. Nycteris lay quite still, and never even saw the animal.

"Now she'll be trodden to death!" said Watho. "That's the way those creatures do."

When the buffalo reached her, he sniffed at her all over, and went away; then came back and sniffed again: then all at once went off as if a demon had him by the tail.

Next came a gnu, a more dangerous animal still, and did much the same; then a gaunt wild boar. But no creature hurt her, and Watho was angry with the whole creation.

At length, in the shade of her hair, the blue-eyes of Nycteris began to come to themselves a little, and the first thing they saw was a comfort. I have told already how she knew the night-daisies, each a sharp-pointed little cone with a red tip; and once she had parted the rays of one of them, with trembling fingers, for she was afraid she was dreadfully rude, and perhaps was hurting it; but she did want, she said to herself, to see what secret it carried so carefully hidden; and she found its golden heart. But now, right under her eyes, inside the veil of her hair, in the sweet twilight of whose blackness she could see it perfectly, stood a daisy with its red tip opened wide into a carmine ring, displaying its heart of gold on a platter of silver. She did not at first recognize it as one of those cones come awake, but a moment's notice revealed what it was. Who then could have been so cruel to the lovely little creature, as to force it open like that, and spread it heart-bare to the terrible death-lamp? Whoever it was, it must be the same that had thrown her out there to be burned to death in its fire! But she had her hair, and could hang her head, and make a small sweet night of her own about her! She tried to bend the daisy down and away from the sun, and to make its petals hang about it like her hair, but she could not. Alas! it was burned and dead already! She did not know that it could not yield to her gentle force because it was drinking life, with all the eagerness of life, from what she called the death-lamp. Oh, how the lamp burned her!

But she went on thinking—she did not know how; and by and by began to reflect that, as there was no roof to the room except that in which the great fire went rolling about, the little Red-tip must have seen the lamp a thousand times, and must know it quite well! and it had not killed it! Nay, thinking about farther, she began to ask the question whether this, in which she now saw it, might not be its more perfect condition. For not only now did the whole seem perfect, as indeed it did before, but every part showed its own individual perfection as well, which perfection made it capable of combining with the rest into the higher perfection of a whole. The flower was a lamp itself! The golden heart was the light, and the silver border was the alabaster globe, skilfully broken, and spread wide to let out the glory. Yes: the radiant shape was plainly its perfection! If, then, it was the lamp which had opened it into that shape, the lamp could not be unfriendly to it, but must be of its own kind, seeing it made it perfect! And again, when she thought of it, there was clearly no little resemblance between them. What if the flower then was the little great-grandchild of the lamp and he was loving it all the time? And what if the lamp did not mean to hurt her, only could not help it? The red tips looked as if the flower had some time or other been hurt: what if the lamp was making the best it could of her—opening her out somehow like the flower? She would bear it patiently, and see. But how coarse the colour of the grass was! Perhaps, however, her eyes not being made for the bright lamp, she did not see them as they were! Then she remembered how different were the eyes of the creature that was not a girl and was afraid of the darkness! Ah, if the darkness would only come again, all arms, friendly and soft everywhere about her! She would wait and wait, and bear, and be patient.

She lay so still that Watho did not doubt she had fainted. She was pretty sure she would be dead before the night came to revive her.

REFUGE

Fixing her telescope on the motionless form, that she might see it at once when the morning came, Watho went down from the tower to Photogen's room. He was much better by this time, and before she left him, he had resolved to leave the castle that very night. The darkness was terrible indeed, but Watho was worse than even the darkness, and he could not escape in the day. As soon, therefore, as the house seemed still, he tightened his belt, hung to it his hunting-knife, put a flask of wine and some bread in his pocket, and took his bow and arrows. He got from the house, and made his way at once up to the plain. But what with his illness, the terrors of the night, and his dread of the wild beasts, when he got to the level he could not walk a step further, and sat down, thinking it better to die than to live. In spite of his fears, however, sleep contrived to overcome him, and he fell at full length on the soft grass.

He had not slept long when he woke with such a strange sense of comfort and security, that he thought the dawn at least must have arrived. But it was dark night about him. And the sky—no, it was not the sky, but the blue eyes of his naiad looking down upon him! Once more he lay with his head in her lap, and all was well, for plainly the girl feared the darkness as little as he the day.

"Thank you," he said. "You are like live armour to my heart; you keep the fear off me. I have been very ill since then. Did you come up out of the river when you saw me cross?"

"I don't live in the water," she answered. "I live under the pale lamp, and I die under the bright one."

"Ah, yes! I understand now," he returned. "I would not have behaved as I did last time if I had understood; but I thought you were mocking me; and I am so made that I cannot help being frightened at the darkness. I beg your pardon for leaving you as I did, for, as I say, I did not understand. Now I believe you were really frightened. Were you not?"

"I was, indeed," answered Nycteris, "and shall be again. But why you should be, I cannot in the least understand. You must know how gentle and sweet the darkness is, how kind and friendly, how soft and velvety! It holds you to its bosom and loves you. A little while ago, I lay faint and dying under your hot lamp.—What is it you call it?"

"The sun," murmured Photogen: "how I wish he would make haste!"

"Ah! do not wish that. Do not, for my sake, hurry him. I can take care of you from the darkness, but I have no one to take care of me from the light.—As I was telling you, I lay dying in the sun. All at once I drew a deep breath. A cool wind came and ran over my face. I looked up. The torture was gone, for the death-lamp itself was gone. I hope he does not die and grow brighter yet. My terrible headache was all gone, and my sight was come back. I felt as if I were new made. But I did not get up at once, for I was tired still. The grass grew cool about me, and turned soft in colour. Something wet came upon it, and it was now so pleasant to my feet, that I rose and ran about. And when I had been running about a long time, all at once I found you lying, just as I had been lying a little while before. So I sat down beside you to take care of you, till your life— and my death—should come again."

"How good you are, you beautiful creature!—Why, you forgave me before ever I asked you!" cried Photogen.

Thus they fell a talking, and he told her what he knew of his history, and she told him what she knew of hers, and they agreed they must get away from Watho as far as ever they could.

"And we must set out at once," said Nycteris.

"The moment the morning comes," returned Photogen.

"We must not wait for the morning," said Nycteris, "for then I shall not be able to move, and what would you do the next night? Besides Watho sees best in the daytime. Indeed, you must come now, Photogen.—You must."

"I can not; I dare not," said Photogen. "I cannot move. If I but lift my head from your lap, the very sickness of terror seizes me."

"I shall be with you," said Nycteris, soothingly. "I will take care of you till your dreadful sun comes, and then you may leave me, and go away as fast as you can. Only please put me in a dark place first, if there is one to be found."

"I will never leave you again Nycteris," cried Photogen. "Only wait till the sun comes, and brings me back my strength, and we will go away together, and never, never part any more."

"No, no," persisted Nycteris; "we must go now. And you must learn to be strong in the dark as well as in the day, else you will always be only half brave. I have begun already—not to fight your sun, but to try to get at peace with him, and understand what he really is, and what he means with me—whether to hurt me or to make the best of me. You must do the same with my darkness."

"But you don't know what mad animals there are away there towards the south," said Photogen. "They have huge green eyes, and they would eat you up like a bit of celery, you beautiful creature!"

"Come, come! you must," said Nycteris, "or I shall have to pretend to leave you, to make you come. I have seen the green eyes you speak of, and I will take care of you from them."

"You! How can you do that? If it were day now, I could take care of you from the worst of them. But as it is, I can't even see them for this abominable darkness. I could not see your lovely eyes but for the light that is in them; that lets me see straight into heaven through them. They are windows into the very heaven beyond the sky. I believe they are the very place where the stars are made."

"You come then, or I shall shut them," said Nycteris, "and you shan't see them any more till you are good. Come. If you can't see the wild beasts, I can."

"You can! and you ask me to come!" cried Photogen.

"Yes," answered Nycteris. "And more than that, I see them long before they can see me, so that I am able to take care of you."

"But how?" persisted Photogen. "You can't shoot with bow and arrow, or stab with a hunting knife."

"No, but I can keep out of the way of them all. Why, just when I found you, I was having a game with two or three of them at once, I see, and scent them too, long before they are near me—long before they can see or scent me."

"You don't see or scent any now, do you?" said Photogen, uneasily, rising on his elbow.

"No—none at present. I will look," replied Nycteris, and sprang to her feet.

"Oh, oh! do not leave me—not for a moment," cried Photogen, straining his eyes to keep her face in sight through the darkness.

"Be quiet, or they will hear you," she returned. "The wind is from the south, and they cannot scent us. I have found out all about that. Ever since the dear dark came, I have been amusing myself with them, getting every now and then just into the edge of the wind, and letting one have a sniff of me."

"Oh, horrible!" cried Photogen. "I hope you will not insist on doing so any more. What was the consequence?"

"Always, the very instant, he turned with flashing eyes, and bounded towards me—only he could not see me, you must remember. But my eyes being so much better than his, I could see him perfectly well, and would run away round him until I scented him, and then I knew he could not find me anyhow. If the wind were to turn, and run the other way now, there might be a whole army of them down upon us, leaving no room to keep out of their way. You had better come."

She took him by the hand. He yielded and rose, and she led him away. But his steps were feeble, and as the night went on, he seemed more and more ready to sink.

"Oh dear! I am so tired! and so frightened!" he would say.

"Lean on me," Nycteris would return, putting her arm round him, or patting his cheek. "Take a few steps more. Every step away from the castle is clear gain. Lean harder on me. I am quite strong and well now."

So they went on. The piercing night-eyes of Nycteris descried not a few pairs of green ones gleaming like holes in the darkness, and many a round she made to keep far out of their way; but she never said to Photogen she saw them. Carefully she kept him off the uneven places, and on the softest and smoothest of the grass, talking to him gently all the way as they went—of the lovely flowers and the stars—how comfortable the flowers looked, down in their green beds, and how happy the stars up in their blue beds!

When the morning began to come, he began to grow better, but was dreadfully tired with walking instead of sleeping, especially after being so long ill. Nycteris too, what with supporting him, what with growing fear of the light which was beginning to ooze out of the east, was very tired. At length, both equally exhausted, neither was able to help the other. As if by consent they stopped. Embracing each the other, they stood in the midst of the wide grassy land, neither of them able to move a step, each supported only by the leaning weakness of the other, each ready to fall if the other should move. But while the one grew weaker still, the other had begun to grow stronger. When the tide of the night began to ebb, the tide of the day began to flow; and now the sun was rushing to the horizon, borne upon its foaming billows. And ever as he came, Photogen revived. At last the sun shot up into the air, like a bird from the hand of the Father of Lights. Nycteris gave a cry of pain, and hid her face in her hands.

"Oh me!" she sighed; "I am *so* frightened! The terrible light stings so!"

But the same instant, through her blindness, she heard Photogen give a low exultant laugh, and the next felt herself caught up: she who all night long had tended and protected him like a child, was now in his arms, borne along like a baby, with her head lying on his shoulder. But she was the greater, for suffering more, she feared nothing.

THE WEREWOLF

At the very moment when Photogen caught up Nycteris, the telescope of Watho was angrily sweeping the table-land. She swung it from her in rage, and running to her room, shut herself up. There she anointed herself from top to toe with a certain ointment; shook down her long red hair, and tied it round her waist; then began to dance, whirling round and round and round faster and faster, growing angrier and angrier, until she was foaming at the mouth with fury. When Falca went looking for her, she could not find her anywhere.

As the sun rose, the wind slowly changed and went round, until it blew straight from the north. Photogen and Nycteris were drawing near the edge of the forest, Photogen still carrying Nycteris, when she moved a little on his shoulder uneasily, and murmured in his ear.

"I smell a wild beast—that way, the way the wind is coming."

Photogen turned, looked back towards the castle, and saw a dark speck on the plain. As he looked, it grew larger: it was coming across the grass with the speed of the wind. It came nearer and nearer. It looked long and low, but that might be because it was running at a great stretch. He set Nycteris down under a tree, in the black shadow of its bole, strung his bow, and picked out his heaviest, longest, sharpest arrow. Just as he set the notch on the string, he saw that the creature was a tremendous wolf, rushing straight at him. He loosened his knife in its sheath, drew another arrow half-way from the quiver, lest the first should fail, and took his aim—at a good distance, to leave time for a second chance. He shot. The arrow rose, flew straight, descended, struck the beast, and started again into the air, doubled like a letter V. Quickly Photogen snatched the other, shot, cast his bow from him, and drew his knife. But the arrow was in the brute's chest, up to the feather; it tumbled heels over head with a great thud of its back on the earth, gave a groan, made a struggle or two, and lay stretched out motionless.

"I've killed it, Nycteris," cried Photogen. "It is a great red wolf."

"Oh, thank you!" answered Nycteris feebly from behind the tree. "I was sure you would. I was not a bit afraid."

Photogen went up to the wolf. It *was* a monster! But he was vexed that his first arrow had behaved so badly, and was the less willing to lose the one that had done him such good service: with a long and a strong pull, he drew it from the brute's chest. Could he believe his eyes? There lay—no wolf, but Watho, with her hair tied round her waist! The foolish witch had made herself invulnerable, as she supposed, but had forgotten that, to torment Photogen therewith, she had handled one of his arrows. He ran back to Nycteris and told her.

She shuddered and wept, and would not look.

ALL IS WELL

There was now no occasion to fly a step farther. Neither of them feared any one but Watho. They left her there, and went back. A great cloud came over the sun, and rain began to fall heavily, and Nycteris was much refreshed, grew able to see a little, and with Photogen's help walked gently over the cool wet grass.

They had not gone far before they met Fargu and the other huntsmen. Photogen told them he had killed a great red wolf, and it was Madam Watho. The huntsmen looked grave but gladness shone through.

"Then," said Fargu, "I will go and bury my mistress."

But when they reached the place, they found she was already buried—in the maws of sundry birds and beasts which had made their breakfast of her.

Then Fargu, overtaking them, would, very wisely, have Photogen go to the king, and tell him the whole story. But Photogen, yet wiser than Fargu, would not set out until he had married Nycteris; "for then," he said, "the king himself can't part us; and if ever two people couldn't do the one without the other, those two are Nycteris and I. She has got to teach me to be a brave man in the dark, and I have got to look after her until she can bear the heat of the sun, and he helps her to see, instead of blinding her."

They were married that very day. And the next day they went together to the king, and told him the whole story. But whom should they find at the court but the father and mother of Photogen, both in high favour with the king and queen. Aurora nearly died for joy, and told them all how Watho had lied, and made her believe her child was dead.

No one knew anything of the father or mother of Nycteris; but when Aurora saw in the lovely girl her own azure eyes shining through night and its clouds, it made her think strange things, and wonder how even the wicked themselves may be a link to join together the good. Through Watho, the mothers, who had never seen each other, had changed eyes in their children.

The king gave them the castle and lands of Watho, and there they lived and taught each other for many years that were not long. But hardly had one of them passed, before Nycteris had come to love the day best, because it was the clothing and crown of Photogen, and she saw that the day was greater than the night, and the sun more lordly than the moon; and Photogen had come to love the night best, because it was the mother and home of Nycteris.

"But who knows," Nycteris would say to Photogen, "that when we go out, we shall not go into a day as much greater than your day as your day is greater than my night?"

13

HARRIET LOUISA CHILDE-PEMBERTON

All my Doing;
or Red Riding-Hood Over Again
(1882)

ARRIET LOUISA CHILDE-PEMBERTON wrote numerous stories, poems, and plays for children during the 1880s and 1890s. Her works such as *Prince, A Story of the American War and Other Narrative Poems* (1883), *Birdie: A Tale of Child-Life* (1888), and *Fire and Water* (1891) tended to be heavily didactic and sentimental. She was a member of the Christian Knowledge Society and decided to modernize fairy tales along suitable Christian lines. Among her publications for this Society are *The Fairy Tales of Every Day* (1882), *Olive Smith; or, an Ugly Duckling* (1883), and *No Beauty* (1884). In her preface to *Fairy Tales of Every Day*, which contains "All my Doing; or, Red Riding-Hood Over Again," she stated that all traditional fairy tales have the same moral: "the reward bestowed after a period of trial, and the triumph of good over evil." Moreover, "the lesson of love lies at the root of them all—that pure unselfish love which makes all things beautiful, all sufferings endurable, all achievement possible." Her avowed intention was to "show that the old fairy-tales which charmed us in our nurseries do not die with our childhood, but may receive new interpretations by the light of our every day experiences." Although she did not know Anne Isabella Ritchie's tales at the time she wrote her own, she acknowledged that she was conducting the same type of experiment with the fairy-tale genre. However, she includes much more didacticism and moralizing in her tales than Ritchie did. Her version of *Little Red Riding Hood* is a fascinating narrative of female self-deprecation upheld in the name of moralism as a warning to young girls in Victorian society.

ALL MY DOING;

OR RED RIDING-HOOD OVER AGAIN

All our lives are in some sense a "might have been"; the very best of us must feel, I suppose, in sad and thoughtful moments, that he might have been transcendently nobler, and greater, and loftier than he is: but while life lasts, every "might have been" should lead, not to vain regrets, but to manly resolution; it should be but the dark background to a "may be" and a "will be" yet.

The Silence and Voices of God, F. W. Farrer

 THINK THE STORY of Red Riding-Hood is one of the stupidest of all the nursery tales," was the criticism which I caught the eldest of my nieces announcing one evening as I unexpectedly walked into the schoolroom.

"Why, Margery?" said I.

Margery, who had evidently just been reading the story in question aloud to one of the little ones, looked up surprised at my unexpected entrance and still more unexpected question. Young people do not often like to be called upon to give an account of their opinions—particularly young people at the shy and awkward age of fifteen, who think more than they care to confess, and are apt to form judgments, more or less hard and fast, without quite knowing why they do so. And so I was not surprised that Margery gave me no answer till I had repeated the question—

"Why do you think Red Riding-Hood the stupidest of all the nursery tales? I used to like it when I was a little girl."

"Oh, so did I when I was a little girl; and so do the children now," replied Margery. "But that's just it. It can't possibly interest any one *but* children. Now some of the others can. But Red Riding-Hood is altogether too unlikely for anything! We don't meet with wolves now, you see, and if we did, we couldn't talk to them. And besides, it's all so exaggerated. Red Riding-Hood was only heedless and silly to talk so, but to be eaten up for that was *much* too severe a punishment."

Margery paused, expecting me to say something in reply. But I sat silent, not a little amused in drawing out this new state of my niece's mind. She was beginning to put away childish things—at least she thought she was—unless they could square somehow with her thoughts upon things that were *not* childish. She was going through a matter-of-fact stage, she was beginning to see the meanings of things, she was learning to set great store by whys and wherefores, causes and effects. Well, it was no wonder, I thought, as I glanced round the schoolroom, and realised that mathematics, and natural philosophy, and political economy played a prominent part in the weekly programme of Margery's education. This glance set me wondering whether, if I had any children to educate, I should have pursued precisely the same plan as found favour in the eyes of my sister-in-law; but *I* had never had much chance of putting my ideas into practice. They had remained ideas—explained at great length very often to certain of my friends—but not going much further. These reflections had carried me far enough away from Red Riding-Hood, but I was recalled to the subject under discussion by Margery's voice—

"And really and truly, auntie, I never quite like reading that story to the children, because it can't possibly be explained to be true in any kind of way, you see! Mamma always says that I ought to be able to show the little ones that there is a *true* meaning, even in their nursery tales; but how can I, when I know in my heart that people don't get put to death themselves or cause the deaths of others simply by being heedless and silly?"

My niece Margery interests me very much. I don't greatly mind at present, as her father does, that her arms and legs are long and awkward, and that she is very careless about brushing her hair and keeping her collars clean, nor am I in a fever of anxiety, like her poor mother, lest she may not know quite as much as other girls of her age. But I like her earnestness and her sincerity, and for the sake of these I can pardon her dogmatic tone, which is only the early outcome of her dawning ideas, and will soften down in time.

And, to tell the truth, Margery is never dogmatic with me. When I begin to talk and tell her things out of my own experience—as I often do, for it has been a varied one—she always listens in rapt attention, and often answers me quite doubtfully and humbly, which surprises me sometimes, I confess, for *I* have never learnt half the things *she* is being taught, and know very little about mathematics and political economy.

"There is something in what you say, Margery dear," said I; "yet I am not at all so sure as you are, that it cannot possibly be explained to be true in any kind of way."

Margery was sitting on the arm of my chair, so I could not see her face, but I knew that it was frowning with perplexity and with the inward dissent which she did not quite like to express aloud.

"Shall I tell you what I think?" I continued. "I think the story of Red Riding-Hood is not intended for the children only, by any means; and as for the meaning, you mustn't expect the little ones to find *that* out. *That* is certainly over their heads at present. And if you think the story the stupidest of all the nursery tales, I suspect the meaning must still be a little over *your* head too."

I felt my niece slip off the arm of my chair, and in another minute she was kneeling before me with her elbows on my lap, looking up at me with just the puzzled sort of look I had expected.

"But *is* there any sensible meaning in it?" she asked.

"You think people don't come by their deaths themselves nor cause the deaths of others by being only heedless and silly?" said I, stroking Margery's rough, untidy hair. "Ah! I wish *I* could think it never had been so!"

Margery looked up at me again, her puzzled gaze having something awestruck in it.

"Why?" she asked, after a pause, "did you really know some one to whom it happened?"

Aye, thought I, I *did* know, all too well, some one to whom it had really happened—or something very like it—some one whose heedlessness and folly had well-nigh ended, indeed, in death and disaster! But what I said to Margery was—

"Shall I tell you a story? Then you can judge for yourself if it is possible to read a meaning in the tale of Red Riding-Hood."

"Oh, yes! please do," said my niece, "*your* stories are always nice."

"It is a true story," said I, "for it happened to myself."

"Oh, auntie!" cried Margery, "you could never have been silly like that!"

"Couldn't I, Margery?" I replied. "Ah, dear, you don't know what sharp teaching it sometimes takes to make people sensible!"

By this time the younger children had all left the room, some for bed, and some to play elsewhere, all except Margery's next sister, Eva, a merry, rosy-cheeked, laughing maiden, her father's pet and plaything, and as thoughtless a little piece of goods as ever I came across! When she heard me speak of a story, she too came and sat down at my feet; and if it sometimes strikes me as strange that Margery shows herself more teachable with me than with any one else, it strikes me as even more so that lively little Eva should be attracted, as she always is, by my sober experiences.

My story, said I, is of more than twenty years ago, at a time when the fashions in dress were just the reverse of what they are now, when crinolines could hardly be worn large enough, when the pork-pie hat was the rage, and when, instead of the sage-greens, the peacock-blues, and rhubarb-reds of the present day, bright scarlet, crude violet, and two new colours called mauve and magenta, found favour in the eyes of those who pretended to taste in the matter of dress.

Amongst these I, who had just grown up, took my place, of course. I wore red stockings, and a violet dress, and a scarlet cloak, and nobody ever thought, as they would now, of calling my taste vulgar. What I must have looked like you can very well imagine, if you can fancy my cheeks a good deal plumper than they are now, my eyes brighter (I had shed very few tears then), and my hair without any streaks of grey. Fortunately, I was not very tall, otherwise the bright colours which took my fancy so would have sat worse upon me than they perhaps did.

That scarlet cloak in particular was my great pride. Cloaks at that time were made in a particular shape, a sort of double cloak, the upper one being shorter than the under, and drawn in at the waist with a rosette—Connemara cloaks I think they were called; and though I am quite ready to admit that the fashions of that date were for the most part hideous and tasteless, the Connemara cloaks were by no means ugly or unbecoming.

They were made in all colours, and when my old bachelor uncle sent me the present he always did on my birthday, I instantly made up my mind to spend it on a Connemara cloak, and a scarlet one. Trotting about in this cloak, with a pair of red stockings, just showing above laced boots, the smallest of small black hats on my head, and my hair drawn back into a chenille net—such was the monstrous fashion of the moment—I must have looked not very unlike Red Riding-Hood herself, I think, and I fancy people took me to be younger than I was.

However, I had plenty to do besides give my attention to dress. You see I was only one among ten brothers and sisters, and a noisy, busy, scrambling family we were. Some large families may be brought up quite carefully and demurely, without any noise or fuss, but it was not so with us. I have heard people remark that we were never brought up at all; and if such people mean by bringing up, doing things at stated times, then certainly we were *not* brought up. We never did anything at stated times. My father never sat down from morning till night. He took his simple meals standing, like the hatter in "Alice in Wonderland," his tea-cup in one hand and his slice of bread and butter in the other. And as for my mother, I think she spent her life in walking up and down-stairs. Nobody looked after us children very regularly, nobody had the leisure to do it; we had governesses at one time, but we didn't get on with any of them, and they didn't much like our scrambling ways, and so after a while they ceased.

After that came a season of anarchy, in which we elder ones were supposed to teach the younger; and you may guess what that amounted to. Then when the boys were being drafted off to school things became a little more manageable; and so we went on till I was grown up. The only person who ever attempted living by any sort of rule was my eldest brother—your father—and a hard time he had of it, with so many against him. I was worse than useless in keeping any kind of order. I liked going my own way, and the easiest way of doing this is generally to let others go theirs. I got into foolish scrapes more than once, but I got out of them again, and no harm came. So I fell into the habit of believing that no harm ever would come, and of thinking that heedlessness and randomness answered just as well as any more careful line of conduct.

Your father used to give me very good advice, if I had only been wise enough to follow it, or even to lay it to heart.

"If you would only try to remember, Pussy," he would say earnestly, "you would find it saved such a lot of time; and if you would think sometimes before you speak, or rush into doing things, it would be so much better."

"What would you have me think about?" I asked.

"Why, the consequences," he replied.

"Oh, bother consequences," I answered flippantly. "Small things don't have any consequences; and if they do, one can't be always stopping to think about them. There isn't time in this house."

Well, one morning as I came down to breakfast late, as was my custom, I met my mother as usual going upstairs. She did not stop, except to give me a hurried kiss, but she just said as she went her way—

"Pussy, your father wants to speak to you."

"What about?" I asked, in some surprise, for nobody ever wanted to speak to anybody at this time in the morning. But by this time my mother was up on the landing.

"Something about a letter from your grandmother," she called out hastily, and before I could inquire further she had vanished down the passage. I went on into the dining-room, where I found my father hearing one of the children say the multiplication table, eating his breakfast rapidly the while, and scanning the morning paper into the bargain. He took hardly any notice of me, but when he had swallowed his last cup of tea, rushed out of the room into the hall, where I heard him wriggling himself into his greatcoat. I followed him.

"What's this about a letter from grandmamma?" I asked.

"Letter from grandmamma?" he repeated. "Oh, yes, to be sure. Wait till I come back; I'm only going to a meeting. Shan't be long." And he, too, vanished.

At this moment my eldest sister came flying down the stairs, her cloak and hat on. She had been up and about for hours, down to the school, into the church, half over the parish for all I knew. I waylaid her.

"What's this about a letter from grandmamma?" I asked.

"Letter from grandmamma?" she repeated in a bewildered tone. "Oh, I know, something about you, I believe."

"But *what* about me?" I asked impatiently.

"I don't know. Let me pass. I'm in a hurry."

Everybody was always in a hurry, and nobody ever attended to any one else. That was the conclusion I arrived at that morning. What was the use of my brother preaching to me about remembering and stopping to think? Nobody here ever remembered, or ever stopped to think; but it all did very well so far as I could see.

So I, like the rest, hurried off on my own devices, quite forgetting that my father had told me to wait for his return. The consequence was, that when he came in, I was far enough away, and only returned to find him cramming a sandwich into his mouth, while his dog-cart was waiting to drive him some eight miles into the country.

If my grandmother expected a prompt answer to her letter, I am afraid she must have been disappointed; for it was some three or four days before there was time found to acquaint me with its contents. It was a pouring wet day, and I think some of us must have got bad colds, probably caught in the reckless rushing about at all moments of the day and night. Nothing less, I am sure, would have found some four or five of us all sitting still in one room together.

"Oh, by the way, we've never answered grandmamma's letter!" said my father, who was sorting a packet he held in his hand.

"No," said I, feeling rather aggrieved, "and you've never told me what was in it either."

"There it is," said my father, who had the most beautiful temper I ever knew, and took the hurry and scramble of his busy life and his large family in the most good-humoured way in the world, never fretting and never putting himself out. "There it is; read it for yourself, Pussy, as it concerns you, and give us the benefit of your opinion."

I took the letter and read it. It contained a proposal from my grandmother, that I should go and live with her. Of course I might see my family as often as they pleased, but my home was to be with her. The reason of the offer was candidly stated—there was a lot of us, and there might be some advantages for one in having a home elsewhere. My grandmother was a fresh, lively old lady, living in a good house in a nice neighbourhood, and she would much like the society of a young thing about her. To be sure she had her dear daughter Rosa, but we all knew, though she did not express this in so many words, that Aunt Rosa's company was sometimes found a little irksome.

My father, in giving me the letter to read, evidently intended the case in all its bearings to be placed before me at once. We had no secrets in our family; everybody told everybody everything—when there was time—except my eldest brother; he sometimes kept things to himself, and had earned the character of loving a mystery. So I took in the situation at a glance—the advantages of being rid of all the children and the scramble, and of living with grandmamma, who had carriages and horses, and entertained her friends in a nice house, and would make me presents of new dresses and hats. And I balanced them all, very rapidly, against Aunt Rosa, of whom I stood rather in awe. The advantages carried the day. After all, if Aunt Rosa bored me beyond endurance, or if I found it more lonely and dull than I expected, I could come home again, of course.

"Well, Pussy," said my father, "how is it to be?"

"I don't think I should mind going to stay with grandmamma," said I.

"Anything for a change, Madcap, I suppose," said my father, chucking me under the chin. "What does everybody else think about it? Grandmamma must be written to to-morrow."

"If Pussy thinks she would like it, I don't see why she shouldn't try," said my mother. "She ought to see a little of life, and go to a few good parties, and really I haven't the time to take her out."

This was perfectly true. No one in their senses could have expected my poor mother, after her long busy days, to sit up till late, while I was amusing myself.

I forget exactly what my brother and sister said; but it left on my mind the impression that the one thought I should derive some benefit to my character from the change, while the other was relieved at the idea of there being one less in our small house to tumble over and get in the way of all the others!

So this change in my life, like everything else, was settled in a hurry, scrambled through without any further debate or consideration. Somebody wrote to my grandmother the next day, and I was to have a fortnight to prepare for my long visit.

These preparations were mainly left to my own care, and resulted in a good many shopping expeditions, and if I remember rightly, the result of one was the scarlet Connemara cloak of which I was so proud. As soon as my leaving home had been settled, my family seemed to forget all about it; it was swallowed up in a score of other interests and occupations, and if it was kept before them at all it was only by passing allusions on my part. The consequence was, that when my last day at home arrived, they were all taken by surprise.

Then suddenly it dawned upon my elder sister that our long companionship was about to be broken up; it had never been very close, perhaps, but still, after a fashion it had been companionship. At a parting it is generally the one left behind with the old work, and the old ways, and the constant associations, who feels the sadder; and when I saw how sad she looked, I was touched and not a little ashamed. I reflected of what very little use or comfort I had been to her, how busy I had always been with my own foolish interests, how slight was the sympathy I had ever shown for the things she cared for!

True, she was always busy and preoccupied, and hurried too; but then, what she did was certainly much better worth being busy about than what I did.

"I shall miss you, Pussy," she said sadly.

"I don't think you can," said I, penitently. "I have never been of any use to you—never!"

"Never mind," she replied, stroking my hair, "it isn't always for the exact amount of *use* people have been to us that we miss them."

My sister was older than I by a year or two, and in a vague kind of way I looked up to her, and cared for what she thought; and when she confessed to missing me, I was pleased, though a little puzzled.

"I wish I could take you with me," I said, for the first time beginning to feel somewhat frightened at the prospect of being cut away from all my old moorings, and sent by myself to a strange place, even though it was only to my own grandmother.

"And papa and mamma, and all the children, Pussy?" she asked. "I daresay you think so just now when the parting is so near; but if you *could*, you know, it wouldn't be the change you're looking forward to."

My father and mother, too, suddenly awoke to the fact that I was going away the next day to a new home and a new life, and that there were some last words which it might be well to speak. Though we all did pretty much as we liked at home, and took care of ourselves, and received less than most the counsels and admonitions which parents generally think it wise to bestow, still home was home, and my father and mother imagined, of course, that they kept their eyes on us all a great deal more than they did.

It was very late that night before my mother wished me good night. She told me some very plain truths, and added many sensible cautions, and a great deal of good advice. The only pity was, that it should have been all left till so late. Such cautions and such advice require to be heard more than once—over and over again, in fact, so that they may soak well in, if they are to produce any effect upon such thoughtless, callous characters as mine. But I had never heard anything of the kind before in my home; there were so many of us, and so much had to be done, and everybody was always in such a hurry; there never was any time to talk to one of us seriously and separately. So I am sorry to say, between being quite unprepared for her admonitory tone, and very sleepy during the lecture, my mother's good counsel went in one ear and out at the other.

What was the good counsel, you want to know? Well, it was mostly a caution against being so heedless and careless, a warning to think sometimes of the possible consequences to myself or to others of my words and deeds. She said a great deal about being discreet and trustworthy, and of trying to be of use to the people I lived with, and of not caring too much about my dress and my amusements. Above all, she advised me to be very careful how I talked to strangers, and not to be too hasty in forming friendships. Though I paid so little attention to it at the time, it has come back to me since, for if my mother had been a prophet she couldn't have spoken words better suited to the circumstances in which I was to be placed.

But I was impatient of it all at the time. I was even more impatient when just before leaving, my brother took me aside, and spoke a few words that were almost an echo of those I had heard on the previous evening. I didn't want to be lectured just then. I wanted to be petted, and told how much I should be missed, and made a fuss over. Perhaps I was impatient because I did not get quite so much of this regret as I had expected; but young people who are always occupied with their own affairs, and never find time to do anything for anybody else, have no right to expect to be keenly missed. Anyhow, I shrugged up my shoulders at my brother, and told him rather pertly that I had no doubt his advice was all very well-meant, but it was a pity he hadn't said it all long ago; there wasn't any time to attend to it now.

"I don't want you to attend to it now, so much as when you are gone," he said kindly. "Think a little of what I have said then, Pussy, will you?"

I forget what I answered, but I escaped from him as soon as I could, and rejoined the rest of the party. And if my family did not express so much regret as I should have liked, it was saying a good deal for the interest they took in what was about to befall me, that they all suspended their own occupations to wish me good-bye, and see me off. My father even went so far as to insist on accompanying me to the station, and as he had only just rushed in from a meeting in the chapter-house (for, as you know, he was a canon, and we lived in a cathedral town), we were ten minutes late in starting, and after making the flyman drive like Jehu, I was barely in time to catch the train. My father flew to get my ticket, while I wrangled with a slow porter. Then I was hurried from platform to platform, hustled into a carriage, gave my father a breathless kiss, and was steaming out from the station before I knew whether I had even got my hand-bag and umbrella safe. If the whole incident had not been completely a piece with the usual circumstances of my daily life, I should have regretted more than I did that I and my father had not had a last word together. Even as it was, for once in my life I felt it a pity that there had not been time to pause!

The journey on which I had thus started by myself was not very long or very formidable. It was to last about two hours and a half, and there would be no changes. My father had seen me off at one end, and my grandmother had promised to send some one to meet me at the other. When I had recovered my breath and began to look around me, I perceived that I was alone in the carriage, except for the company of one lady in the furthest corner by the opposite window. She was rather an austere-looking person, neither young nor old, dressed in more sombre colours than were the fashion at that time, with a brown straw bonnet and a black silk handkerchief round her neck, that when she turned her head left a space of yellow skin visible between the handkerchief and her collar. Why I noticed these little things about her, or why they should dwell so in my mind even now, I do not know, for I thought her a lady of most unprepossessing appearance; I do not think we exchanged two words, and it was a very long time before she even looked my way.

When she did, it was less to look at me than to notice a stranger who was getting in. It was a man, and I thought she seemed rather to resent his presence as an intrusion. That was more than I did, however; I was tired of reading my novel, tired of looking out of the window; I wanted something to vary the monotony of the journey, and I welcomed my new fellow-traveller as a variety.

He was a small man, rather unusually small, and of an age that it was impossible to guess at; he might have been anything from thirty to five-and-forty, or even fifty, for he had that sort of fair hair that, if it has any gray in it, blends both together till the gray becomes indistinguishable, and he had light invisible eyebrows and a very light moustache and "imperial," that imparted a certain indefiniteness to his whole physiognomy. Then he had a habit of screwing up his eyes till it was impossible to guess whether the lines at their corners were due to advancing age or were merely the result of trick. If you ask me *now*, I should say that he was probably nearer fifty than forty, but I did not think so *then*. He was a very dapper little man, too; he was dressed in a neat grey overcoat, and carried a plaid rug, which he spread over his knees when he had settled himself in the carriage. Altogether, I rather liked his looks, and certainly I have had many travelling companions since sitting on the seat opposite me whose aspect was not nearly so pleasant nor their manners so good. I was particularly struck with his manners. They were not forward, not in the least obtrusive; but when he put his bag in the net over my head he apologised for disturbing me, and when I was fumbling with the window he offered to let it down for me. I couldn't understand why the austere female at the other end of the carriage cast such severe and suspicious glances at him; and for the very reason that she looked so glum I felt a perverse inclination to return his good manners with what I thought good manners on my part; never reflecting, of course, that since the net above his own head had nothing in it, there was no need to put his bag above me and to apologise for so doing!

At the next station we came to the austere lady got out. I felt an indescribable satisfaction in seeing her go. Her hard gaze troubled me, and I was annoyed by the black silk handkerchief and the gap of neck visible below it. Yet it might have made all the difference in the world to me, perhaps, if she had remained my travelling companion to the end of my journey. As it was, however, I was pleased to see her go, and I even made some little flippant remark to my opposite neighbour on her very grim appearance.

This broke the ice a little, and when after a while he bought some newspapers, he was polite enough to offer them to me. I did not like to appear ungracious, and so I took them; but with the exception of "Punch" they were not much to my taste. I pretended to read them, and then returned them with a little bow and a "thank you."

So far not much had passed between us, and such as it was it had been very gradual. It had created just enough variety, however, to make me feel how much less dull the journey had appeared during the last half hour than it had before. I found myself wondering whether he would remain my travelling companion to my journey's end, or whether I should again be left to my novel and my own thoughts.

Presently the ticket-collector came for our tickets, and as I gave him mine (taking it from my purse, which I carried in my pocket and not in my hand-bag, for greater safety as I thought), I mentioned, as one often does, the station for which I was bound.

"Ah!" said my companion, repeating the name I had just mentioned, "what a beautiful country it is all round about there, is it not?"

"I don't know much about it," said I. "My home is in the Midlands, and I hardly know the Western counties at all—though they are not very far apart. I'm going on a visit, but I'm so glad to hear it is a nice country."

"Oh, charming—quite charming!" he repeated, screwing up his eyes as if he were dwelling on something that he appreciated very much indeed. "Such lovely ups and downs, such exquisite bits of colouring, such picturesque little villages hidden away where one least expects to find them!"

"Do you know it very well?" I asked.

"Oh, very well indeed," he replied, almost as if there were something laughable in the idea of his *not* knowing it well. "I suppose no one knows it better! It is quite the country for an artist; such a number of ancient churches, and no end of picturesque old houses!"

"Do you draw?" was my next question.

"After a fashion," he replied. "I am passionately fond of it, but am nothing better than an amateur."

"Do you know a village called Cherrybridge?" I asked.

"Cherrybridge," he repeated dubiously; "I seem to have heard *something* in connection with it, but don't think I have ever actually been there."

"Perhaps you have heard of Wyre Hall," said I. "It is a very fine old house, I believe."

"Oh, to be sure! to be sure!" he replied quickly. "Of course I have—a *very* fine old house, so I've been told. I believe the carving over the chimney-piece in the hall is something quite famous, and there's a ceiling, a moulded ceiling, that is very handsome, I believe."

"That is where I am going, to stay with my grandmother, Mrs Brownlow," said I, feeling that such a statement must invest me with some importance in his eyes.

"Are you indeed?" he replied with evident interest. "How I envy you a sight of that old chimney-piece and that splendid ceiling!" Then after a short pause, he added, "I think Mrs Brownlow has only taken the place in the last six months, has she?"

This was perfectly true, and I admitted it was so, but I was surprised that he should be so accurately informed, and wondered if my grandmother knew him.

"Do you know my grandmother, Mrs Brownlow?" I asked.

"I have not that pleasure," he replied politely, "but I used to know old Colonel Malpas, who had the place till he died last summer. He was a very great friend of mind— the poor old colonel—and I have been more than once on the point of staying with him; but somehow the visit never came off. And now I don't suppose I shall ever have the satisfaction of seeing that carving or that fine ceiling." And he gazed a moment out of the window, his eyes opened a little wider than usual, and full of an expression that struck me as rather sad. I supposed he was thinking of the poor old colonel, and of what he had lost by not paying his visit betimes.

I felt a very strong inclination to ask him his name, but, scatter-brained madcap though I was, I did just reflect sufficiently to decide that this would not quite do. If he had been a friend of my grandmother's, it might have been different; but he had distinctly told me he had not the pleasure of her acquaintance.

I do not clearly remember what else we talked about, but I think we carried on the conversation for some time longer; by which you will see that my mother's excellent advice of the previous evening had already been quite forgotten.

As we at last neared the station for which we were both bound, I recollected that my umbrella and a band-box containing my best hat were up in the net above my head, where my travelling companion had also placed his bag. I got up from my seat, and turning my back towards him, made an effort to lift my own things down. Not being tall, however, it *was* an effort, and I could not reach easily.

"Pray let me do that for you," said my companion, and I felt that he was already standing up, close behind me, his left arm almost touching my right one. I remember feeling what I thought was a very slight jolt, and observing that it was impossible to stand steady in a train that was in motion, I sat down again, and in another moment he had lifted down both my things and his own. Then I drew on my scarlet cloak, which I had laid aside, finding it too warm in the railway carriage, and shortly after the train stopped.

"Can I do anything for you?" said my companion as he helped me out of the carriage. "Can I see to your luggage?"

"Oh no, thank you," said I, "my luggage must be all right, it was labelled." He raised his hat very politely, and vanished. When I looked round to see where he was gone I could not trace him anywhere.

And when I came to look for my luggage I found it was anything but all right! The van was ransacked, but my familiar black box was not forthcoming. A second van was ransacked, and still no black box was there! Clearly the slow porter had neglected to put my luggage into the train, and my father, in the hurry of seeing after me, had forgotten to see after the box. No doubt it was still reposing idly on the platform of the station from whence I had started.

The train from which I had just alighted was very long, the station very large, and the platform crowded with people scurrying this way and that. I felt very lonely and bewildered. The porter to whom I had appealed suggested that I should telegraph, and the box would come all right by the next train. This was obviously the thing to do, and instinctively I put my hand in my pocket for my purse.

But there was no purse there! I turned my pocket inside out. There was nothing whatever in it but my pocket-handkerchief and a pencil-case, yet I distinctly remembered having put my purse back in my pocket after I had shown my ticket. In the crowd of rough-looking people through which I had been hurrying up and down the platform in search of my luggage, my pocket must have been picked!

The porter was very civil and very sympathetic, but it was not much consolation to be told "that it was market-day, and that there were generally a sight of pockets picked on market-day." How was I to pay for the telegram? Still worse, how was I to pass out of the station without any ticket to show?

I was almost in tears, for there was no sign of any one having been sent to meet me, and I did not know what to do. Suddenly I heard some one say close beside me—

"Can I be of any use?"

I turned and saw my travelling companion. His courteous tone was an instant relief. I felt that here was some one who would probably know the best way of getting me out of the difficulty.

"My luggage has been left behind," said I, "and my pocket has been picked, and my ticket was in my purse, and I don't know how to telegraph without any money."

"Your pocket picked? Dear me! such a rough crowd as there is about," he replied, adding as he turned to the porter, "I daresay it's common enough on a market-day."

"Oh, bless you, there's a sight o' pockets picked of a Saturday afternoon always," replied the porter, as if it was so much a matter of course it was no use troubling.

"Was there much in the purse?" the stranger asked very kindly.

"Four sovereigns and some silver, and a five pound note, *and* my ticket!" said I.

It was very foolish of me, you will say, to carry so much money in my purse in my pocket. No doubt it was; but no one had ever thought to advise me to put it away elsewhere, and perhaps if they had I should have thought I knew best.

"Dear me!" he said again, "that's a bad business. We must speak to the police. But about your luggage and the telegram; I will see to that, if you tell me what to say."

What could I do but thank him very cordially, and intrust him with the message I had to send. He went away to the telegraph office, and I waited for him to return, that I might thank him again. I knew I owed him a shilling, but that was not a sum that would ruin him, and I felt he would rather I accepted his kind assistance making no allusion to this small debt. In a few minutes he returned with a beaming countenance, holding up something between his thumb and fore-finger.

"See what I've picked up," he said; "your ticket, or I'm very much mistaken. The rascal who picked your pocket has evidently torn it in two and thrown it away as not worth keeping."

Never did I bless any one as I blessed that little man as he gave me back the torn fragments of my ticket. It was bad enough to have been robbed of so much money, but at any rate I should not be kept a prisoner at the station, as I had begun to fear.

"I should advise you to call at the police-station," said my benefactor, "and describe your loss. I would go with you with pleasure, but the train I am going on by is just starting. I am very glad to have been able to render you some slight assistance; I hope you will get your luggage all right by the next train, and get your purse back." So saying he made me a bow, and before I could thank him again he had hurried away to catch his train.

I passed out of the station, and found the brougham which my grandmother had sent to meet me waiting outside, and the coachman wondering what could have happened to me. I explained my disaster, and told him to stop at the police-station, which he did. There I made a statement of my loss, and having received a promise that every inquiry should be made, I went on my way to Wyre Hall.

My box arrived all in due time, and my father, on hearing of my misfortune, very kindly sent me another five-pound note, with a caution to take care of it, and not travel with so much more money in my purse than I could possibly want at one time. And I actually took his advice to heart, and remembered it. But before I go on with my story, I may as well mention that I never saw my purse or its contents again!

And now, of course, you expect me to tell you how I liked my new life with grandmamma and Aunt Rosa. Well, on the whole I liked it very much; there was something about it which contrasted strongly with the sort of life I had led at home, and for awhile the contrast was agreeable. Then I found just what I had expected, a large house, plenty of servants, carriages and horses, a good deal going on in the neighbourhood, and an indulgent grandmamma very ready and willing to make me pretty presents.

She was a large, handsome, good-natured woman, who liked everything about her to be handsome and on a large scale; she habitually wore good silk dresses, and had her rooms filled with choice flowers; her cook was good, and her carriage and horses always smartly turned out. She wore handsome rings, and had her pocket-handkerchief scented with the best eau-de-Cologne. Yet she was hardly to be called an epicure, was my grandmother; she only liked to be comfortable and have nice things about her; and no one was more anxious that others should be comfortable too, and take their share of nice things.

How my grandmother, with her indulgent, take-it-easy ways came to have children so unlike herself on every point, has always been a puzzle to me. That they should not have inherited her height and beauty was nothing strange; but that they should never have found out the advantages of leading a placid, contented, good-humoured existence, and should prefer bustle and worry and hurry, was to me a strange riddle. I have already told you what sort of a man was my father, and except for his beautiful temper, you will have realised that there was little likeness between him and my grandmother. And with Aunt Rosa the unlikeness was even more marked. She bustled about, and fidgeted, and worried from morning till night; but, unlike my father, she had no sweet temper to help her to bear the burden of her worries, and, moreover, she had nothing really to worry about. Her activity, in fact, showed itself in quite a different way to the activity to which I had been accustomed. She had been brought up by force to comfort and leisure, because these things grandmamma *would* have. It would have driven her crazy to see any one take his meals standing, and as for walking up and down-stairs, she would as soon have thought of flying as take the trouble to fetch anything or find anybody if by ringing a bell or sending a message she could get what she wanted done for her. So Aunt Rosa's activity took the form of worrying, and fretting, and bustling about the comforts of the house. Sometimes it would be about the cooking.

"Mamma dear, do try a little of this new pudding. I have written to Mrs So-and-so for the recipe, and such a correspondence as I've had to get the right one; and I've shown the cook exactly how to make it. I've been at it *all* the morning, till I'm quite worn out!"

"Thank you, my dear," grandmamma would say placidly, "but I think I would rather have some of the maraschino jelly." Of course, dear old soul, she greatly preferred what she knew the cook made exceedingly well to a recipe from Mrs So-and-so that Aunt Rosa had been trying her skill upon. Another time it would be—

"Mamma dear, I've been having a new kind of chair made for you, a wicker one, so light that it can be moved from one part of the room to another, so much nicer than the heavy old furniture. I've had it made by a protégé of mine in the village, who has lost both his legs, and I've been down every day for the last fortnight to see how he was getting on. I wish you would try it; I'm sure you would find it very comfortable."

And grandmamma would reply—

"Thank you, dear Rosa, but I am very comfortable where I am." As if it was likely that she would exchange the venerable velvet armchair, which had been her delight for twenty years, for *wicker-work*, at her time of life! It used to amuse me at first to notice the persistent way in which grandmamma quietly declined to be made the victim of Aunt Rosa's restless energy; but after a while it became rather tiresome to see Aunt Rosa affecting the grievance of a martyr, and going about with an expression of stern resignation, that seemed to say it was hard to try and do one's daily duty and never get so much as a word of thanks! I used to long to tell her to leave off trying to do things for people who didn't want to have anything done for them; and once when she had been putting me about sadly by her attempts to make *me* comfortable, I think I *did* tell her so, or something very like it.

"If everybody was as careless and as heedless as *you*, Pussy," Aunt Rosa replied severely, "it's very little comfort any one would enjoy, I'm afraid. If you could be brought to care less for your own amusements, and to try and do something useful for others sometimes, it would be very much better for you, I can assure you."

Aunt Rosa's words reminded me of something of the same kind which my mother had said to me the night before I left home, something about caring less for my own amusements, and trying to be of use to others; but if Aunt Rosa were to point the moral of my mother's advice, if Aunt Rosa were a specimen of trying to be of use to others, "then," thought I, "I would rather go on as I am." True, my family had not seemed much to regret my going away from home; but would grandmamma, I wondered, regret Aunt Rosa? I greatly doubted it. Altogether, I was rather puzzled how to make what I was told square with my present experiences.

So much, then, for the people with whom I actually lived. As for the house, it was just what you would have expected my grandmother to select—large, handsome, and comfortable. There were plenty of rooms, so that we were not obliged to sit all together if we did not like; and there was ample space for the pictures and mirrors and china that my grandmother loved to collect around her as pleasant things to look at.

And sure enough, as my unknown travelling companion had informed me, there was the carved oak chimney-piece in the hall. I noticed that almost as soon as I set foot in the house. As for the moulded ceiling, of which he had also spoken, I did not discover that for a day or two. Then I learnt that it was the ceiling of my grandmother's own particular sitting-room, and was upstairs off the first landing.

I was not much of a judge of these things then, yet even *I* could see that it was an unusually handsome ceiling; and when I found, as I very soon did, that the beauty of the house attracted a good many visitors, I, in my turn, began to value old oak, and to appreciate good moulding. My grandmother was fond of seeing her friends, and when in inviting them she apologised for being "an old woman living in a dull, out-of-the-way place," as she invariably did, she used to throw in something about "artistic beauties." And then when her friends came (and they never seemed to want pressing), she always pretended they came to see the house, and not to see her. Not that this was true in the least, but it was her joke.

Dear old soul! sitting in the velvet chair, with her stiff silk spread out, and her plump, white hands lazily pulling an ivory crochet-needle in and out of magenta wool! I was very fond of her in my way, and I really took the trouble of learning all about the chimney-piece and the ceiling, so as to play the part of show-woman to her guests.

"Here's my grand-daughter knows all about it," she would say, as pleased as Punch. "I never can remember whether the date is 1570 or 1750; but they tell me it makes a great deal of difference, and Pussy knows all about it."

And besides the people who came to stay in the house, we had plenty of pleasant neighbours. One family in particular, who lived only half a mile distant, at a place called the Red House, were very kind, and we saw a great deal of them. There were two girls of my own age, who were inclined to be friendly; and their brother I soon suspected was inclined to be more than friendly. When they joined me for a walk, Herbert frequently came too, and if he could find an excuse for running over from the Red House with a message, or a book, or a piece of music (always from his sisters, of course), he never seemed to lose the opportunity. He was a tall, good-looking young man, in the army, and home from India on leave. I did not at all mind the pleasure he seemed to take in my society, and his being a very great favourite with my grandmother made it very easy for him to come and see her, or me, as often as he pleased.

Yes, he was very nice, was Herbert, rather quiet perhaps, but gentle and courteous and sensible. He had seen and gone through a great deal, and would talk about it in a quiet unobtrusive manner that I liked to listen to; I found myself growing to care a good deal for what he said and what he thought about things and people, and I think I must have thought him pleasanter than at the time I chose to admit.

By-and-by I noticed that grandmamma lost no opportunity of singing his praises to me, and she would contrive little plans for leaving us alone together, plans which I am bound to add Aunt Rosa as often crossed by some contrivance of her own for making matters more comfortable still. As for me, I was sometimes amiable and sometimes perverse, sometimes I was kind to Herbert, and sometimes I was cross. But I know now that if my dear grandmother could have ordered things exactly as she wished, Herbert would have become my husband; and perhaps, perverse though I was, my wishes would not have run counter to hers.

Altogether, my life with grandmamma and Aunt Rosa was a happy one, and by the time I had been with them about three months, I had quite got to look upon Wyre Hall as my home. So much, in fact, was I reckoned at home there, that when it became a question of my grandmother and Aunt Rosa going, as they did every year, for a fortnight to Brighton, they suggested leaving me by myself. To have taken me with them would have been, in some measure, to put out their usual arrangements, and indeed I did not think the change would be very amusing to me. I was given the choice of going to my own people for the fortnight, but on the whole I preferred remaining in my present home. I was exceedingly comfortable there, and, like grandmamma, I appreciated comfort; besides, my friends at the Red House would be very kind to me, and I should see Herbert and his sisters every day. I had no fear of being dull or lonely, there were trustworthy servants, too, to look after the house, and I thought it would be rather fun to play at being mistress for a fortnight.

Well, grandmamma and Aunt Rosa had been gone about ten days, and so far, things had turned out very much as I had expected. I had seen Herbert or his sisters, and generally all three, every day; I had been to luncheon at their house, and had had them to tea with me. I enjoyed being hostess on my own account, and flattered myself that I did the honours very nicely indeed. I half wished that my elder brother and sister could have seen me in my new capacity, presiding over the teapot, and ordering more buttered toast, saying what time I wished the carriage to come round, and offering to drive my young friends home. I thought they would have decided "that Pussy had come on a good deal." But, as you will soon see, Pussy had not yet "come on" to much purpose.

One morning I went out for a stroll by myself. I knew there was not much prospect of my seeing my friends that day, as they were away on a visit—the two sisters and their mother were, at least—and I did not think it very likely that Herbert would come and see me quite alone. So I began the day by wondering how I should get through it—a bad beginning—and whether anything would turn up to make matters livelier. Meanwhile, I rambled through the shrubbery feeling rather doleful.

Just outside the shrubbery was a rising sweep of ground, and when I tell you that the country-folks described it as "a gorsty piece," you will have a pretty good idea of what it was like. In other words, however, it was a patch of wild common, with fern and furze bushes dotted all over it, and a few sheep grazing. It was a picturesque bit of land, and made a very pretty foreground to the view that lay beyond, a view with our shrubbery trees and the Hall on one hand, and the church tower and a line of blue landscape on the other.

So some one else besides myself seemed to think that morning, for as I strolled over the common, I saw a man seated on a camp-stool, sketching the landscape. There was no doubt that he was sketching. I would see his large white block, and the paint-box stuck upon his left thumb, and his head bobbing up and down.

Now this "gorsty piece" was part of our private grounds, though it had the appearance of a common; and therefore this stranger, this artist, or whatever he might be, had no business to come there without first asking grandmamma's leave. I felt very important as I remembered this, and a little bit frightened as I recollected that in my present capacity it was *my* place to inform him that he was trespassing. But the importance carried the day, and I went boldly towards him, making as much noise as I could in walking over the rough ground, so as to warn him that some one was coming.

Apparently he *did* hear me, for as I approached he looked round, then got up from the camp-stool, and with a very polite bow, advanced a step or two towards me. Judge of my surprise when I found myself face to face with my travelling companion of two months back!

We both started on recognising each other, and I did not quite know whether to consider him in the light of an acquaintance, or as a stranger, and I was rather relieved when he spoke first.

"I hope I am not trespassing here?" he asked rather anxiously. "I thought there was a right-of-way when I came through the gate, and it was not till I noticed these palings and the shrubbery close by, that I began to wonder if I was on private ground after all."

"It *is* private ground," said I; "there is no right-of-way through here."

"Then I must apologise most humbly for being where I ought not to be," he said, closing his paint-box. "But I could hardly resist making this sketch; it is so charming, and I may never have another opportunity."

I remembered how he had come to my rescue at a moment of great difficulty; how, too, I was still a shilling in his debt for the telegram I had sent about my luggage, and I could not find it in my heart to be so ungrateful as to tell him he must go with his sketch only just begun!

"Oh, pray don't leave off," I said. "I am sure my grandmother, Mrs Brownlow, would be very sorry that you should."

"You are very kind," he said, with another bow, "but the lights are changing, and I have already done enough for my purpose." He paused a moment, looking at the house through the trees, a slight smile on his lips, and his eyes screwed up very tightly. Then he added, "What a charming old house it is! Such a perfect specimen of its style!"

"This is Wyre Hall, you know," said I; "the house with the fine oak chimney-piece and the moulded ceiling."

"Ah! do I not know it!" he said, shaking his head. "A house that I have been asked to many a time in poor old Colonel Malpas' time!"

A hurried thought rushed through my mind that since he seemed such a genuine lover of artistic beauties, as my grandmother called them, it would be a pity that he should go away without a sight of the carving and the mouldings here, of which he had heard so much; it seemed almost unkind to see him so near, and yet to send him away unsatisfied. Besides, that shilling I owed him was rankling in my conscience. I did not like to allude to it, and yet I felt as if I ought to oblige him in return for what he had done for me.

"Perhaps you would like to come up to the house and have a look at the carved chimney-piece in the hall?" I said. "Mrs Brownlow is not at home just now, but I am sure she would be very pleased if you would."

This I said in perfect simplicity and good faith. It seemed to me that people nearly as complete strangers as this artist had been allowed to look at the carving before now, and I honestly thought that my grandmother was willing that any one should be granted that privilege who desired it.

"Oh, you are very much too kind, but I should like it of all things!" he replied enthusiastically.

The offer had been made and accepted; I could not go back from it now. I turned and led the way across the common and through the shrubbery, and he followed, carrying his camp-stool in one hand and his sketching-bag in the other. I did not quite know how to keep up the conversation, and he evidently thought it was hardly his place to begin. So our little walk was rather a silent one. As we neared the house, however, he said—

"Excuse my asking, but I hope you got your purse back all right?"

"No, indeed!" said I, sadly. "I stopped at the police-station as you advised me, and I believe they made every inquiry; but nothing came of it!"

"How very annoying!" he said. "But I suppose when a thing is taken in a crowd like that, it is very hard to trace."

By this time we had reached the house. The front door was usually locked, and as I did not want to ring the bell, I took my companion in by the garden entrance, which led through the conservatory into a passage. This passage communicated directly with the back stairs, and by a door through which we passed it opened into the hall.

No sooner had my companion set eyes on the carving than he seemed struck dumb with admiration. He had expected something beautiful, no doubt, but nothing so beautiful as this! I told him all I had been taught about it, and which I had repeated to so many people, and felt not a little important at doing it all on my own account this time, not at grandmamma's request.

"I wonder if I might be allowed to make a little sketch of it?" he said suddenly, with a look of enthusiasm. I had known other people make little sketches of it, so it never occurred to me that this man being a perfect stranger was any reason why he should not do as much.

"Oh, certainly, if you like," said I, very graciously. And with many thanks on his part, out came his pencil and sketch-book at once.

I could not guess how long he would be at this work, and I had an idea that artists did not like to be watched while drawing. So I went into the drawing-room, and pretended to be engaged arranging flowers. Once or twice I fancied I heard him move across the hall, but I supposed he was looking for the best point of view, and thought nothing more about it. Presently, when I thought he had finished, I rejoined him; as I approached he was just closing his sketch-book and slipping his pencil into its case.

"I thank you so very much," he said. "I have just been able to get an idea of the design. And the moulded ceiling? I suppose that is in the drawing-room?"

"No," I replied, "you can look into the drawing-room if you like, but I don't think there is anything there to interest you."

And full of my importance as the hostess, I led the way into the drawing-room. He looked all round the room two or three times.

"Plenty to interest any one who is an artist!" he said, pointing to the walls. "Charming pictures!"

"The ceiling of which you have heard so much," said I, "is upstairs in Mrs Brownlow's own sitting-room."

"Oh, ah!" he replied, evidently disappointed, "but of course, in Mrs Brownlow's absence, it is out of the question—"

"Oh no," said I, "if you would like to come up, I am sure she would not mind. It is just on the first landing, opposite the stairs."

So upstairs to grandmamma's sitting-room we went, and he stared at the ceiling with much enthusiasm, and stalked about so as to get a view of the mouldings in every possible position. Like the drawing-room downstairs, this apartment was full of choice and pretty things, and through again was grandmamma's bedroom, containing more valuable things. The door between the one and the other was open, and anybody in the one room could gain an idea of what the other was like.

We did not stay here long; my companion thanked me many times, apologising for the trouble he had given, and I murmured something about one good turn deserving another. Then I let him out by the front door, telling him he might go down the drive if he liked and out by the lodge. Whether he did so or not I cannot tell, for the road made a curve, and he was very soon lost to sight beyond the trees.

By the time he was gone it was nearly the luncheon hour. I had contrived to get through the morning more entertainingly than I could have expected, and I was rather pleased with myself than otherwise. It was strange, I thought, that I should have met my travelling companion again—and so near home—but strange things often *did* happen.

He had hardly been gone half an hour, when I received a telegram from Aunt Rosa, telling me to expect her and my grandmother home again that same day. Like telegrams generally, it was brief, and added no explanation. I had no clue to this sudden change in their plans, but since they *were* coming home that evening I had something to do and think about through the rest of the afternoon.

Late towards evening they arrived, and then I learnt that the reason of the change was my grandmother's health. She had not been so well as usual at Brighton; she had taken a fancy that the air there no longer agreed with her and had suddenly expressed a wish to be taken home, where, if she should become ill, she would at least have all her comforts about her and a doctor she knew to attend her.

I can't say I found her much different to usual. She was tired after her journey, and went to bed at once, but the next day she was downstairs sitting in the velvet arm-chair, and playing with her crochet-needle and magenta wool. In the course of the morning I happened to mention that Herbert was alone at the Red House, his mother and sisters being away. I am not sure that I did not add I had not seen him for two days. Anyhow, she insisted at once that Herbert should be asked to dine and sleep at our house.

"Poor boy!" she exclaimed, "left all alone! I'm so glad you told me, Pussy. The idea of his having his dinner by himself! and spending his evening by himself! Poor Herbert! Write and tell him to come over here."

I did write to him, and he came. He drove over from the Red House about tea-time, and I remember we took a little walk together round the shrubbery. I remember that I had on my scarlet cloak, for it was rather chilly, and he said something about liking the bright colour. I remember, too, that after we had picked some flowers, we strolled through the shrubbery and over the "gorsty piece." The evening shadows were creeping up over the landscape, and a long yellow gleam from a rather stormy sunset lay athwart the middle distance. If I had thought it a fit subject for a sketch on yesterday morning, I thought it doubly so now.

"It *is* a pretty view, certainly," said I. "I almost wonder more people don't come trespassing here to draw it?"

"Do people ever come trespassing here?" asked Herbert.

"Sometimes," said I; "there was a gentleman here yesterday."

"How very unpleasant for you!" said Herbert.

"Oh, not at all," I replied, laughing. "He didn't know he was trespassing, of course; but he was very civil, and wanted to go as soon as he found out his mistake."

"Naturally," Herbert observed, a little drily I thought.

"Oh, but," I continued, "I told him there was no need. I hoped he would finish his sketch, for I was sure grandmamma would wish it."

"Was he a professional artist, do you suppose?" Herbert asked after a pause.

"Oh, no," said I, "he is not a professional, only an amateur."

"It was somebody you knew, then?" he said. Something in his tone annoyed me a little. It seemed to assume that unless I had had an acquaintance with this man I should not, of course, have entered into conversation with him.

"I had met him before," said I. And I said it with a little air as much as to express that it was no business of his whether the man in question was somebody I knew or not.

"What time of day was it?" he asked.

"In the morning."

"Early—quite early, I suppose?"

"No, not so very early; about twelve o'clock, I should think."

"A very odd time for an artist to choose," said Herbert.

"Why?" I asked, not a little puzzled that he should persist in harping on the stranger who had trespassed on our ground. What was it to *him?* Was he jealous that any one should speak to me?

"Because at mid-day the sun is just over one's head," he replied, "and there are no lights or shadows. No true artist would ever choose such a time for making a picture."

"But he was only an amateur," said I.

"Ah—perhaps that might account for it," Herbert replied doubtfully. Then he added, "We always make it a rule never to let trespassers stay on our premises, even though they may only be artists. It is safer, you know."

I laughed outright at him now.

"Why, what *do* you suppose would happen?" I cried. What would he say, I wondered, if he knew that I had allowed this stranger to come up to the house and look at the carved chimney-piece and the moulded ceiling? But for some reason—I know not why exactly—I kept this to myself.

"One never can tell; it is always best to be on the safe side," he answered very quietly, very gently and courteously, in fact, as he always did; nevertheless, I fancied that my flippant laughter at what he had said pained him somewhat. We did not say much more after this, and presently we regained the house.

We parted in the hall, and I went upstairs to sit awhile with grandmamma in her sitting-room, as I usually did before dinner. She was lying on the sofa, and I took off my red cloak, flung it on a chair, and sat down by her side on a low stool. Presently she began to talk about Herbert.

"I'm so glad we asked him to come over this evening," she said, "he always seems so happy to be here."

"Yes, Granny," said I, demurely, "he is very fond of you."

"And of some one else too, I suspect," said grandmamma, patting my cheek. "Don't you think you could care for him a little bit in return, Pussy?"

I don't think that at that moment I realised how far I *did* care for Herbert. So long as I could have him coming to see me continually, so long as I could know for certain how he followed me, and watched me, and waited for my words, and cared greatly whether I was kind or cold, I did not want to ask more or to seek further.

"I like Herbert, Granny," said I, much in the same tone as I might have said I "liked dancing," or I "liked sweetmeats," and not so enthusiastically perhaps. It needed something beyond the happy, placid, untried life I was then leading to show me whether I *loved* or not!

"I'm glad of that, Pussy," said my grandmother, "and if in time you could learn to give him more than mere *liking*, my dear, it would please your poor old granny very much."

"Would it really, Granny?" I said. And in a lazy kind of a way, provided she did not demand too much of me, I felt as if I should like to please her.

So we talked on a little longer about Herbert, about his position and his profession, about his mother and his sisters, till it seemed to me that I had suddenly acquired a new importance in my own eyes. From what grandmamma told me it was clear I could have Herbert at my feet by the mere stretching out of a finger. Well, I would think about it, I thought, and perhaps one of these days I might stretch out the finger. It would be rather amusing to send a letter home to my unsuspecting family, with the announcement that I was engaged to be married!

Full of these ideas, I went away to dress for dinner, quite forgetting to take my red cloak with me. When I got upstairs to my own room, I recollected where I had left it; but it would be all right there, I knew. I often left my things in grandmamma's sitting-room, and she was much too indulgent and good-natured ever to rebuke me for untidiness or forgetfulness.

When I met Herbert again at dinner, any slight feeling of pain which my laughing at him might have caused had passed away. He was cheerful and chatty as usual, very attentive to grandmamma, scrupulously courteous to Aunt Rosa, and something more than either to me.

By degrees his conversation took a turn which startled me. He began talking of one or two extraordinary trials which had lately been held, and from these he went on to relate certain well-known experiences in housebreaking. He described the tricks and dodges of the "swell mob," as they had been revealed by the evidence in these trials, how they imposed on unsuspecting persons, and took in even those who ought to have been on their guard. I was a good deal interested and amused by what he told us, much as I should have been had I been reading some exciting story of adventures and perils and escapes. All of a sudden, however, I felt myself turning hot and cold, and an uneasy sensation seemed to creep all over me from head to foot.

"I'm told there is a gang of these sort of people going about this part of the country," Herbert was saying, "and that they've all sorts of ingenious dodges for getting a look at the insides of houses. So if any strangers come to the house, Mrs Brownlow, I should advise you to caution the servants how they let them in, or leave them alone."

Not one word did he mention of the artist whom I had found sketching just outside the shrubbery, not once did he even look significantly at me. Yet, with the best intentions of sparing me any annoyance, he had contrived to make me far more uncomfortable than if he had openly taxed me with imprudence!

Grandmamma was not easily alarmed by reports; she could not be wrought up to the point of making herself miserable over what after all only *might* happen.

"Fear," she would say, "spoils one's digestion and deprives one of sleep."

So she chuckled over Herbert's stories of accomplice butlers and bamboozled parlour-maids, and treated them just as stories—nothing more. Aunt Rosa, on the other hand, was bristling with belief in the gang all at once, devising busy schemes for baffling rogues and making safety safer. She was for having a policeman to patrol the garden, she was for moving all the plate from the pantry to a cupboard at the top of the house, she was for displacing everybody and everything, so that the robbers might find nothing as they had been led to expect it.

"Indeed, Mamma dear, I think you had better sleep in the blue-room for a night or two, just till the panic has subsided, you know. They'd be sure to go straight to your room, and it would be enough to give you a fit, it would indeed!"

"Thank you, dear Rosa," said grandmamma, in her usual placid way, "but the blue-room hasn't had a fire in it for three weeks, and it looks to the north. If I am to have a fit, I'd rather have it in a bed I'm accustomed to, thank you."

Perhaps, if grandmamma had not treated the whole matter as a jest, and if Aunt Rosa had not taken it up with such intense seriousness, I might have found courage to relate the little episode of my meeting with my former travelling companion, to confess that I had shown him over part of the house, and to ask if they supposed *he* could possibly prove to be one of the gang. But I felt grandmamma would laugh at me, and that I should only have Aunt Rosa to back me up, with whose fears I had no sympathy. So I held my peace, and joined in the laugh against Aunt Rosa. Even Herbert was laughing now.

"Oh, your servants have been with you a long while, haven't they?" he said, "and they are trustworthy probably. These sort of things only happen when some one inside is an accomplice, or has been hoodwinked."

He could not have meant this remark to apply to me, I knew, for he was ignorant of the extent to which I had carried heedlessness; he only thought I had allowed a stranger to trespass on the "gorsty piece." Nevertheless, the word *hoodwinked* distressed me somewhat. Could that quiet, gentlemanlike, artistic person have been one of a gang? Could—oh, *could* he, with his polite manners and his ready help, have actually picked my pocket himself? *Impossible*, was the reply I returned. Burglars and pickpockets were low ruffians, of course. What had *they* to do with travelling first-class, and making water-colour sketches, and raving about oak carving and moulded ceilings? Besides, had not my travelling acquaintance been an intimate friend of old Colonel Malpas? My fears were quieted, and my conscience went to sleep at once.

Well, the evening passed pleasantly enough, and we talked no more of burglars. Herbert and I had some music together, and at half-past ten we all went to bed as usual. My head had hardly been on the pillow five minutes before I was fast asleep.

From this heavy sleep, the sound sleep of a young thing in perfect health, I was suddenly awakened by a long, loud scream. I started up in bed, and almost simultaneously with the scream a bell pealed violently. It was the bell of my grandmother's room, which was situated just below mine! In another moment I had sprung out of bed, and had hurried on to the staircase.

Then I was aware of two figures—two men, rushing frantically down the passage which led past my grandmother's room to the back stairs. There was not much light except from the candle which I held in my hand, but I could see sufficiently to be sure that the hindermost of the two was my travelling companion!

As I was hurrying down the stairs, Herbert dashed past me along the passage, calling out as he went, so as to wake the butler, who slept below. I heard his steps follow those of the burglars, I heard him go through the conservatory and out into the garden, as I rushed on into grandmamma's sitting-room. On the threshold I caught my foot in something which nearly gave me a fall. Stooping down to disentangle myself, I saw it was my own scarlet cloak. I hastily threw it on one side, and ran into the next room.

There I found Aunt Rosa. She alone amongst us had not allowed her fears or her watchfulness to slumber.

My grandmother was sitting up in bed, clutching convulsively at the coverlet, and staring about her with terror-stricken eyes. She was changed as I had never seen her before. Plump and placid as she usually looked, her face seemed now to have suddenly become thin and pinched and drawn. She kept repeating something over and over again, and as I drew nearer I heard her say—

"I thought it was Pussy! I thought it was Pussy!"

"Oh, Aunt Rosa!" I exclaimed, "what has happened?"

"Just what I knew *would* happen," said Aunt Rosa grimly. "Don't stand there gaping, all of you!" she added, turning to a flock of frightened servants who came crowding into the room. "Somebody go for the doctor."

Then she turned again to grandmamma, who was still murmuring—

"I thought it was Pussy! I thought it was Pussy!"

"You must have been dreaming, dear," said Aunt Rosa, soothingly. "You've not been sleeping so well lately, you know, and it must have been all a dream. Why, see, here is Pussy."

"Yes, Granny," said I, "here I am. Did you dream I was in your room? Why, I've been in bed and fast asleep."

"But the scarlet cloak! the scarlet cloak!" she repeated, beating the counterpane with her trembling hands, "and the dreadful face under the hood—the dreadful face—the face of a murderer—the face of a murderer!"

Aunt Rosa looked at me, and I looked at her. She had begun by fearing that grandmamma's mind *had* been unhinged by fright, but it now suddenly struck us both that, terrified though she was, she was trying to tell us what really had occurred.

"I left my cloak in the sitting-room," I said to Aunt Rosa.

"Pussy's cloak—Pussy's cloak," my grandmother repeated, "I saw it in there, and I thought it was Pussy moving about. I had been asleep; and then it came in here, it went up to the table, to my watch and rings; and I saw the face under the hood—the dreadful face—the face of a murderer!" She sank back on her pillow, repeating the last words over and over again.

"Go for the doctor, somebody," said Aunt Rosa again; but nobody would move, they all seemed too terrified to understand, and stood as if fascinated by the sad sight before them, whispering and chattering the while. "Go and chatter somewhere else," said Aunt Rosa, losing patience. "Where's Mr Herbert? He's the only person with any sense."

Curiously enough in our anxiety about grandmamma's condition, we had almost forgotten the burglars, but just as Aunt Rosa asked the question, "Where's Mr Herbert?" a sound reached our ears which made our hearts stand still, and our blood run cold! It was a pistol shot. Sharp, short, clear, it rang out into the silent night, from the lower end of the garden it seemed to come right up to the window-bars. Nothing followed, at least, nothing that we could hear—no shout, no cry for help, no shot fired in return.

I rushed into the next room and flung the window open. All was perfectly still, a beautiful starlight night, with the moon well up in the heavens. I remember it now more distinctly than any night in my whole life, the intense stillness in earth and sky, save for the echo of that one awful sound that had hardly yet died away.

I felt Aunt Rosa's hand laid on my shoulder, and heard her say, "What can it be?"

I turned towards her with a wild, despairing look.

"Oh, Aunt Rosa!" I cried, "he went after them—I saw him—I heard him go down the stairs into the garden. There were two men; they must have shot at him. Oh! do you think they can have killed him? There is no sound. Don't you hear it's all still. Oh, Aunt Rosa!"

I hardly knew what I was saying, but Aunt Rosa's calm, decided manner quieted me and helped me somewhat.

"I will go down and see what has happened," she said. "You stay here and attend to your grandmother, and get some of these gaping idiots to go for the doctor if you can. Try to be of some use, Pussy; I shall not be longer than I can help."

Even at this terrible moment I could not help being struck by the change in Aunt Rosa's manner. All its small needless fussiness had vanished, and her real strength, good sense, and energy, which were wasted every day in meaningless endeavour, rose to the occasion now. I have seen her since active over nothing and busy about trifles, but I have never forgotten her self-possession and courage, and the confidence she inspired at a moment when these were so sorely needed.

I felt just then as if I would gladly be of some use, so I went at once, as she bade me, back to my grandmother's room. Aunt Rosa had sat up all night, convinced when we all went to bed that something was about to happen, so she was dressed for an emergency, and a few minutes later I heard her go down the stairs and hurry across the garden, from whence the sound of the shot had come. Then I remember, after having persuaded one of the servants to go for the doctor, sitting by my grandmother's bedside, and marvelling at Aunt Rosa's courage.

It was not much that I could do for grandmamma; but she had grown somewhat calmer, and lay back on her pillow quite still. I put my hand into hers, which was very cold, and she seemed to like my grasp, clinging to it as if she found strength and protection therein. So she lay, and so I sat, wondering when the doctor would come, and when Aunt Rosa would return to tell me if Herbert were still alive.

Then it was I knew how I loved him, *then* it was I realised how desolate would be my life, how terrible would be the blank, if Herbert really was dead! I never asked myself what it was I should miss, or why I should miss him; but I knew that, with Herbert dead, life could never again be to me what it had been. It was as much as I could do to keep myself from bursting into sobs, and it was only for fear of alarming my grandmother that I restrained myself.

Then it was, too, sitting in that half-darkened room with my grandmother stricken I knew not how sorely, and Aunt Rosa gone out to face I knew not what awful catastrophe, I realised how the blame of it all lay primarily at my door. *I* it was who had heedlessly introduced the plausible stranger into the house. *I* it was who had blindly allowed him to make a plan of the rooms under pretence of sketching the oak. Without me he would have known nothing of the entrance through the conservatory, of the passage and the back staircase, nothing of grandmamma's sitting-room, and her bed-room opening out of it. If only I had attended to my mother's advice to be cautious how I got into conversation with strangers! If only I had taken my brother's words to heart, about stopping to think of *consequences* before I spoke or rushed into doing things! Now that it was too late I could see it all so clearly!

"Little things don't have consequences," I had flippantly said to my brother, and nothing but a lesson, sharp and hard as the one I learnt that terrible night, could have taught me that the littlest things may be fraught with the biggest consequences.

I do not know how long I sat in the stillness and the half-darkness, praying frightened prayers that grandmamma and Herbert might be saved, and breathing vehement resolves never again to be so deaf to all kind advice, so obstinate in my own heedlessness; probably the time seemed longer than it actually was, but the first sound that at last broke the silence was the sound of footsteps crunching the gravel of the garden-paths out in the garden below the window. It seemed to me that there were several feet tramping by. Something told me it was Herbert being brought home, and a shiver shook my whole frame, as with a beating heart I waited to know if they brought a corpse!

I heard them come up the back stairs, and through the door, and along the passage, two men treading heavily, as between a burden, and a lighter footstep following, which I recognised as Aunt Rosa's. I heard her in a low tone indicate the room Herbert had been occupying that night, and the men and their burden passed on there. Grandmamma was holding my hand so tight, clinging to it with nervous shakings as she heard the approach of strange steps, that I could not withdraw it to make my escape for a moment. I still had to sit and wait.

Before long, however, I heard Aunt Rosa in the passage; then followed whisperings and hurryings to and fro. The servants, who had partially recovered their presence of mind, were being sent hither and thither. This gave me a little hope. All was not over with Herbert; there was at least something to be done.

Presently I heard Aunt Rosa calling me from the next room; I gently extricated my hand from grandmamma's grasp, which had loosened its frightened pressure on hearing Aunt Rosa's voice, and hurried to hear what had happened. I could not speak, but I think my wild eyes must have told what I dreaded plainly enough. Oh! the relief it was to hear the tone in which Aunt Rosa spoke!

"It's a bad enough business, but it might have been much worse," she said; "he has been shot in the leg, poor fellow. The wretches were evidently afraid of being identified, for he got very near to them, so the hinder one pulled out a pistol and let fly."

I hardly heard Aunt Rosa's last words in the revulsion of thankfulness that Herbert had only been "shot in the leg." He would not die of *that*. He would suffer, and I should never forgive myself for having been the cause of his suffering; but in time he would recover, and all would be as it had been before!

"Have you sent for the doctor?" asked Aunt Rosa.

"Oh, yes, ever so long ago," I replied. "He ought to be here soon."

"That's right," said Aunt Rosa, and then she went back to grandmamma. She did not tell me what further I could do to be of use; but I felt that the place at grandmamma's bedside was no longer mine to fill. And now, after the long restraint I had put upon my feelings, the reaction set in, and I began to cry. I could not go back to bed, and I did not know what to do, so I sat where Aunt Rosa had left me, sobbing quietly and longing for the doctor to come.

At last he came, and even then I had to wait. I heard him come, I heard his voice, and I heard his step, but I was shut out from the rooms where he was interviewing the two victims of this night's housebreaking. I questioned the servants, but they only answered out of their own terrified imaginations. I could not catch Aunt Rosa, for she was hurrying from one patient to the other, and when she was not moving about, she was giving orders. At last I determined to waylay the doctor, and I did. He was a kindly man, and looked on my misery with pity.

"A nasty case—a nasty case," he said, "but no serious danger to the young gentleman—luckily the villain aimed so low."

"And my grandmother?" I asked breathlessly.

"Ah! Mrs Brownlow's case is the more anxious one of the two, from her advanced age, you see—great shock to the nervous system; but still, I have hopes that she may get over it."

So it was as bad as that! He only had "hopes" that she might get over it. My poor old granny might die,—that might be the outcome of my silly, heedless conduct! As I thought on this my sobs burst forth again.

"Come, come," said the doctor, kindly, "there's every reason to hope for the best; everything is in her favour, all her home comforts about her, and such an excellent nurse as Miss Brownlow. Quiet is the *great* thing—no disturbance, no excitement of any kind, nothing to *distress* her, you know. By the way," he added suddenly, as if with the view of distracting my thoughts a moment, "do you happen to know if the rascals succeeded in taking anything?"

"I hardly know," I replied; "I've not had time to think."

Strangely enough I had been so occupied with my fears for my grandmother and Herbert, so miserable at the thought of the lives and the love that haply might be lost to me, that I had hardly paused to reflect on the lesser loss, the loss of property, which was at the bottom of the whole catastrophe.

"Ah, well," said the doctor, "it would be as well to find out as soon as possible, and let the police know. They're on the track already, I hope, and a man can identify a thief just as well with a broken leg as with a sound one, you know."

The doctor's words put new energy into me. I was satisfied that nothing very serious had happened to Herbert. I was content to leave grandmamma to Aunt Rosa's good nursing, taking care to put a restraint on my own feelings, so as to avoid alarming or distressing the invalid unnecessarily. But from that moment I resolved that it should be *my* business to collect every scrap of evidence I could against the burglars, more particularly against the one who had once been my travelling companion. I felt almost fierce as I made this resolve. After all, he, and he only, was the real cause of my grandmother's illness and Herbert's wound. If she died, or if he was lamed for life, the wrong would lie at that man's door. I had been thoughtless and imprudent and unsuspecting, no doubt, but he had traded on my thoughtlessness and had taken advantage of my innocence. He was a thief, he was all but a murderer, he was a liar and a hypocritical villain! If I could bring him to justice I would, and not for this night's work only, but for my stolen purse three months ago. For that he *had* stolen it I was now unalterably convinced, my conviction being all the stronger that I had hitherto been so slow to open my eyes. People will more readily forgive a direct injury than they will forgive being hoodwinked and deceived and bamboozled; and what lent such a very decided fierceness to my feelings against this man was, not only that he had tried to steal, and done his best to take life, but that he had made a tool of *me*, that he had inspired *me* with confidence and belief in his perfect honesty, that he had contrived out of my very simplicity to make *me* the accomplice of his crimes!

Supposing my evidence should bring him to trial, what sort of a figure should I cut in a court of justice? He might be convicted and get penal servitude for life, and I hoped he would; but everybody would be calling me a little goose and a simpleton for my pains.

Was I perfectly certain, you ask, that the one of the two men who had rushed past me down the passage was the same whom two days before I had let into the house to look at the carving? Oh, yes, perfectly certain. Even in that instant's sight of him, I had recognised the small, slight figure, the colourless hair and eyebrows, the peculiar expression of the half-closed eyes. I should have known that man in ten thousand, his face had stamped itself in my memory with an impress never to be effaced.

So with my new resolve fresh and strong within me, I went back to the sitting-room and carefully searched for any missing property. The first thing I noticed was that the lock of a small cabinet had been picked, and two diamond snuff-boxes and some other valuable curiosities had been abstracted; but Aunt Rosa's sudden and unexpected appearance on the scene had evidently prevented the robbers from taking more. I searched and searched, but nothing further was missing, except my grandmother's gold watch and chain, and the valuable rings she always wore, and which she had left on her dressing-table when she went to bed, where they had been seized by the more audacious of the two men, who, enveloped in my scarlet cloak, had actually penetrated into the room where grandmamma was asleep.

I think I was rather surprised not to find the robbery had been on a more extensive scale, though there was no doubt much more of value in the shape of snuff-boxes, coins, cameos, etc., would have been taken but for grandmamma's scream and Aunt Rosa's appearance. When, however, I had quite satisfied myself on this point, I went downstairs to examine exactly how the burglars had entered the house. It was very simple, almost ridiculously so. The glass door of the conservatory, which opened into the garden, and which was always locked at night, had had a pane taken out. Once inside the conservatory, the rest was easy enough, for the door out of there into the passage was not locked. I believe no one had ever thought of locking it, or at any rate of inquiring whether it were usually locked or not. Furthermore, I reflected with compunction that one of these burglars knew only too well that this particular passage communicated with the back stairs and opened into the hall.

There was no doubt that the robbery had been systematically planned by the gang of which Herbert had spoken, and planned for this particular night, when it was believed that both my grandmother and Aunt Rosa were away in Brighton. Whether the gang was apprised of their return three or four days sooner than they were expected, but having laid its plans, was determined to commit the burglary at all risks, or whether the discovery of grandmamma's presence in her bed was only made at the time of the robbery itself was never completely cleared up. One thing, however, was pretty evident, both from grandmamma's persistent account of what she saw, and from the position in which I found my scarlet cloak: one of the robbers (probably the one who remembered to have seen me wearing that cloak in the train) had slipped it on and drawn the hood over his head, the better to delude my grandmother as to the real person moving about her room. And the audacious dodge seemed to have succeeded admirably, until, having penetrated into the bedroom, the man incautiously allowed too much of his face under the hood to be seen!

Well, we never got the snuff-boxes back again; or the watch, or the rings; they had been passed on to others in the gang, no doubt, without delay, and changed beyond all recognition. The robbers, however, *were* taken, you will be glad to hear; and there was a long trial at the next assizes, which caused a good deal of interest, for the case had been rendered additionally exciting by the attempt on Herbert's life. I had to appear in court, of course, an ordeal to which I sincerely hope I may never be subjected again, and had to bear witness to my own simplicity and thoughtlessness, and to hear some rather unpleasant remarks passed upon my conduct. But at any rate, I as well as Herbert had the satisfaction of identifying one of the prisoners; *he* swore to that being the man who had fired the shot, while *I* swore to his being the same who had rushed past me down the passage, the same whom I had found sketching on the "gorsty piece," the same who had travelled in the railway carriage with me on the day when my pocket was picked. Oh, yes, you may be sure I didn't omit to mention that, and I remember so well as I made the statement there was quite a sensation throughout the court!

It came out in the course of the trial that this man, who had so imposed upon me with his gentlemanlike appearance, his pleasant manners, his agreeable conversation, and his refined tastes, was a well-known leader of a housebreaking gang. He had half-a-dozen different names, and under one or other of them he had come before under the notice of the police. Hitherto, however, he had escaped the punishment of his misdeeds for want of sufficient evidence against him; but his time had come at last, and the shot he had fired at Herbert cost him a sentence of penal servitude for life.

That is the end of my story so far as the robbery is concerned, but that is not quite the end of it so far as it concerns *me* and those who had suffered by my heedless folly.

Between the terrible night and the trial which followed, there was a long and painful period in which my grandmother's life hung on a thread. On her return from Brighton she had not been quite in her usual health, and the violent shock which her nerves had sustained went very near to cost her her life. And the shock was due not so much to the fact that her house had been broken into by thieves, as to the sudden apparition of a man's countenance under the hood which she knew to be mine. This was evident from the manner in which she dwelt upon the incident, hardly opening her lips for days, except to reiterate the same phrases—

"I thought it was Pussy! I thought it was Pussy! The dreadful face under the hood! The face of a murderer! The face of a murderer!"

She made no mention of unexpected footsteps; she never once asked if any of her property had been stolen; she seemed, indeed, hardly to realise that the presence of that man meant robbery; it was connected in her mind, she knew not why, and we never knew exactly why, with an attempt to murder. For my own part, I am inclined to think that when the burglars first effected their entrance, she must have been fast asleep; and that when she *did* awake, the first thing she saw was the figure in the red cloak, which she mistook to be me. And what gave her such a terrible fright was not the suspicion that robbers were stealing her things, but the discovery that the figure in the cloak was not me! Anyhow, for days and weeks she lay prostrated by the shock. Had the doctor not been a clever man, and had Aunt Rosa not proved herself an indefatigable nurse, I doubt if she would ever have recovered. But by degrees, however, she did slowly begin to mend. When she had taken a slight turn for the better, and had asked for me, I was allowed to go into her room for the first time since the night of the catastrophe; and if anything had been needed to make me feel more acutely than I did the full extent of what in my thoughtlessness I had wrought, it was the sight of my poor old granny lying helpless and listless, white and aged and shrunken, on the same pillow where I had been so often accustomed to kiss her plump cheeks, and to see her smile at me with her bright eyes. Those cheeks were wasted now, and those eyes dulled, all her comeliness was gone, and from having looked hardly more than middle-aged, she had suddenly withered into an old woman!

I was not allowed to talk to her, and indeed she seemed to have little energy to speak herself, or even to listen. But as on the first night, so now, I sat by her bedside, with my hand inside hers. She seemed to like this, and thus I used to sit for hours.

And in all those hours, you may suppose, I had a little time to think over my past, and make some resolves for a wiser future. So, perhaps, it was just as well I was forced to sit quite still and silent with my grandmother changed and suffering before me. Willingly would I have undertaken any task, if so be I might have raised her up again to her former health. But this was never to be, Margery. True that in time she left her bed, and even came downstairs; true, too, that she lived for twelve years, and was really quite an old woman when she died, but she never was anything but an invalid. A drive in a carriage, or a turn round the garden in a Bath-chair, was the utmost limit of the exercise she took, and that only on fine, warm days. Perhaps you will say that this was as much as any old woman could expect, but if you had known my grandmother as she was up to the time of the night I have been describing, you would understand how it need not have been so. Even the velvet chair fell into disuse, for she almost habitually lay on her sofa.

Nevertheless, it was much to me that she lived, and if I had been the means of bringing her to this, I am at least thankful to think that I had the opportunity of making some amends by the love and the care which I afterwards gave her.

And it was not the least part of what I had to endure as the consequence of my folly, that it was a long time before I might venture to explain it all to grandmamma. In the first recognition of how much I was to blame, and the first flood of my repentance, I felt as if I could have no peace and no comfort until I had confessed the truth. But I had to put up with unrest and remorse for some while. I told my foolish tale to Aunt Rosa, of course, at the first opportunity, but this was not the same thing as telling it to grandmamma.

But one day, at last, when she was strong enough to talk about it, and indeed was beginning to take an interest in the details of the trial that was then about to come on, I told her everything. And when she had heard it all she only laughed; she chuckled over my simplicity with the comfortable chuckle that reminded me of the days of her health.

"Never mind, Pussy," she said, patting my cheek, "it's just what I should have done myself. When I was a girl I believed everybody told the truth, and listened to what every one said."

But the whole thing was too serious for me to treat it as a jest.

"No, Granny," I said vehemently, "you wouldn't have done anything so silly as I did. You might have been taken in, perhaps, and perhaps it was no wonder *I* was; but I shouldn't have ended by being taken in if I hadn't begun by talking—talking to a stranger—just what mother advised me not to do, without thinking twice about it, or troubling about consequences."

But grandmamma *would* persist in laughing about it, perhaps because she really understood how terribly serious those consequences might have been.

"Well, Pussy," she said, "everything that's worth having must be paid for, and there's nothing more valuable in its way than experience, though it almost always costs one dear. You'll never forget to trouble about consequences in the future, I'll undertake to say."

"No, Granny, I hope I shan't," said I. And I verily believe I kept my word; I verily believe that I grew more prone to look before and after even than Aunt Rosa herself.

And Herbert, what of him? He must have got well, you think, as he appeared in court to identify the prisoners. Oh, yes, he got well—well enough for that, at any rate, and as well as he ever would be. But I know a man, Margery, a fine soldier-like fellow, who loved his profession and was getting on in it, who for twenty years has limped on a wooden leg—and that man is Herbert.

That he is hopelessly lame for life was my doing, that his professional prospects were ruined was my doing. Some people, I daresay, imagine he was wounded in war, others have heard something vaguely of the courage he showed face to face with detected burglars, but *I* know that but for the heedless folly of one silly girl, he need never have been exposed to the peril which cost him a limb and his chosen profession!

We guessed nothing of this at first; while my grandmother was lying so ill we had hardly any thoughts but for her. Herbert had been removed to the Red House, and under the care of his mother and sisters we were told that the wound in his leg was progressing satisfactorily. Then one day a change was spoken of, and then came the terrible news that two London surgeons had been in consultation, and that the leg was to be amputated!

I think no part of my misery and remorse was so overwhelming as on hearing this. After the first moment of horrible suspense when Aunt Rosa went out that night to see what had happened to Herbert, I had never thought that anything very dreadful had befallen him. True, it was no thanks to me that he had not been killed, his death lay on my conscience almost the same as if he were actually dead. But at any rate he would live to tell me he forgave, and to assure me all trace of the injury had passed.

And now they told me he would be a cripple for the rest of his days! The loss of a limb was only one degree less terrible than the loss of life. He would carry to his grave the mark of the injury my heedlessness had wrought! He could never forgive me now! He a soldier; he bright and healthy, and fond of active out-door life—oh, it was dreadful!

And I could do nothing—absolutely nothing. I wrote to him, humbly confessing all the truth, as I had confessed it to my grandmother, but the lowliest contrition could not make him whole again, the bitterest tears could not give him back what he had lost. For at seven-and-twenty the loss of a limb implies a great, great deal more than the loss of the limb itself!

I could not even be of use in doing anything to amuse or relieve the tedium of his recovery; I had not even the opportunity of marking my sense of the irreparable injury I had wrought, by dedicating any portion of my time to him, which I would willingly, oh! so willingly, have done. They had removed him from the Red House to London, that he might be under the treatment of the best surgeons, and shortly after we heard that his family did not mean to return to the Red House, but would make their home in London.

And the hopes that had been so bright in his heart, and the dream which my grandmother had cherished—aye, and the love which I now knew I felt—were never, never to find their fulfilment! Never since the day when the surgeon's knife did its fatal work, never again did my name cross Herbert's lips; those about him forbore to mention me when they saw the pain that it gave him, and it was years before I met him again.

Yet it was not that he could not forgive—oh no! he was too good and too generous for that. I know he forgave, for I have it under his own hand in a precious letter which has been in my keeping for twenty years. Nor was it that he was disappointed, and had recalled his love as a thing that was woefully misplaced, though well might he have done so! But he was a cripple, and a cripple, he said, had no right to ask any woman to chain her love by a sofa-side! I do not know if he realised how willingly I would have chained mine by his sofa; but if he did he was far too proud ever to ask me to do it!

So that was the end of it all. Twenty years have come and gone since then, and Herbert is still a lame old bachelor and I am a lonely old maid!

Thus you see it is sometimes possible to be so heedless and silly as to cause the deaths of other people, and that there may be more in the story of Red Riding-Hood than is to be seen at first sight. For though my grandmother and

Herbert neither of them actually died, it was a very near thing with both of them. Ah! you fancy, perhaps, as I did, that little things have no consequences. Never think it! The slightest word has an echo far beyond what you can hear; the smallest deed casts a shadow broader than you can see.

And of all sad words, none so sad as the wail, Too late! Of all bitter memories, none so bitter as the thought, It never need have been!

14

ANDREW LANG

The Princess Nobody
(1884)

NDREW LANG (1844–1912) was born in Selkirk, Scotland. After attending school in Edinburgh, he went to Oxford and intended to pursue an academic career. However, due to a serious lung problem, he had to spend winters in the south of France and began writing reviews for a literary journal. During the early 1870s he decided to become a free-lance writer and journalist and set up home in London. In 1875 he married Leonore Blanche Alleyne and established his residence in Kensington, where he lived for the rest of his life.

Lang was one of the most prolific and knowledgeable men of letters of his time. Though he wrote on numerous topics, not merely literature, he became most famous for his studies of myth, folk tales, and fairy tales. He was one of the chief proponents of the anthropological school, and he argued that folk tales were the link between literature and anthropology. They provided the documentary evidence of customs and their evolution. In 1889, with the help of his wife, he began publishing the color Fairy Books, a mixture of literary fairy tales and folk tales from the oral tradition, selected from Lang's vast international collection. Lang never thought highly of this series since he was mainly interested in the oral folk tale and scholarly work on the connection between anthropology and literature. However the series, beginning with *The Blue Fairy Book* in 1889 and ending with *The Lilac Fairy Book* in 1910, was a huge success. There were twelve fairy books in all and thirteen others including animal stories, *The Arabian Nights*, and *The Story of King Arthur and his Knights*. Steeped in folklore and the literary tradition, Lang himself wrote four interesting fairy tales for children: *The Princess Nobody* (1884), *The Gold of Fairnilee* (1888), *Prince Prigio* (1889), and *Prince Ricardo of Pantouflia* (1893). About his own work, Lang commented in the preface to *The Lilac Fairy Book*:

> They are rich in romantic adventure, and the Princes always marry the right Princesses and live happily ever afterwards; while the wicked witches, stepmothers, tutors and governesses are *never* cruelly punished, but retire to the country on ample pensions. I hate cruelty; I never put a wicked

grandmother in a barrel and send her tobogganing down a hill. It is true that Prince Ricardo *did* kill the Yellow Dwarf; but that was in fair fight, sword in hand, and the dwarf, peace to his ashes! *died in harness.*

Lang was not an innovative writer. His contribution to folklore and literature lies in his ability to preserve the traditional aspect and optimism of the folk tradition in literary texts. *The Princess Nobody* (originally published with illustrations by Richard Doyle) demonstrates Lang's ability to synthesize folk motifs gracefully within a literary tradition and to develop an intriguing plot to amuse young readers. The first edition included at the end of the tale the following poem by William Allingham which captures Lang's own sentiments.

> ERANT OLIM REX QUIDAM ET REGINA
> *Apuleius*

> *Au Temps jadis*! as Perrault says,
> In half-forgotten Fairy days,—
> "There lived a King once, and a Queen,
> As few there are, as more have been,"—
> Ah, still we love the well-worn phrase,
> Still love to tread the ancient ways,
> To break the fence, to thread the maze,
> To see the beauty we have seen,
>
> > *Au Temps jadis*!

> Here's luck to every child that strays
> In Fairy Land among the Fays;
> That follows through the forest green
> Prince Comical and Gwendoline;
> That reads the tales we used to praise,
>
> > *Au Temps jadis*!

THE PRINCESS NOBODY

The Princess Nobody

 NCE UPON A TIME, when fairies were much more common than they are now, there lived a king and a queen. Their country was close to Fairyland, and very often the little elves would cross over the border, and come into the King's fields and gardens. The girl-fairies would swing out of the bells of the fuchsias, and loll on the leaves, and drink the little drops of dew that fell down the stems.

Now the King and Queen of the country next to Fairyland were very rich, and very fond of each other; but one thing made them unhappy. They had no child, neither boy nor girl, to sit on the throne when they were dead and gone. Often the Queen said she wished she had a child, even if it were no bigger than her thumb; and she hoped the fairies might hear her and help her. But they never took any notice. One day, when the King had been counting out his money all day (the day when the tributes were paid in), he grew very tired. He took off his crown and went into his garden. Then he looked all round his kingdom and said: "Ah, I would give it all for a BABY!"

No sooner had the King said this, than he heard a little squeaking voice near his foot: "You shall have a lovely baby if you will give me what I ask."

The King looked down, and there was the funniest little dwarf that ever was seen. He had a high red cap like a flower. He had a big moustache, and a short beard that curled outwards. His cloak was red, like his cap, and his coat was green, and he rode on a green frog. Many people would have been frightened, but the King was used to fairies.

"You shall have a beautiful baby, if you will give me what I ask," said the dwarf again.

"I'll give you anything you like," said the King.

"Then promise to give me NIENTE," said the dwarf.

"Certainly," said the King (who had not an idea what NIENTE meant). "How will you take it?"

"I will take *it*," said the dwarf, "in my own way, on my own day."

With that he set spurs to his frog, which cleared the garden path at one bound, and he was soon lost among the flowers.

Well, next day, a dreadful war broke out between the ghosts and the giants, and the King had to set forth and fight on the side of his friends the giants.

A long, long time he was away; nearly a year. At last he came back to his own country, and he heard all the church bells ringing merrily. "What *can* be the matter?" said the King, and hurried to his palace, where all the courtiers rushed out and told him the Queen had got a BABY.

"Girl or a boy?" says the King.

"A princess, Your Majesty," says the nurse, with a low curtsy, correcting him.

Well, you may fancy how glad the King was, though he would have *preferred* a boy.

"What have you called her?" he asked.

"Till Your Majesty's return, we thought it better not to christen the Princess," said the nurse, "so we have called her by the Italian name for *Nothing*: NIENTE; the Princess Niente, Your Majesty."

When the King heard *that*, and remembered that he had promised to give NIENTE to the dwarf, he hid his face in his hands and groaned. Nobody knew what he meant, or why he was sad, so he thought it best to keep it to himself. He went in and kissed the Queen, and comforted her, and looked at the BABY. Never was there a BABY so beautiful; she was like a fairy's child, and so light she could sit on a flower and not crush it, and all the birds were fond of her. The peasants and common people (who said they "could not see why the *first* royal baby should be called 'Ninety'") always spoke of her as the Princess Nobody. Only the courtiers called her Niente. The water fairy was her godmother, but (for a fairy reason) they concealed her *real* name and of course she was not *christened* Niente. Great fun she and all her little companions had with the birds. Never was there such a happy country; all birds and babies, playing together, singing, and as merry as the day was long.

Well, this joyful life went on till the Princess Niente was growing quite a big girl; she was nearly fourteen. Then, one day, came a tremendous knock at the palace gates. Out rushed the porter, and saw a little dwarf, in a red cap and a red cloak, riding a green frog.

"Tell the King he is wanted," said the dwarf.

The porter carried this rude message, and the King went trembling to the door.

"I have come to claim your promise; you give me NIENTE," said the dwarf, in his froggy voice.

Now the King had spoken long ago about his foolish promise to the Queen of the Water Fairies, a very powerful person and godmother of his child.

"The dwarf must be one of *my* people if he rides a frog," the Queen of the Water Fairies had said. "Just send him to *me* if he is troublesome."

The King remembered this when he saw the dwarf, so he put a bold face on it.

"That's you, is it?" said the King to the dwarf. "Just you go to the Queen of the Water Fairies; she will have a word to say to you."

When the dwarf heard that, it was *his* turn to tremble. He shook his little fist at the King; he half drew his sword.

"I'll have NIENTE yet," he said, and he set spurs to his frog and bounded off to see the Queen of the Water Fairies.

It was night by the time the dwarf reached the stream where the Queen lived, among the long flags and rushes and reeds of the river.

He and the water fairy had a long talk, and the end of it was that the fairy found only one way of saving the Princess. She flew to the King and said: "I can only help you by making the Princess vanish clean away. I have a bird here on whose back she can fly away in safety. The dwarf will not get her, but you will never see her again, unless a brave prince can find her where she is hidden, and guarded by my water fairies."

Then the poor mother and father cried dreadfully, but they saw there was no hope. It was better that the Princess should vanish away, than that she should be married to a horrid rude dwarf, who rode on a frog. So they sent for the Princess, and kissed her, and embraced her, and wept over her, and gradually she faded out of their very arms and vanished clean away.

CHAPTER TWO

In Mushroom Land

Now all the kingdom next to Fairyland was miserable, and all the people were murmuring, and the King and Queen were nearly melted in tears. They thought of all ways to recover their dear daughter, and at last the Queen hit on a plan.

"My dear," she said to the King, "let us offer to give our daughter for a wife to any prince who will only find her and bring her home."

"Who will want to marry a girl he can't see?" said the King. "If they have not married pretty girls they *can* see, they won't care for poor Niente."

"Never mind; we can only try," said the Queen. So she sent out messengers into all the world, and sent the picture of the Princess everywhere, and proclaimed that the beautiful Princess Niente and no less than three-quarters of the kingdom would be given to the prince that could find the Princess and bring her home. And there was to be a great tournament, or sham fight, at the palace, to amuse all the princes before they went on the search. So many princes gathered together, all full of hope; and they rode against each other with spears and swords, and knocked each other about, and afterwards dined and danced and made merry. Some fairy knights, too, came over the border, and they fought with spears, riding beetles and grasshoppers instead of horses. By all these warlike exercises, they increased their courage till they felt brave enough to fight all the ghosts and all the giants, if only they could save the beautiful Princess.

Well, the tournaments were over, and off all the princes went into Fairyland. What funny sights they saw in Fairyland! They saw a great snail race, the snails running so fast that some of the fairy jockeys fell off on the grass. They saw a fairy boy dancing with a squirrel, and they found all the birds and all the beasts quite friendly and kind, and able to talk like other people. This was the way in old times, but now no beasts talk, and no birds, except parrots only.

Now among all this gallant army of princes, one was ugly, and he looked old and odd, and the rest laughed at him and called him the Prince Comical. But he had a kind heart. One day, when he was out walking alone, and thinking what he could do to find the Princess, he saw three bad little boys teasing a big Daddy-long-legs. They had got hold of one of his legs, and were pulling at it with all their might. When the Prince Comical saw this, he ran up and drove the bad boys away, and rubbed the limb of the Daddy-long-legs, till he gave up groaning and crying. Then the Daddy-long-legs sat up and said in a weak voice: "You have been very kind to me; what can I do for *you?*"

"Oh, help me," said the Prince, "to find the Princess Niente! *You* fly everywhere; don't you know where she is?"

"*I* don't know," said the Daddy-long-legs mournfully. "I have never flown so far. But I know that you are all in a very dangerous part of Fairyland. And I will take you to an aged Black Beetle, who can give you the best advice."

So saying the Daddy-long-legs walked off with the Prince, till they came to the Black Beetle.

"Can *you* tell this prince," said the Daddy-long-legs, "where the Princess Niente is hidden?"

"I know it is in Mushroom Land," said the Beetle; "but he will want a guide."

"Will *you* be my guide?" asked the Prince.

"Yes," said the Beetle; "but what about your friends, the other princes?"

"Oh, they must come too; it would not be fair to leave them behind," said the Prince Comical.

He was *the soul of honour*; and though the others laughed at him, he would not take advantage of his luck and run away from them.

"Well, you *are* a true knight," said the Black Beetle; "but before we go into the depths of Mushroom Land, just you come here with me."

Then the Black Beetle pointed out to the Prince a great, smooth, round, red thing, a long way off.

"That is the first mushroom in Mushroom Land," said the Beetle. "Now come with me, and you shall see what you shall see."

So the Prince followed the Beetle, till they came to the mushroom.

"Climb up and look over," said the Beetle.

So the Prince climbed up and looked over. There he saw a crowned king sound asleep.

"Try to waken him," said the Beetle; "just try."

So the Prince tried to waken the King, but it was of no use.

"Now, take warning by *that*," said the Black Beetle, "and never go to sleep under a mushroom in Mushroom country. You will never wake, if you do, till the Princess Niente is found again."

Well, the Prince Comical said he would remember that, and he and the Beetle went off and found the other princes. They were disposed to laugh at being led by a black beetle; but one of them, who was very learned, reminded them that armies had been led before by woodpeckers and wolves and humming-birds.

So they all moved on, and at night they were very tired.

Now there were no houses, and not many trees, in Mushroom Land, and when night came all the princes wanted to lie down under a very big mushroom.

It was in vain that the Black Beetle and Prince Comical warned them to beware.

"Nonsense," they said. "*You* may sleep out in the open air, if you like; we mean to make ourselves comfortable here."

So they all lay down under the shelter of the mushroom, and Prince Comical slept in the open air. In the morning he wakened, feeling very well and hungry, and off he set to call his friends. But he might as well have called the mushroom itself. There they all lay under its shade; and though some of them had their eyes open, not one of them could move. The Prince shook them, dragged them, shouted at them, and pulled their hair. But the more he shouted and dragged the louder they snored; and the worst of it was that he could not pull them out of the shadow of the magic mushroom. So there he had to leave them, sound asleep.

The Prince thought the elves could help him perhaps, so he went and asked them how to waken his friends. They were all awake, and the fairies were dressing the baby elves. But they only said: "Oh, it's their fault for sleeping under a mushroom! Anybody would know that is a stupid thing to do. Besides, we have no time to attend to them, as the sun will be up soon, and we must get these babies dressed and be off before then."

"Why, where are you going to?" said the Prince.

"Ah, nobody knows where we go to in the day-time!" said the elves.

And nobody does.

"Well, what am I to do now?" said the Prince to the Black Beetle.

"*I* don't know where the Princess is," said the Beetle; "but the Blue Bird is very wise, and *he* may know. Now your best plan will be to steal two of the Blue Bird's eggs, and not give them back till he tells you all he can."

So off they set for Blue Bird's nest; and, to make a long story short, the Prince stole two of the eggs, and would not give them back till the bird promised to tell him all it knew. And the end of it was that the bird carried him to the court of the Queen of Mushroom Land. She was sitting, in her crown, on a mushroom, and she looked very funny and mischievous.

The Prince, with his hat off, kissed the Queen's hair and asked for the Princess.

"Oh, *she*'s quite safe," said the Queen of Mushroom Land; "but what a funny boy you are. You are not *half* handsome enough for the Princess Niente."

The poor Prince blushed. "They call me Prince Comical," said he; "I know I'm not half good enough!"

"You are *good* enough for anything," said the Queen of Mushroom Land; "but you might be prettier."

Then she touched him with her wand, and he became as handsome a prince as ever was seen, in a beautiful red silk doublet, slashed with white, and a long gold-coloured robe.

"*Now* you will do for my Princess Niente," said the Queen of Mushroom Land. "Blue Bird"—and she whispered in the bird's ear—"take him away to the Princess Niente."

So they flew and they flew, all day and all night, and next day they came to a green bower, all full of fairies and butterflies and funny little people. And there, with all her long yellow hair, there sat the Princess Niente. And the Prince Charming laid his crown at her feet, and knelt on one knee, and asked the Princess to be his love and his lady. And she did not refuse him, so they were married in the Church of the Elves, and the glow-worm sent his torches, and all the bells of all the flowers made a merry peal. And soon they were to travel home to the King and the Queen.

CHAPTER THREE

Lost and Found

Now the Prince had found the Princess, and you might think that they had nothing to do but go home again. The father and mother of the Princess were wearying very much to hear about her. Every day they climbed to the bartizan of the castle, and looked across the plain, hoping to see dust on the road, and some brave prince riding back with their daugher. But she never came, and their hair grew grey with sorrow and time. The parents of the other princes, too, who were all asleep under the mushroom, were alarmed about their sons, and feared that they had all been taken prisoners, or perhaps eaten up by some giant. But Princess Niente and Prince Charming were lingering in the enchanted land, too happy to leave the flowers, the brooks and the fairies.

The faithful Black Beetle often whispered to the Prince that it was time to turn homewards, but the Prince paid no more attention to his ally than if he had been an earwig. So there, in the Valley Magical, the Prince and Princess might be wandering to this day but for a very sad accident. The night they were married, the Princess had said to the Prince: "Now you may call me Niente, or any pet name you like; but never call me by my own name."

"But I don't know it," said the Prince. "Do tell me what it is?"

"Never," said the Princess; "you must never seek to know it."

"Why not?" said the Prince.

"Something dreadful will happen," said the Princess, "if ever you find out my name and call me by it."

And she looked quite as if she could be very angry.

Now ever after this the Prince kept wondering what his wife's real name could be, till he made himself quite unhappy.

"Is it Margaret?" he would say, when he thought the Princess was off her guard; or, "Is is Joan?" "Is it Dorothy?" "It can't be Sybil, can it?"

But she would never tell him.

Now, one morning, the Princess awoke very early, but she felt so happy that she could not sleep. She lay awake and listened to the birds singing, and then she watched a fairy-boy teasing a bird, which sang (so the boy said) out of tune, and another fairy-baby riding on a fly.

At last the Princess, who thought the Prince was sound asleep, began to croon softly a little song she had made about him and her. She had never told him about the song, partly because she was shy and partly for another reason. So she crooned and hummed to herself:

> "Oh, hand in hand with Gwendoline,
> While yet our locks are gold,

> He'll fare among the forests green,
> And through the gardens old;
> And when, like leaves that lose their green,
> Our gold has turned to grey,
> Then, hand in hand with Gwendoline,
> He'll fade and pass away!"

"Oh, *Gwendoline* is your name, is it?" said the Prince, who had been wide awake and listening to her song. And he began to laugh at having found out her secret and tried to kiss her.

But the Princess turned very, very cold and white like marble, so that the Prince began to shiver, and he sat down on a fallen mushroom and hid his face in his hands; and in a moment all his beautiful hair vanished, and his splendid clothes, and his gold train, and his crown. He wore a red cap and common clothes, and was Prince Comical once more. But the Princess arose and she vanished swiftly away.

Thus he was punished for being curious and prying. It is natural, you will say, that a man should like to call his wife by her name. But the fairies would not allow it, and, what is more, there are still some nations who will not allow a woman to mention the name of her husband.

Well, here was a sad state of things! The Princess was lost as much as ever, and Prince Charming was changed back into Prince Comical. The Black Beetle sighed day and night, and mingled his tears with those of the Prince. But neither of them knew what to do. They wandered about the Valley Magical, and though it was just as pretty as ever, it seemed quite ugly and stupid to them. The worst of it was that the Prince felt so foolish. After winning the greatest good fortune, and the dearest bride in the world, he had thrown everything away. He walked about crying, "Oh, Gwen—I mean oh, Niente! dear Niente! return to your own Prince Comical, and all will be forgiven!"

It is impossible to say what would have happened; and probably the Prince would have died of sorrow and hunger (for he ate nothing), if the Black Beetle had not one day met a bat, which was the favourite charger of Puck. Now Puck, as all the world knows, is the Jester at the court of Fairyland. He can make Oberon and Titania—the King and Queen—laugh at the tricks he plays, and therefore they love him so much that there is nothing they would not do for him. So the Black Beetle began to talk about his master, the Prince, to the bat Puck commonly rode; and the bat, a good-natured creature, told the story to Puck. Now Puck was also in a good humour, so he jumped at once on his bat's back, and rode off to consult the King and Queen of Fairyland. Well, they were sorry for the Prince—he had only broken one little fairy law after all—and they sent Puck back to tell him what he was to do. This was to find the Blue Bird

again, and get the Blue Bird to guide him to the home of the water fairy, the godmother of the Princess.

Long and far the Prince wandered, but at last he found the Blue Bird once more. And the bird (very good-naturedly) promised to fly in front of him till he led him to the beautiful stream, where the water fairy held her court. So they reached it at last, and then the Blue Bird harnessed himself to the chariot of the water fairy, and the chariot was the white cup of a water-lily. Then he pulled and pulled at the chariot, till he brought her where the Prince was waiting. At first, when she saw him, she was rather angry. "Why did you find out my god-daughter's name?" she said; and the Prince had no excuse to make. He only turned red and sighed. This rather pleased the water fairy.

"Do you love the Princess very much?" said she.

"Oh, more than all the world," said the Prince.

"Then back you go, to Mushroom Land, and you will find her in the old place. But perhaps she will not be pleased to forgive you at first."

The Prince thought he would chance *that*, but he did not say so. He only bowed very low and thanked the water fairy. Then off he set, with the Blue Bird to guide him, in search of Mushroom Land. At long and at last he reached it, and glad he was to see the little sentinel on the border of the country.

All up and down Mushroom Land the Prince searched, and at last he saw his own Princess, and he rushed up and knelt at her feet, and held out his hands to ask pardon for having disobeyed the fairy law.

But she was still rather cross, and down she jumped and ran round the mushroom, and he ran after her.

So he chased her for a minute or two, and at last she laughed and popped up her head over the mushroom, and pursed up her lips into a cherry. And he kissed her across the mushroom, and knew he had won back his own dear Princess, and they felt even happier than if they had never been parted.

"Journeys end in lovers' meeting," and so do stories. The Prince had his Princess once again, and I can tell you they did not wait long this time in the Valley Magical. Off they went straight home, and the Black Beetle guided them flying in a bee-line. Just on the farther border of Mushroom Land they came to all the princes fast asleep. But when the Princess drew near they all wakened and jumped up, and they slapped the fortunate prince on the back and wished him luck, and cried: "Hallo, Comical, old chap; we hardly knew you! Why, you've grown quite handsome!" And so he had; he was changed into Prince Charming again, but he was so happy he never noticed it, for he was not conceited. But the Princess noticed it, and she loved him all the better. Then they all made a procession, with the Black Beetle marching at the head; indeed, they called him "Black Rod" now, and he was quite a courtier.

So with flags flying and music playing they returned to the home of the Princess. And the King and Queen met them at the park gates, and fell on the neck of the Prince and Princess, and kissed them, and laughed, and cried for joy, and kissed them again. You may be sure the old nurse was out among the foremost, her face quite shining with pleasure and using longer words than the noblest there. And she admired the Prince very much, and was delighted that "her girl," as she called the Princess, had got such a good husband. So here we leave them, and that country remained always happy, and so it has neither history nor geography. Therefore you won't find it on any map, nor can you read about it in any book but this book.

15

MARY LOUISA MOLESWORTH

The Story of a King's
Daughter
(1884)

RS MOLESWORTH (née Mary Louisa Stewart, 1839–1921)
received an excellent education from the Reverend
William Gaskell in Manchester, and by the time she was
in her teens, she began submitting short stories to
magazines. However, she never thought of writing as a
career and abandoned her literary pursuits in 1861, when
she married Major Richard Molesworth. She spent the
next decade moving from one army camp to the next while giving birth to seven
children. Upon the death of one of her children, Mrs Molesworth resumed
writing under the pseudonym of Ennis Graham as a means to relieve her
anguish. After publishing a series of undistinguished novels for adults, she
turned her attention to writing for children in 1875 and produced *Tell Me a
Story*, a collection of tales with illustrations by Walter Crane. This work was
soon followed by her two best books *The Cuckoo Clock* (1877) and *The Tapestry
Room* (1879). After the publication of this last fantasy, she separated from her
husband, who had gradually become violent and irrational in his behavior due
to an old head wound, and she moved with her children to Caen, France. From
this point on she divided her time between Caen and Paris and dedicated herself
to her career as professional writer. By 1883 Mrs Molesworth had achieved a
notable reputation in the London literary circles, and two of her best books for
children, *Two Little Waifs* (1883) and *Christmas-Tree Land* (1884) added to her
prominence. It was also at this time that she made London her permanent
home, where she continued writing books primarily for children until her death
in 1921.

An extremely prolific writer—she published approximately 100 books—
Mrs Molesworth tended to moralize and portray the period of childhood as
idyllic. However, her didacticism was never overbearing, and she wrote some
extraordinary visionary novels in the manner of George MacDonald such as
Four Winds Farm (1887) and *The Children of the Castle* (1890) which reveal a
strong utopian impulse and originality. Some of her best fairy tales are
embedded in novels of realism. For instance, "The Goose Girl" is to be found in
Summer Stories (1882), "The Story of a King's Daughter" in *Christmas-Tree Land*

(1884), "The Unselfish Mermaid" in *The Magic Nuts* (1898). These tales were generally intended to add a symbolic dimension to the meaning of the plot. In *Christmas-Tree Land*, Maia and Rollo, two children aged about 10 and 12, have lost their mother, and their father has sent them to a foreign land to be looked after by his cousin, Lady Venelda. The woods surrounding Lady Venelda's castle become their magic realm of freedom where they meet two fairy-like children, Silva and Waldo, and their godmother, a wise, tender, and mysterious woman, who tells them "The Story of a King's Daughter." It is through this fairy tale and the imaginative powers of their godmother that Maia and Rollo receive spiritual guidance and overcome their feelings of loss and alienation. In other works, too, such as *An Enchanted Garden* (1892) and *Fairies Afield* (1911) Mrs Molesworth depicted the escape into fairyland not as a flight from reality but as an effective means to gain distance from disturbing problems. Thus fairyland was the place where cruelty, injustice, and sorrow could be understood and resolved.

THE STORY OF A KING'S
DAUGHTER

Gentle and sweet is she;
As the heart of a rose is her heart,
As soft and as fair and as sweet.

Liliput Lectures

ODMOTHER TURNED TO the little strangers. The two
pairs of blue eyes were still fixed upon her. *Her* eyes looked
very kind and gentle, and yet very "seeing," as she caught
their gaze.

"I believe," thought Maia, "that she can tell all we are
thinking"; and Rollo had something of the same idea, yet
neither of them felt the least afraid of her.

"Rollo and Maia, dear children, too," she said, "we are so pleased to see
you."

"And we are very pleased to be here," said they; "but—" and then they
hesitated.

"You are puzzled how it is I know your names, and all about you, are you
not?" she said, smiling.

"I puzzle most children at first; but isn't it rather nice to be puzzled?"

This was a new idea. Thinking it over, they began to find there was
something in it.

"I think it *is*," both replied, smiling a little.

"If you knew all about everything, and could see through everything, there
wouldn't be much interest left. Nothing to find out or to fancy. Oh, what a dull
world!"

"Are we to find out or to fancy *you*?" asked Maia. She spoke seriously, but
there was a little look of fun in her eyes which was at once reflected in
godmother's.

"Whichever you like," she replied; "but, first of all, you are to kiss me."

Rollo and Maia both kissed the soft white face. It was *so* soft, and there
seemed a sort of fresh, sweet scent about godmother, as if she had been in a room
all filled with violets, only it was even nicer. She smiled, and from a little basket
on her arm, which they had not noticed, she drew out several tiny bunches of
spring flowers, tied with green and white ribbon—so pretty; oh, so very
pretty!

"So you scented my flowers," she said. "No wonder; you have never scented any quite like them before. They come from the other country. Here, dears, catch," and she tossed them up in the air, all four children jumping and darting about to see who would get most. But at the end, when they counted their treasures, it was quite right, each had got three.

"Oh, how sweet!" cried Maia. "May we take them home with us, godmother?" It seemed to come quite naturally to call her that, and Maia did it without thinking.

"Certainly," godmother replied; "but remember this, don't throw them away when they seem withered. They will not be really withered; that is to say, long afterwards, by putting them in the sunshine, they will—some of them, anyway—come out quite fresh again. And even when dried up they will have a delicious scent; indeed, the scent has an added charm about it the older they are—so many think, and I agree with them."

Rollo and Maia looked at their flowers with a sort of awe.

"Then they are *fairy* flowers?" they half whispered. "You said they came from the other country. Do you come from there too, godmother? Are you a fairy?"

Godmother smiled.

"Fancy me one if you like," she said. "Fancy me whatever you like best, you will not be far wrong; but fairyland is only one little part of that other country. You will find that out as you get older."

"Shall we go there some day, then?" exclaimed Maia. "Will you take us, dear godmother? Have Waldo and Silva ever been?"

"Oh, what a lot of questions all at once!" cried godmother. "I can't answer so many. You must be content to find out some things for yourself, my little girl. The way to the other country for one. Shall you go there some day? Yes, indeed, many and many a time, I hope."

Maia clapped her hands with delight.

"Oh, how nice!" she said. "And when? May we go to-day? Oh, Silva, do ask godmother to let us go to-day," she exclaimed, catching hold of Silva in her eagerness. But Silva only smiled, and looked at godmother; and somehow, when they smiled, the two faces—the young one with its bright rich colour, and the old one, white, so white, except for the wonderful, beautiful eyes, that it might have been made of snow—looked strangely alike.

"Silva has learned to be patient," said godmother, "and so she gets to know more and more of the other country. You must follow her example, little Maia. Don't be discouraged. How do you know that you are not already on the way there? What do you think about it, my boy?" she went on, turning to Rollo, who was standing a little behind them listening, but saying nothing.

Rollo looked up and smiled.

"I'd like to find the way myself," he replied.

"That's right," said godmother. And Maia felt more and more puzzled, as it seemed to her that Rollo understood the meaning of godmother's words better than she did.

"Rollo," she exclaimed, half reproachfully.

Rollo turned to her with some surprise.

"You understand and I don't," she said, with a little pout on her pretty lips.

"No," said Rollo, "I don't. But I like to think of understanding some day."

"That is right," said godmother again. "But this is dull talk for you, little people. What is it to be to-day, Silva? What is old godmother to do for you?"

Silva glanced out of the window.

"The day will soon be closing into evening," she said, "and Rollo and Maia cannot stay after sunset. We have not very long, godmother—no time to go anywhere."

"Ah, I don't know about that," godmother replied. "But still—the first visit. What would you like, then, my child?"

"Let us gather round the fire, for it is a little chilly," said Silva, "and you, dear godmother, will tell us a story."

Maia's eyes and Rollo's, too, brightened at this. Godmother had no need to ask if they would like it. She drew the large chair nearer the fireplace, and the four children clustered round her in silence waiting for her to begin.

"It is too warm with my cloak on," she said, and she raised her hand to unfasten it at the neck and loosen it a little. It did not entirely fall off; the dark green hood still made a shade round her silvery hair and delicate face, but the cloak dropped away enough for Maia's sharp eyes to see that the dress underneath was of lovely crimson stuff, neither velvet nor satin, but richer and softer than either. It glimmered in the light of the fire with a sort of changing brilliance that was very tempting, and it almost seemed to Maia that she caught the sparkle of diamonds and other precious stones.

"May I stroke your pretty dress, godmother?" she said softly. Godmother started; she did not seem to have noticed how much of the crimson was seen, and for a moment Maia felt a little afraid. But then godmother smiled again, and the child felt quite happy, and slipped her hand inside the folds of the cloak till it reached the soft stuff beneath.

"Stroke it the right way," said godmother.

"Oh, *how* soft!" said Maia in delight. "What *is* it made of? It isn't velvet, or even plush. Godmother," she went on, puckering her forehead again in perplexity, "it almost feels like *feathers*. Are you perhaps a *bird* as well as a fairy?"

At this godmother laughed. You never heard anything so pretty as her laugh. It was something like—no, I could never tell you what it was like—a very little like lots of tiny silver bells ringing, and soft breezes blowing, and larks trilling, all together and *very* gently, and yet very clearly. The children could not help all laughing, too, to hear it.

"Call me whatever you like," said godmother. "A bird, or a fairy, or a will-o'-the-wisp, or even a witch. Many people have called me a witch, and I don't mind. Only, dears," and here her pretty, sweet voice grew grave, and even a little sad, "never think of me except as loving you and wanting to make you happy and good. And never believe I have said or done anything to turn you from doing right and helping others to do it. That is the only thing that could grieve him. And the world is full of people who don't see things the right way, and blame others when it is their own fault all the while. So sometimes you will find it all rather difficult. But don't forget."

"No," said Maia, "we won't forget, even though we don't quite understand. We will some day, won't we?"

"Yes, dears, that you will," said godmother.

"And just now," said Silva, " it doesn't matter. We needn't think about the difficult world, dear godmother, while we're *here*—ever so far away from it."

"No, we need not," said godmother, with what sounded almost like a sigh, if one could have believed that godmother *could* sigh! If it were one, it was gone in an instant, and with her very prettiest and happiest smile, godmother turned to the children.

"And now, dears," she said, "now for the story."

The four figures drew still nearer, the four pairs of eyes were fixed on the sweet white face, into which, as she spoke, a little soft pink colour began to come. Whether it was from the reflection of the fire or not, Maia could not decide, and godmother's clear voice went on.

"Once—"

"Once upon a time; do say 'once upon a time,'" interrupted Silva.

"Well, well, once upon a time," repeated godmother, "though, by the by, how do you know I was *not* going to say it? Well, then, once upon a time, a long ago once upon a time, there lived a king's daughter."

"A princess," interrupted another voice, Maia's this time. "Why don't you say a princess, dear godmother?"

"Never mind," replied godmother. "I like better to call her a king's daughter."

"And don't interrupt any more, please," said Waldo and Rollo together, quite forgetting that they were actually interrupting themselves.

"And," continued godmother, without noticing this last interruption, "she was very beautiful and very sweet and good, even though she had everything in the world that even a king's daughter could want. Do you look surprised at my saying 'even though,' children? You need not; there is nothing more difficult than to remain unselfish, which is just another word for 'sweet and good,' if one never knows what it is to have a wish ungratified. But so it was with Auréole, for that was the name of the fair maiden. Though she had all her life been surrounded with luxury and indulgence, though she had never known even a crumpled rose-leaf in her path, her heart still remained tender, and she felt for the sufferings of others whenever she knew of them, as if they were her own.

" 'Who knows?' she would say softly to herself, 'who knows but what some day sorrow may come to me, and then how glad I should be to find kindness and sympathy!'

"And when she thought thus there used to come a look in her eyes which made her old nurse, who loved her dearly, tremble and cross herself.

" 'I have never seen that look,' she would whisper, though not so that Auréole could hear it—'I have never seen that look save in the eyes of those who were born to sorrow.'

"But time went on, and no sorrows of her own had as yet come to Auréole. She grew to be tall and slender, with golden fair curls about her face, which gave her a childlike, innocent look, as if she were younger than her real age. And with her years her tenderness and sympathy for suffering seemed to grow deeper and stronger. It was the sure way to her heart. In a glade not far from the castle she had a favourite bower, where early every morning she used to go to feed and tend her pets, of which the best-loved was a delicate little fawn that she had found one day in the forest, deserted by its companions, as it had hurt its foot and could no longer keep pace with them. With difficulty Auréole and her nurse carried it home between them, and tended it till it grew well again and could once more run and spring as lightly as ever. And then one morning Auréole, with tears in her eyes, led it back to the forest where she had found it.

" 'Here, my fawn,' she said, 'you are free as air. I would not keep you a captive. Hasten to your friends, my fawn, but do not forget Auréole, and if you are in trouble come to her to help you.'

"But the fawn would not move. He rubbed himself softly against her, and looked up in her face with eyes that almost spoke. She could not but understand what he meant to say.

" ' 'I cannot leave you. Let me stay always beside you,' was what he tried to express. So Auréole let him follow her home again, and from that day he had always lived in her bower, and was never so happy as when gambolling about her. She had other pets too—numbers of birds of various kinds, none of which she kept in cages, for all of them she had in some way or other saved and protected, and, like the fawn, they refused to leave her. The sweetest, perhaps, were a pair of wood-pigeons which she had one day released from a fowler's snare, where they had become entangled. It was the prettiest sight in the world to see Auréole in her bower every-morning, the fawn rubbing his soft head

against her white dress, and the wood-pigeons cooing to her, one perched on each shoulder, while round her head fluttered a crowd of birds of different kinds—all owing their life and happiness to her tender care. There was a thrush, which she had found half-fledged and gasping for breath, fallen from the nest; a maimed swallow, who had been left behind by his companions in the winter flight. And running about, though still lame of one leg, a tame rabbit which she had rescued from a dog, and ever so many other innocent creatures, all with histories of the same kind, and each vying with the other to express gratitude to their dear mistress as she stood there with the sunshine peeping through the boughs and lighting up her sweet face and bright hair.

"But summer and sunshine do not always last, and in time sorrow came to Auréole as to others.

"Her mother had died when she was a little baby, and her father was already growing old. But he felt no anxiety about the future of his only child, for it had long been decided that she was to marry the next heir to his crown, the Prince Halbert, as by the laws of that country no woman could reign. Auréole had not seen Halbert for many years, when, as children, they had played together; but she remembered him with affection as a bright merry boy, and she looked forward without fear to being his wife.

" 'Why should I not love him?' she said to herself. 'I have never yet known any one who was not kind and gentle, and Halbert will be still more so to me than any one else, for he will be my king and master.'

"And when the day came for the Prince to return to see her again, she waited for him quietly and without misgiving. And at first all seemed as she had pictured it. Halbert was manly and handsome, he had an open expression and winning manners, he was devoted to his gentle cousin. So the old King was delighted, and Auréole said to herself, 'What have I done to deserve such happiness? How can I ever sufficiently show my gratitude?'

"She was standing in her bower when she thought thus, surrounded as usual by her pets. Suddenly among the trees at some little distance she heard a sound of footsteps, and at the same time a harsh voice, which she scarcely recognised, speaking roughly and sharply.

" 'Out of my way, you cur,' it said, and then came the sound of a blow, followed by a piteous whine.

"Auréole darted forward, and in another instant came upon Halbert, his face dark and frowning, while a poor little dog lay bleeding at his feet.

" 'Halbert!' exclaimed Auréole. Her cousin started; he had not heard her come. 'Did *you* do this? Did *you* strike the little dog?'

"Halbert turned towards her; he had reddened with shame, but he tried to laugh it off.

" 'It is nothing,' he said; 'the creature will be all right again directly. Horrid little cur! it rushed out at me from that cottage there and yelped and barked just when I was eagerly hastening to your bower, Princess.'

"But Auréole hardly heard him, or his attempts at excusing himself. She was on her knees before the poor dog.

" 'Why, Fido,' she said, 'dear little Fido, do you not know me?' Fido feebly tried to wag his tail.

" 'Is it *your* dog?' stammered Halbert. 'I had no—not the slightest idea—'

"But Auréole flashed back an answer which startled him. '*My* dog,' she said. 'No. But what has that to do with it? Oh, you cruel man!'

"Then she turned from him, the little dog all panting and bleeding in her arms. Halbert was startled by the look on her face.

" 'Forgive me, Auréole,' he cried. 'I did not mean to hurt the creature. I am hasty and quick-tempered, but you should not punish so severely an instant's thoughtlessness.'

" 'It was not thoughtlessness. It was cowardly cruelty,' replied Auréole slowly, turning her pale face towards him. 'A man must have a cruel nature who, even under irritation, could do what you have done. Farewell,' and she was moving away when he stopped her.

" 'What do you mean by farewell? You are not in earnest?' he exclaimed. But Auréole looked at him with indignation.

" 'Not in earnest?' she repeated. 'Never was I more so in my life! Farewell, Halbert.'

" 'And you will not see me again?' he exclaimed.

" 'I will never see you again,' Auréole replied, 'till you have learnt to feel for the sufferings of your fellow-creatures, instead of adding to them. And who can say if that day will ever come? Farewell again, Halbert.'

"The Prince stood thunderstruck, watching her slight figure as it disappeared among the trees. He felt like a man in a dream. Then, as he gradually became conscious that it was all true, his hot temper broke out in anger at Auréole, in mockery at her absurdity and exaggeration, and he tried to believe what he said, that no man could be happy with so fanciful and unreasonable a wife, and that he had nothing to regret. In his heart he was angry with himself, though to this he would not own, and conscious also that Auréole's instinct had judged him truly. He was selfish and utterly thoughtless for others, and far on the way therefore to becoming actually cruel. He had, like Auréole, been surrounded by luxury and indulgence all his life, but had not, like her, acquired the habit of feeling for others and looking upon his own blessings as to be shared with those who were without them.

"Auréole kept to her word. She would not see Halbert again, though the King, her father, did his utmost to shake her resolution. She remained firm. It was better so for both of them, she repeated. It would kill her to be the wife of such a man, and do him no good. So in bitter and angry resentment, rather than sorrow, Prince Halbert went away, and Auréole's life returned to what it had been before his coming.

"It seemed so at least, but in reality it was very different. Auréole had received a shock which she felt deeply, and which she could not forget. It grieved her, too, to see her father's distress and disappointment, and sometimes she asked herself if perhaps she had done wrong in deciding so hastily. But the sight of the little dog Fido, which had recovered, though with the loss of one eye, always removed these misgivings. 'A man who could be so cruel to a harmless little creature, would have quickly broken my heart,' she said to herself and sometimes to her father. And as time went on, and news came that Prince Halbert was becoming more and more feared and disliked in his own home from the increasing violence of his temper, the old King learnt to be thankful that his dear Auréole was not to be at the mercy of such a man.

" 'But what will become of you, my darling, when I am gone?' he would say.

" 'Fear not for me,' Auréole assured him. 'I have no fear for myself, father, dear. Why, I could live safely in the woods with my dear animals. If I had a little hut, and Fido to guard me, and Lello my fawn, and the little rabbit, and all my pretty birds, I should be quite happy!'

"For the forester to whom Fido belonged had begged Auréole to keep him, as even before its hurt the dog had learnt to love her and spring out to greet her, and wag his tail with pleasure when she passed his master's cottage, which lay on the way to her glade. But though Auréole was not afraid for herself, she was often very miserable when she thought of her country-people, above all the poor and defenceless ones, in the power of such a king as Halbert gave signs of being, after the long and gentle rule of her father. Yet there was nothing to be done, so she kept silence, fearing to cloud with more sorrow and anxiety the last days of the old King.

"They were indeed his last days, for within a year of Halbert's unfortunate visit her father died, and the fair Auréole was left desolate.

"Her grief was great, even though the King had been very old, and she had long known he could not be spared to her for many more years. But she had not much time to indulge in it, for already, before her father was laid in his grave, her sorrow was disturbed by the strange and unexpected events which came to pass.

"These began by a curious dream which came to Auréole the very night of her father's death.

"She dreamt that she was standing in her bower with her pets about her as usual. She felt bright and happy, and had altogether forgotten about her father's death. Suddenly a movement of terror made itself felt among her animals—the birds fluttered closer to her, the little rabbit crept beneath her skirt, the fawn and Fido looked up at her with startled eyes, and almost before she had time to look round their terror was explained. A frightful sound was heard approaching them, the terrible growl of a bear, and in another moment the monster was within a few yards. Even then, in her dream, Auréole's first thought was for her pets. She threw her arms round all that she could embrace, and stood there calmly, watching the creature with a faint hope that if she showed no terror he might pass them by. But he came nearer and nearer, till she almost felt his hot breath on her face, when suddenly, to her amazement, the monster was no longer there, but in his place the Prince Halbert, standing beside her and looking at her with an expression of the profoundest misery.

" 'I have brought it on myself,' he said. 'I deserve it; but pity me, oh, Auréole! Sweet Auréole, pity and forgive me!' Then a cry of irrepressible grief burst from his lips, and at this moment Auréole awoke, to find her eyes wet with tears, her heart throbbing fast with fear and distress.

" 'What can have made me dream of Halbert?' she said to herself. 'It must have been seeing the messengers start yesterday,' and then all came back to her memory, which at the first moment of waking had been confused, and she remembered her father's death and her own loneliness, and the scarcely-dried tears rushed afresh to her eyes.

" 'Has any news come from Prince Halbert?' she inquired of her attendants when they came at her summons. And when they told her 'none,' she felt a strange sensation of uneasiness. For the messengers had been despatched at once on the death of the old King, which had been sudden at the last, to summon his successor, and there had been time already for their return.

"And as the day went on and nothing was heard of them, every one began to think there must be something wrong, till late at night these fears were confirmed by the return of the messengers with anxious faces.

" 'Has the Prince arrived?' was their first question, and when they were told that nothing had been seen of him, they explained the reason of their inquiry.

"Halbert, already informed of the illness of the old King, had quickly prepared to set out with his own attendants and those who had come to summon him. They had ridden through the night, and had nothing untoward occurred, they would have ended their journey by daybreak. But the Prince had lost his temper with his horse, a nervous and restless animal, unfit for so irritable a person to manage.

" 'We became uneasy,' said the messengers, 'on seeing the Prince lashing and spurring furiously the poor animal, who, his sides streaming with blood, no longer understood what was required of him, and at last, driven mad with pain and terror, dashed off at a frantic pace which it was hopeless to overtake. We followed him as best we could, guided for some distance by the branches broken as they passed and the ploughed-up ground, which, thanks to a brilliant moonlight, we were able to distinguish. But at last, where the trees began to grow more thickly—' and here the speaker, who was giving this report to Auréole herself, hesitated—'at last these traces entirely disappeared. We sought on in every direction; when the moon went in we waited for the daylight, and resumed our search. But all to no purpose, and at last we resolved to ride on hither, hoping that the Prince might possibly have found his way before us.'

" 'But this is terrible!' cried Auréole, forgetting all her indignation against Halbert in the thought of his lying perhaps crushed and helpless in some bypath of the forest which his followers had missed. 'We must at once send out fresh horsemen in every direction to scour the country.'

"The captain who had had command of the little troop bowed, but said nothing, and seemed without much hope that any fresh efforts would succeed. Auréole was struck with his manner.

" 'You are concealing something from me,' she said. 'Why do you appear so hopeless? Even at the worst, even supposing the Prince is killed, he must be found.'

" 'We searched too thoroughly,' replied the officer. 'Wherever it was *possible* to get, we left not a square yard unvisited.'

" 'Wherever it was *possible*,' repeated Auréole; 'what do you mean? You do not think—' and she too hesitated, and her pale face grew paler.

"The captain glanced at her.

" 'I see that you have divined our fears, Princess,' he said in a low voice. 'Yes, we feel almost without a doubt that the unfortunate Prince has been carried into the enchanted forest, from whence, as you well know, none have ever been known to return. It is well that his parents have not lived to see this day, for, though he brought it on himself, it is impossible not to feel pity for such a fate.'

"Auréole seemed scarcely able to reply. But she gave orders, notwithstanding all she had heard, to send out fresh horsemen to search again in every direction.

" 'My poor father,' she said to herself; 'I am glad he was spared this new sorrow about Halbert.' And as the remembrance of her strange dream returned to her, 'Poor Halbert,' she added, 'what may he not be suffering?' and she shuddered at the thought.

"For the enchanted forest was the terror of all that country. In reality nothing, or almost nothing, was known of it, and therefore the awe and horror about it were the greater. It lay in a lonely stretch of ground between two ranges of hills, and no one ever passed through it, for there was no pathway or entrance of any kind to be seen. But for longer than any one now living could remember, it had been spoken of as a place to be dreaded and avoided, and travellers in passing by used to tell how they had heard shrieks and screams and groans from among its dark shades. It was said that a magician lived in a castle in the very centre of the forest, and that he used all sorts of tricks to get people into his power, whence they could never again escape. For though several were known to have been tempted to enter the forest, none of them were ever heard of or seen again. And it was the common saying of the neighbourhood, that it would be far worse to lose a child by straying into the forest than by dying. No one had ever seen the magician, no one even was sure that he existed, but when any misfortune came over the neighbourhood, such as a bad harvest or unusual sickness, people were sure to say that the wizard of the forest was at the bottom of it. And Auréole, like every one else, had a great and mysterious terror of the place and its master.

" 'Poor Halbert!' she repeated to herself many times that day. 'Would I could do anything for him!'

"The bands of horsemen she had sent out returned one after the other with the same tidings,—nothing had been seen or heard of the Prince. But late in the day a woodman brought to the castle a fragment of cloth which was recognised as having been torn from the mantle of the Prince, and which he had found caught on the branch of a tree. When asked where, he hesitated, which of itself was answer enough.

" 'Close to the borders of the enchanted forest,' he said at last, lowering his voice. But that was all he had to tell. And from this moment all lost hope. There was nothing more to be done.

" 'The Prince is as lost to us as is our good old King,' were the words of every one on the day of the funeral of Auréole's father. 'Far better for him were he too sleeping peacefully among his fathers than to be where he is.'

"It seemed as if it would have certainly been better for his people had it been so. It was impossible to receive the successor of Halbert as king till a certain time had elapsed, which would be considered as equal to proof of his death. And the next heir to the crown being but an infant living in a distant country, the delay gave opportunity for several rival claimants to begin to make difficulties, and not many months after the death of the old King the once happy and peaceful country was threatened with war and invasion on various sides. Then the heads of the nation consulted together, and decided on a bold step. They came to Auréole offering her the crown, declaring that they preferred to overthrow the laws of the country, though they had existed for many centuries, and to make her, at the point of the sword if necessary, their queen, rather than accept as sovereign any of those who had no right to it, or an infant who would but be a name and no reality.

"Auréole was startled and bewildered, but firm in her refusal.

" 'A king's daughter am I, but no queen. I feel no fitness for the task of ruling,' she replied, 'and I could never rest satisfied that I was where I had a right to be.'

"But when the deputies entreated her to consider the matter, and when she thought of the misery in store for the people unless something were quickly done, she agreed to think it over till the next day.

"The next day came, Auréole was ready, awaiting the deputies. Their hopes rose high as they saw her, for there was an expression on her face that had not been there the day before. She stood before them in her long mourning robe, but she had encircled her waist with a golden belt, and golden ornaments shone on her neck and arms.

" 'It is a good sign,' the envoys whispered, as they remarked also the bright and hopeful light in her eyes, and they stood breathless, waiting for her reply. It was not what they had expected.

" 'I cannot as yet consent to what you wish,' said Auréole; 'but be patient. I set off to-day on a journey from which I hope to return with good news. Till then I entreat you to do your best to keep all peaceful and quiet. And I promise you that if I fail in what I am undertaking, I will return to be your queen.'

"This was all she would say. She was forbidden, she declared, to say more. And so resolute and decided did she appear, that the envoys, though not without murmuring, were obliged to consent to await her return, and withdrew with anxious and uneasy looks.

"And Auréole immediately began to get ready for the mysterious journey of which she had spoken. Her preparations were strange. She took off, for the first time since her father's death, her black dress, and clad herself entirely in white. Then she kissed her old nurse and bade her farewell, at the same time telling her to keep up her courage and have no fear, to which the old dame could not reply without tears.

" 'I do not urge you to tell me the whole, Princess,' she said, 'as it was forbidden you to do so. But if I might but go with you.' Auréole shook her head.

" 'No, dear nurse,' she replied. 'The voice in my dream said, "Alone, save for thy dumb friends." That is all I can tell you,' and kissing again the poor nurse, Auréole set off, none knew whither, and she took care that none should follow her. Some of her attendants saw her going in the direction of her bower, and remarked her white dress. But they were so used to her going alone to see her pets that they thought no more of it. For no one knew the summons Auréole had received. The night before, after tossing about unable to sleep, so troubled was she by the request that had been made to her, she at last fell into a slumber, and again there came to her a strange dream. She thought she saw her cousin; he seemed pale and worn with distress and suffering.

" 'Auréole,' he said, 'you alone can rescue me. Have you courage? I ask it not only for myself, but for our people.'

"And when in her sleep she would have spoken, no words came, only she felt herself stretching out her arms to Halbert as if to reach and save him.

" 'Come, then,' said his voice; 'but come alone, save for thy dumb friends. Tell no one, but fear not.' But even as he said the words he seemed to disappear, and again the dreadful, the panting roar she had heard in her former dream reached Auréole's ears, in another moment the terrible shape of the monster appeared, and shivering with horror she awoke. Yet she determined to respond to Halbert's appeal. She told no one except her old nurse, to whom she merely said that she had been summoned in a dream to go away, but that no harm would befall her. She clad herself in white, as a better omen of success, and when she reached her bower, all her creatures welcomed her joyfully. So, with Fido, Lello the fawn, and the little rabbit gambolling about her feet, the wood-pigeons on her shoulders, and all the strange company of birds fluttering about her. Auréole set off on her journey, she knew not whither.

"But her pets knew. Whenever she felt at a loss Fido would give a little tug to her dress and then run on barking in front, or Lello would look up in her face with his pleading eyes and then turn his head in a certain direction, while the birds would sometimes disappear for a few moments and then, with a great chirping and fluttering, would be seen again a little way overhead, as if to assure her they had been to look if she was taking the right way. So that when night began to fall, Auréole, very tired, but not discouraged, found herself far from home in a part of the forest she had never seen before, though with trembling she said to herself that for all she knew she might already be in the enchanter's country.

" 'But what if it be so?' she reflected. 'I must not be faint-hearted before my task is begun.'

"She was wondering how she should spend the night when a sharp bark from Fido made her look round. She followed to where it came from, and found the little dog at the door of a small hut cleverly concealed among the trees. Followed by her pets Auréole entered it, when immediately, as if pulled by an invisible hand, the door shut to. But she forgot to be frightened in her surprise at what she saw. The hut was beautifully made of the branches of trees woven together, and completely lined with moss. A small fire burned cheerfully in one corner, for the nights were still chilly; a little table was spread with a snow-white cloth, on which were laid out fruits and cakes and a jug of fresh milk; and a couch of the softest moss covered with a rug made of fur was evidently arranged for Auréole's bed. And at the other side of the hut sweet hay was strewn for the animals, and a sort of trellis work of branches was ready in one corner for the birds to roost on.

" 'How pleasant it is!' said Auréole, as she knelt down to warm herself before the fire. 'If this is the enchanted forest I don't think it is at all a dreadful place, and the wizard must be very kind and hospitable.'

"And when she had had some supper and had seen that her pets had all they wanted, she lay down on the mossy couch feeling refreshed and hopeful, and soon fell fast asleep. She had slept for some hours when she suddenly awoke, though what had awakened her she could not tell. But glancing round the hut by the flickering light of the fire, which was not yet quite out, she saw that all her pets were awake, and when she gently called 'Fido, Fido,' the little dog, followed by the fawn and the rabbit, crept across the hut to her, and when she touched them she felt that they were all shaking and trembling, while the birds seemed to be trying to hide themselves all huddled together in a corner. And almost before Auréole had time to ask herself what it could be, their fear was explained, for through the darkness outside came the sound she had twice heard in her dreams—the terrible panting roar of the monster! It came nearer and nearer. Auréole felt there was nothing to do. She threw her arms round the poor little trembling creatures determined to protect them to the last. Suddenly there came a great bang at the door, as if some heavy creature had thrown itself against it, and Auréole trembled still more, expecting the door to burst open. But the mysterious hand that had shut it had shut it well. It did not move. Only a low despairing growl was heard, and then all was silent till a few minutes after, when another growl came from some distance off, and then Auréole felt sure the danger was past: the beast had gone away, for, though she had not seen him, she was certain he was none other than the monster of her dreams. The poor animals cowered down again in their corner, and Auréole, surprised at the quickness with which her terror had passed, threw herself on her couch and fell into a sweet sleep. When she woke, the sun was already some way up in the sky; the door was half open, and a soft sweet breeze fluttered into the hut. All was in order; the little fire freshly lighted, the remains of last night's supper removed, and a tempting little breakfast arranged. Auréole could scarcely believe her eyes. 'Some one must have come in while I was asleep,' she said, and Fido seemed to understand what she meant. He jumped up, wagging his tail, and was delighted when Auréole sat down at the little table to eat what was provided. All her pets seemed as happy as possible, and had quite forgotten their fright. So, after breakfast, Auréole called them all about her and set off again on her rambles. Whither she was to go she knew not; she had obeyed the summons as well as she could, and now waited to see what more to do. The animals seemed to think they had got to the end of their journey, and gambolled and fluttered about in the best of spirits. And even Auréole herself felt it impossible to be sad or anxious. Never had she seen anything so beautiful as the forest, with its countless paths among the trees, each more tempting than the other, the sunshine peeping in through the branches, the lovely flowers of colours and forms she had never seen before, the beautiful birds warbling among the trees, the little squirrels and rabbits playing about, and the graceful deer one now and then caught sight of.

" 'Why,' exclaimed Auréole, '*this* the terrible enchanted forest! It is a perfect fairyland.'

" 'You say true,' said a voice beside her, which made her start. 'To such as *you* it is a fairyland of delight. But to *me*!' and before Auréole could recover herself from her surprise, there before her stood the Prince Halbert! But how changed! Scarcely had she recognised him when every feeling was lost in that of pity.

" 'Oh, poor Halbert,' she cried, 'so I have found you! Where have you been? What makes you look so miserable and ill?'

"For Halbert seemed wasted to a shadow. His clothes, torn and tattered, hung loosely about him. His face was pale and thin, and his eyes sad and hopeless, though, as he saw the pitying look in her face, a gleam of brightness came into his.

" 'Oh, Auréole, how good of you to come! It is out of pity for *me*, who so little deserve it. But will you have strength to do all that is required to free me from this terrible bondage?'

" 'Explain yourself, Halbert,' Auréole replied. 'What is it you mean? What bondage? Remember I know nothing; not even if this is truly the enchanted forest.'

"Halbert glanced at the sun, now risen high in the heavens. 'I have but a quarter of an hour,' he said. 'It is only one hour before noon that I am free.'

"And then he went on to relate as quickly as he could what had come over him. Fallen into the power of the invisible spirits of the enchanted land, whose wrath he had for long incurred by his cruelty to those beneath him, among whom were poor little Fido, and the unhappy horse who had dropped dead beneath him as soon as they entered the forest, his punishment had been pronounced to him by a voice in his dreams. It was a terrible one. For twenty-three hours of the twenty-four which make the day and night, he was condemned to roam the woods in the guise of a dreadful monster, bringing terror wherever he came. 'I have to be in appearance what I was formerly in heart,' he said bitterly. 'You cannot imagine how fearful it is to see the tender innocent little animals fleeing from me in terror, though I would now die rather than injure one of them. And even you, Auréole, if you saw me you too would rush from me in horror.'

" 'I have seen you,' she replied. 'I have twice seen you in my dreams, and now that I know all I shall not fear you.'

" 'Do you indeed think so?' he exclaimed eagerly. 'Your pity and courage are my only hope. For I am doomed to continue this awful life—for hundreds of years perhaps—till twelve dumb animals mount on my back and let me carry them out of this forest. In my despair, when I heard this sentence, I thought of you and your favourites, whom I used to mock at and ill-treat more than you knew. They love and trust you so much that it is possible you may make them do this. But I fear for your own courage.'

" 'No,' said Auréole, 'that will not fail. And Fido is of a most forgiving nature. See here,' she went on, calling to the little dog, 'here is poor Halbert, who wants you to love him. Stroke him, Halbert,' and as the Prince gently did so, Fido looked up in his face with wistful eyes, and began timidly to wag his tail, while Lello and the rabbit drew near, and the birds fluttered, chirping above their heads. It was a pretty picture.

" 'See,' said Auréole, raising her bright face from caressing the good little creatures, 'see, Halbert, how loving and gentle they are! It will not be difficult. In many ways they are wiser than we. But I can never again believe that the spirits of the forest are evil or mischievous. Rather do I now think them good and benevolent. How happy seem all the creatures under their care!'

" 'I know no more than I have told you,' said Halbert; 'but I too believe they must be good, cruelly as they have punished me, for I deserved it. And doubtless all those who are said to have disappeared in the forest have been kept here for good purposes. And such as you, Auréole, have nothing to fear in any country or from any spirits. But I must go,' he exclaimed. 'I would not have you *yet* see me in my other form. You must reflect over what I have said, and prepare yourself for it.'

" 'And when, then, shall I see you again?' she asked.

" 'To-night, at sunset, at the door of your hut, you will see—alas, not *me!*' he whispered, and then in a moment he had disappeared.

"At sunset that evening Auréole sat at the door of the little hut, surrounded by her animals. She had petted and caressed them even more than usual, so anxious was she to prepare them for their strange task. She had even talked of it to Fido and Lello with a sort of vague idea that they might understand a little, though their only answer was for Fido to wag his tail and Lello to rub his soft nose against her. But suddenly both pricked up their ears, and then clinging more closely to their mistress, began to tremble with fear, while the birds drew near in a frightened flock.

" 'Silly birds,' said Auréole, trying to speak in her usual cheerful tone, 'what have *you* to fear? Bears don't eat little birds, and you can fly off in a moment. Not that I want you to fly away'; and she whistled and called to them, at the same time caressing and encouraging the animals, whose quick ears had caught sooner than she had done the dreadful baying roar which now came nearer and nearer. It was exactly the scene of her dreams, and notwithstanding all her determination, Auréole could not help shivering as the form of the monster came in sight. 'Suppose it is not Halbert,' she thought. 'Suppose it is all a trick

of the spirits of this enchanted country for my destruction!' And the idea nearly made her faint as the dreadful beast drew near. He was so hideous, and his roars made him seem still more so. His great red tongue hung out of his mouth, his eyes seemed glaring with rage. It was all Auréole could do to keep her pets round her, and she felt that her terror would take away all her power over them.

"'Oh, Halbert,' she exclaimed, '*is* it you? I know you cannot speak, but can you not make some sign to show me that it is you? I am so frightened.' She had started up as if on the point of running away. The monster, who was close beside her, opened still wider his huge mouth, and gave a roar of despair. Then an idea seemed to strike him—he bent his clumsy knees, and rubbed his great head on the ground at her feet; Auréole's courage returned. She patted his head, and he gave a faint groan of relief. Then by degrees, with the greatest patience, she coaxed the animals to draw near, and at last placed Fido and Lello on the beast's immense back. But though they now seemed less frightened they would not stay there, but jumped off again, and pressed themselves close against her. It was no use; after hours, at least so it seemed to Auréole, spent in trying, she had to give it up.

"'I cannot do it, Halbert,' she said. A groan was his reply. Then another thought struck her.

"'I will climb on your back myself,' she exclaimed; 'and then perhaps I can coax the animals to stay there.'

"The poor beast tried to stoop down still lower to make it easier for Auréole to get on. She managed it without much difficulty, and immediately Fido and Lello and the rabbit saw her mounted, up they jumped, for they had no idea of being left behind. The wood-pigeons came cooing down from the branch where they had taken refuge in their fright, and perched on her shoulders. Auréole looked up, and called and whistled to the other birds. Down they came as if bewitched, and settled round her, all the seven of them on the beast's furry back.

"'Off, Halbert,' cried Auréole, afraid to lose an instant, and off, nothing loath, the beast set. It was hard work to keep on. He plunged along so clumsily, and went so fast in his eagerness, that it was like riding on an earthquake. But when now and then he stopped, and gave a low pitiful roar, as if begging Auréole's pardon for shaking her so, she always found breath to say: 'On, Halbert, on; think not of me.'

"And so at last, after hours of this terrible journey, many times during which Auréole's heart had been in her mouth at the least sign of impatience among the animals, they reached the borders of the enchanted country, and as the panting beast emerged from the forest with his strange burden, poor Auréole slipped fainting off his back. Her task was done.

"When she came back to her senses and opened her eyes, her first thought was for the beast, but he had disappeared. Fido and Lello, and all the others were there, however; the dog licking her hands, the fawn nestling beside her, and at a little distance stood a figure she seemed to know, though no longer miserable and wretched as she had last seen him. It was Halbert, strong and handsome and happy again, but with a look in his eyes of gentleness and humility and gratitude that had never been there in the old days.

" 'Halbert,' said Auréole, sitting up and holding out her hand to him, 'is all then right?'

" 'All is right,' he replied; 'you can see for yourself. But, oh, Auréole, how can I thank you? My whole life would not be long enough to repay or—'

" 'Think not about thanking me,' interrupted Auréole. 'My best reward will be the delight of restoring to my dear country-people a king whose first object will *now*, I feel assured, be their happiness'; and her eyes sparkled with delight at the thought.

"She was right. Nothing could exceed the joy of the nation at the return of Auréole, and thanks to her assurances of his changed character, they soon learned to trust their new king as he deserved.

"No one ever knew the true history of his disappearance, but all admired and respected the noble and unselfish courage of Auréole in braving the dangers of the enchanted forest itself. Her pets all lived to a good old age, and had every comfort they could wish for. It was said that Halbert's only sorrow was that for long he could not persuade Auréole to fulfil her father's wishes by marrying him. But some years later a rumor came from the far-off country where these events happened, telling of the beautiful 'king's daughter' having at last consented to become a king's wife as well, now that she knew Halbert to be worthy of her fullest affection.

"And if this is true, I have no doubt it was for their happiness as well as for that of their subjects, among whom I include the twelve faithful animals."

16
OSCAR WILDE

The Happy Prince
(1888)

 SCAR WILDE (1854–1900) left Dublin in 1874 to study at Oxford, where he came under the influence of John Ruskin and Walter Pater, the foremost social and aesthetic critics in England at that time. They stimulated his thinking in two directions: Ruskin drew Wilde's attention to social questions and the significance of incorporating these questions into art, while Pater demonstrated how private experience is essential for grasping the beautiful and profound nature of the external world. Eventually, Wilde synthesized the notions of these two remarkable thinkers to form his own social concept of aesthetics which received its first full expression in his fairy tales.

Significantly, the publication of *The Happy Prince and Other Tales* (1888) marked the advent of his great creative period: *The Soul of Man Under Socialism* (1891), *The House of Pomegranates* (1891), *The Picture of Dorian Gray* (1891), *Lady Windermere's Fan* (1892), *A Woman of No Importance* (1893), *The Ideal Husband* (1895), and *The Importance of Being Earnest* (1895). It was as though the symbolic form of the fairy tale gave Wilde the necessary distance to conceive his social criticism in an innovative manner. Wilde was deeply disturbed by the hypocrisy of the English upper classes and the Church. Relying heavily on motifs in Hans Christian Andersen's tales which he often reversed to criticize Andersen, Wilde developed a poetical style recalling the rhythm and language of the Bible to expose the narrow-mindedness of the Church. This critique of both Andersen and the Church is most noticeable in the tales "The Young King" and "The Fisherman and his Soul" included in *The House of Pomegranates*. In "The Happy Prince" Wilde was more concerned with the social responsibility of the ruling classes toward society at large, although his Christian socialism plays a role here, too. Indeed, all his fairy tales were artistic endeavors to demonstrate the wanton and indifferent attitudes of the English upper classes toward their so-called inferiors. He juxtaposed the actions of a Christlike figure with the behavior of egocentric characters to reveal social conflicts and contradictions. While the rejection of unjust rulers and snobs is championed in the tales, the Christ figure demonstrates compassion and a possible mode of action to combat exploitation. It is first by perceiving how human beings are degraded by social convention, Wilde believed, that one can begin to struggle against human degradation. Such a perception is the motivating force behind the happy prince, who unfortunately endeavors to rectify social injustice when it is too late.

THE HAPPY PRINCE

IGH ABOVE THE city, on a tall column, stood the statue of the Happy Prince. He was gilded all over with thin leaves of fine gold, for eyes he had two bright sapphires, and a large red ruby glowed on his sword-hilt.

He was very much admired indeed. "He is as beautiful as a weathercock," remarked one of the Town Councillors who wished to gain a reputation for having artistic tastes; "only not quite so useful," he added, fearing lest people should think him unpractical, which he really was not.

"Why can't you be like the Happy Prince?" asked a sensible mother of her little boy who was crying for the moon. "The Happy Prince never dreams of crying for anything."

"I am glad there is some one in the world who is quite happy," muttered a disappointed man as he gazed at the wonderful statue.

"He looks just like an angel," said the Charity Children as they came out of the cathedral in their bright scarlet cloaks, and their clean white pinafores.

"How do you know?" said the Mathematical Master, "you have never seen one."

"Ah! but we have, in our dreams," answered the children; and the Mathematical Master frowned and looked very severe, for he did not approve of children dreaming.

One night there flew over the city a little Swallow. His friends had gone away to Egypt six weeks before, but he had stayed beind, for he was in love with the most beautiful Reed. He had met her early in the spring as he was flying down the river after a big yellow moth, and had been so attracted by her slender waist that he had stopped to talk to her.

"Shall I love you?" said the Swallow, who liked to come to the point at once, and the Reed made him a low bow. So he flew round and round her, touching the water with his wings, and making silver ripples. This was his courtship, and it lasted all through the summer.

"It is a ridiculous attachment," twittered the other Swallows, "she has no money, and far too many relations"; and indeed the river was quite full of Reeds. Then, when the autumn came, they all flew away.

After they had gone he felt lonely, and began to tire of his lady-love, "She has no conversation," he said, "and I am afraid that she is a coquette, for she is always flirting with the wind." And certainly, whenever the wind blew, the Reed made the most graceful curtsies. "I admit that she is domestic," he continued, "but I love travelling, and my wife, consequently, should love travelling also."

"Will you come away with me?" he said finally to her; but the Reed shook her head, she was so attached to her home.

"You have been trifling with me," he cried, "I am off to the Pyramids. Good-bye!" and he flew away.

All day long he flew, and at night-time he arrived at the city. "Where shall I put up?" he said; "I hope the town has made preparations."

Then he saw the statue on the tall column. "I will put up there," he cried; "it is a fine position with plenty of fresh air." So he alighted just between the feet of the Happy Prince.

"I have a golden bedroom," he said softly to himself as he looked round, and he prepared to go to sleep; but just as he was putting his head under his wing a large drop of water fell on him. "What a curious thing!" he cried, "there is not a single cloud in the sky, the stars are quite clear and bright, and yet it is raining. The climate in the north of Europe is really dreadful. The Reed used to like the rain, but that was merely her selfishness."

Then another drop fell.

"What is the use of a statue if it cannot keep the rain off?" he said; "I must look for a good chimney-pot," and he determined to fly away.

But before he had opened his wings, a third drop fell, and he looked up, and saw—Ah! what did he see?

The eyes of the Happy Prince were filled with tears, and tears were running down his golden cheeks. His face was so beautiful in the moonlight that the little Swallow was filled with pity.

"Who are you?" he said.

"I am the Happy Prince."

"Why are you weeping then?" asked the Swallow; "you have quite drenched me."

"When I was alive and had a human heart," answered the statue, "I did not know what tears were, for I lived in the Palace of Sans-Souci, where sorrow is not allowed to enter. In the daytime I played with my companions in the garden, and in the evening I led the dance in the Great Hall. Round the garden ran a very lofty wall, but I never cared to ask what lay beyond it, everything about me was so beautiful. My courtiers called me the Happy Prince, and happy indeed I was, if pleasure be happiness. So I lived, and so I died. And now that I am dead they have set me up here so high that I can see all the ugliness and all the misery of my city, and though my heart is made of lead yet I cannot choose but weep."

"What, is he not solid gold?" said the Swallow to himself. He was too polite to make any personal remarks out loud.

"Far away," continued the statue in a low musical voice, "far away in a little street there is a poor house. One of the windows is open, and through it I can see a woman seated at a table. Her face is thin and worn, and she has coarse, red hands, all pricked by the needle, for she is a seamstress. She is embroidering passion-flowers on a satin gown for the loveliest of the Queen's maids-of-honour to wear at the next Court-ball. In a bed in the corner of the room her little boy is lying ill. He has a fever, and is asking for oranges. His mother has nothing to give him but river water, so he is crying. Swallow, Swallow, little Swallow, will you not bring her the ruby out of my sword-hilt? My feet are fastened to this pedestal and I cannot move."

"I am waited for in Egypt," said the Swallow. "My friends are flying up and down the Nile, and talking to the large lotus-flowers. Soon they will go to sleep in the tomb of the great King. The King is there himself in his painted coffin. He is wrapped in yellow linen, and embalmed with spices. Round his neck is a chain of pale green jade, and his hands are like withered leaves."

"Swallow, Swallow, little Swallow," said the Prince, "will you not stay with me for one night, and be my messenger? The boy is so thirsty, and the mother so sad."

"I don't think I like boys," answered the Swallow. "Last summer, when I was staying on the river, there were two rude boys, the miller's sons, who were always throwing stones at me. They never hit me, of course; we swallows fly far too well for that, and besides, I come of a family famous for its agility; but still, it was a mark of disrespect."

But the Happy Prince looked so sad that the little Swallow was sorry. "It is very cold here," he said; "but I will stay with you for one night, and be your messenger."

"Thank you, little Swallow," said the Prince.

So the Swallow picked out the great ruby from the Prince's sword, and flew away with it in his beak over the roofs of the town.

He passed by the cathedral tower, where the white marble angels were sculptured. He passed by the palace and heard the sound of dancing. A beautiful girl came out on the balcony with her lover. "How wonderful the stars are," he said to her, "and how wonderful is the power of love!" "I hope my dress will be ready in time for the State-ball," she answered; "I have ordered passion-flowers to be embroidered on it; but the seamstresses are so lazy."

He passed over the river, and saw the lanterns hanging to the masts of the ships. He passed over the Ghetto, and saw the old Jews bargaining with each other, and weighing out money in copper scales. At last he came to the poor house and looked in. The boy was tossing feverishly on his bed, and the mother had fallen asleep, she was so tired. In he hopped, and laid the great ruby on the table beside the woman's thimble. Then he flew gently round the bed, fanning the boy's forehead with his wings. "How cool I feel," said the boy, "I must be getting better"; and he sank into a delicious slumber.

Then the Swallow flew back to the Happy Prince, and told him what he had done. "It is curious," he remarked, "but I feel quite warm now, although it is so cold."

"That is because you have done a good action," said the Prince. And the little Swallow began to think, and then he fell asleep. Thinking always made him sleepy.

When day broke he flew down to the river and had a bath. "What a remarkable phenomenon," said the Professor of Ornithology as he was passing over the bridge. "A swallow in winter!" And he wrote a long letter about it to the local newspaper. Every one quoted it, it was full of so many words that they could not understand.

"To-night I go to Egypt," said the Swallow, and he was in high spirits at the prospect. He visited all the public monuments, and sat a long time on top of the church steeple. Wherever he went the Sparrows chirruped, and said to each other, "What a distinguished stranger!" so he enjoyed himself very much.

When the moon rose he flew back to the Happy Prince. "Have you any commissions for Egypt?" he cried; "I am just starting."

"Swallow, Swallow, little Swallow," said the Prince, "will you not stay with me one night longer?"

"I am waited for in Egypt," answered the Swallow, "Tomorrow my friends will fly up to the Second Cataract. The river-horse couches there among the bulrushes, and on a great granite throne sits the God Memnon. All night long he watches the stars, and when the morning star shines he utters one cry of joy, and then he is silent. At noon the yellow lions come down to the water's edge to drink. They have eyes like green beryls, and their roar is louder than the roar of the cataract."

"Swallow, Swallow, little Swallow," said the Prince, "far away across the city I see a young man in a garret. He is leaning over a desk covered with papers, and in a tumbler by his side there is a bunch of withered violets. His hair is brown and crisp, and his lips are red as a pomegranate, and he has large and dreamy eyes. He is trying to finish a play for the Director of the Theatre, but he is too cold to write any more. There is no fire in the grate, and hunger has made him faint."

"I will wait with you one night longer," said the Swallow, who really had a good heart. "Shall I take him another ruby?"

"Alas! I have no ruby now," said the Prince; "my eyes are all that I have left. They are made of rare sapphires, which were brought out of India a thousand years ago. Pluck out one of them and take it to him. He will sell it to the jeweller, and buy food and firewood, and finish his play."

"Dear Prince," said the Swallow, "I cannot do that"; and he began to weep.

"Swallow, Swallow, little Swallow," said the Prince, "do as I command you."

So the Swallow plucked out the Prince's eye, and flew away to the student's garret. It was easy enough to get in, as there was a hole in the roof. Through this he darted, and came into the room. The young man had his head buried in his hands, so he did not hear the flutter of the bird's wings, and when he looked up he found the beautiful sapphire lying on the withered violets.

"I am beginning to be appreciated," he cried; "this is from some great admirer. Now I can finish my play," and he looked quite happy.

The next day the Swallow flew down to the harbour. He sat on the mast of a large vessel and watched the sailors hauling big chests out of the hold with ropes. "Heave a-hoy!" they shouted as each chest came up. "I am going to Egypt!" cried the Swallow, but nobody minded, and when the moon rose he flew back to the Happy Prince.

"I am come to bid you good-bye," he cried.

"Swallow, Swallow, little Swallow," said the Prince, "will you not stay with me one night longer?"

"It is winter," answered the Swallow, "and the chill snow will soon be here. In Egypt the sun is warm on the green palm-trees, and the crocodiles lie in the mud and look lazily about them. My companions are building a nest in the Temple of Baalbec, and the pink and white doves are watching them, and cooing to each other. Dear Prince, I must leave you, but I will never forget you, and next spring I will bring you back two beautiful jewels in place of those you have given away. The ruby shall be redder than a red rose, and the sapphire shall be as blue as the great sea."

"In the square below," said the Happy Prince, "there stands a little match-girl. She has let her matches fall in the gutter, and they are all spoiled. Her father will beat her if she does not bring home some money, and she is crying. She has no shoes or stockings, and her little head is bare. Pluck out my other eye, and give it to her, and her father will not beat her."

"I will stay with you one night longer," said the Swallow, "but I cannot pluck out your eye. You would be quite blind then."

"Swallow, Swallow, little Swallow," said the Prince, "do as I command you."

So he plucked out the Prince's other eye, and darted down with it. He swooped past the match-girl, and slipped the jewel into the palm of her hand. "What a lovely bit of glass," cried the little girl; and she ran home, laughing.

Then the Swallow came back to the Prince. "You are blind now," he said, "so I will stay with you always."

"No, little Swallow," said the poor Prince, "you must go away to Egypt."

"I will stay with you always," said the Swallow, and he slept at the Prince's feet.

All the next day he sat on the Prince's shoulder, and told him stories of what he had seen in strange lands. He told him of the red ibises, who stand in long rows on the banks of the Nile, and catch gold fish in their beaks; of the Sphinx, who is as old as the world itself, and lives in the desert, and knows everything;

of the merchants, who walk slowly by the side of their camels, and carry amber beads in their hands; of the King of the Mountains of the Moon, who is as black as ebony, and worships a large crystal; of the great green snake that sleeps in a palm-tree, and has twenty priests to feed it with honey-cakes; and of the pygmies who sail over a big lake on large flat leaves, and are always at war with the butterflies.

"Dear little Swallow," said the Prince, "you tell me of marvellous things, but more marvellous than anything is the suffering of men and of women. There is no Mystery so great as Misery. Fly over my city, little Swallow, and tell me what you see there."

So the Swallow flew over the great city, and saw the rich making merry in their beautiful houses, while the beggars were sitting at the gates. He flew into dark lanes, and saw the white faces of starving children looking out listlessly at the black streets. Under the archway of a bridge two little boys were lying in one another's arms to try and keep themselves warm. "How hungry we are!" they said. "You must not lie here," shouted the Watchman, and they wandered out into the rain.

Then he flew back and told the Prince what he had seen.

"I am covered with fine gold," said the Prince, "you must take it off leaf by leaf, and give it to my poor; the living always think that gold can make them happy."

Leaf after leaf of the fine gold the Swallow picked off, till the Happy Prince looked quite dull and grey. Leaf after leaf of the fine gold he brought to the poor, and the children's faces grew rosier, and they laughed and played games in the street. "We have bread now!" they cried.

Then the snow came, and after the snow came the frost. The streets looked as if they were made of silver, they were so bright and glistening; long icicles like crystal daggers hung down from the eaves of the houses, everybody went about in furs, and the little boys wore scarlet caps and skated on the ice.

The poor little Swallow grew colder and colder, but he would not leave the Prince, he loved him too well. He picked up crumbs outside the baker's door when the baker was not looking, and tried to keep himself warm by flapping his wings.

But at last he knew that he was going to die. He had just strength to fly up to the Prince's shoulder once more. "Good-bye, dear Prince!" he murmured, "will you let me kiss your hand?"

"I am glad that you are going to Egypt at last, little Swallow," said the Prince, "you have stayed too long here; but you must kiss me on the lips, for I love you."

"It is not to Egypt that I am going," said the Swallow. "I am going to the House of Death. Death is the brother of Sleep, is he not?"

And he kissed the Happy Prince on the lips, and fell down dead at his feet.

At that moment a curious crack sounded inside the statue, as if something had broken. The fact is that the leaden heart had snapped right in two. It certainly was a dreadfully hard frost.

Early the next morning the Mayor was walking in the square below in company with the Town Councillors. As they passed the column he looked up at the statue: "Dear me! how shabby the Happy Prince looks!" he said.

"How shabby indeed!" cried the Town Councillors, who always agreed with the Mayor, and they went up to look at it.

"The ruby has fallen out of his sword, his eyes are gone, and he is golden no longer," said the Mayor; "in fact, he is little better than a beggar!"

"Little better than a beggar," said the Town Councillors.

"And here is actually a dead bird at his feet!" continued the Mayor. "We must really issue a proclamation that birds are not to be allowed to die here." And the Town Clerk made a note of the suggestion.

So they pulled down the statue of the Happy Prince. "As he is no longer beautiful he is no longer useful," said the Art Professor at the University.

Then they melted the statue in a furnace, and the Mayor held a meeting of the Corporation to decide what was to be done with the metal. "We must have another statue, of course," he said, "and it shall be a statue of myself."

"Of myself," said each of the Town Councillors, and they quarrelled. When I last heard of them they were quarrelling still.

"What a strange thing!" said the overseer of the workmen at the foundry. "This broken lead heart will not melt in the furnace. We must throw it away." So they threw it on a dust-heap where the dead Swallow was also lying.

"Bring me the two most precious things in the city," said God to one of His Angels; and the Angel brought Him the leaden heart and the dead bird.

"You have rightly chosen," said God, "for in my garden of Paradise this little bird shall sing for evermore, and in my city of gold the Happy Prince shall praise me."

17

LUCY LANE CLIFFORD

Wooden Tony
(1892)

 UCY LANE CLIFFORD (1853–1929) was born in Barbados and went to London in her late teens to study art. In 1875 she married William Kingdon Clifford, a gifted mathematician, and when he died four years later, she was left with two daughters to support and very little money. Consequently, she turned to writing romantic novels, verse, plays, and short stories to provide for herself and her children. In addition she built a reputation as hostess of a fine London literary salon and became close friends with George Eliot, Henry James, Rudyard Kipling, and James Russell Lowell. Though she wrote some bestsellers, such as *Love-Letters of a Worldly Woman* (1891), *Aunt Anne* (1892), *A Flash of Summer* (1893), *A Woman Alone* (1898), and *Miss Fingal* (1919), most of her works were standard melodramatic narratives with a dose of moral sentiment to justify the contrived sensational scenes.

Mrs Clifford's best writing was in the area of children's literature. She published several books such as *Anyhow Stories* (1882), *Under Mother's Wings* (1885), *Very Short Stories and Verses for Children* (1886), and *Dear Mr. Ghost* (1895), which contain unusual tales with psychological sophistication. Undoubtedly her best work is *Anyhow Stories*, in which she dealt with the indeterminable boundaries between inanimate and animate worlds and between morality and immorality. In "Wooden Tony," which first appeared in *The Last Touches and Other Stories* (1892), she reflects her own ambivalence—and perhaps a Victorian ambivalence—toward imaginative children, who do not conform to the work ethic of Victorian society. Though the narrative is a chilling demonstration of what happens to wayward children, who live for and in their dreams, it also enables readers to judge the stern moral rigor of Victorian society.

WOODEN TONY

ONY WAS THE idlest boy in Switzerland. Other boys of his age chopped wood, gathered edelweiss, looked after goats and cattle; carried parcels for the strangers, guided them on short expeditions; and earned pence in many ways. But Tony did none of these things, and when his mother tried to make him useful he looked so frightened that at last she left him alone and let him do as he pleased. Gradually he grew to look quite stupid, as if his wits had gone a-wandering: and he was called the "Wooden-head' —that was the name by which all the neighbours knew him.

"Poor little Wooden-head! he's no use at all to you," they said to his mother; and at this she waxed angry, for though she often called him Wooden-head herself, she did not like to hear others do so.

"Perhaps he thinks more than he cares to say," she would answer.

"But he never tells of what he thinks; and a thinker who says nothing is like a signpost that points no way, and has nought written on it to guide him who looks up," old Gaspard said one morning.

"The signpost was made before the writing, and the talking that is worth hearing only comes after much thinking. He'll tell us enough some day," the mother answered. But though she spoke up bravely she was sad at heart. "I love thee dearly, my little son," she said. "I love thy pale face and wide open eyes, looking as though they expected to see Heaven's door creak on its hinges so that thou mightest know what the heavenly city was like; but who besides will care for thee if thou art stupid? And if thou art useless who will want thee? Even thy father gets impatient." Tony turned from the faggot that was beginning to crackle and merrily lick with its long flames the black soup-pot hung over it.

"Could I be with thee and yet far off?" he asked. "I long to be far off."

"Dear mercy!" his mother exclaimed. "But why dost thou want to be far off, Tony?"

"Then would I be little and could lie in thy arms; and none would want me to do the things I cannot do and forget to do."

"But how would being far off make thee little, my son?"

"All the people are little far off," he answered. "I often watch the strangers come down the pathway from the big house. They grow bigger and bigger as they come near; they pass the door and go on by the gorge, getting smaller and smaller till they are as little as the figures in the wood that my father cuts away in the winter. When they return they grow bigger and bigger again as they come near. Yes—I want to be very little and far off."

"My son, thou art a fool," his mother said. "Is thy father ever smaller, dost thou think? It is only the distance that makes the strangers seem as thou hast said; if thou drew near them thou wouldst see that they had neither grown smaller nor larger." But Tony shook his head and would not understand.

"They are little to me," he said. "I would like to go away and be little to thee again, and then thou wouldst not be always asking me to do this thing and that, and be angry at my forgetting. There are so many things in my head that come before my eyes and make my hands useless."

"Thou are no good if thou art useless," his mother sighed. "All things have a reason for staying in the world, and the reason for the young and strong is that they are useful." But Tony answered only,—

"Some day I will go far off and be very little," and went to the sunshine and sat down on his little stool by the door. Presently he began to sing a song learnt in some strange fashion unknown to any near him, as a solitary bird might learn from its own little lonely heart.

"Ah, dear child," his mother said sadly as she listened. "He is no fool in spite of his talk, or if he be one, then his voice is sweeter than the wisest; there is not room for an evil thought anywhere within sound of it. While I listen to him I could even forgive Gaspard's wife for getting the fine linen to be washed for the English lady. It was a small thing to quarrel about."

But you do not know yet where Tony lived. In the summer his home was far up a high mountain in Switzerland. Beneath was a valley abounding in little meadows and winding pathways that had at one end a waterfall. The waterfall fell over a mountain side and was like a dream forgotten before waking-time, for though the spray went down and down, it never reached the bottom, but scattered itself in the sunshine and was lost. Tony used to watch the falling water, and try to feel as he imagined it felt—caught by the breeze and carried away in its arms. Sometimes he could almost fancy himself journeying with it—on and on, till he lost all likeness to himself, and, meeting the great winds, he became a part of them, and swept over the far-off sea. All about the valley and here and there on the mountains were the chålets or dark wooden houses of the peasants. Some were built on piles, so that when the storms and floods came the herdsmen and their beasts might still keep themselves dry; and some had heavy stones on their roofs, so that the winds might not blow them away.

When Tony was very little, and before he had seen the builders at work, he thought that the piles were wooden legs on which the chälets had walked up in the darkness and stillness of the night, and that the two little windows in most of their fronts were eyes with which they had looked out to guide themselves. He often wished that he could see them staggering step by step upward along the zig-zag pathways. When he grew older it was almost a grief to know that human hands had built them on the mountain and in the valley, and that they would stay where they first rose till the winds and rains had done their worst. There was a little heap of rubbish on one side of the mountain; he had often wondered what it meant, but at last he knew, and then he stood looking at it and thought sadly of the children crouching over the fire, while the herdsman watched the sweeping storm gather to shatter their home and leave it in the past.

Just above his father's chälet was a big stone house, called the Alpine Hotel, where strangers came and stayed in the summer. The strangers talked among themselves in a language Tony did not understand, and were curious about the country round, professing to love it much, and day after day they walked over little bits of it. It seemed odd to Tony that they should travel from far countries to see the things he had lived among all his life—just the hills and valleys, the snow and the edelweiss, the sunshine and the infinite stillness. Was it really for these that the strangers came? He wondered sometimes what more might be in the distances beyond his home, and in what strange forms the great world stretched itself. Yet he did not trouble often about either the strangers or the world they came from, but silent and lonely let the days and nights slip by as one that swims with but just enough movement to keep himself from drowning. So Tony seemed to swim through time, and to find each day as difficult to remember from the one that went before or came after it as he would have found it to tell one mile of sea from another. Sometimes he wondered if the strangers were people easy to break, or to kill, or to get lost, for though they never ceased praising the beauty of the mountains, yet they were afraid to go alone up the steep paths or on the snow-plains that he could have wandered over in his sleep. But it was good that they had so little courage, for they gave his father money to show them the mountain ways, to carry their food, and pull them across the little precipices and crevasses that Tony scarce noticed, to cut steps on the sheer ice to which his feet clung surely, to take care of them altogether, those foolish strangers who professed to love the mountains and yet were afraid to be alone among them. All day long while his father was away Tony stayed in the chälet watching his mother scrub and clean and wash, and make the soup ready for his father at night. Or he would sit by the doorway, listening to the falling avalanche, and letting the warm sun fall on his closely-cropped head. Happy Tony! the trees made pictures and he saw them, the wind blew and he understood: surely he belonged to the winds and the trees, and had once been a part of them? Why should he trouble to work? Vaguely his heart knew that not to work as his father and mother worked had he journeyed into the world from the mists beyond it. Had he not been very little once when he set out on that first journey? Some day, when he had done his resting on the mountain, he would go into the distance, and be very little once more. And there were, besides, other thoughts than these that came into his heart, for he and nature were so near akin—thoughts of which those about him knew nothing; but he had few words with which to talk; even the easy ones of daily life his lips found difficult to use.

When the evening came, and the soup was eaten, he stood by the doorway, listening to his father's stories of what the strangers had said and done. Sometimes when they had been niggardly or very silent or the day a disappointing one, his father would be cross and grumble at the soup, or reproach Tony for being idle; but his mother always took his part.

"Nay, nay, do not be hard on him," she would say. "Now he is as one called too soon, before his sleep has satisfied him, and his dreams overtake his waking hours. Let him get his dreaming done, and he will rouse to work as men do in the morning time."

"Ah, nonsense," the father would answer; "we can any of us dream who are too stupid to wake and too idle to work. If it were not that he could sing I would have no patience with him."

The strange thing about Tony's song was that no one knew how he had come by it. He sang a little bit of it in the days when he looked for edelweiss on the mountain. To the highest ridges he went to seek for the little white flowers that grow on the edge of the snow on the Alps, and when he brought any back they were tied in bunches and offered for sale to the strangers. That was before he had grown so silent, before the time when the great cobweb seemed to have wrapped him round, before he had wandered into a dream and shut the door on the waking world. One day he came back with his basket empty.

"But where is the edelweiss?" his mother asked.

"I did not see any," he answered, and sat down beside the smoking wood. Then he began the song he had known since he could sing at all; but this time there was something that his mother had never heard before.

"Where didst thou learn that?" she asked, but Tony would not speak.

"It is hard on thee," Gaspard's wife said, "that thy son should be a fool."

"Nay, he is no fool," the mother answered.

"But he cannot tell even where he learnt his song," the woman said.

"He learnt it in the clouds, or on the mountain side, farther up than our feet can climb—what may be there—only the like of Tony can tell," and she waited scornfully for Gaspard's wife to go; but then she sighed sadly enough.

"Surely he will some day awaken," she thought, "or what will be the good of him?" But from that time Tony forgot more and more the things he was told to do, and lived among his dreams, which grew so tangled that even he could not tell the sleeping from the waking ones.

It was only in the summer that the days passed thus. When the storms came and the snow descended, the hotels and all the chälets on the mountains were closed, and the peasants and the herdsmen and their families and their flocks went down to the valley for the winter. Tony and his parents lived with a neighbour at the entrance to the village, all of them huddled together in a little wooden dwelling. The floods came, and the winds swept past, and the snow-drift piled higher and higher against the windows till it was hardly possible for any light to enter the close and smoky room. Tony used to watch his father cutting bits of wood: chip by chip he seemed to take away the walls that held little animals and men and women in prison. He never realized that his father's sharp knife and precise eye shaped the toys, or understood that it was just for the sake of the money they would bring that his mother placed them away so carefully till the dealer from Geneva came to buy them, or till it was time to put them on a tray outside the chälet door so that the strangers might see and bargain for them.

One winter there was a dark knotty morsel of wood that fascinated him. Every morning as he drank his milk his eyes wandered towards it. In the evening as he crouched shiveringly by the smouldering fire beneath the black soup-pot, he kept his eyes fixed on it and wondered what strange thing it concealed. One day his father took it up, and, turning it over and over, began to cut, till there came forth the figure of a little woman who had on her face an expression of listening and waiting. Tony's father looked at her and held her up before him when he had taken off the last bits of wood that clung to her.

"Maybe thou are expecting some one to come and bear thee company," he said, speaking to it affectionately, as though it were a child; "but I do not know of any thou canst have, unless Tony here will please thee?"

Tony shrinking back fancied that the woman's eyes turned towards him.

"She is only wood, my lad," his mother said, "and to-morrow she will be sent to the dealer's far off—there is nothing to be afraid of, she cannot move, and in things that cannot move no danger lies. All things that live and move have power to frighten, but not this bit of wood that has been shaped by thy father's knife."

But Tony crept out of the chälet and trampled the soft snow under foot, and he was afraid of the little wooden woman lying still and wide-eyed in the smoky chälet. When he went back his mother looked up and said, just as if she had divined his thoughts, "Our neighbour Louis has gone to Geneva to look for mules for the summer; he has taken all thy father's carving with him, so thou needst not be afraid of the little woman any more."

This had happened more than a year ago, and Tony had forgotten the piece of wood and what had come from it. Now his father was carving again, and making ready for the dealer who arrived once a year to buy their winter's work from the peasants; and if the dealer would not buy, the little figures would be put away in a drawer ready for the strangers.

"If I were but like one of them," Tony used to think as he saw them wrapped in soft paper, "to be always little, to be handled tenderly and put to sleep in a drawer till the summer, and then to be warmed through and through by the sun. Why should they have legs that never ache and hands that never work?"

It was a cold morning when the dealer came—a dark, silent man, black haired, with overhanging eye-brows.

"Who is this?" he asked, looking at Tony.

"He is my son," the father said; "but little enough good is he save to sing."

"Is he the boy whose song the goatherds say was learnt in the clouds?"

"It may be."

"Ah, Tony's song is known all down the valley and over the mountain too," his mother said.

"A stranger came to Geneva once and tried to sing it," the dealer said, "but he could not remember it all."

"It is no good to Tony," the father said, "he is only a fool, and will not use his hands and feet." Then the mother spoke up for her son.

"Don't judge him harshly," she said. "Surely, some are made to use their hands and some their feet, and some it may be just their hearts to feel and their lips to speak. Does he not sing a song he has fetched from the clouds? Let that travel instead of his feet and work instead of his hands?"

"He is called the Wooden-head," the father went on, unheeding, "and he might well be all wooden but for his song. The rest of him is no good—"

"A song has sometimes lived longer than the strongest hands that ever worked for bread, and travelled farther than the swiftest runner," said the mother.

"—And he would be like one of those," the father added, pointing to the little carved figures he had made.

"They were hidden in a block of wood, just as thy song is hidden in thee," his mother said, looking at Tony fondly.

"He would be better without his song," his father said. "He might dream less and work more."

The dealer considered and was silent, and when he spoke again he spoke slowly.

"Let him go to the city with me—to Geneva," he said, "and I will take the song from his lips and send it over the world."

"Tony," asked his father, "wilt thou go to Geneva? Perhaps there thou wouldst get thy wish to be far off and very little."

"Ah!" said the mother, with a heart that stood still, "but I have heard it said that a wish and its fulfillment sometimes find themselves strange company. But go if thou wilt, dear lad, there is much in the world. I would not keep thee from seeing it."

The peasants came out of their chälets and stood at their doors watching Tony as he went through the village with the dealer; but Tony did not see them. He walked as one who was dazed. The icicles hung like a fringe on the waterfall, and everywhere the sun had kissed it there rested a little golden star; but he did not look up as he passed by. He kept his eyes towards the long, straight road, and wondered if in the stems of the fir-trees beside it there dwelt strange figures like those his father had set free with his knife. The dealer pulled some wire from his pocket and fashioned it carefully as he walked on, but he said no word until the village was far behind and they could no longer hear the trickle of the unfrozen water. Then he looked up and said,

"Sing."

Mechanically, as though he were a puppet, of which the string had been pulled, Tony began to sing, and the dealer twanged the wire in his hands till it almost echoed the song. But Tony did not hear it. Over his senses had stolen a great rest; he walked as though before him he saw the land of his dreams and presently would enter its gateway.

Twang, twang, went the wire.

The fir-trees swayed a very little in the breeze; more and more as the twilight deepened, as the night came on. Tony turned his face towards them; he felt as if he knew them, he wanted to go to them, to walk among them as his friends, but something held him and he could not. The trees knew him and held out their arms: they whispered a message but he did not understand it. But he was going to understand them, to learn their language and ponder their secrets.

Twang, twang, went the wire.

The trees were wrapped in darkness at last, but Tony did not stop, he went on, on and on without stopping, into the blackness till that too was behind, and towards him slowly stole the morning light. There was a range of low mountains far in the distance. They rose higher and higher as he drew near as if to greet him.

"Sing," said the dealer.

But his song was different, it seemed no longer to come from his heart but only from his lips, and as he sang he heard the notes repeated. The song was going out of him and on to the dealer's wire. He did not look towards it, he did not care; he felt nothing keenly. His legs were growing stiff and his feet were hard, yet lighter to lift than they had been. He was not tired, or warm, or cold, or glad, or sorry, but only in a dream.

The fir-trees were far, far behind now. Tony and the dealer had passed other villages than the one from which they had started yesterday. They were nearer to the mountains that had looked so low at first, and before them was a blue lake reflecting the bluer sky. Beside the lake was a long road that led to the city of Geneva—the city towards which they were journeying. But there were more villages and little towns to go through first—towns with white houses on the hill-side and others low down close to the water's edge. There were carved wooden balconies to some of them, and some were built altogether of wood. Tony wondered in what strange forest the trees of which they were made had grown. He seemed to have more and more kinship with the things that belonged to Nature's firstness—with the sky and the lake and the trees, nay, even with the dead wood that had been used on human dwelling-places. But towards human beings he felt a strangeness spring up in his heart as if between him and them had begun a separation. They seemed to be made of a different texture, of different flesh and blood from himself, and they—these people— were so tall, they overshadowed him; they took long steps and carried great loads that would have crushed him. And yet they did not look bigger than his father and mother, it was only when they were beside him that he realized the difference in height. It did not surprise him, for nothing surprised him now, or stirred his pulse, or made his heart beat quicker. He went on, on.

The dealer twanged the wire, and the music of it grew more and more to resemble Tony's song. But Tony tramped in silence looking at the lake and sky, while the sun shone, and the mountains rose higher and higher. He felt as if they were his parents or had been once in a far-off time, and now they were reaching out to him trying once more to bring him back to themselves before it was for ever too late. Too late for what? He did not know, he could not answer himself. His heart was growing still and slow, his lips were growing dumb.

"Sing," said the man again.

Then Tony opened his mouth, but the words of his song had gone, he could not remember them, he could not say them, only the notes came forth, but they had no meaning that could be written down in words, and each listener heard them differently. Gradually instead of singing he listened, for his song was all around and about, but did not come from his lips any more. It seemed as if it came from behind him, but when he tried to turn he could not. He was clasped everywhere by the wire, and in the midst of its cold tangle he walked, strange and rigid, as if in a dream. One arm hung by his side, he could not move it; one hand was in his pocket, he could not pull it out. His clothes seemed to have changed, to have grown as stiff as he, and to be separate from him no more. Only his feet moved just enough to carry him forward, and that was all.

But now the last miles of the road were behind, and the sounds of a city were before him with lines of houses standing up high and white, and many little windows like gaping mouths talking in the air or lidless eyes looking out on the people in the streets. Lower down there were windows, reaching to the ground, filled with all manner of things to please those who had money to go in and buy. Tony walked by all scarcely knowing: but he understood, for he had seen his shadow: he was in the distance towards which he had looked so often from his mountain home.

He was far off and very little.

He knew that he was bound and a prisoner, but it did not matter, he did not care. It was only part of a new life in the new world that he had entered. Suddenly with a jerk he stopped by one of the great windows; a door opened and he entered. All about him was wooden—wooden houses and people and animals—and everywhere a sound of ticking. Tick, tick, tick. He was lifted by the dealer's hand on to a height. Before him was a house, a chälet, with a flight of stairs outside leading to a balcony.

"Go up," the dealer said, and slowly stair by stair he went, his feet growing stiffer and stiffer with every step upward. He rested on the balcony; there were two little doors leading into the house, they opened suddenly and disclosed a little room behind. In the room waiting—surely waiting for him—was the strange little woman Tony had seen his father take from the block of wood. He remembered that he used to be afraid of her. How foolish he had been; now he was afraid of nothing. He took his place beside her, he felt that they would never be apart again unless great change or sorrow came: surely it was like a marriage? He saw that the little woman was as big as he, had she grown? or had he—but he could not think or reason. He was jerked back, the wire twanged, the doors closed, and all was still. He was in the darkness waiting too, but for what or how long he did not know: all time was the same to him, he could measure it no more.

In the distance he heard other wires twanging, and presently the melody of his song came from many directions, as though the place were full of it. He could hear the people in the street; they hummed it as they passed by. Once far off he heard a band playing it. But he did not listen long, for all things grew faint as they would have grown dim too had he been in the light to see and know. For Tony's life had gone into his song; only a simple little song, just as his had been a simple little life.

Life is not only in nodding heads, and work is not only for hands that move and feet that walk; it is in many other things.

After a time there were sounds of fitting and tapping over Tony's head, a loud ticking—tick, tick, tick unceasingly, and then a strange whirring, and an iron tongue struck out clang-clang up to eleven. As the last stroke fell the little doors flew open and Tony and his companion were jerked out by the wire that bound them on to the balcony at the top of the stairs by which he had mounted, and stood together while all around and above the song was played—the song that never would come from his lips again. Before them, separating the place in which their dwelling was from the street, was a great window letting in a flood of light, and on the outer side against the glass were pressed eager faces watching; but Tony and his companion did not know this; as the last note died away they were jerked back into the little room and all was darkness till another hour had passed, and then it all happened again. Hour after hour it was always the same, day after day, week after week, month after month, in light and dark, in heat and cold.

Two weary faces once were pressed against the window, those of a woman and a man, and as the doors opened and the two little figures came forth on the clock and stood while the song was played, the woman cried.

"It is Tony, it is Tony, it is his song; there beside him is the woman you made, and he is wooden too—he is wooden."

"Thou art dreaming," said the man; "Tony is gone into the world, and we will go and seek him."

"No, no," the woman cried in despair, "his song has gone into the world, but Tony is there," and she pointed to the clock; "he is wooden—he is wooden." The man looked long and silently.

"He had always a wooden head," he answered slowly; "maybe the rest of him has gone wooden too, for he did not move enough to keep quickened. But he was useless," he added, trying to comfort his wife; "didst thou not say thyself that his song would work instead of his hands, and journey instead of his feet?"

"Ah, that was well enough for those who did not love him" said the mother, "but it does not comfort me. It is Tony that I want, my son Tony who sat by the door and sang, or by the fire watching the wood smoulder." While she spoke the song ceased, the figures were jerked into the darkness, and the doors closed: before the man and woman lay the long road and the weary miles that led back to the village and the mountain.

18

RUDYARD KIPLING

The Potted Princess
(1893)

UDYARD KIPLING (1865–1936) was born in India, where he spent the first six years of his life. It was there that he learned to speak Hindustani as his second language and developed a great sensitivity for Indian customs and folklore. Between the ages of 6 and 17 he was educated in England and returned to India in 1881 to work on the newspaper *Lahore Gazette*. His job as journalist enabled him to gather material that he used in much of his verse and tales for young readers. By 1886 he began making a name for himself when his book, *Departmental Ditties*, received positive reviews in England. Two years later he recorded even more success with the publication of *Plain Tales from the Hills* and *Wee Willie Winkie*. Most of the stories in the volumes were modelled after the work of Juliana Horatia Ewing, who gave a military setting to many of her tales. When Kipling returned to England he found himself famous and continued writing stories and novels for young readers. Among his best known works are: *Stalky and Co* (1899), *Just So Stories* (1902), *Kim* (1900), *Puck of Pook's Hill* (1906), and *Rewards and Fairies* (1910).

"The Potted Princess" is not a well-known Kipling tale, and yet it is very characteristic of his work in theme and style. Published first in the *St. Nicholas Magazine* (1893), it weaves Indian folklore into the English literary tradition. Kipling combines traditional European fairy-tale motifs with Indian lore to form a remarkable tale about the magic of simplicity and humility. Moreover, his narrative offers an entertaining lesson in the art of storytelling, a tradition that he felt must be kept alive by children.

THE POTTED PRINCESS

OW THIS IS THE true tale that was told to Punch, and Judy his sister, by their nurse, in the city of Bombay. They were playing in the veranda, waiting for their mother to come back from her evening drive. The big pink crane, who generally lived by himself at the bottom of the garden because he hated horses and carriages, was with them too, and the nurse who was called the ayah, was making him dance by throwing pieces of mud at him. Pink cranes dance very prettily until they grow angry. Then they peck.

This pink crane lost his temper, opened his wings, and clattered his beak, and the ayah had to sing a song which never fails to quiet all the cranes in Bombay. It is a very old song, and it says:

> Buggle baita nuddee kinara,
> Toom-toom mushia kaye,
> Nuddee kinara kanta lugga
> Tullaka-tullaka ju jaye.

That means: A crane sat by the river-bank, eating fish *toom-toom*, and a thorn in the river-bank pricked him, and his life went away *tullaka-tullaka*—drop by drop. The ayah and Punch and Judy always talked Hindustani because they understood it better than English.

"See now," said Punch, clapping his hands. "He knows, and he is ashamed. Tullaka-tullaka, ju jaye! Go away!"

"Tullaka-tullaka!" said little Judy, who was five; and the pink crane shut up his beak and went down to the bottom of the garden to the coco-nut palms and the aloes and the red peppers. Punch followed, shouting "Tullaka-tullaka!" till the crane hopped over an aloe hedge and Punch got pricked by the spikes. Then he cried, because he was only seven, and because it was so hot that he was wearing very few clothes and the aloes had pricked a great deal of him; and Judy cried too, because Punch was crying, and she knew that meant something worth crying for.

"Ohoo!" said Punch, looking at both his fat little legs together, "I am very badly pricked by the very bad aloe. Perhaps I shall die!"

"Punch will die because he has been pricked by the very bad aloe, and then there will be only Judy," said Judy.

"No," said Punch, very quickly, putting his legs down. "Then you will sit up to dinner alone. I will not die; but, ayah, I am very badly pricked. What is good for that?"

The ayah looked down for a minute, just to see that there were two tiny pink scratches on Punch's legs. Then she looked out across the garden to the blue water of Bombay harbour, where the ships are, and said:

"Once upon a time there was a rajah." "Rajah" means king in Hindustani, just as "ranee" means queen.

"Will Punch die, ayah?" said Judy. She too had seen the pink scratches, and they seemed very dreadful to her.

"No," said Punch. "Ayah is telling a tale. Stop crying, Judy."

"And the Rajah had a daughter," said the ayah.

"It is a new tale," said Punch. "The last Rajah had a son, and he was turned into a monkey. Hssh!"

The ayah put out her soft brown arm, picked Judy off the matting of the veranda, and tucked her into her lap. Punch sat cross-legged close by.

"That Rajah's daughter was very beautiful," the ayah went on.

"How beautiful? More beautiful than Mamma? Then I do not believe this tale," said Punch.

"She was a fairy princess, Punch baba, and she was very beautiful indeed; and when she grew up the Rajah her father said that she must marry the best prince in all India."

"Where did all these things happen?" said Punch.

"In a big forest near Delhi. So it was told to me," said the ayah.

"Very good," said Punch. "When I am big I will go to Delhi. Tell the tale, ayah."

"Therefore the King made a talk with his magicians—men with white beards who do *jadoo* (magic), and make snakes come out of baskets, and grow mangoes from little stones, such as you, Punch, and you, Judy baba, have seen. But in those days they did much more wonderful things: they turned men into tigers and elephants. And the magicians counted the stars under which the Princess was born."

"I—I do not understand this," said Judy, wriggling on the ayah's lap. Punch did not understand either, but he looked very wise.

The ayah hugged her close. "How should a baby understand?" she said softly. "It is in this way. When the stars are in one position when a child is born, it means well. When they are in another position, it means, perhaps, that the child may be sick or ill-tempered, or she may have to travel very far away."

"Must I travel far away?" said Judy.

"No, no. There were only good little stars in the sky on the night that Judy baba was born—little home-keeping stars that danced up and down, they were so pleased."

"And I—I—I! What did the stars do when I was born?" said Punch.

"There was a new star that night. I saw it. A great star with a fiery tail all across the sky. Punch will travel far."

"That is true. I have been to Nassik in the railway train. Never mind the Princess's stars. What did the magic-men do?"

"They consulted the stars, little impatient, and they said that the Princess must be shut up in such a manner that only the very best of all the princes in India could take her out. So they shut her up, when she was sixteen years old, in a big, deep grain-jar of dried clay, with a cover of plaited grass."

"I have seen them in the Bombay market," said Judy. "Was it one of the *very* big kind?" The ayah nodded, and Judy shivered, for her father had once held her up to look into the mouth of just such a grain-jar, and it was full of empty darkness.

"How did they feed her?" said Punch.

"She was a fairy. Perhaps she did not want food," the ayah began.

"All people want food. This is not a true tale. I shall go and beat the crane." Punch got up on his knees.

"No, no. I have forgotten. There was plenty of food—plantains, red and yellow ones, almond curd, boiled rice and peas, fowl stuffed with raisins and red pepper, and cakes fried in oil with coriander seeds, and sweetmeats of sugar and butter. Is that enough food? So the Princess was shut up in the grain-jar, and the Rajah made a proclamation that whoever could take her out should marry her and should govern ten provinces, sitting upon an elephant with tusks of gold. That proclamation was made through all India."

"We did not hear it, Punch and I," said Judy. "Is this a true tale, ayah?"

"It was before Punch was born. It was before even I was born, but so my mother told it to me. And when the proclamation was made, there came to Delhi hundreds and thousands of princes and rajahs and great men. The grain-jar with the cover of the plaited grass was set in the middle of all, and the Rajah said that he would allow to each man one year in which to make charms and learn great things that would open the grain-jar."

"I do not understand," said Judy again. She had been looking down the garden for her mother's return, and had lost the thread of the tale.

"The jar was a magic one, and it was to be opened by magic," said Punch. "Go on, ayah. I understand."

The ayah laughed a little. "Yes, the Rajah's magicians told all the princes that it was a magic jar, and led them three times round it, muttering under their beards, and bade them come back in a year. So the princes and the subadars and the wazirs and the maliks rode away east and west and north and south, and consulted the magicians in their fathers' courts, and holy men in caves."

"Like the holy men I saw at Nassik on the mountain? They were all *nungapunga* (naked), but they showed me their little gods, and I burned stuff that smelt in a pot before them all, and they said I was a Hindu, and—" Punch stopped, out of breath.

"Yes. Those were the men. Old men smeared with ashes and yellow paint did the princes consult, and witches and dwarfs that live in caves, and wise tigers and talking horses and learned parrots. They told all these men and all these beasts of the Princess in the grain-jar, and the holy men and the wise beasts taught them charms and spells that were very strong magic indeed. Some of the princes they advised to go out and kill giants and dragons, and cut off their heads. And some of the princes stayed for a year with the holy men in forests, learning charms that would immediately split open great mountains. There was no charm and no magic that these princes and subadars did not learn, for they knew that the Rajah's magicians were very strong magicians, and therefore they needed very, very strong charms to open the grain-jar. So they did all these things that I have told, and also cut off the tails of the little devils that live on the sand of the great desert in the north; and at last there were very few dragons and giants left, and poor people could plough without being bewitched any more.

"Only there was one prince that did not ride away with the others, for he had neither horse nor saddle, nor any men to follow him. He was a prince of low birth, for his father had married the daughter of a potter, and he was the son of his mother. So he sat down on the ground, and the little boys of the city driving the cattle to pasture threw mud at him."

"Ah!" said Punch, "mud is nice. Did they hit him?"

"I am telling the tale of the Princess, and if there are so many questions, how can I finish before bedtime? He sat on the ground, and presently his mother, the Ranee, came by, gathering sticks to cook bread, and he told her of the Princess and the grain-jar. And she said: 'Remember that a pot is a pot, and thou art the son of a potter.' Then she went away with those dry sticks, and the Potter-Prince waited till the end of the year. Then the princes returned, as many of them as were left over from the fights that they had fought. They brought with them the terrible cut-off heads of the giants and dragons, so that people fell down with fright; and the tails of all the little devils, bunch by bunch, tied up with string; and the feathers of magic birds; and their holy men and dwarfs and talking beasts came with them. And there were bullock-carts full of the locked books of magic incantations and spells. The Rajah apppointed a day, and his magicians came, and the grain-jar was set in the middle of all, and the princes began, according to their birth and the age of their families, to open the grain-jar by means of their charm-work. There were very many princes, and the charms were very strong, so that as they performed the ceremonies the lightning ran about the ground as a broken egg runs over the cook-house floor, and it was thick, dark night, and the people heard the voices of devils and djinns and talking tigers, and saw them running to and fro about the grain-jar till the ground shook. But, none the less, the grain-jar did not open. And the next day the ground was split up as a log of wood is split, and great rivers flowed up and down the plain, and magic armies with banners walked in circles—so great was the strength of the charms. Snakes too crawled round the grain-jar and hissed, but none the less the jar did not open. When morning came the holes in the ground had closed up, and the rivers were gone away, and there was only the plain. And that was because it was all magic charm-work which cannot last."

THE INCANTATION.

"Aha!" said Punch, drawing a deep breath. "I am glad of that. It was only magic, Judy. Tell the tale, ayah."

"At the very last, when they were all wearied out and the holy men began to bite their nails with vexation, and the Rajah's magicians laughed, the Potter-Prince came into the plain alone, without even one little talking beast or wise bird, and all the people made jokes at him. But he walked to the grain-jar and cried 'A pot is a pot, and I am the son of a potter!' and he put his two hands upon the grain-jar's cover and he lifted it up, and the Princess came out! Then the people said 'This is very great magic indeed'; and they began to chase the holy men and the talking beasts up and down, meaning to kill them. But the Rajah's magicians said: 'This is no magic at all, for we did not put any charm upon the jar. It *was* a common grain-jar; and it *is* a common grain-jar such as they buy in the bazaar; and a child might have lifted the cover one year ago, or on any day since that day. Ye are too wise, O Princes and Subadars, who rely on holy men and the heads of dead giants and devils' tails, but do not work with your own hands! Ye are too cunning! There was no magic, and now one man has taken it all away from you because he was not afraid. Go home, princes, or, if ye will, stay to see the wedding. But remember that a pot is a pot!' "

There was a long silence at the end of the tale.

"But the charms were very strong," said Punch doubtfully.

"They were only words, and how could they touch the pot. Could words turn you into a tiger, Punch baba?"

"No, I am Punch."

"Even so," said the ayah. "If the pot had been charmed, a charm would have

opened it. But it was a common bazaar pot. What did it know of charms? It opened to a hand on the cover."

"Oh!" said Punch; and then he began to laugh, and Judy followed his example. "Now I quite understand. I will tell it to Mamma."

When Mamma came back from her drive, the children told her the tale twice over, while she was dressing for dinner; but as they began in the middle and put the beginning first, and then began at the end and put the middle last, she became a little confused.

"Never mind," said Punch; "I will show." And he reached up to the table for the big eau-de-Cologne bottle that he was strictly forbidden to touch, and pulled out the stopper and upset half the scent down the front of his dress, shouting: "A pot is a pot, and I am the son of a potter!"

19

LAURENCE HOUSMAN

The Rooted Lover
(1894)

AURENCE HOUSMAN (1865–1959) was born in Bromsgrove, Worcestershire, the second youngest of seven children. Among his brothers and sisters were A. E. Housman, the famous poet, and Clemence Housman, an accomplished engraver and novelist. In 1883 Housman went to London to study at the Lambeth School of Art. During his initial period in London he had very little money and only gradually began to earn a living by writing poetry and illustrating books. Exposed to poverty and a more liberal world than the conservative surroundings of Bromsgrove, Housman was drawn to socialism, and his early works of the 1890s reflect a strong interest in questions of injustice and self-fulfillment. In particular his two collections of fairy tales, *A Farm in Fairyland* (1894) and *The House of Joy* (1895), which he himself illustrated, contain magical stories in which gifted characters display great fortitude in realizing their deepest wishes. With these works and others he established a solid reputation as writer and illustrator and obtained the position of art critic for the *Manchester Guardian*, a post he held until 1911. A third volume of fairy tales entitled *The Field of Clover* appeared in 1898, and it was apparent in such tales as "The Passionate Puppets" that Housman was becoming more critical of social conditions in England. He also played an active role with George Bernard Shaw and H. G. Wells in the development of the Fabian Society. Like his contemporary Fabians, Housman deplored the hypocrisy of the upper classes and often sought to provoke high society with outrageous works. In 1900 his book *An Englishwoman's Love-Letters*, published under a pseudonym, caused a sensation because it attacked the stringent sexual code of Victorian society. In his next book of fairy tales, *The Blue Moon* (1904), he wrote erotic tales like "The White Doe," "The Rat-Catcher's Daughter," and "White Birch" to question the double standards of Victorian society. His attitude toward art, as depicted in "A Chinese Fairy Tale," demanded that artists possess the integrity to use their imaginative powers to expose the ugly side of truth as well as suggesting alternatives to bleak conditions. Though Housman rarely compromised his own art, he wrote so many occasional pieces and became so

absorbed by politics that many of his works lack polish and depth. In the early part of the twentieth century he led the men's section of the extremist Women's Social and Political Union. During World War I he became a pacifist and worked for socialist causes. He incorporated many of his political ideas in plays which were continually banned by the English censor. His best work after the war, among numerous stories, poems, essays, and plays, was his autobiography *The Unexpected Years* (1937), which captured the spirit of the last phase of Victorianism and portrayed the leading figures in the world of art and literature.

In Housman's introduction to the Grimms' *Gammer Grethel's Fairy Tales* in 1905 he stated that "the true end and object of a fairy tale—if that can be said to have an object which moves by instinct to its goal—is the expression of the joy of living. There begins and ends the morality of the fairy tale: its value consists in its optimism." Certainly this principle is at work in "The Rooted Lover" taken from *A Farm in Fairyland*. Housman's narrative and illustration reveal the exhilaration of love that triumphs against the odds. The ploughboy in this tale is characteristic of many of Housman's fairy-tale protagonists, whose success and happiness depend on the nobility of their striving.

THE ROOTED LOVER

ORNING AND EVENING a ploughboy went driving his team through a lane at the back of the palace garden. Over the hedge the wind came sweet with the scents of a thousand flowers, and through the hedge shot glimpses of all the colours of the rainbow, while now and then went the sheen of silver and gold tissue when the Princess herself paced by with her maidens. Also above all the crying and calling of the blackbirds and thrushes that filled the gardens with song, came now and then an airy exquisite voice flooding from bower to field; and that was the voice of the Princess Fleur-de-lis herself singing.

When she sang all the birds grew silent; new flowers came into bud to hear her and into blossom to look at her; apples and pears ripened and dropped down at her feet; her voice sang the bees home as if it were evening: and the ploughboy as he passed stuck his face into the thorny hedge, and feasted his eyes and ears with the sight and sound of her beauty.

He was a red-faced boy, red with the wind and the sun: over his face his hair rose like a fair flame, but his eyes were black and bold, and for love he had the heart of a true gentleman.

Yet he was but a ploughboy, rough-shod and poorly clad in coat of frieze, and great horses went at a word from him. But no word from him might move the heart of that great Princess; she never noticed the sound of his team as it jingled by, nor saw the dark eyes and the bronzed red face wedged into the thorn hedge for love of her.

"Ah! Princess," sighed the ploughboy to himself, as the thorns pricked into his flesh, "were it but a thorn-hedge which had to be trampled down, you should be my bride to-morrow!" But shut off by the thorns, he was not a whit further from winning her than if he had been kneeling at her feet.

He had no wealth in all the world, only a poor hut with poppies growing at the door; no mother or father, and his own living to get. To think at all of the Princess was the sign either of a knave or a fool.

No knave, but perhaps a fool, he thought himself to be. "I will go," he said at last, "to the wise woman who tells fortunes and works strange cures, and ask her to help me."

So he took all the money he had in the world and went to the wise woman in her house by the dark pool, and said, "Show me how I may win Princess Fleur-de-lis to be my wife, and I will give you everything I possess."

"That is a hard thing you ask," said the wise woman; "how much dare you risk for it?"

"Anything you can name," said he.

"Your life?" said she.

"With all my heart," he replied; "for without her I shall but end by dying."

"Then," said the wise woman, "give me your money, and you shall take your own risk."

Then he gave her all.

"Now," said she, "you have but to choose any flower you like, and I will turn you into it; then, in the night I will take you and plant you in the palace garden; and if before you die the Princess touches you with her lips and lays you as a flower in her bosom, you shall become a man again and win her love; but if not, when the flower dies you will die too and be no more. So if that seems to you a good bargain, you have but to name your flower, and the thing is done."

"Agreed, with all my heart!" cried the ploughboy. "Only make me into some flower that is like me, for I would have the Princess to know what sort of a man I am, so that she shall not be deceived when she takes me to her bosom."

He looked himself up and he looked himself down in the pool which was before the wise woman's home; at his rough frieze coat with its frayed edges, his long supple limbs, and his red face with its black eyes, and hair gleaming at the top.

"I am altogether like a poppy," he said, "what with my red head, and my rough coat, and my life among fields which the plough turns to furrow. Make a poppy of me, and put me in the palace garden, and I will be content."

Then she stroked him down with her wand full couthly, and muttered her wise saws over him, for she was a wonderful witch-woman; and he turned before her very eyes into a great red poppy, and his coat of frieze became green and hairy all over him, and his feet ran down into the ground like roots.

The wise woman got a big flower-pot and a spade; and she dug him up out of the ground and planted him in the pot, and having watered him well, waited till it was quite dark.

As soon as the pole-star had hung out its light she got across her besom, tucked the flower-pot under her arm, and sailed away over hedge and ditch till she came to the palace garden.

There she dug a hole in a border by one of the walks, shook the plough-boy out of his flower-pot, and planted him with his feet deep down in the soil. Then giving a wink all round, and a wink up to the stars, she set her cap to the east, mounted her besom, and rode away into thin space.

But the poppy stood up where she had left him taking care of his petals, so as to be ready to show them off to the Princess the next morning. He did not go fast asleep, but just dozed the time away, and found it quite pleasant to be a flower, the night being warm. Now and then small insects ran up his stalks, or a mole passed under his roots, reminding him of the mice at home. But the poppy's chief thought was for the morning to return; for then would come the Princess walking straight to where he stood, and would reach out a hand and gather him, and lay her lips to his and his head upon her bosom, so that in the shaking of a breath he could turn again to his right shape, and her love would be won for ever.

Morning came, and gardeners with their brooms and barrows went all about, sweeping up the leaves, and polishing off the slugs from the gravel-paths. The head gardener came and looked at the poppy. "Who has been putting this weed here?" he cried. And at that the poppy felt a shiver of red ruin go through him; for what if the gardener were to weed him up so that he could never see the Princess again?

All the other gardeners came and considered him, twisting wry faces at him. But they said, "Perhaps it is a whim of the Princess's. It's none of our planting." So after all they let him be.

The sun rose higher and higher, and the gardeners went carrying away their barrows and brooms; but the poppy stood waiting with his black eye turned to the way by which the Princess should come.

It was a long waiting, for princesses do not rise with the lark, and the poppy began to think his petals would be all shrivelled and old before she came. But at last he saw slim white feet under the green boughs and heard voices and shawm-like laughter and knew that it was the Princess coming to him.

Down the long walks he watched her go, pausing here and there to taste a fruit that fell or to look at a flower that opened. To him she would come shortly, and so bravely would he woo her with his red face, that she would at once bend down and press her lips to his, and lift him softly to her bosom. Yes, surely she would do this.

She came; she stopped full and began looking at him: he burned under her gaze. "That is very beautiful!" she said at last. "Why have I not seen that flower before? Is it so rare, then, that there is no other?" But, "Oh, it is too common!" cried all her maids in a chorus; "it is only a common poppy such as grows wild in the fields."

"Yet it is very beautiful," said the Princess; and she looked at it long before she passed on. She half bent to it. "Surely now," said the poppy, "her lips to mine!"

"Has it a sweet smell?" she asked. But one of her maids said, "No, only a poor little stuffy smell, not nice at all!" and the Princess drew back.

"Alas, alas," murmured the poor poppy in his heart, as he watched her departing, "why did I forget to choose a flower with a sweet smell? then surely at this moment she would have been mine." He felt as if his one chance were gone, and death already overtaking him. But he remained brave: "At least," he said, "I will die looking at her; I will not faint or wither, till I have no life left in me. And after all there is to-morrow." So he went to sleep hoping much, and slept late into the morning of the next day.

Opening his eyes he was aware of a great blaze of red in a border to his right. Ears had been attentive to the words of Princess Fleur-de-lis, and a whole bed of poppies had been planted to gratify her latest fancy. There they were, in a thick mass, burning the air around them with their beauty. Alas! against their hundreds what chance had he?

And the Princess came and stood by them, lost in admiration, while the poppy turned to her his love-sick eye, trying to look braver than them all. And she being gracious, and not forgetful of what first had given her pleasure, came and looked at him also, but not very long; and as for her lips, there was no chance for him there now. Yet for the delight of those few moments he was almost contented with the fate he had chosen—to be a flower, and to die as a flower so soon as his petals fell.

Days came and went; they were all alike now, save that the Princess stayed less often to look at him or the other poppies which had stolen his last chance from him. He saw autumn changes coming over the garden: flowers sickened and fell, and were removed, and the nights began to get cold.

Beside him the other poppies were losing their leaves, and their flaming tops had grown scantier; but for a little while he would hold out still: so long as he had life his eye should stay open to look at the Princess as she passed by.

The sweet-smelling flowers were gone, but the loss of their fragrant rivalry gave him no greater hopes: one by one every gorgeous colour dropped away; only when a late evening primrose hung her lamp beside him in the dusk did he feel that there was anything left as bright as himself to the eye. And now death was taking hold of him, each night twisting and shrivelling his leaves; but still he held up his head, determined that, though but for one more day, his eye should be blessed by a sight of his Princess. If he could keep looking at her he believed he should dream of her when dead.

At length he could see that he was the very last of all the poppies, the only spot of flame in a garden that had gone grey. In the cold dewy mornings cobwebs hung their silvery hammocks about the leaves, and the sun came through mist, making them sparkle. And beautiful they were, but to him they looked like the winding-sheet of his dead hopes.

Now it happened just about this time that the Prince of a neighbouring country was coming to the Court to ask Princess Fleur-de-lis' hand in marriage. The fame of his manners and of his good looks had gone before him, and the Princess being bred to the understanding that princesses must marry for the good of nations according to the bidding of their parents, was willing, since the King her father wished it, to look upon his suit with favour. All that she looked for was to be wooed with sufficient ardour, and to be allowed time for a becoming hesitancy before yielding.

A great ball was prepared to welcome the Prince on his arrival; and when the day came, Princess Fleur-de-lis went into the garden to find some flower that she might wear as an adornment of her loveliness. But almost everything had died of frost, and the only flower that retained its full beauty was the poor bewitched poppy, kept alive for love of her.

"How wonderfully that red flower has lasted!" she said to one of her maidens. "Gather it for me, and I will wear it with my dress to-night."

The poppy, not knowing that he was about to meet a much more dangerous rival than any flower, thrilled and almost fainted for bliss as the maid picked him from the stalk and carried him in.

He lay upon Princess Fleur-de-lis' toilet-table and watched the putting on of her ballroom array. "If she puts me in her breast," he thought, "she must some time touch me with her lips; and then!"

And then, when the maid was giving soft finishing touches to the Princess's hair, the beloved one herself took up the poppy and arranged it in the meshes of gold. "Alas!" thought the poppy, even while he nestled blissfully in its warm depths, "I shall never reach her lips from her; but I shall dream of her when dead; and for a ploughboy, that surely is enough of happiness."

So he went down with her to the ball, and could feel the soft throbbing of her temples, for she had not yet seen this Prince who was to be her lover, and her head was full of gentle agitation and excitement to know what he would be like. Very soon he was presented to her in state. Certainly he was extremely passable: he was tall and fine and had a pair of splendid mustachios that stuck out under his nostrils like walrus-tusks, and curled themselves like ram's horns. Beyond a slight fear that these might sweep her away when he tried to kiss her, she favoured his looks sufficiently to be prepared to accept his hand when he offered it.

Then music called to them invitingly, and she was led away to the dance.

As they danced the Prince said: "I cannot tell how it is, I feel as if someone were looking at me."

"Half the world is looking at you," said the Princess in slight mockery. "Do you not know you are dancing with Princess Fleur-de-lis?"

"Beautiful Princess," said the Prince, "can I ever forget it? But it is not in that way I feel myself looked at. I could swear I have seen somewhere a man with a sunburnt face and a bold black eye looking at me."

"There is no such here," said the Princess; and they danced on.

When the dance was over the Prince led her to a seat screened from view by rich hangings of silken tapestry; and the Princess Fleur-de-lis knew that the time for the wooing was come.

She looked at him; quite clearly she meant to say "yes." Without being glad, she was not sorry. If he wooed well she would have him.

"It is strange," said the Prince, "I certainly feel that I am being looked at."

The Princess was offended. "I am not looking at you in the least," she said slightingly.

"Ah!" replied the other, "if you did, I should lose at once any less pleasant sensation; for when your eyes are upon me I know only that I love you—you, Princess, who are the most beautiful, the most radiant, the most accomplished, the most charming of your sex! Why should I waste time in laying my heart bare before you? It is here; it is yours. Take it!"

"Truly," thought the Princess, "this is very pretty wooing, and by no means ill done." She bent down her head, and she toyed and she coyed, but she would not say "yes" yet.

But the poppy, when he heard the Prince's words, first went all of a tremble, and then giving a great jump fell down at the Princess's feet. And she, toying and coying, and not wishing to say "yes" yet, bent down and taking up the poppy from where it had fallen, brushed it gently to and fro over her lips to conceal her smiles, and then tucking her chin down into the dimples of her neck began to arrange the flower in the bosom of her gown.

As she did so, all of a sudden a startled look came over her face. "Oh! I am afraid!" she cried. "The man, the man with the red face, and the strong black eyes!"

"What is the matter!" demanded the Prince, bending over her in the greatest concern.

"No, no!" she cried, "go away! Don't touch me! I can't and I won't marry you! Oh, dear! oh, dear! what is going to become of me?" And she jumped up and ran right away out of the ballroom, and up the great staircase, where she let the poppy fall, and right into her own room, where she barred and bolted herself in.

In the palace there was the greatest confusion: everybody was running about and shaking heads at everybody else. "Heads and tails! has it come to this?" cried the King, as he saw a party of serving men turning out a ploughboy who by some unheard-of means had found his way into the palace. Then he went up to interview his daughter as to her strange and sudden refusal of the Prince.

The Princess wrung her hands and cried: she didn't know why, but she couldn't help herself: nothing on earth should induce her to marry him.

Then the King was full of wrath, and declared that if she were not ready to obey him in three days' time, she should be turned out into the world like a beggar to find a living for herself.

So for three days the Princess was locked up and kept on nothing but bread and water; and every day she cried less, and was more determined than ever not to marry the Prince.

"Whom do you suppose you are going to marry then?" demanded the King in a fury.

"I don't know," said the Princess, "I only know he is a dear; and has got a beautiful tanned face and bold black eyes."

The King felt inclined to have all the tanned faces and bold black eyes in his kingdom put to death: but as the Princess's obstinacy showed no signs of abating he ended by venting all his anger upon her. So on the third day she was clothed in rags, and had all her jewelry taken off her, and was turned out of the palace to find her way through the world alone.

And as she went on and on, crying and wondering what would become of her, she suddenly saw by the side of the road a charming cottage with poppies growing at the door. And in the doorway stood a beautiful man, with a tanned face and bold black eyes, looking as like a poppy as it was possible for a man to look.

Then he opened his arms: and the Princess opened her arms: and he ran, and she ran. And they ran and they ran and they ran, till they were locked in each other's arms, and lived happily ever after.

20

KENNETH GRAHAME

The Reluctant Dragon
(1898)

 ENNETH GRAHAME (1859–1932) lived with his two brothers and sister in the vicinity of Edinburgh until his mother died in 1864. Since his father, a wealthy lawyer and an alcoholic, was unable to care for his children, he sent them to live with their maternal grandmother in a small English town in Berkshire. From 1868 to 1876 Grahame attended St Edward's School in Oxford and looked forward to continuing his education at the University of Oxford. However, his father had depleted the family finances, and Grahame was compelled to enter the offices of his uncle John Grahame, a Westminster parliamentary agent. Then, in 1879, he began working as a clerk in the Bank of England. Although he was a remarkably competent banker and rose swiftly up through the ranks, Grahame aspired to become a writer and spent his leisure time among Bohemians and intellectuals. At one point he made the acquaintance of James Furnivall, founder of the Early English Text Society and a member of the Christian Socialist movement. He introduced Grahame to the writings of Malory, Ruskin, and William Morris and gave him encouragement to write. After trying his hand at poetry, Grahame had some essays and sketches published in various magazines, and they were eventually collected in his first book *Pagan Papers* (1893). Between 1894 and 1897 he wrote nostalgic essays and stories about his childhood for *The Yellow Book*, and they comprised the selections in his second book *The Golden Age* (1895). This work was followed by *Dream Days* (1898), which included "The Reluctant Dragon," a tale that many critics consider his finest work. The year 1898 also marked his promotion to the post of Secretary of the Bank of England, a position he held until 1908, when he was obliged to retire due to ill health. In 1899 he married Elspeth Tomson, and in 1900 they had a son Alastair. Because of Grahame's long separations from his son while conducting business, he wrote him a series of letters about Mole, Badger, Rat, and Toad, who became the major characters in his great novel of fantasy for children, *The Wind in the Willows* (1908). This book capped his fame as a writer of nostalgia, and he apparently attracted readers in England because of his ability to capture a general mood of longing for

bygone days and carefree nature. Interestingly, the publication of this book occurred in the same year that Grahame retired from the bank and virtually abandoned writing. He moved with his wife and son to Blewbury in Berkshire, approximately fifty-five miles outside London, and wrote occasional sketches. The idyllic setting for his retirement was disturbed by the suicide of his son Alastair in 1919. Thereafter, he and his wife took an extended trip to Italy from 1920 to 1924. When they returned to England, they settled in the little village of Pangbourne and lived the eccentric lives of recluses until Grahame died in 1932.

Grahame's writings focus on a pursuit of childhood and innocent nature, almost as though the trajectory of his own life as banker had been a mistake. Writing was his way of breaking out and away from the drudgery of banking. Certainly, the escapist and rebellious tendency is strong in his works, but it is also balanced by a common-sense attitude that always strikes a happy compromise with his imaginative longings. *Dream Days* is typical of this philosophic position. It contains eight reminiscences of childhood concerning five brothers and sisters: Edward, Selima, Charlotte, Harold, and the unnamed narrator. As a sequel to *The Golden Age*, all the pieces seek to reformulate the rites of passage during childhood from the idealistic viewpoint of the adult who would like to recapture the past, extolling the virtues of youth in contrast to the petty societal demands of the present. Accordingly, the Boy in "The Reluctant Dragon" acts as Grahame's moral arbiter, who confidently satisfies the expectations of his society while protecting the innocent nature of fantasy. But it was not only the Boy who championed Grahame's views of youth, but the fairy-tale form itself that he employed in a deft and unusual manner to defend the realm of imagination.

THE RELUCTANT DRAGON

OOTPRINTS IN THE SNOW have been unfailing provokers of sentiment ever since snow was first a white wonder in this drab-coloured world of ours. In a poetry-book presented to one of us by an aunt, there was a poem by one Wordsworth in which they stood out strongly with a picture all to themselves, too—but we didn't think very highly either of the poem or the sentiment. Footprints in the sand, now, were quite another matter, and we grasped Crusoe's attitude of mind much more easily than Wordsworth's. Excitement and mystery, curiosity and suspense—these were the only sentiments that tracks, whether in sand or in snow, were able to arouse in us.

We had awakened early that winter morning, puzzled at first by the added light that filled the room. Then, when the truth at last finally dawned on us and we knew that snow-balling was no longer a wistful dream, but a solid certainty waiting for us, outside, it was a mere brute fight for the necessary clothes, and the lacing of boots seemed a clumsy invention, and the buttoning of coats an unduly tedious form of fastening, with all that snow going to waste at our very door.

When dinner-time came we had to be dragged in by the scruff of our necks. The short armistice over, the combat was resumed; but presently Charlotte and I, a little weary of contests and of missiles that ran shuddering down inside one's clothes, forsook the trampled battlefield of the lawn and went exploring the blank virgin spaces of the white world that lay beyond. It stretched away unbroken on every side of us, this mysterious soft garment under which our familiar world had so suddenly hidden itself. Faint imprints showed where a casual bird had alighted, but of other traffic there was next to no sign; which made these strange tracks all the more puzzling.

We came across them first at the corner of the shrubbery, and pored over them long, our hands on our knees. Experienced trappers that we knew ourselves to be, it was annoying to be brought up suddenly by a beast we could not at once identify.

"Don't you know?" said Charlotte rather scornfully. "Thought you knew all the beasts that ever was."

This put me on my mettle, and I hastily rattled off a string of animal names embracing both the arctic and the tropic zones, but without much real confidence.

"No," said Charlotte, on consideration; "they won't any of 'em quite do. Seems like something *lizardy*. Did you say a iguanodon? Might be that, p'raps. But that's not British, and we want a real British beast. *I* think it's a dragon!"

" 'Tisn't half big enough," I objected.

"Well, all dragons must be small to begin with," said Charlotte: "like everything else. P'raps this is a little dragon who's got lost. A little dragon would be rather nice to have. He might scratch and spit, but he couldn't *do* anything really. Let's track him down!"

So we set off into the wide snow-clad world, hand in hand, our hearts big with expectation,—complacently confident that by a few smudgy traces in the snow we were in a fair way to capture a half-grown specimen of a fabulous beast.

We ran the monster across the paddock and along the hedge of the next field, and then he took to the road like any tame civilized tax-payer. Here his tracks became blended with and lost among more ordinary footprints, but imagination and a fixed idea will do a great deal, and we were sure we knew the direction a dragon would naturally take. The traces, too, kept reappearing at intervals—at least Charlotte maintained they did, and as it was *her* dragon I left the following of the slot to her and trotted along peacefully, feeling that it was an expedition anyhow and something was sure to come out of it.

Charlotte took me across another field or two, and through a copse, and into a fresh road; and I began to feel sure it was only her confounded pride that made her go on pretending to see dragon-tracks instead of owning she was entirely at fault, like a reasonable person. At last she dragged me excitedly through a gap in a hedge of an obviously private character; the waste, open world of field and hedgerow disappeared, and we found ourselves in a garden, well-kept, secluded, most undragonhaunted in appearance. Once inside, I knew where we were. This was the garden of my friend the circus-man, though I had never approached it before by a lawless gap, from this unfamiliar side. And here was the circus-man himself, placidly smoking a pipe as he strolled up and down the walks. I stepped up to him and asked him politely if he had lately seen a Beast.

"May I inquire" he said, with all civility, "what particular sort of a Beast you may happen to be looking for?"

"It's a *lizardy* sort of Beast," I explained. "Charlotte says it's a dragon, but she doesn't really know much about beasts."

The circus-man looked round about him slowly. "I don't *think*," he said, "that I've seen a dragon in these parts recently. But if I come across one I'll know it belongs to you, and I'll have him taken round to you at once."

"Thank you very much," said Charlotte, "but don't *trouble* about it, please, 'cos p'raps it isn't a dragon after all. Only I thought I saw his little footprints in the snow, and we followed 'em up, and they seemed to lead right in here, but maybe it's all a mistake, and thank you all the same."

"Oh, no trouble at all," said the circus-man cheerfully. "I should be only too pleased. But of course, as you say, it *may* be a mistake. And it's getting dark, and he seems to have got away for the present, whatever he is. You'd better come in and have some tea. I'm quite alone, and we'll make a roaring fire, and I've got the biggest Book of Beasts you ever saw. It's got every beast in the world, and all of 'em coloured; and we'll try and find *your* beast in it!"

We were always ready for tea at any time, and especially when combined with beasts. There was marmalade, too, and apricot jam, brought in expressly for us; and afterwards the beast-book was spread out, and, as the man had truly said, it contained every sort of beast that had ever been in the world.

The striking of six o'clock set the more prudent Charlotte nudging me, and we recalled ourselves with an effort from Beast-land, and reluctantly stood up to go.

"Here, I'm coming along with you," said the circus-man. "I want another pipe, and a walk'll do me good. You needn't talk to me unless you like."

Our spirits rose to their wonted level again. The way had seemed so long, the outside world so dark and eerie, after the bright warm room and the highly-coloured beast-book. But a walk with a real Man—why, that was a treat in itself! We set off briskly, the Man in the middle. I looked up at him and wondered whether I should ever live to smoke a big pipe with that careless sort of majesty! But Charlotte, whose young mind was not set on tobacco as a possible goal, made herself heard from the other side.

"Now, then," she said, "tell us a story, please, won't you?"

The Man sighed heavily and looked about him. "I knew it," he groaned. "I *knew* I should have to tell a story. Oh, why did I leave my pleasant fireside? Well, I *will* tell you a story. Only let me think a minute."

So he thought a minute, and then he told us this story:

Long ago—might have been hundreds of years ago—in a cottage half-way between this village and yonder shoulder of the Downs up there, a shepherd lived with his wife and their little son. Now the shepherd spent his days—and at certain times of the year his nights too—up on the wide ocean-bosom of the Downs, with only the sun and the stars and the sheep for company, and the friendly chattering world of men and women far out of sight and hearing. But his little son, when he wasn't helping his father, and often when he was as well, spent much of his time buried in big volumes that he borrowed from the affable gentry and interested parsons of the country round about. And his parents were very fond of him, and rather proud of him too, though they didn't let on in his hearing, so he was left to go his own way and read as much as he liked; and instead of frequently getting a cuff on the side of the head, as might very well have happened to him, he was treated more or less as an equal by his parents, who sensibly thought it a very fair division of labour that they should supply the practical knowledge, and he the book-learning. They knew that book-learning often came in useful at a pinch, in spite of what their neighbours said. What the Boy chiefly dabbled in was natural history and fairy-tales, and he just took them as they came, in a sandwichy sort of way, without making any distinctions; and really his course of reading strikes one as rather sensible.

One evening the shepherd, who for some nights past had been disturbed and preoccupied, and off his usual mental balance, came home all of a tremble, and, sitting down at the table where his wife and son were peacefully employed, she with her seam, he in following out the adventures of the Giant with no Heart in his Body, exclaimed with much agitation:

"It's all up with me, Maria! Never no more can I go up on them there Downs, was it ever so!"

"Now don't you take on like that," said his wife, who was a *very* sensible woman: "but tell us all about it first, whatever it is as has given you this shake-up, and then me and you and the son here, between us, we ought to be able to get to the bottom of it!"

"It began some nights ago," said the shepherd. "You know that cave up there—I never liked it, somehow, and the sheep never liked it neither, and when sheep don't like a thing there's generally some reason for it. Well, for some time past there's been faint noises coming from that cave—noises like heavy sighings, with grunts mixed up in them; and sometimes a snoring, far away down—*real* snoring, yet somehow not *honest* snoring, like you and me o' nights, you know!"

"*I* know," remarked the Boy quietly.

"Of course I was terrible frightened," the shepherd went on; "yet somehow I couldn't keep away. So this very evening, before I come down, I took a cast round by the cave, quietly. And there—O Lord! there I saw him at last, as plain as I see you!"

"Saw *who*?" said his wife, beginning to share in her husband's nervous terror.

"Why *him*, I'm a-telling you!" said the shepherd. "He was sticking half-way out of the cave, and seemed to be enjoying of the cool of the evening in a poetical sort of way. He was as big as four cart-horses, and all covered with shiny scales—deep-blue scales at the top of him, shading off to a tender sort o' green below. As he breathed, there was a sort of flicker over his nostrils that you see over our chalk roads on a baking windless day in summer. He had his chin on his paws, and I should say he was meditating about things. Oh, yes, a peaceable sort o' beast enough, and not ramping or carrying on or doing anything but what was quite right and proper. I admit all that. And yet, what am I to do? Scales, you know, and claws, and a tail for certain, though I didn't see that end of him—I ain't *used* to 'em, and I don't *hold* with 'em, and that's a fact!"

The Boy, who had apparently been absorbed in his book during his father's recital, now closed the volume, yawned, clasped his hands behind his head, and said sleepily:

"It's all right, father. Don't you worry. It's only a dragon."

"Only a dragon?" cried his father. "What do you mean, sitting there, you and your dragons? *Only* a dragon indeed! And what do *you* know about it?"

" 'Cos it *is*, and 'cos I *do* know," replied the Boy quietly. "Look here, father, you know we've each of us got our line. *You* know about sheep, and weather, and things; *I* know about dragons. I always said, you know, that that cave up there was a dragon-cave. I always said it must have belonged to a dragon some time, and ought to belong to a dragon now, if rules count for anything. Well, now you tell me it *has* got a dragon, and so *that's* all right. I'm not half as much surprised as when you told me it *hadn't* got a dragon. Rules always come right if you wait quietly. Now, please, just leave this all to me. And I'll stroll up to-morrow morning—no, in the morning I can't, I've got a whole heap of things to do—well, perhaps in the evening, if I'm quite free, I'll go up and have a talk to him, and you'll find it'll be all right. Only please, don't you go worrying round there without me. You don't understand 'em a bit, and they're very sensitive, you know!"

"He's quite right, father," said the sensible mother. "As he says, dragons is his line and not ours. He's wonderful knowing about book-beasts, as every one allows. And to tell the truth, I'm not half happy in my own mind, thinking of that poor animal lying alone up there, without a bit o' hot supper or anyone to change the news with; and maybe we'll be able to do something for him; and if he ain't quite respectable our Boy'll find it out quick enough. He's got a pleasant sort o' way with him that makes everybody tell him everything."

Next day, after he'd had his tea, the Boy strolled up the chalky track that led to the summit of the Downs; and there, sure enough, he found the dragon, stretched lazily on the sward in front of his cave. The view from that point was a magnificent one. To the right and left, the bare and billowy leagues of Downs; in front, the vale, with its clustered homesteads, its threads of white roads running through orchards and well-tilled acreage, and, far away, a hint of grey old cities on the horizon. A cool breeze played over the surface of the grass, and the silver shoulder of a large moon was showing above distant junipers. No wonder the dragon seemed in a peaceful and contented mood; indeed, as the Boy approached he could hear the beast purring with a happy regularity. "Well, we live and learn!" he said to himself. "None of my books ever told me that dragons purred!"

"Hullo, dragon!" said the Boy quietly, when he had got up to him.

The dragon, on hearing the approaching footsteps, made the beginning of a courteous effort to rise. But when he saw it was a Boy, he set his eyebrows severely.

"Now don't you hit me," he said; "or bung stones, or squirt water, or anything. I won't have it, I tell you!"

"Not goin' to hit you," said the Boy wearily, dropping on the grass beside the beast: "and don't, for goodness' sake, keep on saying 'Don't'; I hear so much of it, and it's monotonous, and makes me tired. I've simply looked in to ask you how you were and all that sort of thing; but if I'm in the way I can easily clear out. I've lots of friends, and no one can say I'm in the habit of shoving myself in where I'm not wanted!"

"No, no, don't go off in a huff," said the dragon hastily; "fact is—I'm as happy up here as the day's long; never without an occupation, dear fellow, never without an occupation! And yet, between ourselves, it *is* a trifle dull at times."

The Boy bit off a stalk of grass and chewed it. "Going to make a long stay here?" he asked politely.

"Can't hardly say at present," replied the dragon. "It seems a nice place enough—but I've only been here a short time, and one must look about and reflect and consider before settling down. It's rather a serious thing, settling down. Besides—now I'm going to tell you something! You'd never guess it if you tried ever so!—fact is, I'm such a confoundedly lazy beggar!"

"You surprise me," said the Boy civilly.

"It's the sad truth," the dragon went on, settling down between his paws and evidently delighted to have found a listener at last: "and I fancy that's really how I came to be here. You see all the other fellows were so active and *earnest* and all that sort of thing—always rampaging, and skirmishing, and scouring the desert sands, and pacing the margin of the sea, and chasing knights all over the place, and devouring damsels, and going on generally—whereas I liked to get my meals regular and then to prop my back against a bit of rock and snooze a bit, and wake up and think of things going on and how they kept going on just the same, you know! So when it happened I got fairly caught."

"When *what* happened, please?" asked the Boy.

"That's just what I don't precisely know," said the dragon. "I suppose the earth sneezed, or shook itself, or the bottom dropped out of something. Anyhow there was a shake and a roar and a general stramash, and I found myself miles away underground and wedged in as tight as tight. Well, thank goodness, my wants are few, and at any rate I had peace and quietness and wasn't always being asked to come along and *do* something. And I've got such an active mind—always occupied, I assure you! But time went on, and there was a certain sameness about the life, and at last I began to think it would be fun to work my way upstairs and see what you other fellows were doing. So I scratched and burrowed, and worked this way and that way and at last I came out through this cave here. And I like the country, and the view, and the people—what I've seen of 'em—and on the whole I feel inclined to settle down here."

"What's your mind always occupied about?" asked the Boy. "That's what I want to know."

The dragon coloured slightly and looked away. Presently he said bashfully: "Did you ever—just for fun—try to make up poetry—verses, you know?"

" 'Course I have," said the Boy. "Heaps of it. And some of it's quite good, I feel sure, only there's no one here cares about it. Mother's very kind and all that, when I read it to her, and so's father for that matter. But somehow they don't seem to—"

"Exactly," cried the dragon; "my own case exactly. They don't seem to, and you can't argue with 'em about it. Now you've got culture, you have, I could tell it on you at once, and I should just like your candid opinion about some little things I threw off lightly, when I was down there. I'm awfully pleased to have met you, and I'm hoping the other neighbours will be equally agreeable. There was a very nice old gentleman up here only last night, but he didn't seem to want to intrude."

"That was my father," said the boy, "and he *is* a nice old gentleman, and I'll introduce you some day if you like."

"Can't you two come up here and dine or something to-morrow?" asked the dragon eagerly. "Only, of course, if you've got nothing better to do," he added politely.

"Thanks awfully," said the Boy, "but we don't go out anywhere without my mother, and, to tell you the truth, I'm afraid she mightn't quite approve of you. You see there's no getting over the hard fact that you're a dragon, is there? And when you talk of settling down, and the neighbours, and so on, I can't help feeling that you don't quite realize your position. You're an enemy of the human race, you see!"

"Haven't got an enemy in the world," said the dragon cheerfully. "Too lazy to make 'em, to begin with. And if I *do* read other fellows my poetry, I'm always ready to listen to theirs!"

"Oh, dear!" cried the boy, "I wish you'd try and grasp the situation properly. When the other people find you out, they'll come after you with spears and swords and all sorts of things. You'll have to be exterminated, according to their way of looking at it! You're a scourge, and a pest, and a baneful monster!"

"Not a word of truth in it," said the dragon, wagging his head solemnly. "Character'll bear the strictest investigation. And now, there's a little sonnet-thing I was working on when you appeared on the scene—"

"Oh, if you *won't* be sensible," cried the Boy, getting up, "I'm going off home. No, I can't stop for sonnets; my mother's sitting up. I'll look you up to-morrow, sometime or other, and do for goodness' sake try and realize that you're a pestilential scourge, or you'll find yourself in a most awful fix. Good night!"

The Boy found it an easy matter to set the mind of his parents at ease about his new friend. They had always left that branch to him, and they took his word without a murmur. The shepherd was formally introduced and many compliments and kind enquiries were exchanged. His wife, however, though expressing her willingness to do anything she could—to mend things, or set the cave to rights, or cook a little something when the dragon had been poring over sonnets and forgotten his meals, as male things *will* do, could not be brought to recognize him formally. The fact that he was a dragon and "they didn't know who he was" seemed to count for everything with her. She made no objection, however, to her little son spending his evenings with the dragon quietly, so long as he was home by nine o'clock: and many a pleasant night they had, sitting on the sward, while the dragon told stories of old, old times, when dragons were quite plentiful and the world was a livelier place than it is now, and life was full of thrills and jumps and surprises.

What the Boy had feared, however, soon came to pass. The most modest and retiring dragon in the world, if he's as big as four cart-horses and covered with blue scales, cannot keep altogether out of the public view. And so in the village tavern of nights the fact that a real live dragon sat brooding in the cave on the Downs was naturally a subject for talk. Though the villagers were extremely frightened, they were rather proud as well. It was a distinction to have a dragon of your own, and it was felt to be a feather in the cap of the village. Still, all were agreed that this sort of thing couldn't be allowed to go on. The dreadful beast must be exterminated, the country-side must be freed from this pest, this terror, this destroying scourge. The fact that not even a hen-roost was the worse for the dragon's arrival wasn't allowed to have anything to do with it. He was a dragon, and he couldn't deny it, and if he didn't choose to behave as such that was his own look-out. But in spite of much valiant talk no hero was found willing to take sword and spear and free the suffering village and win deathless fame; and each night's heated discussion always ended in nothing. Meanwhile the dragon, a happy Bohemian, lolled on the turf, enjoyed the sunsets, told antediluvian anecdotes to the Boy, and polished his old verses while meditating on fresh ones.

One day the Boy, on walking into the village found everything wearing a festal appearance which was not to be accounted for in the calendar. Carpets and gay-coloured stuffs were hung out of the windows, the church-bells clamoured noisily, the little street was flower-strewn, and the whole population jostled each other along either side of it, chattering, shoving, and ordering each other to stand back. The Boy saw a friend of his own age in the crowd and hailed him.

"What's up?" he cried. "Is it the players, or bears, or a circus, or what?"

"It's all right," his friend hailed back. "He's a-coming."

"*Who's* a-coming?" demanded the Boy, thrusting into the throng.

"Why, St George, of course," replied his friend. "He's heard tell of our dragon, and he's comin' on purpose to slay the deadly beast, and free us from his horrid yoke. O my! won't there be a jolly fight!"

Here was news indeed! The Boy felt that he ought to make quite sure for himself, and he wriggled himself in between the legs of his good-natured elders, abusing them all the time for their unmannerly habit of shoving. Once in the front rank, he breathlessly awaited the arrival.

Presently from the far-away end of the line came the sound of cheering. Next, the measured tramp of a great war-horse made his heart beat quicker, and then he found himself cheering with the rest, as, amidst welcoming shouts, shrill cries of women, uplifting of babies, and waving of handkerchiefs, St George paced slowly up the street. The Boy's heart stood still and he breathed with sobs, the beauty and the grace of the hero were so far beyond anything he had yet seen. His fluted armour was inlaid with gold, his plumed helmet hung at his saddle-bow, and his thick fair hair framed a face gracious and gentle beyond expression till you caught the sternness in his eyes. He drew rein in front of the little inn, and the villagers crowded round with greetings and thanks and voluble statements of their wrongs and grievances and oppressions. The Boy heard the grave gentle voice of the Saint, assuring them that all would be well now, and that he would stand by them and see them righted and free them from their foe; then he dismounted and passed through the doorway and the crowd poured in after him. But the Boy made off up the hill as fast as he could lay his legs to the ground.

"It's all up, dragon!" he shouted as soon as he was within sight of the beast. "He's coming! He's here now! You'll have to pull yourself together and *do* something at last!"

The dragon was licking his scales and rubbing them with a bit of house-flannel the Boy's mother had lent him, till he shone like a great turquoise.

"Don't be *violent*, Boy," he said without looking round. "Sit down and get your breath, and try and remember that the noun governs the verb, and then perhaps you'll be good enough to tell me *who's* coming?"

"That's right, take it coolly," said the Boy. "Hope you'll be half as cool

when I've got through with my news. It's only St George who's coming that's all; he rode into the village half an hour ago. Of course you can lick him—a great big fellow like you! But I thought I'd warn you, 'cos he's sure to be round early, and he's got the longest, wickedest-looking spear you ever did see!" And the Boy got up and began to jump round in sheer delight at the prospect of the battle.

"O deary, deary me," moaned the dragon; "this is too awful. I won't see him, and that's flat. I don't want to know the fellow at all. I'm sure he's not nice. You must tell him to go away at once, please. Say he can write if he likes, but I can't give him an interview. I'm not seeing anybody at present."

"Now, dragon, dragon," said the Boy imploringly, "don't be perverse and wrong-headed. You've *got* to fight him some time or other, you know, 'cos he's St George and you're the dragon. Better get it over and then we can go on with the sonnets. And you ought to consider other people a little, too. If it's been dull up here for you, think how dull it's been for me!"

"My dear little man," said the dragon solemnly, "just understand, once for all, that I can't fight and I won't fight. I've never fought in my life, and I'm not going to begin now, just to give you a Roman holiday. In old days I always let the other fellows—the *earnest* fellows—do all the fighting, and no doubt that's why I have the pleasure of being here now."

"But if you don't fight he'll cut your head off!" gasped the Boy, miserable at the prospect of losing both his fight and his friend.

"Oh, I think not," said the dragon in his lazy way. "You'll be able to arrange something. I've every confidence in you, you're such a *manager*. Just run down, there's a dear chap, and make it all right. I leave it entirely to you."

The Boy made his way back to the village in a state of great despondency. First of all, there wasn't going to be any fight; next, his dear and honoured friend the dragon hadn't shown up in quite such a heroic light as he would have liked; and lastly, whether the dragon was a hero at heart or not, it made no difference, for St George would most undoubtedly cut his head off. "Arrange things indeed!" he said bitterly to himself. "The dragon treats the whole affair as if it was an invitation to tea and croquet."

The villagers were straggling homewards as he passed up the street, all of them in the highest spirits, and gleefully discussing the splendid fight that was in store. The Boy pursued his way to the inn, and passed into the principal chamber, where St George now sat alone, musing over the chances of the fight, and the sad stories of rapine and of wrong that had so lately been poured into his sympathetic ears.

"May I come in, St George?" said the Boy politely, as he paused at the door. "I want to talk to you about this little matter of the dragon, if you're not tired of it by this time."

"Yes, come in, Boy," said the Saint kindly. "Another tale of misery and wrong, I fear me. Is it a kind parent, then, of whom the tyrant has bereft you? Or some tender sister or brother? Well, it shall soon be avenged."

"Nothing of the sort," said the Boy. "There's a misunderstanding somewhere, and I want to put it right. The fact is, this is a *good* dragon."

"Exactly," said St George, smiling pleasantly, "I quite understand. A good *dragon*. Believe me, I do not in the least regret that he is an adversary worthy of my steel, and no feeble specimen of his noxious tribe."

"But he's *not* a noxious tribe," cried the Boy distressedly. "Oh dear, oh dear, how *stupid* men are when they get an idea into their heads! I tell you he's a *good* dragon, and a friend of mine, and tells me the most beautiful stories you ever heard, all about old times and when he was little. And he's been so kind to mother, and mother'd do anything for him. And father likes him too, though father doesn't hold with art and poetry much, and always falls asleep when the dragon starts talking about *style*. But the fact is, nobody can help liking him when once they know him. He's so engaging and so trustful, and as simple as a child!"

"Sit down, and draw your chair up," said St George. "I like a fellow who sticks up for his friends, and I'm sure the dragon has his good points, if he's got a friend like you. But that's not the question. All this evening I've been listening, with grief and anguish unspeakable, to tales of murder, theft, and wrong; rather too highly coloured, perhaps, not always quite convincing, but forming in the main a most serious roll of crime. History teaches us that the greatest rascals often possess all the domestic virtues; and I fear that your cultivated friend, in spite of the qualities which have won (and rightly) your regard, has got to be speedily exterminated."

"Oh, you've been taking in all the yarns those fellows have been telling you," said the Boy impatiently. "Why, our villagers are the biggest story-tellers in all the country round. It's a known fact. You're a stranger in these parts, or else you'd have heard it already. All they want is a *fight*. They're the most awful beggars for getting up fights—it's meat and drink to them. Dogs, bulls, dragons—anything so long as it's a fight. Why, they've got a poor innocent badger in the stable behind here, at this moment. They were going to have some fun with him to-day, but they're saving him up now till *your* little affair's over. And I've no doubt they've been telling you what a hero you were, and how you were bound to win, in the cause of right and justice, and so on; but let me tell you, I came down the street just now, and they were betting six to four on the dragon freely!"

"Six to four on the dragon!" murmured St George sadly, resting his cheek on his hand. "This is an evil world, and sometimes I begin to think that all the wickedness in it is not entirely bottled up inside the dragons. And yet—may not this wily beast have misled you as to his real character, in order that your good report of him may serve as a cloak for his evil deeds? Nay, may there not be, at this very moment, some hapless Princess immured within yonder gloomy cavern?"

The moment he had spoken, St George was sorry for what he had said, the Boy looked so genuinely distressed.

"I assure you, St George," he said earnestly, "there's nothing of the sort in the cave at all. The dragon's a real gentleman, every inch of him, and I may say that no one would be more shocked and grieved than he would, at hearing you talk in that—that *loose* way about matters on which he has very strong views!"

"Well, perhaps I've been over-credulous," said St George. "Perhaps I've misjudged the animal. But what are we to do? Here are the dragon and I, almost face to face, each supposed to be thirsting for each other's blood. I don't see any way out of it, exactly. What do you suggest? Can't you arrange things, somehow?"

"That's just what the dragon said," replied the Boy, rather nettled. "Really, the way you two seem to leave everything to me—I suppose you couldn't be persuaded to go away quietly, could you?"

"Impossible, I fear," said the Saint. "Quite against the rules. *You* know that as well as I do."

"Well, then, look here," said the Boy, "it's early yet—would you mind strolling up with me and seeing the dragon and talking it over? It's not far, and any friend of mine will be most welcome."

"Well, it's *irregular*," said St George, rising, "but really it seems about the most sensible thing to do. You're taking a lot of trouble on your friend's account," he added good-naturedly, as they passed out through the door together. "But cheer. up! Perhaps there won't have to be any fight after all."

"Oh, but I hope there will, though!" replied the little fellow wistfully.

"I've brought a friend to see you, dragon," said the Boy rather loud.

The dragon woke up with a start. "I was just—er—thinking about things," he said in his simple way. "Very pleased to make your acquaintance, sir. Charming weather we're having!"

"This is St George," said the Boy, shortly. "St George, let me introduce you to the dragon. We've come up to talk things over quietly, dragon, and now for goodness' sake do let us have a little straight common sense, and come to some practical business-like arrangement, for I'm sick of views and theories of life and personal tendencies, and all that sort of thing. I may perhaps add that my mother's sitting up."

"So glad to meet you, St George," began the dragon rather nervously, "because you've been a great traveller, I hear, and I've always been rather a stay-at-home. But I can show you many antiquities, many interesting features of our countryside, if you're stopping here any time—"

"I think," said St George in his frank, pleasant way, "that we'd really better take the advice of our young friend here, and try to come to some understanding, on a business footing, about this little affair of ours. Now don't you think that after all the simplest plan would be just to fight it out, according to the rules, and let the best man win? They're betting on you, I may tell you, down in the village, but I don't mind that!"

"Oh, yes, *do*, dragon," said the Boy delightedly; "it'll save such a lot of bother!"

"My young friend, you shut up," said the dragon severely. "Believe me, St George," he went on, "there's nobody in the world I'd sooner oblige than you and this young gentleman here. But the whole thing's nonsense, and conventionality, and popular thick-headedness. There's absolutely nothing to fight about, from beginning to end. And anyhow I'm not going to, so that settles it!"

"But supposing I make you?" said St George, rather nettled.

"You can't," said the dragon triumphantly. "I should only go into my cave and retire for a time down the hole I came up. You'd soon get heartily sick of sitting outside and waiting for me to come out and fight you. And as soon as you'd really gone away, why, I'd come up again gaily, for I tell you frankly, I like this place, and I'm going to stay here!"

St George gazed for a while on the fair landscape around them. "But this would be a beautiful place for a fight," he began again persuasively. "These great bare rolling Downs for the arena—and me in my golden armour showing up against your big blue scaly coils! Think what a picture it would make!"

"Now you're trying to get at me through my artistic sensibilities," said the dragon. "But it won't work. Not but what it would make a very pretty picture, as you say," he added, wavering a little.

"We seem to be getting rather nearer to *business*," put in the Boy. "You must see, dragon, that there's got to be a fight of some sort, 'cos you can't want to have to go down that dirty old hole again and stop there till goodness knows when."

"It might be arranged," said St George thoughtfully. "I *must* spear you somewhere, of course, but I'm not bound to hurt you very much. There's such a lot of you that there must be a few *spare* places somewhere. Here, for instance, just behind your foreleg. It couldn't hurt you much, just here!"

"Now you're tickling, George," said the dragon coyly. "No, that place won't do at all. Even if it didn't hurt—and I'm sure it would, awfully—it would make me laugh, and that would spoil everything."

"Let's try somewhere else, then," said St George patiently. "Under your neck, for instance—all these folds of thick skin,—if I speared you here you'd never even know I'd done it!"

"Yes, but are you sure you can hit off the right place?" asked the dragon anxiously.

"Of course I am," said St George, with confidence. "You leave that to me!"

"It's just because I've *got* to leave it to you that I'm asking," replied the dragon rather testily. "No doubt you would deeply regret any error you might make in the hurry of the moment; but you wouldn't regret it half as much as I should! However, I suppose we've got to trust somebody, as we go through life, and your plan seems, on the whole, as good a one as any."

"Look here, dragon," interrupted the Boy, a little jealous on behalf of his friend, who seemed to be getting all the worst of the bargain: "I don't quite see where *you* come in! There's to be a fight, apparently, and you're to be licked; and what I want to know is, what are *you* going to get out of it?"

"St George," said the dragon, "just tell him, please—what will happen after I'm vanquished in the deadly combat?"

"Well, according to the rules I suppose I shall lead you in triumph down to the market-place or whatever answers to it," said St George.

"Precisely," said the dragon. "And then—?"

"And then there'll be shoutings and speeches and things," continued St George. "And I shall explain that you're converted, and see the error of your ways, and so on."

"Quite so," said the dragon. "And then—?"

"Oh, and then—" said St George, "why, and then there will be the usual banquet, I suppose."

"Exactly," said the dragon; "and that's where *I* come in. Look here," he continued, addressing the Boy, "I'm bored to death up here, and no one really appreciates me. I'm going into Society, I am, through the kindly aid of our friend here, who's taking such a lot of trouble on my account; and you'll find I've got all the qualities to endear me to people who entertain! So now that's all settled, and if you don't mind—I'm an old-fashioned fellow—don't want to turn you out, but—"

"Remember, you'll have to do your proper share of the fighting, dragon!" said St George, as he took the hint and rose to go; "I mean ramping, and breathing fire, and so on!"

"I can *ramp* all right," replied the dragon confidently; "as to breathing fire, it's surprising how easily one gets out of practice; but I'll do the best I can. Good night!"

They had descended the hill and were almost back in the village again, when

St George stopped short. "*Knew* I had forgotten something," he said. "There ought to be a Princess. Terror-stricken and chained to a rock, and all that sort of thing. Boy, can't you arrange a Princess?"

The Boy was in the middle of a tremendous yawn. "I'm tired to death," he wailed, "and I *can't* arrange a Princess, or anything more, at this time of night. And my mother's sitting up, and *do* stop asking me to arrange more things till to-morrow!"

Next morning the people began streaming up to the Downs at quite an early hour, in their Sunday clothes and carrying baskets with bottle-necks sticking out of them, every one intent on securing good places for the combat. This was not exactly a simple matter, for of course it was quite possible that the dragon might win, and in that case even those who had put their money on him felt they could hardly expect him to deal with his backers on a different footing to the rest. Places were chosen, therefore, with circumspection and with a view to a speedy retreat in case of emergency; and the front rank was mostly composed of boys who had escaped from parental control and now sprawled and rolled about on the grass, regardless of the shrill threats and warnings discharged at them by their anxious mothers behind.

The Boy had secured a good front place, well up towards the cave, and was feeling as anxious as a stage-manager on a first night. Could the dragon be depended upon? He might change his mind and vote the whole performance rot; or else, seeing that the affair had been so hastily planned without even a rehearsal, he might be too nervous to show up. The Boy looked narrowly at the cave, but it showed no sign of life or occupation. Could the dragon have made a moonlight flitting?

The higher portions of the ground were now black with sightseers, and presently a sound of cheering and a waving of handkerchiefs told that something was visible to them which the Boy, far up towards the dragon-end of the line as he was, could not yet see. A minute more and St George's red plumes topped the hill, as the Saint rode slowly forth on the great level space which stretched up to the grim mouth of the cave. Very gallant and beautiful he looked on his tall war-horse, his golden armour glancing in the sun, his great spear held erect, the little white pennon, crimson-crossed, fluttering at its point. He drew rein and remained motionless. The lines of spectators began to give back a little, nervously; and even the boys in front stopped pulling hair and cuffing each other, and leaned forward expectant.

"Now then, dragon!" muttered the Boy impatiently, fidgeting where he sat. He need not have distressed himself, had he only known. The dramatic possibilities of the thing had tickled the dragon immensely, and he had been up from an early hour, preparing for his first public appearance with as much heartiness as if the years had run backwards, and he had been again a little dragonlet, playing with his sisters on the floor of their mother's cave, at the game of saints-and-dragons, in which the dragon was bound to win.

A low muttering, mingled with snorts, now made itself heard; rising to a bellowing roar that seemed to fill the plain. Then a cloud of smoke obscured the mouth of the cave, and out of the midst of it the dragon himself, shining, sea-blue, magnificent, pranced splendidly forth; and everybody said, "Oo-oo-oo!" as if he had been a mighty rocket! His scales were glittering, his long spiky tail lashed his sides, his claws tore up the turf and sent it flying high over his back, and smoke and fire incessantly jetted from his angry nostrils. "Oh, well done, dragon!" cried the Boy excitedly. "Didn't think he had it in him!" he added to himself.

St George lowered his spear, bent his head, dug his heels into his horse's sides, and came thundering over the turf. The dragon charged with a roar and a squeal,—a great blue whirling combination of coils and snorts and clashing jaws and spikes and fire.

"Missed!" yelled the crowd. There was a moment's entanglement of golden armour and blue-green coils and spiky tail, and then the great horse, tearing at his bit, carried the Saint, his spear swung high in the air, almost up to the mouth of the cave.

The dragon sat down and barked viciously, while St George with difficulty pulled his horse round into position.

"End of Round One!" thought the Boy. "How well they managed it! But I hope the Saint won't get excited. I can trust the dragon all right. What a regular play-actor the fellow is!"

St George had at last prevailed on his horse to stand steady, and was looking round him as he wiped his brow. Catching sight of the Boy, he smiled and nodded, and held up three fingers for an instant.

"It seems to be all planned out," said the Boy to himself. "Round Three is to be the finishing one, evidently. Wish it could have lasted a bit longer. Whatever's that old fool of a dragon up to now?"

The dragon was employing the interval in giving a ramping performance for the benefit of the crowd. Ramping, it should be explained, consists in running round and round in a wide circle, and sending waves and ripples of movement along the whole length of your spine, from your pointed ears right down to the spike at the end of your long tail. When you are covered with blue scales, the effect is particularly pleasing; and the Boy recollected the dragon's recently expressed wish to become a social success.

St George now gathered up his reins and began to move forward, dropping the point of his spear and settling himself firmly in the saddle.

"Time!" yelled everybody excitedly; and the dragon, leaving off his ramping, sat up on end, and began to leap from one side to the other with huge ungainly bounds, whooping like a Red Indian. This naturally disconcerted the horse, who swerved violently, the Saint only just saving himself by the mane; and as they shot past the dragon delivered a vicious snap at the horse's tail which sent the poor beast careering madly far over the Downs, so that the language of the Saint, who had lost a stirrup, was fortunately inaudible to the general assemblage.

Round Two evoked audible evidence of friendly feeling towards the dragon. The spectators were not slow to appreciate a combatant who could hold his own so well and clearly wanted to show good sport; and many encouraging remarks reached the ears of our friend as he strutted to and fro, his chest thrust out and his tail in the air, hugely enjoying his new popularity.

St George had dismounted and was tightening his girths, and telling his horse, with quite an Oriental flow of imagery, exactly what he thought of him, and his relations, and his conduct on the present occasion; so the Boy made his way down to the Saint's end of the line, and held his spear for him.

"It's been a jolly fight, St George!" he said, with a sigh. "Can't you let it last a bit longer?"

"Well, I think I'd better not," replied the Saint. "The fact is, your simple-minded old friend's getting conceited, now they've begun cheering him, and he'll forget all about the arrangement and take to playing the fool, and there's no telling where he would stop. I'll just finish him off this round."

He swung himself into the saddle and took his spear from the Boy. "Now don't you be afraid," he added kindly. "I've marked my spot exactly, and *he's* sure to give me all the assistance in his power, because he knows it's his only chance of being asked to the banquet!"

St George now shortened his spear, bringing the butt well up under his arm; and, instead of galloping as before, he trotted smartly towards the dragon, who crouched at his approach, flicking his tail till it cracked in the air like a great cart-whip. The Saint wheeled as he neared his opponent and circled warily round him, keeping his eye on the spare place; while the dragon, adopting similar tactics, paced with caution round the same circle, occasionally feinting with his head. So the two sparred for an opening, while the spectators maintained a breathless silence.

Though the round lasted for some minutes, the end was so swift that all the Boy saw was a lightning movement of the Saint's arm, and then a whirl and a confusion of spines, claws, tail, and flying bits of turf. The dust cleared away, the spectators whooped and ran in cheering, and the Boy made out that the dragon was down, pinned to the earth by the spear, while St George had dismounted, and stood astride of him.

It all seemed so genuine that the Boy ran in breathlessly, hoping the dear old dragon wasn't really hurt. As he approached, the dragon lifted one large eyelid, winked solemnly, and collapsed again. He was held fast to earth by the neck, but the Saint had hit him in the spare place agreed upon, and it didn't even seem to tickle.

"Bain't you goin' to cut 'is 'ed orf, master?" asked one of the applauding crowd. He had backed the dragon, and naturally felt a trifle sore.

"Well, not *to-day*, I think," replied St George pleasantly. "You see, that can be done at *any* time. There's no hurry at all. I think we'll all go down to the village first, and have some refreshment, and then I'll give him a good talking-to, and you'll find he'll be a very different dragon!"

At that magic word *refreshment* the whole crowd formed up in procession and silently awaited the signal to start. The time for talking and cheering and betting was past, the hour for action had arrived. St George, hauling on his spear with both hands, released the dragon, who rose and shook himself and ran his eye over his spikes and scales and things, to see that they were all in order. Then the Saint mounted and led off the procession, the dragon following meekly in the company of the Boy, while the thirsty spectators kept at a respectful interval behind.

There were great doings when they got down to the village again, and had formed up in front of the inn. After refreshment St George made a speech, in which he informed his audience that he had removed their direful scourge, at a great deal of trouble and inconvenience to himself, and now they weren't to go about grumbling and fancying they'd got grievances, because they hadn't. And they shouldn't be so fond of fights, because next time they might have to do the fighting themselves, which would not be the same thing at all. And there was a certain badger in the inn stables which had got to be released at once, and he'd come and see it done himself. Then he told them that the dragon had been thinking over things, and saw that there were two sides to every question, and he wasn't going to do it any more, and if they were good perhaps he'd stay and settle down there. So they must make friends, and not be prejudiced, and go about fancying they knew everything there was to be known, because they didn't, not by a long way. And he warned them against the sin of romancing, and making up stories and fancying other people would believe them just because they were plausible and highly-coloured. Then he sat down, amidst much repentant cheering, and the dragon nudged the Boy in the ribs and whispered that he couldn't have done it better himself. Then every one went off to get ready for the banquet.

Banquets are always pleasant things, consisting mostly, as they do, of eating and drinking; but the specially nice thing about a banquet is, that it comes when something's over, and there's nothing more to worry about, and to-morrow seems a long way off. St George was happy because there had been a fight and he hadn't had to kill anybody; for he didn't really like killing, though he generally had to do it. The dragon was happy because there had been a fight, and so far from being hurt in it he had won popularity and a sure footing in Society. The Boy was happy because there had been a fight, and in spite of it all his two friends were on the best of terms. And all the others were happy because there had been a fight, and—well, they didn't require any other reasons for their happiness. The dragon exerted himself to say the right thing to everybody, and proved the life and soul of the evening; while the Saint and the Boy, as they looked on, felt that they were only assisting at a feast of which the honour and the glory were entirely the dragon's. But they didn't mind that, being good fellows, and the dragon was not in the least proud or forgetful. On the contrary, every ten minutes or so he leant over towards the Boy and said impressively: "Look here! you *will* see me home afterwards, won't you?" And the Boy always nodded, though he had promised his mother not to be out late.

At last the banquet was over, the guests had dropped away with many good nights and congratulations and invitations, and the dragon, who had seen the last of them off the premises, emerged into the street followed by the Boy, wiped his brow, sighed, sat down in the road and gazed at the stars. "Jolly night it's been!" he murmured. "Jolly stars! Jolly little place this! Think I shall just stop here. Don't feel like climbing up any beastly hill. Boy's promised to see me home. Boy had better do it then! No responsibility on my part. Responsibility all Boy's!" And his chin sank on his broad chest and he slumbered peacefully.

"Oh, *get* up, dragon," cried the Boy piteously. "You *know* my mother's sitting up, and I'm so tired, and you made me promise to see you home, and I never knew what it meant or I wouldn't have done it!" And the Boy sat down in the road by the side of the sleeping dragon, and cried.

The door behind them opened, a stream of light illumined the road, and St George, who had come out for a stroll in the cool night-air, caught sight of the two figures sitting there—the great motionless dragon and the tearful little Boy.

"What's the matter, Boy?" he inquired kindly, stepping to his side.

"Oh, it's this great lumbering *pig* of a dragon!" sobbed the Boy. "First he makes me promise to see him home, and then he says I'd better do it, and goes to sleep! Might as well try to see a *hay-stack* home! And I'm so tired, and mother's—" Here he broke down again.

"Now don't take on," said St George. "I'll stand by you, and we'll *both* see him home. Wake up, dragon!" he said sharply, shaking the beast by the elbow.

The dragon looked up sleepily. "What a night, George!" he murmured; "what a—"

"Now look here, dragon," said the Saint firmly. "Here's this little fellow waiting to see you home, and you *know* he ought to have been in bed these two hours, and what his mother'll say *I* don't know, and anybody but a selfish pig would have *made* him go to bed long ago—"

"And he *shall* go to bed!" cried the dragon, starting up. "Poor little chap, only fancy his being up at this hour! It's a shame, that's what it is, and I don't think, St George, you've been very considerate—but come along at once, and don't let us have any more arguing or shilly-shallying. You give me hold of your hand, Boy—thank you, George, an arm up the hill is just what I wanted!"

So they set off up the hill arm-in-arm, the Saint, the Dragon, and the Boy. The lights in the little village began to go out; but there were stars, and a late moon, as they climbed to the Downs together. And, as they turned the last corner and disappeared from view, snatches of an old song were borne back on the night-breeze. I can't be certain which of them was singing, but I *think* it was the Dragon!

"Here we are at your gate," said the man abruptly, laying his hand on it. "Good night. Cut along in sharp, or you'll catch it!"

Could it really be our own gate? Yes, there it was, sure enough, with the familiar marks on its bottom bar made by our feet when we swung on it.

"Oh, but wait a minute!" cried Charlotte. "I want to know a heap of things. Did the dragon really settle down? And did—"

"There isn't any more of that story," said the man, kindly but firmly. "At least, not to-night. Now be off! Good-bye!"

"Wonder if it's all true?" said Charlotte, as we hurried up the path. "Sounded dreadfully like nonsense, in parts!"

"P'raps it's true for all that," I replied encouragingly.

Charlotte bolted in like a rabbit, out of the cold and the dark; but I lingered a moment in the still, frosty air, for a backward glance at the silent white world without, ere I changed it for the land of firelight and cushions and laughter. It was the day for choir-practice, and carol-time was at hand, and a belated member was passing homewards down the road, singing as he went:

> Then St George: ee made rev'rence: in the stable so dim,
> Oo vanquished the dragon: so fearful and grim.
> So-o grim: and so-o fierce: that now may we say
> All peaceful is our wakin': on Chri-istmas Day!

The singer receded, the carol died away. But I wondered, with my hand on the door-latch, whether that was the song, or something like it, that the dragon sang as he toddled contentedly up the hill.

21

EDITH NESBIT

The Last of the Dragons
(c. 1900)

 DITH NESBIT (1858–1924) was born in London, where her father was the head of an agricultural college. After his death in 1862 her mother directed the college until 1867 while also raising five children. At this point she resigned from her post and took her family to the Continent. Edith, who was placed in various boarding schools in France and Germany, was unhappy and kept running away. When the family returned to England in 1871 and established residence in a large country mansion in Kent, she felt more at home and enjoyed the freedom to explore the countryside and follow her literary pursuits. By the time she was 15, she began publishing poems in various London magazines and aspired to become a great poet. In 1880 she married Hubert Bland, a young businessman, and soon after their marriage Nesbit had to support him and their newborn son because Bland had contracted small pox. She made Christmas cards, gave recitals of her poetry, and co-authored stories with Bland, who had lost his money in a bad business venture. In 1884 Nesbit and Bland became founding members of the Fabian Society and mixed with such writers as George Bernard Shaw, H.G. Wells, and G.K. Chesterton. Nesbit's commitment to the socialist causes of the Fabian Society was superficial. She liked playing the rebellious Bohemian and made her home into a literary salon. In order to entertain her guests and raise three children (along with two of Bland's illegitimate children), she wrote an inordinate number of poems, stories, and novels, largely for adults. It was not until she published *The Treasure Seekers* (1898), which became an immediate success, that she discovered her talent as a writer for children. The book recounted the unusual adventures of the Bastable children in a realistic manner and maintained a child's viewpoint on most incidents. From this point, Nesbit alternated between writing novels of realism for children such as *The Wouldbegoods* (1901), *The New Treasure Seekers* (1904), and *The Railway Children* (1906) and fantasy works such as *The Story of the Amulet* (1905), *The Enchanted Castle* (1907), and *The Magic City* (1910). No matter what genre she chose, Nesbit always focused on ingenuous middle-class children who were to exhibit values associated with fairness, loyalty, compassion, and self-sacrifice. Her main

goal was to convey both a sense of freedom and responsibility to children, and more than half of the hundred books that she wrote during her lifetime were directed at children.

Though Nesbit published numerous fantasy works with fairy-tale elements, she wrote only three books of fairy tales: *The Book of Dragons* (1900), *Nine Unlikely Tales for Children* (1901), and *The Old Nursery Tales* (1908). In most of these tales she blended features of modern English society with aspects of the traditional fairy tale in a humorous fashion, although at times she revealed a condescending attitude toward her child readers. "The Last of the Dragons" was published posthumously in *Five of Us—and Madeleine* (1925). It was probably written about 1900 when Nesbit was writing her other dragon tales. Unlike in those tales, however, she did not portray the dragon as sinister but worked in a vein similar to Kenneth Grahame's "The Reluctant Dragon." Her tale is an experiment in role reversals which leads to an alternative way of dealing with alien creatures. Important here is the theme of compassion that is central to most of her works.

THE LAST OF THE DRAGONS

F COURSE YOU KNOW that dragons were once as common as motor-omnibuses are now, and almost as dangerous. But as every well-brought-up prince was expected to kill a dragon, and rescue a princess, the dragons grew fewer and fewer till it was often quite hard for a princess to find a dragon to be rescued from. And at last there were no more dragons in France and no more dragons in Germany, or Spain, or Italy, or Russia. There were some left in China, and are still, but they are cold and bronzy, and there were never any, of course, in America. But the last real live dragon left was in England, and of course that was a very long time ago, before what you call English History began. This dragon lived in Cornwall in the big caves amidst the rocks, and a very fine dragon it was, quite seventy feet long from the tip of its fearful snout to the end of its terrible tail. It breathed fire and smoke, and rattled when it walked, because its scales were made of iron. Its wings were like half-umbrellas—or like bat's wings, only several thousand times bigger. Everyone was very frightened of it, and well they might be.

Now the King of Cornwall had one daughter, and when she was sixteen, of course she would have to go and face the dragon: such tales are always told in royal nurseries at twilight, so the Princess knew what she had to expect. The dragon would not eat her, of course—because the prince would come and rescue her. But the Princess could not help thinking it would be much pleasanter to have nothing to do with the dragon at all—not even to be rescued from him. "All the princes I know are such very silly little boys," she told her father. "Why must I be rescued by a prince?"

"It's always done, my dear," said the King, taking his crown off and putting it on the grass, for they were alone in the garden, and even kings must unbend sometimes.

"Father, darling?" said the Princess presently, when she had made a daisy chain and put it on the King's head, where the crown ought to have been.

"Father, darling, couldn't we tie up one of the silly little princes for the dragon to look at—and then *I* could go and kill the dragon and rescue the prince? I fence much better than any of the princes we know."

"What an unladylike idea!" said the King, and put his crown on again, for he saw the Prime Minister coming with a basket of new-laid Bills for him to sign. "Dismiss the thought, my child. I rescued your mother from a dragon, and you don't want to set yourself up above her, I should hope?"

"But this is the *last* dragon. It is different from all other dragons."

"How?" asked the King.

"Because he *is* the last," said the Princess, and went off to her fencing lessons, with which she took great pains. She took great pains with all her lessons—for she could not give up the idea of fighting the dragon. She took such pains that she became the strongest and boldest and most skilful and most sensible princess in Europe. She had always been the prettiest and nicest.

And the days and years went on, till at last the day came which was the day before the Princess was to be rescued from the dragon. The Prince who was to do this deed of valour was a pale prince, with large eyes and a head full of mathematics and philosophy, but he had unfortunately neglected his fencing lessons. He was to stay the night at the palace, and there was a banquet.

After supper the Princess sent her pet parrot to the Prince with a note. It said:

> Please, Prince, come on to the terrace. I want to talk to you without anybody else hearing.—The Princess.

So, of course, he went—and he saw her gown of silver a long way off shining among the shadows of the trees like water in starlight. And when he came quite close to her he said: "Princess, at your service," and bent his cloth-of-gold-covered knee and put his hand on his cloth-of-gold-covered heart.

"Do you think," said the Princess earnestly, "that you will be able to kill the dragon?"

"I will kill the dragon," said the Prince firmly, "or perish in the attempt."

"It's no use your perishing," said the Princess.

"It's the least I can do," said the Prince.

"What I'm afraid of is that it'll be the most you can do," said the Princess.

"It's the only thing I can do," said he, "unless I kill the dragon."

"Why you should do anything for me is what I can't see," said she.

"But I want to," he said. "You must know that I love you better than anything in the world."

When he said that he looked so kind that the Princess began to like him a little.

"Look here," she said, "no one else will go out tomorrow. You know they tie me to a rock and leave me—and then everybody scurries home and puts up the shutters and keeps them shut till you ride through the town in triumph shouting that you've killed the dragon, and I ride on the horse behind you weeping for joy."

"I've heard that that is how it is done," said he.

"Well, do you love me well enough to come very quickly and set me free—and we'll fight the dragon together?"

"It wouldn't be safe for you."

"Much safer for both of us for me to be free, with a sword in my hand, than tied up and helpless. *Do* agree?"

He could refuse her nothing. So he agreed. And next day everything happened as she had said.

When he had cut the cords that tied her to the rock they stood on the lonely mountain-side looking at each other.

"It seems to me," said the Prince, "that this ceremony could have been arranged without the dragon."

"Yes," said the Princess, "but since it has been arranged with the dragon—"

"It seems such a pity to kill the dragon—the last in the world," said the Prince.

"Well then, don't let's," said the Princess; "let's tame it not to eat princesses but to eat out of their hands. They say everything can be tamed by kindness."

"Taming by kindness means giving them things to eat," said the Prince. "Have you got anything to eat?"

She hadn't, but the Prince owned that he had a few biscuits. "Breakfast was so very early," said he, "and I thought you might have felt faint after the fight."

"How clever," said the Princess, and they took a biscuit in each hand. And they looked here, and they looked there, but never a dragon could they see.

"But here's its trail," said the Prince, and pointed to where the rock was scarred and scratched so as to make a track leading to a dark cave. It was like cart-ruts in a Sussex road, mixed with the marks of sea-gull's feet on the sea-sand. "Look, that's where it's dragged its brass tail and planted its steel claws."

"Don't let's think how hard its tail and its claws are," said the Princess, "or I shall begin to be frightened—and I know you can't tame anything, even by kindness, if you're frightened of it. Come on. Now or never."

She caught the Prince's hand in hers and they ran along the path towards the dark mouth of the cave. But they did not run into it. It really was so very *dark*.

So they stood outside, and the Prince shouted: "What ho! Dragon there! What ho within!" And from the cave they heard an answering voice and great clattering and creaking. It sounded as though a rather large cotton-mill were stretching itself and waking up out of its sleep.

The Prince and Princess trembled, but they stood firm.

"Dragon—I say, dragon!" said the Princess, "do come out and talk to us. We've brought you a present."

"Oh yes—I know your presents," growled the dragon in a huge rumbling voice. "One of those precious princesses, I suppose? And I've got to come out and fight for her. Well, I tell you straight, I'm not going to do it. A fair fight I wouldn't say no to—a fair fight and no favour—but one of those put-up fights where you've got to lose—no! So I tell you. If I wanted a princess I'd come and take her, in my own time—but I don't. What do you suppose I'd do with her, if I'd got her?"

"Eat her, wouldn't you?" said the Princess, in a voice that trembled a little.

"Eat a fiddle-stick end," said the dragon very rudely. "I wouldn't touch the horrid thing."

The Princess's voice grew firmer.

"Do you like biscuits?" she said.

"No," growled the dragon.

"Not the nice little expensive ones with sugar on the top?"

"*No*," growled the dragon.

"Then what *do* you like?" asked the Prince.

"You go away and don't bother me," growled the dragon, and they could hear it turn over, and the clang and clatter of its turning echoed in the cave like the sound of the steam-hammers in the Arsenal at Woolwich.

The Prince and Princess looked at each other. What *were* they to do? Of course it was no use going home and telling the King that the dragon didn't want princesses—because His Majesty was very old-fashioned and would never have believed that a new-fashioned dragon could ever be at all different from an old-fashioned dragon. They could not go into the cave and kill the dragon. Indeed, unless he attacked the Princess it did not seem fair to kill him at all.

"He must like something," whispered the Princess, and she called out in a voice as sweet as honey and sugar-cane:

"Dragon! Dragon dear!"

"WHAT?" shouted the dragon. "Say that again!" and they could hear the dragon coming towards them through the darkness of the cave. The Princess shivered, and said in a very small voice:

"Dragon—Dragon dear!"

And then the dragon came out. The Prince drew his sword, and the Princess drew hers—the beautiful silver-handled one that the Prince had brought in his motor-car. But they did not attack; they moved slowly back as the dragon came out, all the vast scaly length of him, and lay along the rock—his great wings halfspread and his silvery sheen gleaming like diamonds in the sun. At last they could retreat no further—the dark rock behind them stopped their way—and with their backs to the rock they stood swords in hand and waited.

The dragon drew nearer and nearer—and now they could see that he was not breathing fire and smoke as they had expected—he came crawling slowly towards them wriggling a little as a puppy does when it wants to play and isn't quite sure whether you're not cross with it.

And then they saw that great tears were coursing down its brazen cheek.

"Whatever's the matter?" said the Prince.

"Nobody," sobbed the dragon, "ever called me 'dear' before!"

"Don't cry, dragon dear," said the Princess. "We'll call you 'dear' as often as you like. We want to tame you."

"I *am* tame," said the dragon—"that's just it. That's what nobody but you has ever found out. I'm so tame that I'd eat out of your hands."

"Eat what, dragon dear?" said the Princess. "Not biscuits?" The dragon slowly shook his heavy head.

"Not biscuits?" said the Princess tenderly. "What, then, dragon dear?"

"Your kindness quite undragons me," it said. "No one has ever asked any of us what we like to eat—always offering us princesses, and then rescuing them—and never once, 'What'll you take to drink the King's health in?' Cruel hard I call it," and it wept again.

"But what would you like to drink our health in?" said the Prince. "We're going to be married today, aren't we, Princess?"

She said that she supposed so.

"What'll I take to drink your health in?" asked the dragon. "Ah, you're something like a gentleman, you are, sir. I don't mind if I do, sir. I'll be proud to drink your and your good lady's health in a tiny drop of"—its voice faltered— "to think of you asking me so friendly like," it said. "Yes, sir, just a tiny drop of puppuppuppuppupetrol—tha-that's what does a dragon good, sir—"

"I've lots in the car," said the Prince, and was off down the mountain like a flash. He was a good judge of character and knew that with this dragon the Princess would be safe.

"If I might make so bold," said the dragon, "while the gentleman's away— p'raps just to pass the time you'd be so kind as to call me Dear again, and if you'd shake claws with a poor old dragon that's never been anybody's enemy but his own—well, the last of the dragons'll be the proudest dragon that's ever been since the first of them."

It held out an enormous paw, and the great steel hooks that were its claws closed over the Princess's hand as softly as the claws of the Himalayan bear will close over the bit of bun you hand it through the bars at the Zoo.

And so the Prince and Princess went back to the palace in triumph, the dragon following them like a pet dog. And all through the wedding festivities no one drank more earnestly to the happiness of the bride and bridegroom than the Princess's pet dragon—whom she had at once named Fido.

And when the happy pair were settled in their own kingdom, Fido came to them and begged to be allowed to make himself useful.

"There must be some little thing I can do," he said, rattling his wings and stretching his claws. "My wings and claws and so on ought to be turned to some account—to say nothing of my grateful heart."

So the Prince had a special saddle or howdah made for him—very long it was—like the tops of many tramcars fitted together. One hundred and fifty seats were fitted to this, and the dragon, whose greatest pleasure was now to give pleasure to others, delighted in taking parties of children to the seaside. It flew through the air quite easily with its hundred and fifty little passengers— and would lie on the sand patiently waiting till they were ready to return. The children were very fond of it, and used to call it Dear, a word which never failed to bring tears of affection and gratitude to its eyes. So it lived, useful and respected, till quite the other day—when someone happened to say, in his hearing, that dragons were out-of-date, now so much new machinery had come in. This so distressed him that he asked the King to change him into something less old-fashioned, and the kindly monarch at once changed him into a mechanical contrivance. The dragon, indeed, became the first aeroplane.

22

EVELYN SHARP

*The Spell of the
Magician's Daughter
(1902)*

EVELYN SHARP (1869–1955) was born in London, the ninth child of a respectable middle-class family. Her father, James, was a wealthy slate merchant, and her mother, Jane, supervised the upbringing of the children in a town outside London. Sharp developed an early proclivity for writing, and she loved to travel. By 1894 she left home to settle in London, where she earned her keep as a private tutor for students. Within a couple of years, Sharp began to publish stories and fairy tales for children such as *The Making of a School Girl* (1897), *Wymps and Other Fairy Tales* (1897), and *All the Way to Fairyland* (1898). She soon became a member of the circle of writers who wrote for the innovative magazine *The Yellow Book* and was on friendly terms with Kenneth Grahame, Laurence Housman, and John Lane. Like many of these writers, Sharp was disturbed by the impact of the industrial revolution on English society. Aside from projecting the need for social reform in her writings, she joined the suffragette movement and became one of the leaders in the Women's Social and Political Union. When she became a reporter for the *Manchester Guardian*, she found that she could not separate herself from the women's protest movements about which she reported. Thus she not only wrote such books as *Rebel Women* (1910), a collection of stories, but she was also imprisoned for her active participation in demonstrations by the suffragettes.

During World War I Sharp was a dedicated pacifist, and after the War she was one of the founding members of the United Suffragists. As a reporter for the *Manchester Guardian*, she journeyed to such countries as Germany, Ireland, and Russia and wrote about the harrowing postwar conditions of inflation and chaos in those countries. Although she published a play, *The Loafer and the Loaf* (1927), a novel, *The London Child* (1928), and a non-fiction work, *Here We Go Round: The Story of Dance* (1928), most of her activities were now of a political and journalistic nature. In 1933 she married Henry Nevinson, a noted political journalist, with whom she had been friends for many years, and she also published her important memoirs, *Unfinished Adventure*. Indeed, her life's adventure was unfinished, for she continued her pacifist and antifascist work in the 1930s and 1940s, wrote for various newspapers, and remained an outspoken champion of women until her death in 1955.

Sharp's early fairy-tale writings are not as explicitly political as her own life became. Yet, there is a sense in both her two most important collections, *Wymps* and *All the Way to Fairyland*, that rebellion against the accepted notions of behavior and propriety may lead to greater self-awareness. Oppression will not be tolerated. Certainly, in "The Spell of the Magician's Daughter," Firefly realizes her full potential as a unique woman by exercising her imaginative powers and striving to overcome tyranny.

THE SPELL OF THE
MAGICIAN'S DAUGHTER

HERE WAS ONCE A magician, who lived in a pine forest and frightened everyone who came near him. This did not matter so much as it might have done, perhaps, for it was such a very thick forest that nobody ever did come near him; still, a magician is a magician, as all the world knows, and there is no doubt that he would have been an extremely frightening magician, if he could have found anybody to frighten. As it was, he had to be a nice, fatherly magician instead; for most of his time was taken up in teaching his four daughters to be witches. Now, the three elder daughters were very anxious to be witches; they thought it would be good fun to turn people into frogs and toads, and to go to the christenings of Princes uninvited, and to do all the uncomfortable things that witches love to do. But the magician's youngest daughter was of a very different opinion.

"It is too much trouble to be a witch," she said with a pout. "Who wants to learn a lot of stupid spells and things? Besides, I haven't the right kind of chin; it is round instead of hooked, and nobody could possibly be a witch without a hooked chin."

"The magician will alter the shape of your chin, if you ask him," suggested her eldest sister.

"Oh, but I do not want to ask him!" said little Firefly, hastily; and she stroked her small pink chin with her finger.

"What are you going to do when you grow up?" asked her three sisters. "You must do something, if you are not a witch."

Firefly rose to her feet and gave her short red frock a tug, to try and make it as long as a grown-up person's frock.

"If I must do something," she said in a resigned tone, "I will marry the King's son." And when her three sisters burst out laughing at the idea, she turned and walked away indignantly into the forest.

Now, of course, the magician's forest was by no means an ordinary forest;

and one of the most remarkable things about it was the way it managed to suit the mood of everybody who went into it. So when the magician's youngest daughter took her crossness and her grievances into the wood, that afternoon, the sunshine brought her the warm strong scent of the pine trees, and the breeze brought her the sound that lives at the top of the pine trees, and the fairies brought her the secrets of the grass at her feet—and Firefly was a nice little girl again. Then, just as the last bit of her crossness went floating away into nothing at all, the forest suddenly changed into quite another sort of forest. A small white cloud dropped over the sun like a thin muslin curtain, and the trees stopped putting their heads together, which is a favourite habit of pine trees, and the bees stopped whirring; and there was no doubt whatever that something was really going to happen. And the very next minute it did happen, for there came a crackling and a rustling in the underwood; and out into the open, just in front of the little girl in the short red frock, sprang a tall, eager-looking boy.

"Dear me!" exclaimed Firefly, for it was most unusual to meet anyone in the magician's forest. "What are you doing here?"

"I am running away from home," answered the boy, breathlessly. "I am running as fast as ever I can. Do you not see what a tremendous hurry I am in?"

"Why are you running away from home?" demanded the magician's daughter. "It seems to me a very stupid thing to do."

"It is not half so stupid as staying at home, when your country is being enchanted by a most objectionable giant," retorted the boy. Then he looked at her and sighed. "It is a pity," he said in a disappointed tone, "that you are only a girl."

"I do not think it is a pity at all," cried Firefly. "I would *much* rather be a girl, thank you."

"Well, you see," explained the boy, "if you were not a girl you might help me to disenchant my country; as it is, I am only wasting my time in talking to you." Then he made her a very grand bow and ran away again.

Firefly called after him to stop. "It is very evident," she exclaimed in an offended tone, "that you do not know who I am."

The boy looked round impatiently. "Of course I don't," he said; "but it doesn't matter, does it?"

"It matters very much," replied Firefly, stamping her foot angrily; "for I am the magician's daughter."

The boy came back at once. "Why did you not say so before?" he inquired. "Girls are so fond of wasting other people's time! All this while, you might have been helping me to disenchant my country."

Firefly was not at all sure that she knew how to disenchant anybody's country, and she consequently found herself in an awkward fix, which is what may happen to any of us if we do not learn our lessons properly. However, she did her best to look as wise as a magician's daughter should, and she asked the boy to tell her all about the giant.

"The wymps sent him," he explained sadly. "They had a grudge against the King, because he told tales about them in Fairyland when they played tricks with his fruit trees. No doubt, it was very annoying for the King to see all his apples and pears ripening on one side and not on the other, just because it amused the wymps to make the sun shine only on one side of the royal orchard; but it is ever so much worse to be obliged to put up with a giant who won't go away, and lives on nothing but fruit. There he sits in his castle on the top of the biggest hill in the kingdom, and every orchard in the place is being stripped in order to give him enough to eat. You have no idea how difficult it is to feed a giant who never touches anything but fruit! A cartload of strawberries is only just enough for his breakfast, and he eats a melon as we should eat a grape. All the houses are being pulled down and the streets are being made into orchards and gardens, so that the giant may have his food; and if any ordinary person is found swallowing so much as a red currant, he is instantly beheaded. You must agree that it is not pleasant to live in a country with a giant of this description."

"It must be most unpleasant," agreed Firefly; "but why do you not starve the giant instead of feeding him? Perhaps, he would go away if he had no fruit to eat."

The boy shook his head. "The King thought of that," he answered; "but the giant pointed out, most politely, that when he could not get any fruit to eat he always ate kings and other members of the royal family, so his Majesty instantly dropped the subject. Then we sent the whole of the army to kill him, and the giant thought it was a review, and he looked out of the window with great interest until the soldiers told him why they had come. He did not seem to mind the idea of being killed at all, but he explained to them that there were plenty of other giants in the world, and that the next one might eat babies or schoolboys or something like that; so of course the army marched back again. After that, we tried to make terms with the wymps; and they gave in so far as to say that they would remove the giant, if any one could invent a joke that would make him laugh."

"That would surely not be difficult," remarked the magician's daughter.

"It is more difficult than you think," said the boy. "To begin with, the giant is of such a melancholy disposition that any ordinary joke merely depresses him. I have known him to weep bitterly for hours at one of the King's very best jokes, so there is not much chance for any one else in the country."

"Have *you* not tried to make a joke for the giant?" asked Firefly.

"It would be no good," sighed the boy; "everybody says I am much too stupid. But I thought I might find a joke if I came out into the world to look for it, and then I could take it back and disenchant the kingdom, you see. I did not know," he added with a little smile, "that I should be so lucky as to meet a real magician's daughter. Now I have met you, no doubt you will be good enough to tell me what I must do in order to meet with a joke."

Firefly tried harder than ever to look like a magician's daughter, and she gave her frock another tug to show how important she was feeling. All the same, she could not in the least remember the spell for conjuring up a joke, though the magician had given it her to learn, over and over and over again. So there was nothing for it but to invent a new one, and that was how the magician's youngest daughter came to invent her very first spell.

"To begin with, you must find a girl," she told him, "a really nice sort of girl. And when you have kissed the five fingers of her left hand, she will doubtless tell you the way to the nicest, greenest, and wisest dragon in the world. And when you have told the dragon how nice and green and wise he is, no doubt he will tell you the way to the dwarf who has been trying all his life to make a noise in the world. And if you will assure the dwarf that he is making a most terrific noise in the world, you may be sure that he will tell you the way home again."

"But where shall I find my joke?" demanded the boy, impatiently.

"Oh, well," said Firefly, carelessly, "if you haven't found a joke by that time, you never will."

The boy repeated the spell over again, just to fix it in his mind; then he looked down at the little girl in the short red frock, and a twinkle shone in his eyes.

"Are *you* a really nice sort of girl?" he asked.

Firefly gave a jump. "Oh, I never thought of that," she cried in dismay, quite forgetting that she was supposed to be a witch. "I—I think it ought to be some other girl."

"I don't," laughed the boy, and he promptly took her left hand and kissed it five times on the finger-tips. "Now," he continued, "will you please tell me the way to the nicest, greenest, and wisest dragon in the world?"

Firefly was truly in a fix this time. No doubt the nice, green, wise dragon lived somewhere; but it was quite impossible for a lazy little girl, who had never bothered to learn her lessons, to say where he did live. So she stopped feeling important, and began to pout.

"I never met such a tiresome boy in my life," she complained. "You do nothing but ask questions!"

"But that is exactly what you told me to do," protested the boy.

There was certainly something in what he said, and it was not a bit of good grumbling at the spell she had invented out of her own head; so with a very bad grace she told him to go straight on until he came to the dragon. The boy looked at her suspiciously.

"Your spell is certainly a very funny kind of spell," he remarked. "Are you quite sure you are the magician's daughter?"

Firefly drew herself up and turned her back on him. "If my spells are not good enough for you," she remarked with much dignity, "you can go and try somebody else's spells."

The boy drew near to her and held out his hand coaxingly. "Pray do not be angry," he begged her; "if there is any thing odd about your spell, no doubt it is because you are not yet a full-grown magician's daughter."

But Firefly walked straight home to supper, and left him to find the dragon by himself. "Clearly, I must marry the King's son when I grow up," she muttered to herself. "*Anything* would be better than trying to be a witch!"

When she reached home, she found her three sisters eating their bread-and-milk, while the magician told them stories about the things that were happening at that very moment in the world beyond the pine forest. That is the best of having a magician for a father; because, of course, any ordinary father can only tell stories about the things that happened yesterday or the day before.

"The country is just being ordered to go into mourning," said the magician, as Firefly sat down with her bowl of bread-and-milk. "The King's son has run away from home in search of a good joke, and he is never expected to return. It is a pity, for, until he does return, my magic tells me that the country will not be disenchanted."

"Was that the King's son?" exclaimed Firefly, in a tone of the greatest astonishment. "Well, I *am* disappointed!"

"Shall you not marry him, little sister, when you grow up?" teased the magician's eldest daughter.

Firefly let her spoon fall into the milk with a splash, and looked away among the tall red trunks of the pine trees. "I have changed my mind," she answered slowly; "perhaps I shall be a witch, after all."

When her three sisters went to bed, she lingered behind and caressed the long white beard of the old magician. "The King's son will never come back," she said, "because I have sent him wandering over the world to work out a spell that isn't a real spell."

The magician smiled, for of course he knew fast enough what she had been doing. "It is a real spell, little daughter," he answered, "because you took it straight from your head and your heart and wove it round the King's son."

"But how can anyone find the nice green dragon and the dwarf who wants to make a noise in the world, when I only invented them myself?" cried Firefly.

"No doubt," admitted the magician, "you must give them time to get there before you can expect anybody to find them; for it always takes longer to find things you have only just invented than it takes to find things that somebody else invented ever so long ago. As for the King's son, he will never find them at all, because the spell is yours and not his. But that is of no consequence."

"N-no," said Firefly, doubtfully; and she looked away again at the tall red trunks of the pine trees. Then she sprang to her feet and gave herself a determined little shake. "If I find the stupid things first, will the King's son be able to find them afterwards?" she demanded.

"He will be very foolish if he doesn't," answered the magician.

"Then I shall go out into the world and search for them, this very minute," declared his little daughter. "That is only fair, since it is my fault that the King's son is looking for things that are not there. All the same," she added with a sigh, "I do wish he were not quite such an unpleasant boy!"

So, the very next morning, as soon as the sun came up and began shining sideways through the tall, straight trunks of the pine trees, the magician's daughter kissed her father and her three sisters, and started on her travels.

"Will you not take a spell or two with you, just to help you on your way?" they called after her. But Firefly shook her head. She had had enough of spells for the present; and besides, she was so ignorant that she would not have known what to do with other people's spells. So she went empty-handed through the forest, and her sisters stayed at home and learned their lessons.

Now, it was all very well to go out into the world to help a King's son to find a dragon that never need have been invented, but before many days had passed the magician's lazy little daughter began to feel extremely tired of the task she had set herself. "If I had only known that I should have to work out my own spell, I should have made it a *very* different kind of spell," she thought disconsolately. Then she sat down under a hedge, and seriously considered how she should manage to get to her journey's end without any more trouble to herself. "It is quite certain," she reflected, "that I cannot get there by witchcraft, for I have never learned to be a witch. But if I cannot be a witch, there is no reason why I should not pretend to be one." And when a large eagle suddenly swooped down in front of her, as she sat under the hedge, she at once seized the opportunity to pretend she was a witch.

"What a magnificent bird you are!" she began in her softest voice. "How is it that you have grown so handsome and so strong?"

"By eating little girls," answered the eagle, sternly. Firefly secretly trembled; for she was decidedly little, and the eagle was decidedly big. However, she managed to go on smiling, and she reached out her hand and stroked his feathers boldly.

"That is hardly the way to speak to a magician's daughter," she said carelessly. "How would you like to be turned into a soft woolly lamb and carried off by your wife for her supper?"

It was fortunate for her that the eagle did not like it at all, for she certainly could not have done what she threatened. As it was, he shivered all over at the bare idea, and instantly became as polite as possible.

"When I said little girls," he hastened to explain, "I was not referring to any one so important as yourself. Is there anything I can do for you on my way home?"

"Yes," said Firefly, condescendingly, "you may fly with me to the nicest, greenest, and wisest dragon in the world. And you may start this very minute, if you like."

The eagle looked a little crestfallen. "That is not exactly on my way home," he remarked.

"Ah!" smiled Firefly, "then you *do* want to be turned into a nice woolly lamb, do you?"

The eagle immediately gave in, and allowed her to jump on his back; and then he rose into the air and swept up with her to the warm blue sky overhead. For days and days and days the great bird darted onward; and Firefly lay upon his back and wondered what the King's son was doing, and dreamed about so many things that she lost count of the time altogether. At last, the day came when the eagle suddenly bent his head and dived towards the earth, down, down, down, until he touched the ground; and there he lay exhausted, while the magician's daughter slipped off his back and stretched herself.

"If you follow the path down to the sea-shore," panted the bird, "you will find the dragon waiting for you. I cannot carry you any further, for you have grown so tall since we started that my back is not strong enough to bear you. Will you let me go home now?"

"First of all," said Firefly, "you must find the King's son. I do not know where he is, but you will soon meet him somewhere or other. And you must show him the way to the nicest, greenest, and wisest dragon in the world. Then you may go home. But whatever you do, you must not tell the King's son that I sent you."

The eagle promised to obey her, and he rose into the air once more, while the magician's daughter followed the path down to the sea-shore. The first thing she saw was the nicest and the greenest and the wisest dragon in the world. He was lying on the pebbles in the hot sunshine, blinking his eyes at the waves; and he never so much as swished his tail when he saw the little girl in the red frock coming towards him. He was certainly not a very active dragon; but then, a dragon who had been invented by the magician's youngest daughter would naturally be an extremely lazy sort of dragon.

"Why," exclaimed Firefly, "I never expected to find you like this! I always thought that dragons lived in caves."

"So they do when they have been properly invented," answered the dragon,

in a hurt tone. "You never said anything about a cave when you invented *me*, you see."

"I'm very sorry," said Firefly, apologetically. "I was in such a hurry at the time that I invented you just anyhow. However, if you will tell me the way to the dwarf who wants to make a noise in the world, I will ask the magician to invent you a cave, directly I get home."

"He lives on the other side of the sea," answered the dragon; and he winked one eye solemnly at the little girl in the red frock. "I am afraid you will have to swim across to get there," he added; and he winked both his eyes at once, as though it amused him to think that someone as lazy as himself was going to do some work.

"I shall do nothing of the sort," answered Firefly; and she walked down to the edge of the water and hailed the first fish that came swimming along. This happened to be a fine handsome young whale with a pleasant smile.

"I should be delighted," he said, when she asked him to carry her across the ocean; "but unfortunately, I am going in the opposite direction."

"Dear me!" remarked Firefly, "one would never think that I was a magician's daughter and could turn you into an octopus at a moment's notice. Do you know what would happen to you, if you were an octopus? Your own father would not know you, and he would eat you up for his supper."

"What a bother it is!" grumbled the whale. "One is never safe from witches nowadays. Would you like to travel on the top of the sea, or along the bottom?"

"The top, please," answered Firefly, arranging herself on his back, "and if you so much as let a drop of water come near me, I will turn you into—"

"All right," said the whale, hastily; and the next moment they were skimming swiftly along the top of the waves. For days and days and days they went on crossing the ocean, and the magician's daughter sat perched on the whale's back, and wondered more than ever what the King's son was doing, and dreamed about so many things that she lost count of the time altogether. At last they arrived on the other side of the sea, and the whale drew a long breath of relief as the little girl in the red frock jumped ashore.

"That's a good thing!" he gasped. "You have grown so much since we started that I could not have carried you another minute."

"That is what the eagle said," thought Firefly. "Have I really grown any taller?" It was quite impossible to know how tall she was, however, without having someone else to measure herself against; so she gave up wondering, and asked the whale where the dwarf lived.

"Follow the path up the beach till you come to him," answered the whale. "May I go home now?"

"First of all, you must look for the King's son," replied Firefly. "You will find him talking to the dragon, and then you will bring him here. After that, you may go home. But whatever you do, you must not tell the King's son that I sent you."

Then the whale went back to fetch the King's son, and the magician's daughter strolled up the beach until she came to the dwarf who wanted to make a noise in the world. She was surprised to find him sitting disconsolately under a gorse bush, with a dissatisfied expression on his face.

"Dear me!" exclaimed Firefly. "What have you done with your house? I always thought that dwarfs lived in neat little houses, with gardens in front of them."

"That depends on the person who invented them," answered the dwarf, crossly. "I was invented so carelessly that I have no home at all. And how am I to make a noise in the world when there is nothing to make a noise with? People ought to be more careful when they invent things!"

"Never mind," said Firefly, soothingly. "If you will wait for the King's son and tell him to follow the path over the field until he comes to me, I will ask the magician to invent you the neatest little house in the world, directly I get home. And I will make him send you such a pair of creaking boots that you will be heard for miles round whenever you go for a stroll. Won't that be a nice easy way of making a noise in the world?"

The dwarf beamed with joy, for, having been invented by the magician's lazy little daughter, he naturally wanted to make a noise in the world with as little trouble as possible. So he promised to wait for the King's son, and Firefly passed on and followed the path across the field, until it brought her to the foot of the biggest hill in the kingdom. On the top of the hill was a castle, and out of the castle window looked a giant with a melancholy face. All round her stretched the most beautiful country she had ever seen, for there were no crowded streets in it, and no houses, and nothing to make it sad or ugly or dull; it was covered, instead, with the most charming orchards and the most delightful fruit gardens; and all the people in the kingdom lived in the open air, because there was nowhere else to live; and all the children played together under the fruit trees; and everyone was happy and gay from morning till night. Truly, no one would have said that the country was under a spell; but then, it must be remembered that it was the wymps who had bewymped it, and that explains a good deal. As for Firefly, she clapped her hands at the sight of it, for right away at the edge of this beautiful country she could see a line of tall straight pine trees against the blue clear sky.

"I have come home again," she murmured; and then she climbed the hill and sat down by the castle wall to wait for the King's son.

Nobody knows how long she waited, for she thought about him so much that she quite forgot to count the days. But one morning, as she was looking down the hillside as usual, wishing that the boy she was waiting for was not quite such an unpleasant boy, she saw a man striding along the path that led across the field. He was tall and brave-looking, and as he came up the hill-side she saw to her amazement that it was the King's son grown into a man; and she quite forgot that he was the boy who had teased her so unpleasantly in the forest. Now that there was someone to measure herself against, she saw, too, that the bird and the whale had spoken the truth, for she was nearly as tall as the King's son; and when she looked down for her short red frock, she found that it had been changed into a beautiful, soft white gown, fit for a Princess to go to court in.

"What a wonderful witch-woman you are!" said the King's son, as he stooped and kissed the five fingers of her left hand.

"I am not a witch at all," confessed the magician's daughter. "I have only been pretending to be a witch ever since I first saw you. It was extremely hard work," she added dolefully, "for I had to wander round the world in front of you, just to make that tiresome spell come true. I hope I shall never have to invent another spell as long as I live!"

"Then there would not have been a spell at all, unless we had made it up as we went along!" cried the King's son; and the idea tickled him so much that he broke into a peal of laughter. At the same moment a tremendous noise, like several thunder-storms and half-a-dozen gales of wind, sounded from the castle above; and there was the melancholy old giant, laughing just as heartily as the King's son.

"You absurd children!" roared the giant. "That is the best joke I ever heard in my life, and I must go straight off to Wympland to tell it to the wymps."

And without waiting so much as to pack his portmanteau, the giant marched straight out of the country and was never heard of again.

The King's son turned to the magician's daughter, and took her right hand as well, and kissed it five times on the finger-tips.

"Little witch-girl," he murmured, "your spell has disenchanted my country, after all!"

"That is impossible," laughed the magician's daughter, "for it was not a real spell, and I am not a real witch."

Then the King's son answered her as the magician had done, long ago in the pine forest.

"You are a real witch," he declared, "for you took a spell straight from your head and your heart, and you have woven it round the King's son."

Then he took her home and married her; and they chose the finest fruit garden in the kingdom for their own, and they lived in the middle of it, just as all the other people were living in their gardens. But the garden of the King's son was the finest of all, for it was full of baked-apple trees, and preserved-cherry trees, and blackberry-jam bushes, and sugar-candy canes; and best of all, there were almond-and-raisin trees, that always had more almonds than raisins on them.

So the magician's youngest daughter did marry the King's son, when she was grown up. But there is no doubt that she also became a witch, for to this day she can do what she likes with the King's son.

SELECT BIBLIOGRAPHY

FAIRY TALES AND WORKS OF FANTASY

A.L.O.E. ("A Lady of England," pseudonym of Charlotte Maria Tucker). *Fairy Know-a-bit*. London: Nelson, 1866.

Andersen, Hans Christian. *Wonderful Stories for Children*. London: Bentley, 1846.

Anstey, F. (pseudonym of Thomas Anstey Guthrie). *The Talking Horse and Other Tales*. London: Smith, Elder, 1892.

———. *The Giant's Robe*. London: Smith, Elder, 1894.

———. *Paleface and Redskin*. London: Grant, Richards, 1898.

Barlow, Jane. *The End of Elfin-Town*. London: Macmillan, 1894.

Bayley, F. W. N. *Comic Nursery Tales*. London: W. S. Orr, 1844.

Bethell, Augusta. *Echoes of an Old Bell and Other Tales of Fairy Lore*. London: Griffith & Farran, 1865.

———. *Feathers and Fairies, or Stories from the Realms of Fancy*. London: Griffith & Farran, 1874.

———. *Among the Fairies*. London: Sonnerschein, 1883.

Browne, Frances. *Granny's Wonderful Chair, and the Tales It Told*. London: Griffith, Farran, Okeden, & Welsh, 1856.

Browne, Maggie (pseudonym of Margaret Hammer). *Wanted—a King*. London: Cassell, 1890.

Burkhardt, C. B. *Fairy Tales and Legends of Many Nations*. New York: Scribner, 1849.

Burnett, Frances Hodgson. *Children I Have Known and Giovanni and the Other*. London: Osgood, McIlvaine, 1892.

Carroll, Lewis (pseudonym of Charles Lutwidge Dodgson). *Alice's Adventures in Wonderland*. London: Macmillan, 1865.

———. "Bruno's Revenge." In *Aunt Judy's Magazine*, December, 1867.

———. *Through the Looking Glass, and What Alice Found There*. London: Macmillan, 1871.

———. *Sylvie and Bruno*. London: Macmillan, 1889.

———. *Sylvie and Bruno Concluded*. London: Macmillan, 1893.

Chatelain, Clara de Pontigny. *The Silver Swan*. London: Grant & Griffith, 1847.

———. *Child's Own Book of Fairy Tales*. New York: Hurst, 1850.

———. *Merry Tales for Little Folk*. London: Addey, 1851.

———. *Little Folks' Books*. New York: Leavitt & Allen, 1857.

———. *The Sedan-Chair: Sir Wilfred's Seven Flights*. London: Routledge, 1866.

Childe-Pemberton, Harriet. *The Fairy Tales of Every Day*. London: Christian Knowledge Society, 1882.

———. *Olive Smith; or, an Ugly Duckling*. London: Christian Knowledge Society, 1883.

———. *No Beauty*. London: Christian Knowledge Society, 1884.

Clifford, Lucy Lane. *Anyhow Stories*. London: Macmillan, 1882.

———. *Very Short Stories and Verses for Children*. London: Walter Scott, 1886.

———. *The Last Touches and Other Stories*. London: Adam & Charles Black, 1892.

Comfort, Lucy Randall. *Folks and Fairies*. New York: Harper, 1868.

Corkran, Alice. *The Adventures of Mrs. Wishing-to-be; and Other Stories*. London: Blackie & Son, 1883.

———. *Down the Snow Stairs*. London: Blackie & Son, 1887.

Craik, Dinah Mulock. *Alice Learnmont. A Fairy Tale*. London: Macmillan, 1852.

———. *Romantic Tales*. London: Smith, Elder, 1859.

———. *The Fairy Book*. London: Macmillan, 1863.

———. *The Little Lame Prince*. London: Daldy, Isbister, 1874.

Crane, Walter. *Walter Crane's New Toybook*. London: Routledge, 1874.

Crowquill, Alfred (pseudonym of Alfred Henry Forrester). *Crowquill's Fairy Book*. New York: Hurst, 1840.

———. *Tales of Magic and Meaning*. London: Griffith & Farran, 1856.

———. *The Giant Hands*. London: Routledge, 1856.

———. *Fairy Tales*. London: Routledge, 1857.

———. *Fairy Footsteps; or Lessons from Legends*. London: H. Lea, 1860.

Cruikshank, George. *George Cruikshank's Fairy Library*. London: David Bogne, 1853–4.

———. *The Cruikshank Fairy-Book*. London: G. Bell, 1885.

D'Aulnoy, Madame. *The Fairy Tales of Madame D'Aulnoy*. Tr. Annie Macdonell. Introduction by Anne Thackeray Ritchie. London: Lawrence & Bullen, 1895.

De Morgan, Mary. *On a Pincushion*. London: Seeley, Jackson & Halliday, 1877.

———. *The Necklace of Princess Fiorimonde*. London: Macmillan, 1880.

———. *The Windfairies*. London: Seeley, 1900.

Dickens, Charles. *A Christmas Carol*. London: Routledge, 1843.

———. *Holiday Romance*. Published in four parts in *Our Young Folks. An Illustrated Magazine for Boys and Girls*, IV, January–May, 1868.

Doyle, Richard. *Jack the Giant Killer*. London: Eyre & Spottiswoode, 1842.

Ewing, Juliana Horatia. *Old-Fashioned Fairy Tales*. London: Society for Promoting Christian Knowledge, 1882.

Francis, Beata. *The Gentlemanly Giant and Other Denizens of the Never, Never Forest*. London: Hodder & Stoughton, 1897.

Gatty, Mrs Alfred. *The Fairy Godmothers and Other Tales*. London: George Bell, 1851.

Grahame, Kenneth. *Dream Days*. London: John Lane, 1898.

Grimm, Jacob and Wilhelm. *German Popular Stories, Translated from the Kinder und Haus Märchen*. Tr. Edgar Taylor. London: C. Baldwin, 1823.

———. *Household Stories from the Collection of the Brothers Grimm*. Tr. Lucy Crane. London: Macmillan, 1882.

———. *Grimm's Fairy Tales*. Tr. Mrs H. B. Paull. London: Frederick Warne, 1887.

———. *Fairy Tales from Grimm.* Introduction by S. Baring-Gould. London: Wells Gardner, Darnton, 1894.

———. *Gammer Grethel's Fairy Tales.* Introduction by Laurence Housman. London: Alexander Moring, 1905.

Harrison, Mrs Burton. *Folk and Fairy Tales.* London: Ward & Downey, 1885.

Hood, Thomas. *Fairy Realm.* London: Cassell, Peter, & Galpin, 1865.

———. *Petsetilla's Posy. A Fairy Tale for the Nineteenth Century.* London: Routledge, 1870.

———. *Harlequin, Little Red Riding Hood, or The Wicked Wolf and the Wirtuous Woodcutter.* London: Scott, 1870.

Hood, Thomas and Jane Hood. *Fairy Land, or Recreation for the Rising Generation.* London: Griffith & Farran, 1882.

Housman, Laurence. *A Farm in Fairyland.* London: Kegan Paul, 1894.

———. *The House of Joy.* London: K. Paul, Trench, Trübner, 1895.

———. *The Field of Clover.* London: John Lane, 1898.

———. *The Blue Moon.* London: John Murray, 1904.

Ingelow, Jean. *Mopsa the Fairy.* London: Longmans, Green, 1869.

———. *The Little Wonder-Horn. A New Series of Stories Told to a Child.* London: Henry S. King, 1872.

———. *The Fairy Who Judged Her Neighbours and As the Crow Flies.* London: Griffith, Farran, Okeden, & Welsh, 1887.

Inman, Herbert E. *Up the Spider's Web.* London: J. Clarke, 1893.

———. *The One-Eyed Griffin and other Fairy Tales.* London: Frederick Warne, 1897.

———. *The Owl King and Other Fairy Stories.* London: Frederick Warne, 1898.

———. *The Two-Eyed Griffin.* London: Frederick Warne, 1900.

———. *The Admiral and I: A Fairy Story.* London: Ward, Lock, 1902.

———. *The Did of Didn't Think.* London: Frederick Warne, 1913.

Jones, Harry. *Prince Boohoo and Little Smuts.* London: Gardner Darton, 1896.

Keary, Annie and E. *Little Wanderlin and Other Fairy Tales.* London: Macmillan, 1865.

Kingsley, Charles. *The Water Babies. A Fairy Tale for a Land-Baby.* London: Macmillan, 1863.

———. *Madame How and Lady Why.* London: Macmillan, 1870.

Kipling, Rudyard. "The Potted Princess." In *St. Nicholas Magazine,* January, 1893.

———. *Just So Stories.* London: Macmillan, 1902.

———. *Puck of Pook's Hill.* London: Macmillan, 1906.

———. *Rewards and Fairies.* London: Macmillan, 1910.

Kirby, Mary, and Elizabeth Kirby. *The Talking Bird.* London, 1856.

Knatchbull-Hugessen, Edward H. (Lord Brabourne). *Stories for My Children.* London: Macmillan, 1869.

———. *Crackers for Christmas.* London: Macmillan, 1870.

———. *Moonshine.* London: Macmillan, 1871.

———. *Tales at Tea Time.* London: Macmillan, 1872.

———. *Queer Folk.* London: Macmillan, 1874.

———. *River Legends.* London: Dalby, Isbister, 1875.

———. *Higgedly-Piggedly.* London: Longmans, Green, 1875.

———. *Whispers from Fairyland.* London: Longmans, Green, 1875.

——. *Uncle Joe's Stories*. London, 1879.

——. *Other Stories*. London: Routledge, 1880.

——. *The Mountain Sprite's Kingdom*. London: Routledge, 1881.

——. *Ferdinand's Adventure and Other Stories*. London: Routledge, 1882.

——. *Friends and Foes from Fairy Land*. London: Longmans, Green, 1886.

——. *The Magic Oak Tree and Prince Filderkin*. London: T. Fisher Unwin, 1894.

Lang, Andrew. *The Princess Nobody*. London: Longmans, 1884.

——. *The Gold of Fairnilee*. Bristol: Arrowsmith, 1888.

——. *Prince Prigio*. Bristol: Arrowsmith, 1889.

——. *Prince Ricardo of Pantouflia: Being the Adventures of Prince Priglio's Son*. Bristol: Arrowsmith, 1893.

——. *The Blue Fairy Book*. London: Longmans, 1889.

——. *The Red Fairy Book*. London: Longmans, 1890.

——. *The Green Fairy Book*. London: Longmans, 1892.

——. *The Yellow Fairy Book*. London: Longmans, 1894.

——. *The Pink Fairy Book*. London: Longmans, 1897.

——. *The Grey Fairy Book*. London: Longmans, 1900.

——. *The Violet Fairy Book*. London: Longmans, 1901.

——. *The Crimson Fairy Book*. London: Longmans, 1903.

——. *The Brown Fairy Book*. London: Longmans, 1904.

——. *The Orange Fairy Book*. London: Longmans, 1906.

——. *The Olive Fairy Book*. London: Longmans, 1907.

——. *The Lilac Fairy Book*. London: Longmans, 1910.

——. *The Arabian Nights Entertainment*. London: Longmans, 1898.

——. *The Book of Princes and Princesses*. London: Longmans, 1908.

Lemon, Mark. *The Enchanted Doll. A Fairy Tale for Little People*. London: Bradbury & Evans, 1849.

——. *Tinykin's Transformations*. London: Bradbury & Evans, 1869.

Lucas, E. V. *Old Fashioned Tales*. London: Wells Gardner, 1905.

Lucas, F. Lancaster. *The Fish Crown in Dispute. A Submarine Fairy Tale*. London: Skeffington, 1901.

Lucas, J. Templeton. *Prince Ubbely Bubble's Fairy Tales*. London: Frederick Warne, 1871.

Lushington, Henrietta. *Hacco the Dwarf, or The Tower on the Mountain, and Other Tales*. London: Griffith & Farran, 1865.

MacDonald, George. *Dealings with the Fairies*. London: Alexander Strahan, 1867.

——. *The Princess and the Goblin*. London: Blackie & Son, 1872.

——. *The Light Princess and Other Stories*. London: Dalby, Isbister, 1874.

——. *The Wise Woman*. London: Alexander Strahan, 1875.

——. *The Princess and Curdie*. London: Chatto & Windus, 1883.

——. *The Gifts of the Christ Child and Other Tales*. 2 vols. London: Sampson Low, 1882.

Macleod, Norman. *The Gold Thread*. Edinburgh, 1861.

Molesworth, Mary. *Tell Me a Story*. London: Macmillan, 1875.

——. *The Tapestry Room*. London: Macmillan, 1879.

——. *Christmas-Tree Land*. London: Macmillan, 1884.

——. *The Children of the Castle*. London: Macmillan, 1890.

——. *An Enchanted Garden.* New York: Cassell, 1892.

——. *Fairies Afield.* London: Macmillan, 1911.

Montalba, Anthony (pseudonym of W. R. Whitehill). *Fairy Tales of All Nations.* London, 1849.

Morley, Henry. *Fables and Fairy Tales.* London: Cassell, 1859.

——. *Oberon's Horn: A Book of Fairy Tales.* London: Cassell, 1860.

Nesbit, Edith. *The Book of Dragons.* London: Harper, 1900.

——. *Nine Unlikely Tales for Children.* London: T. Fisher Unwin, 1901.

——. *The Magic World.* London: Macmillan, 1912.

——. *Five of Us—and Madeleine.* London: T. Fisher Unwin, 1925.

Paget, Francis Edward. *The Hope of the Katzekopfs.* London: The Juvenile Englishman's Library, 1844.

Parr, Harriet. *Legends from Fairyland.* London: Frederick Warne, 1860.

——. *The Wonderful Adventures of Tuflongbo.* London: Frederick Warne, 1861.

——. *Tuflongbo's Journey in Search of Ogres.* London: Frederick Warne, 1862.

——. *Holme Lee's Fairy Tales.* London: Frederick Warne, 1868.

Pennell, Cholmondeley, ed. *The Family Fairy Tales; or Glimpses of Elfland at Heatherston Hall.* London: John Camden Hotten, 1863.

Planché, J. R *An Old Fairy Tale Told Anew.* London: Routledge, 1865.

Pollock, Lady Juliet, W. K. Clifford, and W. W. Pollock. *The Little People.* London, 1874.

Quiller-Couch, Sir Arthur. *The Sleeping Beauty and Other Fairy Tales.* London: Hodder & Stoughton, 1910.

Ritchie, Anne Isabella. *Five Old Friends and a Young Prince.* London: Smith, Elder, 1868.

——. *Bluebeard's Keys and Other Stories.* Smith, Elder, 1874.

Ritson, Joseph. *Fairy Tales.* London: Payne & Foss, 1831.

Rossetti, Christina. *The Goblin Market.* London: Blackie & Son, 1862.

——. *Speaking Likenesses.* London: Macmillan, 1874.

Ruskin, John. *The King of the Golden River.* London: J. Wiley, 1841.

Selous, Henry Courtney. *Granny's Story-Box.* London: Griffith & Farran, 1874.

Sewell, Elizabeth M. *Uncle Peter's Fairy Tale for the Nineteenth Century.* London: Longmans, Green, 1869.

Sewell, William. *The Giant.* London, 1871.

Sharp, Evelyn. *All the Way to Fairyland.* London: John Lane, 1898.

——. *The Other Side of the Sun.* London: John Lane, 1900.

——. *Round the World to Wympland.* London: John Lane, 1902.

——. *The Story of the Weathercock.* London: Blackie & Son, 1916.

Sinclair, Catherine. *Holiday House. A Book for the Young.* London: Ward, Lock, 1839.

Summerly, Felix (pseudonym of Sir Henry Cole). *Beauty and the Beast.* London: Joseph Cundall, 1843.

——. *The Chronicle of the Valiant Feats, Wonderful Victories and Bold Adventures of Jack the Giant-Killer.* London: Joseph Cundall, 1843.

——. *The Traditional Fairy Tales of Little Red Riding Hood, Beauty and the Beast, and Jack and the Bean Stalk.* London: Joseph Cundall, 1845.

Tabart, Benjamin. *Popular Fairy Tales; or, A Lilliputian Library.* London: Phillips, 1818.

Thackeray, William Makepeace. *The Rose and the Ring, or The History of Prince Giglio and*

Prince Bulbo. London: Smith, Elder, 1855.

Wilde, Oscar. *The Happy Prince and Other Tales*. London: David Nutt, 1888.

———. *The House of Pomegranates*. London: Osgood, McIlvaine, 1891.

Yonge, Charlotte. *The History of Thomas Thumb*. London: Hamilton, Adams, 1855.

CRITICAL STUDIES

Alderson, Brian. "Tracts, Rewards and Fairies: The Victorian Contribution to Children's Literature." In *Essays in the History of Publishing*, edited by Asa Briggs, 248–82. London: Longman, 1977.

Altick, Richard Daniel. *The English Common Reader: A Social History of the Mass Reading Public, 1800–1900*. Chicago: University of Chicago Press, 1957.

Avery, Gillian. *Victorian People: In Life and Literature*. New York: Holt, Rinehart & Winston, 1970.

———. *Childhood's Pattern. A Study of the Heroes and Heroines of Children's Fiction 1770–1950*. London: Hodder & Stoughton, 1975.

Avery, Gillian, and Angela Bull. *Nineteenth-Century Children; Heroes ad Heroines in English Children's Stories 1780–1900*. London: Hodder & Stoughton, 1965.

Baer, Elizabeth R. "The Sisterhood of Jane Eyre and Antoinette Cosway." In *The Voyage In: Fictions of Female Development*, edited by Elizabeth Abel, Marianne Hirsch, and Elizabeth Langland, 131–48. Hanover: University Press of New England, 1983.

Barry, Florence V. *A Century of Children's Books*. London: Croom Helm, 1981.

Bell, Anthea. *E. Nesbit*. London: Bodley Head, 1960.

Best, Geoffrey. *Mid-Victorian Britain 1851–1875*. Rev. ed. London: Panther Books, 1973.

Bettelheim, Bruno. *The Uses of Enchantment: The Meaning and Importance of Fairy Tales*. New York: Knopf, 1976.

Blount, Margaret. *Animal Land: The Creatures of Children's Fiction*. New York: Avon, 1974.

Bratton, Jacqueline S. *The Impact of Victorian Children's Fiction*. London: Croom Helm, 1981.

Briggs, K. M. *The Fairies in Tradition and Literature*. London: Routledge & Kegan Paul, 1967.

———. "The Folklore of Charles Dickens." *Journal of the Folklore Institute*, VII (1970): 3–20.

———. *A Dictionary of Fairies*. London: Allen Lane, 1976.

Buckley, Jermone H., ed. *The Worlds of Victorian Fiction*. Cambridge, Mass. Harvard University Press, 1975.

Cadogan, Mary, and Patricia Craig. *You're a Brick Angela! A New Look at Girls' Fiction from 1839 to 1975*. London: Victor Gollancz, 1975.

Carpenter, Humphrey. *Secret Gardens. The Golden Age of Children's Literature*. London: George Allen & Unwin, 1985.

Carpenter, Humphrey, and Mari Prichard. *The Oxford Companion to Children's Literature*. Oxford: Oxford University Press, 1984.

Cott, Jonathan, ed. *Beyond the Looking Glass: Extraordinary Works of Fairy Tale and Fantasy.* New York: Stonehill, 1973.

Coveney, Peter. *The Image of Childhood.* Harmondsworth: Penguin, 1967.

Crouch, Marcus. *Treasure Seekers and Borrowers.* London: The Library Association, 1962.

Darton, F. J. Harvey. *Children's Books in England.* 3rd rev. ed. by Brian Alderson. Cambridge: Cambridge University Press, 1982.

Demers, Patricia, ed. *A Garland from the Golden Age: An Anthology of Children's Literature from 1850 to 1900.* Toronto: Oxford University Press 1983.

Duffy, Maureen. *The Erotic World of Faery.* London: Hodder & Stoughton, 1972.

Engen, Rodney K. *Walter Crane As a Book Illustrator.* London: Academy Editions, 1975.

———. *Laurence Housman.* Stroud: Catalpa, 1983.

Evans, R. J. *The Victorian Age 1815–1914.* London: Edward Arnold, 1950.

Filstrup, Jane Merrill. "Thirst for Enchanted Views in Ruskin's *The King of the Golden River.*" *Children's Literature,* 8 (1980): 68–79.

Fraser, James H., ed. *Society and Children's Literature.* Boston: David Godine, 1978.

Gallagher, Catherine. *The Industrial Reformation of English Fiction: Social Discourse and Narrative Form.* Chicago: University of Chicago Press, 1985.

Gérin, Winifred. *Anne Thackeray Ritchie.* Oxford: Oxford University Press, 1981.

Gilbert, Sandra M., and Susan Gubar. *The Mad Woman in the Attic: The Woman Writer and the Nineteenth-Century Imagination.* New Haven: Yale University Press, 1979.

Green, Roger Lancelyn. *Andrew Lang. A Critical Biography.* Leicester: Ward, 1946.

———. *Tellers of Tales.* Rev. ed. New York: Franklin Watts, 1946.

———. *J. M. Barrie.* London: Bodley Head, 1960.

———. *Lewis Carroll.* London: Bodley Head, 1960.

———. *Andrew Lang.* London: Bodley Head, 1962.

Houghton, Walter. *The Victorian Frame of Mind.* New Haven: Yale University Press, 1957.

Inglis, Fred. *The Promise of Happiness. Value and Meaning in Children's Fiction.* Cambridge: Cambridge University Press, 1981.

Jan, Isabelle. *On Children's Literature.* New York: Schocken, 1974.

Jones, Michael Wynn. *George Cruikshank: His Life and London.* London: Macmillan, 1978.

Julian, Philippe. *Oscar Wilde.* London: Constable, 1969.

Knoepflmacher, U. C. "The Balancing of Child and Adult: An Approach to Victorian Fantasies for Children." *Nineteenth-Century Fiction,* 37 (March 1983): 497–530.

———. "Little Girls without their Curls: Female Aggression in Victorian Children's Literature." *Children's Literature,* 11 (1983): 14–31.

———. "Introduction." In *A Christmas Carol by Charles Dickens and Other Victorian Fairy Tales by John Ruskin, W. M. Thackeray. George MacDonald, and Jean Ingelow.* New York: Bantam, 1983.

———. "Resisting Growth through Fairy Tale in Ruskin's *King of the Golden River.*" *Children's Literature,* 13 (1985): 3–30.

Kotzin, Michael C. "The Fairy Tale in England, 1800–1870." *Journal of Popular Culture,* 4 (Summer, 1970): 130–54.

———. *Dickens and the Fairy Tale.* Bowling Green: Bowling Green University Popular Press, 1972.

Lanes, Selma. *Down the Rabbit Hole.* New York: Atheneum, 1971.

Langstaff, Eleanor De Selms. *Andrew Lang.* Boston: Twayne, 1978.

Laski, Marghanita. *Mrs. Ewing, Mrs. Molesworth and Mrs. Hodgson Burnett.* New York: Oxford University Press, 1951.

Lawrence, Elizabeth. *The Origins and Growth of Modern Education.* Harmondsworth: Penguin, 1970.

Lerner, Laurence, ed. *The Victorians.* New York: Holmes & Meier, 1978.

Lochhead, Marion. *Their First Ten Years: Victorian Childhood.* London: John Murray, 1956.

———. *Young Victorians.* London: John Murray, 1959.

———. *The Renaissance of Wonder in Children's Literature.* Edinburgh: Canongate, 1977.

MacDonald, Greville. *George MacDonald and his Wife.* London: George Allen, 1924.

Manlove, C. N. *Modern Fantasy.* London: Cambridge University Press, 1975.

Marcus, Stephen. *The Other Victorians: A Study of Sexuality and Pornography in Mid-Nineteenth-Century England.* New York: Basic Books, 1964.

Martin, Robert K. "Oscar Wilde and the Fairy Tale: 'The Happy Prince' as Self-Dramatization." *Studies in Short Fiction,* 16 (1979): 74–77.

Meigs, Cornelia, Anne Thaxter Eaton, Elizabeth Nesbitt, and Ruth Hill Viguers. *A Critical History of Children's Literature.* New York: Macmillan, 1953.

Miller, Patricia. "The Importance of Being Earnest: The Fairy Tale in Nineteenth-Century England," *ChLA Quarterly,* 7 (Summer, 1982): 11–14.

Moss, Anita. "Varieties of Literary Fairy Tale." *ChLA Quarterly,* 7 (Summer, 1982): 15–17.

Muir, Percy. *English Children's Books 1600–1900.* New York: Praeger, 1954.

Opie, Iona, and Peter Opie, eds. *The Classic Fairy Tales.* Oxford: Oxford University Press, 1974.

Petzold, Dieter. *Das englische Kunstmärchen im neunzehnten Jahrhundert.* Tübingen: Niemeyer, 1981.

Phillips, Robert, ed. *Aspects of Alice.* New York: Vanguard, 1971.

Pickering, Samuel F., Jr. *John Locke and Children's Books in Eighteenth-Century England.* Knoxville: University of Tennessee Press, 1981.

Pinchbeck, Ivy, and Margaret Hewitt. *Children in English Society.* 2 vols. London: Routledge & Kegan Paul, 1969.

Prickett, Stephen. *Victorian Fantasy.* London: Harvester, 1979.

Quayle, Eric. *Early Children's Books.* London: David & Charles, 1983.

Quintus, J. A. "The Moral Prerogative in Oscar Wilde: A Look at the Tales." *Virginia Quarterly Review,* 53 (1977): 708–17.

Reis, Richard H. *George MacDonald.* New York: Twayne, 1972.

Richardson, Selma K., ed. *Research About Nineteenth-Century Children and Books.* Champaign: University of Illinois Graduate School of Library Science, 1980.

Roe, F. Gordon. *The Victorian Child.* London: Phoenix House, 1959.

Rose, Jacqueline. *The Case of Peter Pan, or the Impossibility of Children's Fiction.* London: Macmillan, 1984.

Rowe, Karen E. "Feminism and Fairy Tales." *Women's Studies,* 6 (1979): 237–57.

———. " 'Fairy-born and human-bred': Jane Eyre's Education in Romance." In *The Voyage In: Fictions of Female Development,* edited by Elizabeth Abel, Marianne Hirsch, and Elizabeth Langland, 69–89. Hanover: University Press of New England, 1983.

Rustin, Michael. "A Defence of Children's Fiction: Another Reading of Peter Pan." *Free Associations*, 2 (1985): 128–48.

Sale, Roger. *Fairy Tales and After: From Snow White to E. B. White*. Cambridge, Mass: Harvard University Press, 1978.

Showalter, Elaine. *A Literature of Their Own: British Women Novelists from Brontë to Lessing*. Princeton: Princeton University Press, 1977.

Smith, Lillian H. *The Unreluctant Years: A Critical Approach to Children's Literature*. Chicago: American Library Association, 1953.

Stone, Harry. *Dickens and the Invisible World: Fairy Tales, Fantasy, and Novel-Making*. Bloomington: University of Indiana Press, 1979.

Sullivan, Paula. "Fairy Tale Elements in Jane Eyre." *Journal of Popular Culture*, 12 (1978): 61–74.

Summerfield, Geoffrey. *Fantasy and Reason. Children's Literature in the Eighteenth Century*. London: Methuen, 1984.

Supple, Barry. "The Governing Framework: Social Class and Institutional Reform in Victorian Britain." In *The Victorians*, edited by Laurence Lerner, 90–119. New York: Holmes & Meier, 1978.

——. "Material Development: The Condition of England 1830–1860." In *The Victorians*, edited by Laurence Lerner, 49–69. New York: Holmes & Meier, 1978.

Sutcliff, Rosemary. *Rudyard Kipling*. London: Bodley Head, 1960.

Thwaite, Mary F. *From Primer to Pleasure in Reading: An Introduction to the History of Children's Books in England from the Invention of Printing to 1914*. Boston: Horn Book, 1972.

Townsend, John Rowe. *Written for Children: An Outline of English Children's Literature*. London: Garnet Miller, 1965.

Whalley, Joyce Irene. *Cobwebs to Catch Flies: Illustrated Books for the Nursery and Schoolroom 1700–1900*. London: Elek, 1974.

Zipes, Jack. *Fairy Tales and the Art of Subversion: The Classical Genre for Children and the Process of Civilization*. London: Heinemann, and New York: Methuen, 1983.